Embodying Antiracist Christianity

Keun-joo Christine Pae • Boyung Lee
Editors

Embodying Antiracist Christianity

Asian American Theological Resources
for Just Racial Relations

Editors
Keun-joo Christine Pae
The Department of Religion
and Women's and Gender Studies
Denison University
Granville, OH, USA

Boyung Lee
Iliff School of Theology
Denver, CO, USA

ISBN 978-3-031-37263-6   ISBN 978-3-031-37264-3   (eBook)
https://doi.org/10.1007/978-3-031-37264-3

© The Editor(s) (if applicable) and The Author(s), under exclusive licence to Springer Nature Switzerland AG 2023
This work is subject to copyright. All rights are solely and exclusively licensed by the Publisher, whether the whole or part of the material is concerned, specifically the rights of translation, reprinting, reuse of illustrations, recitation, broadcasting, reproduction on microfilms or in any other physical way, and transmission or information storage and retrieval, electronic adaptation, computer software, or by similar or dissimilar methodology now known or hereafter developed.
The use of general descriptive names, registered names, trademarks, service marks, etc. in this publication does not imply, even in the absence of a specific statement, that such names are exempt from the relevant protective laws and regulations and therefore free for general use.
The publisher, the authors, and the editors are safe to assume that the advice and information in this book are believed to be true and accurate at the date of publication. Neither the publisher nor the authors or the editors give a warranty, expressed or implied, with respect to the material contained herein or for any errors or omissions that may have been made. The publisher remains neutral with regard to jurisdictional claims in published maps and institutional affiliations.

This Palgrave Macmillan imprint is published by the registered company Springer Nature Switzerland AG.
The registered company address is: Gewerbestrasse 11, 6330 Cham, Switzerland

Paper in this product is recyclable.

Preface

Embodying Antiracist Christianity is the product of years-long friendship, sisterhood, and collective caring. Friendship becomes stronger during a time of crisis like COVID-19 when collaborative caring is needed. While caring for one another in 2020, Asian/American feminist theologians Keun-joo Christine Pae, Boyung Lee, Nami Kim, and Wonhee Anne Joh conceived an antiracist Asian/American feminist theology project. We wanted to present Asian/American Christian theologians' collective antiracist resources to academic and public audiences.

At the beginning of the COVID lockdown, the alarming rate of anti-Asian hate incidents, particularly against women across the United States, troubled us deeply, although we were not surprised. Such attacks on people of Asian descent have a long-lived history in this country, which American society has ignored for centuries. As a result, anti-Asian racism has generally become invisible to the American public. Asian/Americans are the only people whose immigration to the United States and access to citizenship had been legally banned until the mid-twentieth century, despite the Asian presence in this land since the sixteenth century. In the nineteenth century, a massive influx of Asians in the United States—mostly from British and American colonies and occupied territories in Asia (i.e., the Philippines) fueled the US nation-building. These Asian migrants had "offered" cheap labor for the industrialization of every part of the US economy since the outlawing of British slavery and the abolition of American slavery. However, due to their racial and cultural differences, so-called Asian "guest" workers or "coolies" (i.e., non-White/Christian immigrants) suddenly became a threat to the United States when their forced service for the rising empire was no longer needed. So, the United States imposed various legal prohibitions, such as the Page Act (1875) and the Chinese Exclusion Act (1882), on Asian/Americans and implemented these anti-Asian immigration laws as governing policies. Such discrimination against Asian/Americans continues until this day.

Sadly, microaggressions Asian/Americans experience daily, even at progressive workplaces dominated by white majorities, become normal to many of us even if these organizations advocate for diversity, equity, and inclusion. On the other hand, the violence that Asian/Americans have experienced since the global pandemic seems to occur at different levels and has shaken us to the core. For example, physical or verbal attackers were not hesitant to insult Asian Americans. Instead, they justified their "right" to use violence against ordinary people of Asian descent, just as Robert Aaron Young justified his killing of eight people, including six women of Asian descent. White supremacist political and religious leaders touted visible and invisible anti-Asian violence. When many Asian/Americans experience personal attacks or hear news about anti-Asian incidents here and there, their immediate reactions might be fear and sometimes indifference. At first, the four of us felt distressed. However, the friendship and trust that we have nurtured for years rescued us from fear and apathy. Furthermore, we could embark on a journey to build a beloved community for ALL beyond the circle of our immediate friends and communities. The first step was to interrogate the complex of anti-Asian racism, co-constitutive with anti-Black racism, white settler colonialism, anti-Muslim hatred, and other various forms of oppression sustained by the US empire-building.

As critical Asian/American feminist scholars, we seriously discussed the shortcomings of Asian/American communities and their various counterparts' dealing with anti-Asian violence. As you can see later, several authors of this book critically examine Asian/American Christian communities' failure to be attentive to other minoritized peoples' experiences of centuries-long racism, heteropatriarchy, exploitation, and violence. If we fail to comprehend the complexities of anti-Asian violence in larger historical contexts, our fight for racial justice will perpetuate white supremacy, the fundamental problem of the United States. White supremacy often pits minoritized communities against each other in the arena of the oppression Olympics.

Since the pandemic, some of the known misogynistic and homophobic (mostly) male leaders of mega Asian/American churches have become the spokespeople for matters of anti-Asian violence because the mainstream American media often chooses to hear only these "important" people's opinions. Thus, the most marginalized voices within our Asian/American communities continue to be silenced, although they are most vulnerable to anti-Asian violence and structural oppression. This book is our small effort to create a platform to bring unheard voices.

A similarly problematic approach to responding to the uptick of anti-Asian hate is found among many well-meaning non-Asian/American colleagues or antiracist allies. These people advocate for cross-racial solidarity often without paying critical attention to authentic solidarity-building work with racially minoritized people. For instance, many allies against anti-Asian racism adopt Asian/American scholars' work in their teaching and research. To be sure, we appreciate their efforts to engage with Asian/American perspectives. However, we are simultaneously worried that they often read Asian/Americans' complex experiences detached from particular historical contexts. Namely, anti-Asian racism, Asian/American heteropatriarchy, and the hypersexualization of the Asian female body are treated as ahistorical, as if we were perpetually oppressed, powerless, and invisible. Some Asian American so-called feminist theologians present Asian women in a similarly invisible and powerless woman image. Allies' selective work with the body of Asian/American theological scholarship rarely highlights Asian/American women's persistent work for global justice. Hence, work by non-Asian/American scholarly allies unintentionally becomes transactional, often benefiting them more than us. They should be more cautious when engaging with Asian American theology. Since Asian/American histories and contributions to the United States and the global community are hardly taught in the American education system, their well-meaning but not-so-helpful approach is understandable. Still, this reality should not be an excuse for allies not to do necessary self-education.

Observing these approaches and personally experiencing anti-Asian incidents, the four of us started spending intentional time together to process our experiences and explore Asian/American feminist responses to the current interracial conflict. We agreed that anti-Asian hate could be understood and interrogated only in co-constitutive ways with anti-Black racism, settler colonialism, anti-Muslim hatred, discrimination against immigrants of color, and heteropatriarchy sustained by white heteropatriarchal supremacy. We felt the urgency of promoting antiracism work from Asian American perspectives that also show interconnectedness among all forms of oppression, as most Americans do not have many opportunities to learn about Asian/American histories and narratives. As the second step, we decisively brought our private conversation to more public space through webinars and writing projects, including this book, accessible to both academic and general audiences. Our conversation extended to a larger circle of Asian American feminist theologians and religious studies scholars whom we have known through the Pacific, Asian, and North American Asian Women in Theology and Ministry (PANAAWTM).

We applied for the Louisville Institute's Research Grant for a more structured conversation and book project. The institute's generous support enabled us to invite eleven Asian/American Christian feminist colleagues for deepened discussion toward a book project. For two years, the fifteen of us had a monthly Zoom meeting, sharing our journey stories, creating a space for grief and mutual support, reflecting on our individual and communal experiences, and generating writing topics through communal discernment. The virtual space allowed us to read each other's work, provide critical and constructive feedback with care and respect, and explore practical ways to work with our communities and world toward just racial relations. The result is *Embodying Antiracist Christianity: Asian American Theological Resources for Just Racial Relations,* which early career and more seasoned Christian feminist scholar-activists of Asian heritage have generated together. The book delivers eleven essays critically examining anti-Asian racism in connection with xenophobia, anti-Black racism, settler colonialism, heterosexual patriarchy, and US overseas militarism. Recognizing the limitations of the analytical voices presented in this book, we, the project's leaders, hope to launch a second book project to interrogate anti-Asian racism co-constructive upon anti-Muslim hatred, misogyny, anti-poverty, and ecological destruction. Additionally, we want to explore these issues with other racially minoritized colleagues for authentic cross-racial feminist solidarity for justice without compartmentalizing any of us. We are committed to that work now.

The clouds of communities supported this anthology. First of all, the editors express deep gratitude to PANAAWTM for excitedly endorsing this project as the fourth anthology of the group. We especially thank PANAAWTM for creating a virtual forum after the Atlanta Spa shooting spree. The forum indeed provided a much-needed space for mutual support among Asian/American women in theology and ministry, many of whom worked in isolation. In addition, the Iliff School of Theology generously hosted the webinar on anti-Asian racism from Korean American feminist perspectives after the Atlanta shooting incidents. Once again, we acknowledge the Louisville Institute's generosity that helped us actualize this project.

We cannot thank all the contributors to this book for their critical intelligence, honesty, and labor of love enough! **The fantastic 11** made this historical anthology! We are incredibly thankful to Dr. Kwok Pui Lan, one of the co-founders of PANAAWTM, for reading our initial project statement and giving us helpful feedback. She has been promoting this work with enthusiasm ever since. Dr. Su Yon Pak is another PANAAWTM sister-mentor who recommended our project to the Louisville Institute. We thank our colleagues and students at Denison University and Iliff School of Theology for their support and challenges. Christine particularly feels grateful to her Religion Department colleagues at Denison, Dave Woodyard, John Jackson, John Cort, Jue Liang, Joan Novak, and Jodi Weibel as well as colleagues at Women's and Gender Studies, Clare Jen and Isis Nussair for supporting her scholarship and sharing heavy burdens with her during the pandemic. We sincerely thank Amy Invernizzi, an awesome editor at Palgrave, who believed in our book project from the beginning and has supported it throughout the collective writing journey. Michael Pettinger is another gracious person who professionally edited all the essays in this book. We thank you!

Above all, we are grateful to our family for having not stopped believing in us and our work. Through thick and thin, they have been our unconditional cheerleaders. Christine is deeply thankful to Jinwoo, her partner, and their two young children, Juahn Julian and Jubin Lucas. They inspired her to launch this project and physically, emotionally, and spiritually sustained her throughout her writing journey. Boyung feels immensely blessed to be a parent of two young adults, Clara and Landon, with whom she discusses, debates, and proves ways to dismantle racism and white supremacy at many dinner tables and during their visits. Our family's just love charges and recharges us to keep going. Thank you! We are also grateful for the kinship-friendship we have built together, so hard conversations and critical feedback are embraced with respect and love.

We hope many conversations in this book incite anger, frustration, confusion, and discomfort in many of you before embellishing any false hope, as these emotional and intellectual reactions are the normal process of true antiracism work. We pray that staying together in a difficult space created by this book will lead us—authors and readers—to develop a love for one another. In this love, we build solidarity for just racial relations.

Granville, OH, USA　　　　　　　　　　　　　　　　　　　　Keun-joo Christine Pae
Denver, CO, USA　　　　　　　　　　　　　　　　　　　　　　　　　　Boyung Lee

Contents

1   Introduction: Problematizing a Problem 1
       Keun-joo Christine Pae and Boyung Lee

Part I   Settler Colonialism, Anti-Black Racism, and Anti-Asian Racism

2   America, the New Jerusalem, and Anti-immigrant Discourse 15
       Yii-Jan Lin

3   Waves of Memory and Possibility: Remembering New Songs,
       Re-forming Old Ones as Asian Settlers 39
       SueJeanne Koh

4   The Cosmopolitics of Belonging: Model Minority Superheroes
       and Theological Imagination 53
       B. Yuki Schwartz

5   An Antiracist and Antiwar Feminist Theology: When the
       US Military Empire Divides Us 73
       Keun-joo Christine Pae

Part II   Cross-Racial and Cross-Border Solidarity

6   Intimate Encounters at the Unhomely Home: Reading
       Morrison's *Home* and the Gospel of John's Homecoming Story 95
       Jin Young Choi

7   Beyond Siloed Solidarity: The Place of Asian Americans
       in the Struggle for Racial Justice 111
       Jessica Wai-Fong Wong

8   The Confines of "Antiracism" Work in the Intersectional
       Realities of "Anti-Asian" Violence 131
       Nami Kim

Part III Rereading Memories and Creative Activism

9 **Tasting Me/You: Sensory-Affective Multiracial Identity Formations** 151
 Heike Peckruhn

10 **Toward Solidarity-Creating Narratives: Anti-Racist Identity Formation in Korean Immigrant Churches**............. 177
 Boyung Lee

11 **Under the Master's Table: An Anti-darkness and Caste Interpretation of the Canaanite Woman**............... 195
 Sharon Jacob

12 **Who Is Family? Where Asian North American Christians Are in Empathizing with Black People**...................... 211
 Courtney T. Goto

Name Index 233

Subject Index... 235

Notes on Contributors

Jin Young Choi   is Professor of New Testament and Christian Origins and the Baptist Missionary Training School Professorial Chair in Biblical Studies at the Colgate Rochester Crozer Divinity School. By weaving biblical narratives together with diverse interpretative threads, Choi's work focuses on the intersections of race/ethnicity, gender/sexuality, class, empire, and early Christianity, employing postcolonial feminist criticism and diaspora studies. She is the author of *Postcolonial Discipleship of Embodiment: An Asian and Asian American Feminist Reading of the Gospel of Mark* (Palgrave Macmillan, 2015). Her co-edited volumes include *Minoritized Women Reading Race and Ethnicity: Intersectional Approaches to Constructed Identity and Early Christian Texts* (Lexington, 2020), *Faith, Class, and Labor: Intersectional Approaches in a Global Context* (Pickwick, 2020), and *Activist Hermeneutics of Liberation in the Bible: A Global Intersectional Perspective* (Routledge, 2023).

Courtney T. Goto   (she/her/hers) is Associate Professor of Religious Education at the Boston University School of Theology and a co-director for the Center for Practical Theology. She is the author of *Taking on Practical Theology: The Idolization of Context and the Hope of Community* (Brill 2018), as well as *The Grace of Playing: Pedagogies for Leaning into God's New Creation* (Pickwick, 2016). Her research interests include racism and relating across race; issues of power and practical theological method; aesthetic teaching and creative learning; as well as intersections between faith and culture.

Sharon Jacob   is Visiting Professor of New Testament and Postcolonial Studies at Claremont School of Theology. She is the author of *Reading Mary alongside Indian Surrogate Mothers* (Palgrave Macmillan, 2015), and a co-author of "Flowing from breast to breast: An Examination of Dis/placed Motherhood in Black and Indian Wet Nurses," in *Womanist Biblical Interpretations* (Society of Biblical Literature Press, 2016). Her essay, "Imagined Nations, Real Women: Politics of Culture and Women's Bodies: A Postcolonial, Feminist, and Indo-Western Interpretation of 1 Timothy 2:8-15" appears in *Handbook to Asian American Biblical Hermeneutics* (T & T Clark, 2019). Sharon serves on the board of the *Electronic Journal for Feminist*

Studies in Religion (EFSR) where she regularly contributes and blogs on various topics connected to religion and feminism.

Nami Kim is Professor of Religious Studies and chair of the Department of Philosophy and Religious Studies at Spelman College. She is the author of *The Gendered Politics of the Korean Protestant Right: Hegemonic Masculinity* (Palgrave Macmillan, 2016) and the coeditor of *Feminist Praxis against U.S. Militarism* (Lexington, 2020) and *Critical Theology against U.S. Militarism in Asia: Decolonization and Deimperialization* (Palgrave Macmillan, 2016).

SueJeanne Koh is the Graduate Futures Program Director of the Humanities Center at the University of California, Irvine. She develops programming for humanities doctoral students on professional development and diverse career pathways. She is also the Director of Adult Education and Resident Theologian for St. Mark and New Hope Presbyterian Churches in Orange County. Her research interests focus on the intersections of religion, theology, critical ethnic studies, and gender and sexuality studies, along with graduate education reform. Sue Jeanne has written an introductory essay on Asian American Christianity titled, "Asian American Christian theology: Topographies, trajectories, and possibilities" (*Religion Compass*) and a recent, co-written article, "Care Work is Not Conditional: Contingent Labor and 'Vocation' in Theology and Religious Studies."

Boyung Lee is Professor of Practical Theology and was the Senior Vice President for Academic Affairs and Dean of the Faculty from 2017 to 2022 at the Iliff School of Theology. She is ordained United Methodist clergy who served churches in both Korea and the United States. Lee is the immediate past president of the Religious Education Association and is the board chair of the Pacific, Asian, and North American Asian Women in Theology and Ministry. Her published works include *Transforming Congregations through Community: Faith Formation from the Seminary to the Church* (2013), "Diversity Within Korean Diaspora" in *The Oxford Handbook of the Bible in Korea* (Oxford, 2022), "Exploring a Transnational Practical Theology" in *Theologies of the Multitude for Multitudes* (Claremont 2021), and "What and How Shall We Teach to Undo Violent Extremisms" in *Teaching in a World of Violent Extremism* (Wipf & Stock, 2021).

Yii-Jan Lin is Associate Professor of New Testament at Yale Divinity School. She specializes in textual criticism, the Revelation of John, critical race theory, gender and sexuality, and immigration. Her book, *The Erotic Life of Manuscripts* (Oxford 2016), examines how metaphors of race, family, evolution, and genetic inheritance have shaped the goals and assumptions of New Testament textual criticism from the eighteenth century to the present. Her forthcoming book, *Immigration and Apocalypse: The Revelation of John in the History of American Immigration* (Yale University Press), focuses on the use of Revelation in political discourse surrounding American immigration—in conceptions of America as the New Jerusalem and of unwanted immigrants as the filthy, idolatrous horde outside the city walls.

Keun-joo Christine Pae is Associate Professor of Religion/Ethics and Women's and Gender Studies and Chair of the Department of Religion at Denison University (Granville, OH). Taking social ethics as a discipline, she has researched and taught transnational feminist ethics, religious ethics of peace and war, US overseas militarism, military prostitution, faith-based peace activism, and Asian and Asian American feminist theology and ethics. She is the author of *Transpacific Imagination of Theology, Ethics, and Spiritual Activism: Doing Ethics Transnationally* (Palgrave Macmillan, 2024) and an ordained Episcopal priest.

Heike Peckruhn is a bi-racial queer immigrant who grew up in Germany and is now living in the United States. She studied theology in Switzerland and Colorado and is interested in the ways in which embodiment and experience create meaning and meaningful action in the world. Located in the Shenandoah Valley in Virginia, she teaches religion, theology, and ethics, with a focus on how disability, race, sex, and gender impact our communal lives. She is a former chair of the Religion Department at Daemen University. She enjoys spending time with her family of two- and four-legged beings, hiking, and working in her wood shop.

B. Yuki Schwartz is Assistant Professor of Constructive and Political Theologies and a Louisville Institute Postdoctoral Scholar, 2022–23, at Claremont School of Theology. They are also an ordained minister in the United Church of Christ. Their research interests include Asian American theologies and histories of resistance, Asian North American and diasporic literature and pop culture, affect theory, decolonization and decoloniality, and practices of imagination and collective belonging. Schwartz received PhD in Theology and Ethics from Garrett-Evangelical Theological Seminary and is a previous FTE North American Dissertation Fellow. Currently, Yuki is working to turn their dissertation on the colonizing politics of shame into a book and is researching different theopolitical aspects of Asian North American model minority identity and identifications.

Jessica Wai-Fong Wong is Associate Professor of Systematic Theology at Azusa Pacific University and works in political and liberation theologies with a focus on race, gender, society, and visual theory. She is an ordained ruling elder in the Presbyterian Church (United States) and holds degrees in Christian theology and ethics from Duke Divinity School and Duke University. She is the author of *Disordered: The Holy Icon and Racial Myths* (Baylor University Press, 2021) and co-author of the curriculum *Lamenting Racism: A Christian Response to Racial Injustice* (MennoMedia, 2021). Her current research project—*Black Monsters, Yellow Ghosts*—considers the racial and sociopolitical dynamics of Asian American invisibility and Black hypervisibility as they function to create docile subjects and maintain established systems of power.

List of Figures

Fig. 2.1 T-O map of the world, detail from folio 17r of an astrological and medical compilation, end of the fifteenth century, England, mssHM 64. Huntington Library   17

Fig. 2.2 W. A. Rogers, "The Dragon's Choice," *Harper's Weekly*, 44 no. 2278 (August 18, 1900): cover image   30

Fig. 2.3 H. Knackfuss, "The Yellow Peril," *Harper's Weekly* 42, no. 2144 (January 22, 1898): 76   31

1
Introduction: Problematizing a Problem

Keun-joo Christine Pae and Boyung Lee

Problematizing a Problem of Asian America

In his classic *The Souls of Black Folk*, first published in 1903, W.E.B. DuBois asked, "How does it feel to be a problem?"[1] This question posits race as one of the most critical issues of the twentieth century in the United States. A century later, in 2008, Moustafa Bayoumi published a book, *How Does It Feel to Be a Problem*, posing the same question about America's "new problem," Arabs and Muslims.[2] In post-September 11 America, Muslims, or anyone who looks "Middle Eastern," and thus, allegedly a potential "terrorist," has been policed, surveilled, and detained as a security threat or "banned" from entering the United States.[3] Asian Americans of South, Central, and West Asian descent have been disproportionately affected by post-9/11

---

[1] W. E. B. DuBois, *The Souls of Black Folk* (Chicago: A. C. McClurg & Co., 1903).

[2] Moustafa Bayoumi, *How Does It Feel to Be a Problem: Being Young and Arab in America* (New York: Penguin Books, 2008).

[3] The American war on terror allowed the American public to racially profile Arabs, Muslims, and Sikhs as terrorists and threats to US security. As a result, these groups endured countless physical and verbal forms of violence, public harassment, bigotry, death threats, vandalism to their religious sites and institutions, and bomb threats. See, Jasleen Singh, "Desire, Patriotism, and Sikh Subjectivity," *Sikh Formations* 13 no. 4 (2017): 255, https://doi.org/10.1080/17448727.2017.1382632; Ironically, the first victim of racially motivated hate crime after September 11 terrorists' attacks was Balbir Singh Sodhi, who had a beard and wore a turban and ran the family gas station in Mesa, Arizona. See, Jatinder Dhillon, Shrai Popoat, and David Reimers, "My Dad Was Killed in First Hate-Crime after 9/11," *BBC News*, September 13, 2021, https://www.bbc.com/news/av/world-us-canada-58514967.

K. C. Pae (✉)
The Department of Religion and Women's and Gender Studies, Denison University, Granville, OH, USA
e-mail: paec@denison.edu

© The Author(s), under exclusive license to Springer Nature Switzerland AG 2023
K. C. Pae, B. Lee (eds.), *Embodying Antiracist Christianity*, https://doi.org/10.1007/978-3-031-37264-3_1

racist hatred. In 2020, As the COVID-19 pandemic swept North America as well as other parts of the world, Americans of East Asian descent struggled with the same question: *How does it feel to be a problem, Asian America?* A more accurate question would be: *How does it feel to be a problem again and again, Asian America?*

Since its foundation, the United States has constantly faced problems in its perceived times of crisis: Native Americans, Blacks, Chinese, Japanese, Germans, communists, Muslims, Arabs, feminists, gays and lesbians, and Mexicans, to name only a few. The exhausting list of problems shows similar patterns. The American public singles out racial, ethnic, religious, or sexual minorities from so-called good Americans, problematizes these populations, and blames them for bringing crises, from economic recession to war, moral decadence, climate change, and even God's wrath.[4] Thus, these problems, more precisely "problematic peoples," should be contained, prohibited, banned, and erased for the sake of public safety. This is what former president Donald Trump's Executive Order signed on January 27, 2017, barred the entry of any refugee who was awaiting resettlement in the United States for 120 days; prohibited all Syrian refugees from entering the United States until further notice; and banned the citizens of seven Muslim-majority countries—Iraq, Iran, Syria, Somalia, Sudan, Libya, and Yemen—from entering the United States under any visa category.[5] Barring, prohibiting, banning, and incarcerating have been shared experiences of Asian Americans since we stepped on American soil.

In almost all crisis cases, the blamed populations are not responsible for threatening public security but are "problematized" and scapegoated out of a public fear often incited by irresponsible politicians and religious leaders. The uptick of anti-Asian hate during the COVID-19 pandemic is a perfect example of problematizing Asians' right to life. In a critical response to anti-Asian hate, Asian American scholars of critical Christian studies have collectively produced *Embodying Antiracist Christianity*, analyzing what has problematized us, and searching for how we can dismantle anti-Asian racism, co-constitutive with anti-Black racism, xenophobia, anti-Muslim hatred, settler colonialism, and so forth. Through Asian American theological reflection and actions, namely praxis, we reclaim our communities' livelihood, interdependent on the well-being of all "problematized" groups.

---

[4] An extreme case of blaming a minoritized population and so-called secular politics could come from Christian fundamentalists Reverend Jerry Falwell and Pat Robertson, who claimed that "an angry God had allowed the terrorists to succeed in their deadly mission because the United States had become a nation of abortion, homosexuality, secular schools and courts, and the American civil liberties union." See, Laurie Goodstein, "Falwell: Blame Abortionists, Feminists, and Gays," *New York Times*, September 19, 2001; reprinted in *The Guardian*, https://www.theguardian.com/world/2001/sep/19/september11.usa9.

[5] Krishnadev Calamur, "What Trump's Executive Order on Immigration Does—and Doesn't Do," *The Atlantic*, January 30, 2017, https://www.theatlantic.com/news/archive/2017/01/trump-immigration-order-muslims/514844.

B. Lee
Iliff School of Theology, Denver, CO, USA
e-mail: blee@iliff.edu

Diseases and Historical Trace of Anti-Asian Racism

East Asians, or particularly anyone who looks "Chinese," have been blamed for spreading COVID-19 and, as a result, become subject to bullying, and intimidation, not to mention verbal and physical attacks in various locations in North America. Since the origin of COVID-19 was tied to Wuhan, China, the American public has racialized the virus as the "Chinese virus," "Wuhan virus," or "Kung Flu virus." This racialization has historical precedents. Between 1900 and 1905, Chinese/Americans in San Francisco's Chinatown were quarantined because of an outbreak of bubonic plague (black death). Bubonic plague was called an "Oriental disease," although European Americans had memories of its deadly power in Medieval Europe.[6] Historian Guenter Risse summarizes the public health officials' management of bubonic plague in San Francisco:

> Following the California gold rush of 1849, Chinatown was repeatedly condemned for its filth and bad smells, which were believed to breed disease. For more than half a century, such discourse, heavily tinged with racial prejudice and amplified by sensational print media, found widespread acceptance. Playing on public anxiety regarding contagion, the periodic rants not only dehumanized an entire population but also motivated local authorities to employ *muscular strategies of social isolation, control, and removal. Sanitary representations and the employment of stereotypes came to underpin political, economic, and cultural considerations designed to negatively portray Chinese in California, becoming a potent and permanent component of anti-Asian prejudice* (emphasis added by the author).[7]

Risse's description of racialized (or Orientalized) bubonic plague resembles the American public's anxieties over global diseases such as SARS, Ebola, and MERS in the twenty-first century. As history teaches us, the American public has greatly feared diseases crossing oceans. Ellis Island in New York City and Angel Island off the shore of San Francisco were forts to protect Americans from foreign disease carriers. For example, between 1910 and 1940, Chinese immigrants experienced humiliating medical check-ups at Angel Island. Doctors and nurses searched their bodies for physical defects and looked for "parasitic 'Oriental' diseases that were not contagious but were grounds for exclusion if untreated after arrival."[8] Americans (read as white Americans) were considered innocent and vulnerable to unknown diseases carried by bodies of color, and thus innocent Americans had to be protected from outside invaders.

Innocence, protection, and invasion can all be read through theological, military, and gendered imaginations. Innocence portrays the moral purity of the vulnerable, who could be easily feminized or represented by the "pure" white female body. The

---

[6] Becky Little, "Trump's 'Chinese' Virus Is Part of a Long History of Blaming Other Countries for Disease," *Time*, March 20, 2020, https://time.com/5807376/virus-name-foreign-history/?fbclid=IwAR2QVvyMguaUDFMTqAwzNOk2eaGA1L-MEdT16X3bx5RzY0%20WlAEgvqSsodlU.

[7] Guenter Risse, *Plague, Fear, and Politics in San Francisco's Chinatown* (Baltimore: Johns Hopkins University Press, 2012), 1, doi:10.1353/book.14337.

[8] Erika Lee, *America for Americans: A History of Xenophobia in the United States* (New York: Basic Books, 2019), 109.

innocent must be protected theologically, morally, and physically. Protectors are usually associated with images of rational, intelligent, and responsible men who should make "tough" decisions to fight against evil.[9] Argentinian queer feminist theologian Marcella Althaus-Reid shows how innocence and protection collapse in heteropatriarchal theology, which, in fact, has justified the destruction of poor people, gender queers, and racial/ethnic minorities in the Latin American context. According to Althaus-Reid, the Virgin iconized in a white female body has been detached from the real lives of (poor) women and queer folk, particularly in Latin America, where Virgin worship is popular.[10] The colonialist representation of the Virgin portrays the brutal massacre of Indigenous women, men, and children as an innocent act, an act of faith, or even God's will. Moreover, the Virgin Mary's apparitions continued with the support of military dictatorship, as seen in Chilean dictator Augusto Pinochet who constantly evoked the Virgin.[11] The same name must have been evoked in the midst of bubonic plague in Medieval Europe and early twentieth-century San Francisco, as well as the COVID-plagued world in the 2020s. If religious stories, symbols, metaphors, and rituals have the power to create material realities, as many contributors to this anthology argue, the Virgin's name evoked during times of contagious diseases may provoke fears and hatred toward dark-skinned people whose bodies cannot be assimilated with the Virgin. Just as Althaus Reid argues that the Virgin Mary closets the Church's heterosexual patriarchy, the Virgin closets the destructive power of the American public's presumed innocence that has killed Black, Indigenous, and people of color (BIPOC) inside and outside the United States. Theology always matters when it comes to social (in)justice because theological stories have the power to (re)make a world, (re)shape moral values, and strengthen human (in)dignity.

To be certain, this book is not about public health from Asian American perspectives but about centuries-old anti-Asian violence along with other forms of racist hate that have repeatedly exploded during various social crises. For example, during the first month of the COVID-19 outbreak, Stop AAPI Hate, an online reporting forum that started on March 18, 2020, received "more than 650 direct reports of discrimination against primarily Asian Americans."[12] Through March 2022, Stop

---

[9] Feminist international studies scholar Cynthia Enloe has critically analyzed the masculinized political sphere, especially militarized US foreign affairs. She argues that to unravel the masculinized US foreign policy knot, both congressional and presidential policymakers should stop equating "security" with military superiority. This argument applies to the Trump administration's militant approach to controlling COVID-19, already practiced in controlling bubonic plague in San Francisco 100 years ago. See Cynthia Enloe, *The Curious Feminist: Searching for Women in a New Age of Empire* (Berkeley: University of California Press, 2004), 125–30.

[10] Marcella Althaus-Reid, *Indecent Theology: Theological Perversions in Sex, Gender, and Politics* (London, UK: Routledge, 2000), 46 & 59.

[11] Althaus-Reid, *Indecent Theology*, 58–59.

[12] Caitlin Yoshiko Kandil, "Asian Americans Report over 650 Racist Acts over Last Week, New Data Says," *NBC News*, March 26, 2020, https://www.nbcnews.com/news/asian-america/asian-americans-report-nearly%20500-racist-acts-overlast-week-n1169821?fbclid=IwAR2yYRyjZ0HG-9O6GnlzebhqueI2KV_Hbmd0J6ruVQ-x90uRcw_Ryy7QseI.

AAPI Hate collected almost 11,500 incidents.[13] According to Stop AAPI's 2022 national report, Asian American women are disproportionately impacted by racial hatred, ranging from physical violence to verbal abuse, showing that racism is gendered.[14] In addition to mounting xenophobia and anti-Asian racism, the disproportionate impacts of COVID-19 on Black, Brown, and Indigenous communities expose many existing and enduring structural problems, namely, the interlocking of racism, poverty, environmental destruction, urban/rural ghettos, sexism, and so on. Furthermore, we continue to witness state-sanctioned violence against BIPOC and gender non-conforming people at the hands of police and white vigilantes.

Toward Antiracist Asian American Theology

If tenacious racist violence has hurt BIPOC communities for a long time, what resources can Asian American theology offer to heal these communities, dismantle the causes of racist violence, and renew radically inclusive theological visions? As Asian American woman scholars who critically engage in Christian theology, ethics, and biblical studies, the contributors to this book delineate from their various social locations how to respond to the co-constitutive nature of white supremacy that differentially affects nonwhite communities. The contributors' critical analyses of Christianity's roles in constructing racist ideologies and maintaining racist realities offer opportunities to build up cross-racial solidarity and activism for just racial relations. Thus, this book wrestles with the questions of what steps would be necessary for Asian American Christians to build coalitional solidarity for just racial relations domestically and globally and how we can educate the American public about anti-Asian racism and antiracist work.

Embodying Antiracist Christianity shares antiracist resources informed by Asian/North American feminist theology and biblical scholarship with multiracial audiences, including whites, who want to learn about America's racism through the Asian American eye and dismantle racism from where they stand. Although scholarly books and articles on Asian American theology (broadly defined) in response to contemporary ethical, political, and cultural issues have been prolific, there have been few concerted efforts to interrogate or dismantle anti-Asian racism inseparable from racialized and sexualized discrimination against Blacks, Latinx, Native Americans, Arabs, and gender queers that has significantly undermined the communal spirit and vitality of Christian churches. Hence, this anthology makes up for the current paucity of work with critical discussions on the multiple facets of

---

[13] Stop AAPI Hate, "National Report: Two Years and Thousands of Voices: What Community-Generated Data Tells Us about Anti-AAPI Hate," https://stopaapihate.org/wp-content/uploads/2022/07/Stop-AAPI-Hate-Year-2-Report.pdf.
[14] See Wendy Lu, "This Is What It's Like to Be an Asian Woman in The Age of the Coronavirus," *Asian Voices*, March 31, 2020, https://www.huffpost.com/entry/asian-women-racism-coronavirus_n_5e822d41c5b66ea70fda8051.

racism from Asian American theological perspectives. Contributors deepen inter/transdisciplinary approaches concerning dismantling racist theological teachings, biblical interpretations, liturgical presentations, and the Christian church's leadership structure.

The eleven chapters in the book aim to (1) detail discussions and conversations on how anti-Asian racism is intricately connected to anti-Black racism and white settler colonialism in North America; (2) examine how differently racialized groups can be complicit in perpetuating each other's oppression in general and, in particular, the various ways Asian/North Americans perpetuate anti-Blackness through the model minority myth coded in the hetero-patriarchal, binary gender system; (3) interrogate how Christian theology in general, and Asian/North American theological discourse in particular, has been part of the "problem" rather than a "solution" to racial/gender/economic injustice; and (4) constructively offer critical and creative theological resources developed by Asian/North American women in theology for radical possibilities of cross-racial solidarity in resistance to various forms of structural violence. Some chapters will discuss all four aspects, while most chapters highlight one or two. More specifically, through the lens of gender and sexuality interlocked with race, contributors reflect on a wide range of topics, including racial formations of Asian American Christians, Asian American Christian activism for racial justice, Asian American complicity in anti-Black racism and settler colonialism, Christianity's role either as an enforcer of God's creation order in a heterosexist and racist way or as resistance to such order, and practical, pedagogical guidance for antiracist work within Christian communities and beyond. Essays in this book pave meaningful ways for many Christian churches and people of Christian faith to discuss the urgent and relevant issues related to racial justice intersecting with gender justice, sexual justice, economic justice, disability justice, and environmental justice. All of these will involve challenging dominant theological narratives, languages, liturgies, and metaphors that revolve around exclusive claims on God's chosen people and land, God's providence, redemption, and what it means to be human, among others.

Structure of the Book

The editors of this book have organized its eleven chapters in three interconnected parts in order to invite readers to reflect on similar and dissimilar issues in different lights. The chapters in "Part I Settler Colonialism, Anti-Black Racism, and Anti-Asian Racism," trace the historical and cultural roots of multifaceted racism. Yii-Jan Lin's chapter, "America, The New Jerusalem and Anti-Immigrant Discourse," reads the Book of Revelation in juxtaposition to documented anti-Chinese immigration in American history. Lin successfully shows how the ideation of America as the New Jerusalem, as a walled, secure, and wealthy *city*, feeds into racist, white nativist discourse and fearmongering, and anti-immigrant rhetoric. Asians/Asian Americans, as unassimilable, disease-ridden, and idolatrous foreigners, could be compared to those kept out of the heavenly city in Revelation. Although Lin's essay focuses on the history of Chinese immigration to the United States, the implications apply to all immigrants unwanted by white nativists. With Lin, readers can examine racial purity transferred to moral purity in the Christian imagination of "heaven" and the impact of this imagination on interracial relations in the Church and American society.

SueJeanne Koh's chapter, "Waves of Memory and Possibility," examines settler colonialist sentiment among Asian Americans. By looking at American popular music in postwar Korea as a formative factor in the Korean immigrant imagination, Koh argues that such music highlighted white settler emotions. Skillfully interweaving her memories of her father's immigration stories with historical and cultural analysis, Koh reveals how American pop music instilled among Asian/Korean immigrants the image of the United States as a land of freedom of possibility. This vision depended on the erasure of Indigenous Americans. Asian Christian settlers have a moral responsibility to consider their relationship with Indigenous Americans and to begin the work of relationship building and solidarity between communities. Koh's essay challenges readers to reflect on their (un)conscious participation in settler colonialism even while pursuing just racial relations.

Comic and graphic novel readers would gain critical theological perspectives on superheroes by reading Yuki Schwartz's chapter, "The Cosmopolitics of Belonging." Schwartz examines the process of shaping and reshaping US theological imagination through comic book superheroes and the role that Asian and Asian North American superhero characters play in that theological work. Asian American superhero narratives that dwell within what Cathy Park Hong calls "minor feelings"—specifically the minor feeling of shame—reveal the contradictions and hybridities, capacities and limitations, and critical choices about identity, power, and care that make communal belonging possible. In addition, Schwartz makes superheroes' racial identities more visible. Through Schwartz's essay, readers can strengthen their "theological literacy"—by tracing invisible theological images embedded in American pop culture, readers can see how these images shape and reshape racial/gender/class politics.

Keun-joo Christine Pae's chapter, "An Antiracist and Antiwar Feminist Theology," is premised on the critical observation that US militarism is a persistent cause of xenophobia, racism, and interracial conflict at home and abroad. America's "hot wars" in Asia during the Cold War militarized and racialized Black-Asian relations and still influence interracial conflict domestically and internationally. Pae searches for possibilities of revitalizing Christian internationalism to dismantle militarized racism and racialized militarism. Critical theo-ethical reflection on the Women's International Democratic Federation's antiwar and anti-imperialist work at the height of McCarthyism helps Pae imagine these possibilities with a liberative God emerging from popular activism in the transpacific space. This chapter encourages readers to reexamine America's war stories and (re)tell new Christian stories (i.e., myths and good news) highlighting Christians' international solidarity work for peace and justice. Thus, readers can critically reflect on what antiracist/ antiwar work they have done (or can do) at their respective social locations. Pae's chapter creates a bridge toward Part II.

Part II Cross-Racial and Cross-Border Solidarity expands and sheds new light on the topics analyzed and reflected upon in Part I. The chapters in Part II critically interrogate barriers and opportunities of cross-racial solidarity for just racial relations. Like Koh's and Pae's chapters, Jin Young Choi's "Intimate Encounters at Unhomely Homes" takes the Korean War as a critical moment to analyze Black-Asian relations. Through Frank Money, the protagonist of Toni Morrison's novel *Home* (2012), Choi contemplates a racially minoritized community's trauma and healing. Choi places the suffering endured by African Americans in the transpacific space of US imperialist politics. Choi juxtaposes *Home* to the Jesus story in the Gospel of John. Unlike the synoptic gospels, John adds the story of *the homecoming of Jesus* and his disciples to Jesus' post-resurrection apparitions. This unhomely home is where remembering and healing can take place. Choi argues that stories of trauma and healing in the ancient and present times provide minoritized communities with space for collective restoration. Readers can contemplate the possibilities for Asian and Black American communities together to overcome the historical trauma caused by racist violence. These communities' healing journeys are intergenerationally and transnationally bound with each other.

Jessica Wai-Fong Wong's "Beyond Siloed Solidarity" actively searches for the Asian American voice and space in antiracist activism. As racial discourse and solidarity work in the United States are often trapped in the Black-White dichotomy, Asian Americans are welcomed into the conversation but pushed toward a form of white advocacy or encouraged to pursue racial justice with and for other Asian Americans. Wong explores one possible reason behind this dynamic: the concept of race at the center of the racial logic dominating Western modernity remains a powerful organizing idea within the very justice groups aimed at challenging said logic. The presence of this concept, with its definitive and organizing power, produces notable parallels between the given racial system and these antiracist efforts. Hence, Wong presents an alternative logic of identity and belonging, one rooted in the transgressive character of the holy order of God.

Nami Kim challenges well-intentioned Korean American Christian leaders' antiracist activism, especially in response to shooting incidents in Atlanta in 2021. From an intersectional and transnational feminist perspective, Kim's chapter, "The Confines of 'Antiracism' Work in the Intersectional Realities of 'Anti-Asian' Violence," argues that antiracist work based solely on shared racial identity cannot end or prevent violent incidents such as the killings of six women of Asian descent in Atlanta. As Kim accentuates for effective antiracism work, material conditions and other intersecting structures of oppression that produce differences must be named. Additionally, minority nationalism, stemming from the singularity of race as an operating principle, is frequently conjoined with the notion of "national belonging" or "inclusion," concomitant with the binary of deserving and undeserving persons. Arguing that such a binary is a constitutive part of the "theology of decency," Kim proposes that rejection of a theology of decency is a necessary step for a Christian praxis of solidarity across differences. Kim's efforts to complicate antiracism work in order to increase its effectiveness and her proposal of an indecent antiracist theology would motivate readers to reexamine their communities' antiracist work.

The four essays in "Part III Rereading Memories and Creative Activism" challenge inherited cultural wisdom about race and search for holistic ways of dismantling racist culture, politics, and theology. This section begins with Heike Peckruhn's essay, "Tasting Me/You." Like Schwartz and Koh, Peckruhn interweaves her autobiographic theology with critical race theory and affect theory. For Peckruhn, the racialization of Thais and Thai Americans (a minority among minorities) is analogous to the Orientalization of Thai food in the US global market. This analogy leads her to recognize race and racism as state technologies of affect (i.e., visceral feelings, emotions, etc.). Peckruhn argues for interracial/complex racial embodiment and bodily encounters as pluralities of experience and identity formations. Utilizing affective forces focuses on producing "felt" spaces in which affective agency is harnessed for reconfigurations of affective economies and emotional investments in antiracist, anti-oppression habits, and practices. Readers can critically see the complex racial polities revealed on a plate of Thai food.

Boyung Lee critically analyzes Korean immigrant Christians' foundational identity narratives in "Toward Solidarity-Creating Personhood." Utilizing narrative identity formation theories, she identifies indifference, self-excuse, and Christian nationalistic orientation toward Korea as the ideological and historical identity markers of Korean American Christians. Such ideologies have formed Korean American meta-narratives marked with the uniqueness and struggles of Korean Americanhood while allowing Korean Americans to be silent on anti-Black racism, white supremacy, and colonialism. Lee endeavors to develop solidarity-creating identity formation narratives among Korean Americans in struggles with other minoritized communities to disturb the white supremacy entangled with Christian nationalism. Readers would find it useful to compare Lee's antiracist strategies to those suggested by Kim's elaboration of an indecent theology for antiracism. Lee's essay would also help readers explore new narratives forming their antiracist identities.

Sharon Jacob's "Under the Master's Table" probes and teases out the nuances between caste, religion, and color that are intricately intertwined to construct anti-darkness sentiments among South Asians. Critically reflecting on her social location, Jacob argues that anti-darkness sentiments might have emerged in the Indian context but have successfully traversed and settled within South Asian American communities. Like Pae, Jacob looks for the roots of anti-Black racism in Asian American communities in the transpacific space. Using anti-darkness as a lens, Jacob reinterprets the narrative of the Canaanite woman, who was compared to a dog by Jesus (Matthew 15: 21–28). Her interpretation shows how generationally accumulated narratives, learned behaviors, and encultured attitudes toward others are duplicated, institutionalized, and turned into stringent systems that seek effectively to dehumanize entire communities and peoples. Readers may engage Jacob's chapter in conjunction with Lin's and Choi's essays to explore antiracist readings of biblical stories.

The last chapter, "Who Is Family?" by Courtney Goto critically explores Asian North American (ANA) Christians' complicated relationships with Black people as "family"—people with whom they empathize. Goto categorizes three diverges of ANA Christians' empathy with Black folk: supporting Blacks as fellow victims of racism, partially relating to Black experiences, and actively or implicitly discriminating against Black people. These three ways of relating are not only found among ANA Christians, but often also within individuals as conflicting feelings about relating to their Black neighbors. Goto facilitates honest conversations among ANA Christians about what motivates and/or keeps us from deeper relationships with Black people. The life of Yuri Kochiyama, who is a "saintly" figure in the Jamesian sense, serves as a case study for "introspection" (Kohut) and shared reflection in ANA congregations. Readers will appreciate Goto's detailed practical steps of exercising empathy for just racial relations. Her chapter expands the practicality of previous chapters, particularly those of Pae, Choi, and Wong.

What impact will the stories of our communities have? What can you take away from our stories? Melissa Wilcox, a queer scholar of religion, stresses the critical power of stories that can "make the world, unmake it, and remake it in a different form" as well as "erase people, places, and events or add them in, elevate or downplay their importance, retell or reinterpret them."[15] According to Wilcox, transgender studies, queer studies, and religious studies can equip people with powerful insights to comprehend "how stories can give life, and how they can kill."[16] *Embodying Antiracist Christianity* is a collection of Asian American stories that aim to make a world with just racial relations by challenging and reinterpreting familiar stories such as biblical narratives, the foundation stories of America, comic superheroes, the saga of fallen American soldiers abroad, food, popular songs, and more. Yet, the stories we tell in the anthology make familiar stories unfamiliar too. Our personal and communal stories, interwoven with critical race theories, religious/theological studies, feminist studies, and Asian American studies, help readers comprehend the power of stories and the unfamiliarity of familiar stories. Our stories will also show various ways of embodying antiracist Christianity in Asian American communities and beyond.

How to Use This Book: Some Suggestions

Each chapter offers three to five discussion questions for readers to (re)examine their antiracism work in various social institutions, including faith communities, colleges, graduate schools, and seminaries. These questions also invite readers to challenge the authors' analyses and suggestions for just racial relations. However,

---

[15] Melissa M. Wilcox, *Queer Religiosities: An Introduction to Queer and Transgender Studies in Religion* (Lanham, MD: Rowman and Littlefield, 2021), 1.

[16] Wilcox, *Queer Religiosities*, 62.

before rushing into discussion questions, spend enough time closely reading the essay, in order to understand the historical contexts and structural complexities behind it. Additionally, be in imaginative conversation with each author and make a connection between different chapters. This book would work the best when you read it holistically and discuss questions with others in the classroom or in other group settings.

As editors, we are keenly aware of the limited scope of the stories *Embodying Antiracist Christianity* presents. When the project was conceived in 2020, we were a group of fifteen women committed to antiracist work at diverse institutional and social contexts. In the intervening three years, some members were unable to finish writing manuscripts due to unforeseen circumstances, although their commitment to antiracism work remains unchanged. The book could have delivered more ethnically diverse stories. We regret that the majority of the stories come from East Asian/American experiences. Despite its limits, we are confident that *Embodying Antiracist Christianity* will generate new conversations on American racism both in domestic and transnational contexts and Christians' collective responsibility to see and act against any forms of racist violence on every level of human life. We hope that this book will encourage readers to normalize practices for just racial relations from where they stand.

Bibliography

Althaus-Reid, Marcella. 2000. *Indecent Theology: Theological Perversions in Sex, Gender, and Politics*. London, UK: Routledge.
Bayoumi, Moustafa. 2008. *How Does It Feel to Be a Problem: Being Young and Arab in America*. New York: Penguin Books.
Calamur, Krishnadev. 2017. What Trump's Executive Order on Immigration Does—and Doesn't Do. *The Atlantic*, January 30. https://www.theatlantic.com/news/archive/2017/01/trump-immigration-order-muslims/514844/.
Dhillon, Jatinder, Shrai Popoat, and David Reimers. 2021. My Dad Was Killed in First Hate-Crime After 9/11. *BBC News*, September 13. https://www.bbc.com/news/av/world-us-canada-58514967.
DuBois, W.E.B. 1903. *The Souls of Black Folk*. Chicago: A. C. McClurg & Co.
Goodstein, Laurie. 2001. Falwell: Blame Abortionists, Feminists, and Gays. *New York Times*, September 19; reprinted in *The Guardian*. https://www.theguardian.com/world/2001/sep/19/september11.usa9.
Enloe, Cynthia. 2004. *The Curious Feminist: Searching for Women in a New Age of Empire*. Berkeley: University of California Press.
Kandil, Caitlin Yoshiko. 2020. Asian Americans Report Over 650 Racist Acts over Last Week, New Data Says. *NBC News*, March 26. https://www.nbcnews.com/news/asian-america/asian-americans-report-nearly-500-racist-acts-over-last-week-n1169821.
Lee, Erika. 2019. *America for Americans: A History of Xenophobia in the United States*. New York: Basic Books.
Little, Becky. 2020. Trump's 'Chinese' Virus Is Part of a Long History of Blaming Other Countries for Disease. *Time*, March 20. https://time.com/5807376/virus-name-foreign-history/?fbclid=IwAR2QVvyMguaUDFMTqAwzNOk2eaGA1L-MEdT16X3bx5RzY0%20WlAEgvqSsodlU.

Lu, Wendy. 2020. This Is What It's Like to Be an Asian Woman in the Age of The Coronavirus. *Asian Voices*, March 31. https://www.huffpost.com/entry/asian-women-racism-coronavirus_n_5e822d41c5b66ea70fda8051.

Risse, Guenter. 2012. *Plague, Fear, and Politics in San Francisco's Chinatown*. Baltimore: Johns Hopkins University Press. https://doi.org/10.1353/book.14337.

Singh, Jasleen. 2017. Desire, Patriotism, and Sikh Subjectivity. *Sikh Formations* 13 (4): 254–267. https://doi.org/10.1080/17448727.2017.1382632.

Stop AAPI Hate. National Report: Two Years and Thousands of Voices: What Community-Generated Data Tells Us about Anti-AAPI Hate. https://stopaapihate.org/wp-content/uploads/2022/07/Stop-AAPI-Hate-Year-2-Report.pdf.

Wilcox, Melissa M. 2021. *Queer Religiosities: An Introduction to Queer and Transgender Studies in Religion*. Lanham, MD: Rowman and Littlefield.

Part I
Settler Colonialism, Anti-Black Racism, and Anti-Asian Racism

2
America, the New Jerusalem, and Anti-immigrant Discourse

Yii-Jan Lin

Introduction

What does apocalypse have to do with American immigration? And what do I mean by "apocalypse"? Whether the term "apocalypse" is used in its broader, popular sense or in its narrower, ancient sense, it relates to immigration. On a popular level, the word brings to mind world-ending catastrophe or glorious entry into a heavenly utopia—both of which are possibilities in immigrant imagination and discourses of the American dream/nightmare. In the study of ancient literature and biblical studies, the term *apocalypse* refers to a genre of ancient Jewish literature that includes elements such as a heavenly ascent, angelic guides, the revelation of other realities, and prophecies—both indictments of oppressive empires and predictions of the end of empires and the beginning of the full reign of God. These also relate to American immigration, particularly through the Book of Revelation, which has undeniably shaped American national identity. Explorers, colonists, and political and religious leaders have all described and identified America and the United States as the heavenly New Jerusalem of Revelation, the ultimate seat of God's reign, and the dwelling place of God's people. But, like the double-edged sword coming from the mouth of the Son of Man (Rev 1:16, 2:12), this glorious American identification with the heavenly city cuts both ways. The ideation of America as an apocalyptic destination has also brought with it apocalyptic violence through the gatekeeping discourse of American immigration. Those who have claimed America as the new holy city have likewise claimed it as an exclusive destination to be defended against outside threats.

In the mid-nineteenth century, as Chinese immigrants arrived in America to work in the mines and railway construction of the West, the apocalyptic language used to

Y.-J. Lin (✉)
Yale Divinity School, New Haven, CT, USA
e-mail: yii-jan.lin@yale.edu

glorify America as the New Jerusalem turned to target the Chinese as a prime threat to the heavenly city. Congressional speeches, novels, newspaper articles, and political cartoons depicted Chinese peoples as a heathen Yellow Peril and China as the demonic Dragon, both threatening God's city. The tactics using Revelation's rhetoric and discourse to exclude Chinese immigrants have become the blueprint for violent anti-immigration rhetoric in America ever since.

Apocalyptic "Discovery"

The history of America as the New Jerusalem starts with the first wave of immigrants to the Americas in the last millennium, beginning with Christopher Columbus's first voyage in 1492.[1] But long before Columbus made landfall in Guanahani, modern San Salvador, European theologians and cartographers had unconsciously and proleptically created a place for the Americas in the geographical imaginary of the fifteenth century. This theologically charged geography placed the Holy City of Jerusalem at the center of the world—not only in recognition of its centrality in Christian salvation history but also in proclaiming its *future* as the city to be retaken by Christians and the location of Christ's return and millennial reign.[2] This is expressed with the neatness of the symbolism often found in maps of the world (*mappaemundi*), common throughout Europe at the time.[3]

---

[1] Archaeologists estimate that the first human arrivals to the Americas date to 21,000–23,000 years ago. See Matthew R. Bennett, et al., "Evidence of Humans in North America during the Last Glacial Maximum," *Science* 373:6562 (2021): 1528–1531, https://www.science.org/doi/10.1126/science.abg7586. Evidence of a brief Viking settlement in Newfoundland dates to 1021 CE. See Margot Kuitems, et al., "Evidence for European presence in the Americas in AD 1021," *Nature* 601 (2022): 388–391, https://www.nature.com/articles/s41586-021-03972-8.

[2] See David Woodward, "Medieval *Mappaemundi*" in *The History of Cartography*, ed. J. B. Harley and David Woodward (Chicago: University of Chicago Press, 1987), 341: "Thus, while there is a clear biblical justification for centering these maps on Jerusalem and an empirical reason for doing so (it did occur roughly in the middle of the then known world), the idea does not seem to have been taken as literally as was previously thought …The strengthening of the idea of Jerusalem as the spiritual center, a natural outcome of the Crusades, may have been responsible for the noticeable shift in the structure of *mappaemundi* from 1100 to 1300, toward centering maps on Jerusalem." See also John Kirtland Wright, *The Geographical Lore of the Time of the Crusades: A Study in the History of Medieval Science and Tradition in Western Europe* (New York: American Geographical Society, 1927), 259–260.

[3] While other types of maps, such as portolan (navigational) and topographical maps, were certainly in use during Columbus's time, symbolic T-O maps were also important in that time period for understanding and *interpreting* the world, with T-O maps accounting for over 50 percent of the extant *mappaeumundi* from the fifteenth century (around 330 maps). See Woodward, "Medieval *Mappaemundi*," 286–370, especially Fig. 18.8 and 18.9 on 298.

2 America, the New Jerusalem, and Anti-immigrant Discourse

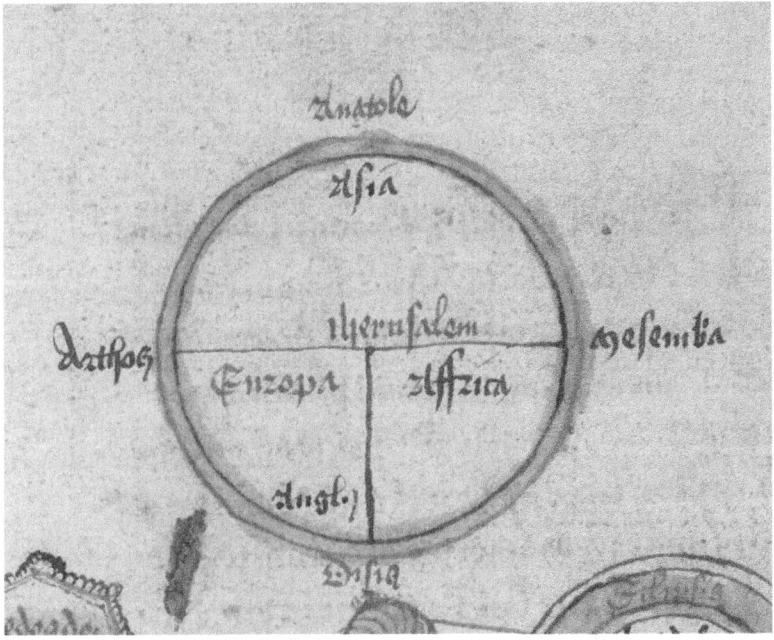

Fig. 2.1 T-O map of the world, detail from folio 17r of an astrological and medical compilation, end of the fifteenth century, England, mssHM 64. Huntington Library

Figure 2.1 is an Isidoran T-O map of the world from around the year 1500.[4] This map does not, obviously, convey much geographical information—its power lies in its symbolic presentation of the world.[5] The map shows an encircling ocean—the O—divided by a T made up of rivers (the horizontal line of the Nile and the Don) and the Mediterranean Sea (running perpendicularly downward). These waters separate Asia, Europe, and Africa, placing the city of Jerusalem at its physical, geographical, and theological center. Asia forms the top half of the circle, with the rising of the Sun (here labeled *Anatole*) at the highest point of the map.[6]

As mentioned above, this tripartite map neatly encapsulates with a few simple strokes the key elements of Christian chronology: the East, representing Eden at the creation of the world; Jerusalem, as the Israelite center of power, the location of the

---

[4] Isidoran because it is based on Isidore of Seville's descriptions of the world in *De natura rerum* and *Etymologiae*. See John Williams, "Isidore, Orosius, and the Beatus Map," *Imago Mundi* 49 (1997): 7–32; also Woodward, "Medieval *Mappaemundi*," 301–302.

[5] Woodward, "Medieval *Mappaemundi*," 342: "the function of *mappaemundi* was primarily didactic and moralizing and lay not in the communication of geographical facts."

[6] The other points of the compass here are *Arthos* [sic] for *Arctos* (north) to the left, *Mesembria* (south) to the right, and *Disis* (Greek: δύσις, west, "sunset") at the bottom. The city name at the lower left-hand side is *Anglia* (England).

temple, and the site of the crucifixion and resurrection of Christ—emphasized by the T lines forming the cruciform and the crucified body of Christ[7]; and finally Jerusalem-yet-to-be, widely understood as the eventual site of Christ's return and earthly reign (Rev 20:1-6).

Christopher Columbus began his travels within this symbolic context, with this geographical and theological vision of the world. Both literally and hermeneutically, Columbus aimed for two destinations—the same two highlighted on medieval T-O maps: Jerusalem and Paradise. It was his belief, informed by the apocalypticism of abbot and mystic Joachim of Fiore (c. 1135–1202) and the Franciscans, not only that the end of the world was rapidly approaching, but also that certain prophecies had yet to be fulfilled to usher in the eschaton.[8]

First, Jerusalem must be taken from the infidels and brought under Christian rule; and second, the Christian gospel must reach all people on earth. Columbus considered himself the primary instrument God was using to bring these two events to fulfillment. In Columbus's mind, his voyage across the ocean was inspired by the Holy Spirit so that he could fulfill these two prophecies. By sailing westward, he would reach rich lands in the East. Consequently, he could bring home the funds for a final crusade to take back Jerusalem. At the same time, the gospel would reach the peoples found at the ends of the earth. That he should have conceived of finding lands at all by sailing to the West, Columbus in fact credits the Revelation of John and divine vision, writing after his third voyage, "Of the new heaven and earth of which Our Father spoke through Saint John in the Apocalypse, after it was spoken through the mouth of Isaiah, he made me messenger and showed me that place."[9]

Therefore, in Columbus's imagination, when he reached the islands of the Caribbean, they were no less than the apocalyptic lands that Revelation had "shown him," signaling the fulfillment of his predictions. Thus, via the Revelation of John, Columbus framed his discovery as ultimate and apocalyptic in three ways: these lands were literally, to him and Europe, a new earth that nearly touched heaven; they were the Edenic Terrestrial Paradise, full of riches for a New Jerusalem crusade; and they contained the final peoples to be converted before the apocalypse. Ultimately,

---

[7] Jonathan T. Lanman, "The Religious Symbolism of the T in T-O Maps," *Cartographica* 18:4 (1981): 18–22. See also Woodward, "Medieval *Mappaemundi*," 334.

[8] See John Leddy Phelan, "The Apocalypse in the Age of Discovery," 17–28 in *The Millennial Kingdom of the Franciscans in the New World*, 2nd ed. (Berkeley: University of California Press, 1970); Abbas Hamdani, "Columbus and the Recovery of Jerusalem," *Journal of the American Oriental Society* 99.1 (1979): 39–48; and Carol Delaney, "Columbus's Ultimate Goal: Jerusalem," *Comparative Studies in Society and History* 48.2 (2006): 260–292.

[9] In a letter to Doña Juana de la Torre, Christopher Columbus, *Cristóbal Colón, Textos y documentos completos: Relaciones de viajes, cartas y memoriales*, ed. and comm. Consuelo Varela (Madrid: Alianza Editorial, 1984, 2a ed.), 243. Quoted and translated in Margarita Zamora, *Reading Columbus* (Berkeley: University of California Press, 1993), 141.

when Columbus envisioned these lands, he saw Jerusalem as the destination—and the New Jerusalem beyond that as the final end of his task.[10]

What the arrival of Columbus and other Europeans meant to the native peoples who watched these immigrants arrive on their shores was devastation and death through disease and warfare, and the destruction of their home by the violent reinterpretation and appropriation of it as a Terrestrial Paradise. Nevertheless, through the passionate belief of the Spanish explorers and then later missionaries and converts, the identification of this New World with the New Jerusalem had been irrevocably established. Through a collision of prophetic imagination with fulfillment, of navigation with hermeneutics, Columbus's landing entrenched the understanding that "the New World equals the end of the world," that the New World is the New Jerusalem.[11]

Pilgrimage to the New Jerusalem

A little more than a century after Columbus, groups of colonizers were arriving on the shores of Wampanoag, Narragansett, Mohegan, and Pequot lands, among others. While English immigrants were quite differently motivated than Columbus in their takeover of territories, there were a few striking similarities. English churchmen, broadly called "Puritans" in American history, were also seeking the New Jerusalem, both allegorically and literally. In the apocalyptic view of these colonizers, indigenous peoples were either heathens to be converted or, as was more often the case, expendable lives to be cleared for the "better growth" of God's people.[12]

New Haven colony co-founder John Davenport declared in his writings that the Congregational assembly he strove to build would truly embody the New Jerusalem,

---

[10] As Zamora, *Reading Columbus*, 143, eloquently states: ... the Indies is not only on the figurative way to Jerusalem, it is also in the vicinity of Paradise. Such a geography makes sense only in the context of a paradigmatic cartographic discourse in which spatiotemporal coordinates are determined ideologically rather than empirically. Columbus describes the voyage's trajectory from west (Spain) to far east (the presumed Asiatic mainland) as an ascent up the slope of a pear-shaped southern hemisphere toward a Terrestrial Paradise, situated at the very top, on the spot closest to heaven."

[11] Quotation from Phelan, *Millennial Kingdom of the Franciscans*, 24: "Only after the equation 'the New World equals the end of the world' is understood can some new light be thrown on the origins of one of the most celebrated New World myths; namely, that the Indians were the descendants of the ten lost tribes of Israel." The lost tribes are just one aspect of the many apocalyptic beliefs surrounding the New World and, later, America and the United States, that should be understood in light of this equation.

[12] See Daniel Denton, *A Brief Description of New-York* (London: John Hancock, 1670), 12, who described disease that killed indigenous peoples as the process of clearing the land "of those pernicious creatures to make room for better growth."

"measured" as the heavenly city is, by a "golden reed."¹³ Davenport intended all layers of life in New Haven—from civic and ecclesial governance to doctrinal "purity" to the literal urban structures of everyday life—to comply with the golden measurements of the New Jerusalem.¹⁴ This was, after all, the enterprise John Cotton (1585–1652) had promised him when urging him to sail from his exile in Holland to New England.

Cotton, the leading minister of Boston and the Massachusetts Bay Colony, boasted in a letter to Davenport that "the Order of the Churches, and the Common-Wealth, was now so settled in New-England, by common Consent, that it brought into [Cotton's] Mind the New Heaven, and the New Earth, wherein dwells Righteousness."¹⁵ Thus motivated, Davenport set out to establish the New Haven colony and "did all that was possible to render the Renowned Church of New Haven, like the New Jerusalem."¹⁶

This conception of American colonies as the New Jerusalem connects from Davenport back to John Cotton and, back further still, through different national and religious networks, to Columbus. It connects forward in time to the apocalyptic patriotism and martyrdom of the Revolution¹⁷ and the identification of America with Zion throughout the Civil War.¹⁸ Heavenly imagery and metaphor continued with

---

¹³ John Davenport, *The Power of the Congregational Churches Asserted and Vindicated* (London: [s.n.], 1672 [written ca. 1648]), 57.

¹⁴ On Puritan colonists' intention to merge state and church governance, see Michael P. Winship, *Godly Republicanism: Puritans, Pilgrims, and a City on a Hill* (Cambridge, MA: Harvard University Press, 2012); on Davenport's hopes for New Haven and surrounding regions specifically, see Francis J. Bremer, *Building a New Jerusalem: John Davenport, a Puritan in Three Worlds* (New Haven: Yale University Press, 2012), 181–219.

¹⁵ This is a quotation of John Cotton, recorded by his grandson: Cotton Mather, *Magnalia Christi Americana or The Ecclesiastical History of New-England from Its First Planting in the Year 1620 unto the Year of our Lord, 1698* (London: Thomas Parkhurst, 1702), Book 3.53.

¹⁶ Ibid., Book 3.55.

¹⁷ See James P. Byrd, "'The Fierceness and Wrath of the Almighty God': Revelation in the Revolution" in *Sacred Scripture, Sacred War: The Bible and the American Revolution* (Oxford: Oxford University Press, 2013), 143–163. Byrd demonstrates that while Revelation was not among the most quoted biblical books during the American Revolution, it still provided rhetorically effective imagery and language to stir up morale, such as the call to martyrdom in the opening seven letters to seven churches (Rev 2–3), the woman's flight from the dragon to the wilderness (Rev 12), and the militant Christ (Rev 19:11–21): 163: "Through these apocalyptic visions, including the victorious charge of a militant Christ, ministers proclaimed a bellicose Christianity that endowed patriotic sacrifice with sacred martyrdom" (163).

¹⁸ On the conflation of America with Zion see Eran Shalev, *American Zion: The Old Testament as a Political Text from the Revolution to the Civil War* (New Haven: Yale University Press, 2013). For more on Julia Ward Howe's writing of "The Battle Hymn of the Republic" (1862) and its use of Revelation, see Ernest Lee Tuveson, *Redeemer Nation: The Idea of America's Millennial Role* (Chicago: University of Chicago Press, 1968), 197–202. The winepress imagery comes not only from Revelation 14:9-10, 18-20, 19:15 but also from Isaiah 63:1-6, Joel 3:13, and Lamentations 1:15.

American expansion westward, with the patriotic goddess Columbia lighting the way in John Gast's 1872 painting *American Progress*.

But while the rhetoric of America-as-the-New-Jerusalem works to inspire nationalist pride, it can be even more effective when used to exclude, to suppress, and to banish. No apocalyptic text exists without violence in its visions and metaphors, with destruction aimed at those it labels outsiders and evildoers. Thus, the New Jerusalem metaphor has also been used in American political discourse for violence and destruction.

Bones and Bodies

Toano, Nevada, lies among the foothills close to the Utah border, an arid desert landscape dotted with sagebrush. It is now a ghost town, with no remaining structures standing, but in 1870 it was connected to the city of Elko, Nevada, by the Central Pacific Railroad, about seventy-five miles away. January 5, 1870, was probably a cold day, but railway workers in Toano probably preferred the chill for the cargo they were loading onto a six-car train headed west to Elko and on to San Francisco. They had to ensure that each car was packed with the dead remains of Chinese railroad workers—packed as full as possible, so the Central Pacific Rail could be well paid for the load, according to the *Elko Independent*, a twice-weekly newspaper that ran from 1869 to 1872. "We understand that the Chinese companies pay the Railroad Company ten dollars for carrying to San Francisco each dead Chinaman. Six cars, well stuffed with this kind of freight, will be a good day's work." The paper went on to state, with the same astonishing casualness, "The remains of the females are left to rot in shallow graves, while every defunct male is carefully preserved for shipment to the Occident."[19]

The western section of the transcontinental railroad had reached completion the prior year—largely through the labor of Chinese workers.[20] The remains of laborers who had died, either by sickness, construction accidents, harsh conditions, or

---

[19] "Dead Chinamen," *Elko Independent*, January 5, 1870, 3. Cited in CPPR.org, "FAQs: How Many Died Building the Central Pacific Railroad," *Central Pacific Railroad Photographic History Museum*, http://cprr.org/Museum/FAQs.html#died, accessed June 13, 2022.

[20] On the history of Chinese workers and the transcontinental railroad, see Gordon H. Chang, *Ghosts of Gold Mountain: The Epic Story of the Chinese Who Built the Transcontinental Railroad* (Boston: Houghton Mifflin, 2019); Gordon H. Chang and Shelly Fisher Fishkin, eds., *The Chinese and the Iron Road: Building the Transcontinental Railroad* (Stanford: Stanford University Press, 2019); Manu Karuka, *Empire's Tracks: Indigenous Nations, Chinese Workers, and the Transcontinental Railroad* (Oakland: University of California Press, 2019); David R. Roediger and Elizabeth D. Esch, *Production of Difference: Race and the Management of Labor in U.S. History* (New York: Oxford University Press, 2012).

outright murder, were collected to be shipped back to China.[21] Not all bodies made it across the Pacific, however. The remains of some Chinese workers have been discovered, quite by accident. Such was the case when a landowner began construction on a site in Carlin, Nevada, to build a new house, unearthing the remains of thirteen men.[22] These remains belonged to a community of immigrants who had already been settled in the area for decades by the time of burial—Chinese miners had worked in Nevada's silver mines starting in the 1850s, after the California Gold Rush of 1849.[23] But unlike the Puritans of New Haven and New England, these Chinese who came to America would not become part of an essential, patriotic national narrative, nor would they or their descendants by default belong to the citizenry of the United States.[24]

In fact, the same year the bodies of Chinese railroad workers were shipped from Nevada to San Francisco, on July 4, 1870, Congress voted not to allow Chinese

---

[21] Other newspaper reports of the cargo of dead Chinese workers include "Bones in Transit," *Sacramento Reporter*, June 30, 1870, which notes that "accumulated bones of perhaps 1,200 Chinamen" weighing "20,000 pounds" were in by train, noting that Chinese custom requires burial in China; "Bones of Defunct Chinamen," *Sacramento Union*, June 30, 1870, which reports "fifty defunct Chinamen … to be interred in Conboie's private cemetery, as have been already the bones of about one hundred others similarly deceased." Whether these reports tell of the same shipment (and the numbers of one or the other are mistaken or exaggerated) or of different cargo trains is unknown. Both are cited in CPPR.org, "FAQs: How Many Died Building the Central Pacific Railroad?" which states that the report of 1200 dead Chinese workers is highly dubious given the two conflicting reports, although the possibility that these were two different trains with different destinations (Conboie's cemetery in Sacramento vs. China via San Francisco) is not considered. The museum site is run by descendants of Lewis R. Clement, an engineer and surveyor of the Central Pacific Railroad. On the dangers that led to the death of Chinese railroad workers, see Chang, *Ghosts of Gold Mountain*, especially 225–226.

[22] The landowner first unearthed five bodies on his property, which led to the discovery of thirteen total bodies on his land and a neighbor's property. See Sue Fawn Chung, Fred P. Frampton, and Timothy W. Murphy, "Venerate These Bones: Chinese American Funerary Practices as Seen in Carlin, Elko County, Nevada," in *Chinese American Death Rituals: Respecting the Ancestors*, Sue Fawn Chung and Priscilla Wegars eds. (Lanham, MD: AltaMira Press, 2005), 107–145, on the discovery of these graves and their analysis. See also Ryan P. Harrod and John J. Crandall, "Rails Built of the Ancestors' Bones: The Bioarchaeology of the Overseas Chinese Experience," *Historical Archaeology* 49.1 (2015): 148–161, on the analysis of these remains and the evidence of hard labor in rough environments.

[23] The earliest dated tombstone housed in the crypt of the Center Church on the Green belongs to "Ms. Sarah Trowbridge," who died in 1687. New Haven was "founded" in 1638. See M. Reynard Georgevitch, "Sarah (Rutherford) Trowbridge, 1641-1687," *Tales from the Crypt: A Cata-Blog of Stones and Stories form the Basement of Center Church*, July 20, 2014, https://ctcryptkeeper.wordpress.com/2014/07/20/sarah-rutherford-trowbridge-1641-1687/. The graves of Chinese discovered in Carlin Nevada date from before 1900 through 1924, according to Chung, Frampton, and Murphy, "Venerate these Bones." On Chinese immigrants heading east after working mines in California, see ibid., 108–111.

[24] Birthright citizenship was codified in the Supreme Court ruling in *United States v. Wong Kim Ark*, 1898.

immigrants to be naturalized.[25] During that Senate debate, Senator George Williams (R-OR) could not imagine that anyone would want Chinese people to belong to the nation, stating, "Is there anybody who will say that the Chinese is a desirable population? ... Mongolians, no matter how long they may stay in the United States, will never lose their identity as a peculiar and separate people. They will never amalgamate with persons of European descent."[26] Williams, in that statement, captures succinctly the racialization of Chinese (and Asian) peoples as perpetual foreigners throughout their history in the United States up to and beyond this writing.

At the end of the nineteenth century, the Chinese were not the latest newcomer, only the greatest perceived threat in the minds of white residents in the western states. With the end of the Gold Rush in California, the closing of certain mines in Nevada, and the completion of the transcontinental railroad, Chinese laborers moved into other areas of work, and their communities continued to expand.[27] While Chinese immigrants had faced discrimination and harassment—social, legal, and civic—since their arrival,[28] the shift of Chinese labor from the railroads plus the continued arrival of Chinese in California prompted still greater violence and hate against them.[29]

Earlier, when the railroad companies needed workers for hard and dangerous jobs, they welcomed and recruited Chinese immigrants—after all, "w[ould] the white man, in this country, follow such employments? Never," stated the *Daily*

---

[25] The Naturalization Act of 1870, passed in Congress as H.R. 2201. This extended the ability to be naturalized to those of African descent, but Congress rejected any amendment that would allow those of Chinese descent to be naturalized. Similarly, although birthright naturalization had existed by *jus soli* in the United States and then codified in both the Civil Rights Act of 1868 and the Fourteenth Amendment's Citizenship Clause, the children born of Chinese immigrants in the United States were not regarded as legal citizens as a matter of course. See, for example, the case *In re Look Tin Sing* (1884) of the California federal circuit court, in which American-born Look Tin Sing's citizenship had to be established in court before he could be legally readmitted in the country. It was not until *United States vs. Wong Kim Ark* (1898) that birthright citizenship was established for all born in the United States—although that right has been questioned in recent decades with regard to the children of "illegal" immigrants. See Chap. 4.

[26] 41st Congress, 2nd Session, Congressional Globe 5156, July 4, 1870. Also quoted in Martin B. Gold, *Forbidden Citizens: Chinese Exclusion and the U.S. Congress: A Legislative History* (Alexandria, VA: TheCapitol.Net, 2012), §1.13, p. 17.

[27] See Donald L. Hardesty, "Archaeology and the Chinese Experience in Nevada," *South Dakota History*, Ethnic Oasis: The Chinese in the Black Hills, Special Historic Preservation Issue, 33.4 (2003): 363–379; Chang, *Ghosts of Gold Mountain*, 209–236; D. Michael Bottoms, *An Aristocracy of Color: Race and Reconstruction in California and the West: 1850–1890* (Norman, OK: University of Oklahoma Press), 137–138; Alexander Saxton, *The Indispensable Enemy: Labor and Anti-Chinese Movement in California* (Berkeley: University of California Press, 1995), 70–71.

[28] See Saxton, *The Indispensable Enemy*, 136–137, and Paul Spickard, *Almost All Aliens: Immigration, Race, and Colonialism in American History and Identity* (New York: Routledge, 2007), 161.

[29] Bottoms, *An Aristocracy of Color*, 138: The Chinese population in California increased by 50 percent in the 1870s, although their number did not account for more than 10 percent of the total population.

California Chronicle, in 1854. But the Chinese "were such a people."[30] Leland Stanford, railroad investor and politician, assured President Andrew Johnson in 1865 that the Chinese were "quiet, peaceable, patient, industrious and economical ... ready and apt to learn all the different kinds of work required in railroad building" and "contented with less wages."[31] Then the Burlingame Treaty of 1868 further opened up immigration and commerce between the United States and China. But with the completion of the railroad in 1869, the labor that Chinese immigrants provided became viewed as a threat. In arguments in the Senate, anti-Chinese speeches dwelled on the "hordes" of Chinese, who were flooding the United States, what Senator Thomas Bayard (D-DE) called an "inundation of countless numbers and of a race wholly different" who will "destroy the labor of our own people."[32] The "inundation" by the Chinese Bayard speaks of never amounted to more than one-twentieth of all the immigrants arriving in the United States.[33] Nevertheless, Chinese peoples were the first racial-ethnic group targeted by federal immigration law.

The Page Law of 1875 effectively barred Chinese women from entering the United States by assuming them to be sex workers and morally corrupting.[34] Then the Chinese Exclusion Act of 1882 further restricted the entry of Chinese immigrants by denying entry to Chinese laborers.[35] While this may have addressed some fears regarding an incoming flood of Chinese workers, it did not account for the lives of the Chinese already within the country and their vulnerability in an environment of violent racist hatred.[36]

---

[30] *Daily California Chronicle,* April 22, 1854. Quoted in Chang, *Ghosts of Gold Mountain,* 44.

[31] Leland Stanford, *Statement Made to the President of the United States, and Secretary of the Interior, on the Progress of Work, October 10, 1865* (Sacramento: H. S. Crocker & Co, 1865), 990. Quoted in Chang, *Ghosts of Gold Mountain,* 86.

[32] 47th Congress, First Session, Congressional Record vol. 13.2, 2616, April 5, 1882.

[33] Spickard, *Almost All Aliens,* 165.

[34] See Susan Koshy, *Sexual Naturalization: Asian Americans and Miscegenation* (Stanford: Stanford University Press, 2004), 10–11. The Page Law also effectively tamped down the growth of Chinese communities and populations. See also George Anthony Peffer, "Forbidden Families: Emigration Experiences of Chinese Women under the Page Law," *Journal of American Ethnic History* 6.1 (1986): 28–46.

[35] While widely known as the Chinese Exclusion Act, historian Beth Lew-Williams uses the term "Chinese Restriction Act" to capture more accurately the phases of legislation against Chinese and Asian immigration: "Historians, with their eyes trained on what Chinese exclusion would become, have overlooked the distinction between the Restriction Period (1882-1888) and Exclusion Period (1888–1943). To understand the radicalism of Chinese exclusion and the contingent history of its rise, we must recognize the period of restriction experimentation, and contestation that preceded it." Beth Lew-Williams, *The Chinese Must Go: Violence, Exclusion, and the Making of the Alien in America* (Cambridge, MA: Harvard University Press, 2018), 8–9.

[36] See R. Gregory Nokes, *Massacred for Gold: The Chinese in Hells Canyon* (Corvallis, OR: Oregon State University Press, 2009), 76: "But although the Exclusion Act effectively blocked new laborers, it failed to protect the estimated 132,300 Chinese who remained. If anything, violence and mistreatment became worse."

Chinese immigrants had already experienced violence and expulsion from towns through intimidation and harassment in the 1870s. The brutality reached a climax in the 1880s, during which Chinese were shot, lynched, and tortured, not only in California but in Oregon, Washington, Idaho, Wyoming, and other western territories.[37] In 1885, a group of 150 white men killed at least 28 Chinese coal miners in Rock Springs, Wyoming, whom they shot, dismembered, and burned alive.[38] In 1887, a gang of white men tortured, mutilated, and murdered at least thirty-four Chinese miners in Hells Canyon, Oregon.[39] No convictions were brought against those responsible for this butchery, in either the Rock Springs or the Hells Canyon massacres, or after murders, lynchings, and mass expulsions in Los Angeles, Truckee, and Denver.[40]

This hate manifested itself in legislation in 1884 and 1888, which furthered restricted Chinese entry,[41] and then with the Geary Act of 1892, which renewed and strengthened the 1882 Act by requiring all Chinese laborers (which later meant all Chinese) within the United States to carry proof they were in the country legally—thereby implementing the first such federal requirement of documentation.[42] Without a certificate, a Chinese laborer could be forced to do hard labor and be deported, and they could not post bail or serve as witnesses in a trial.

The Geary Act was extended indefinitely in 1902, made permanent in 1904, and was not to be repealed until 1943. In the decades between the passage of the Chinese Exclusion Act in 1882 and 1904, there proliferated, throughout American political speeches, news media, literature, and art, depictions of Chinese peoples and China as a looming, pernicious, ugly threat: the Yellow Peril.[43]

---

[37] See Lew-Williams, *The Chinese Must Go*, particularly the map "Sites of Anti-Chinese Expulsion, 1885–1886," page 2, and Appendix A: Sites of Anti-Chinese Expulsions and Attempted Expulsions, 1885–1887, pages 247–251.

[38] See *U.S. House Report* (1885–1886), 49th Congress, 1st Session, no. 2044, 28–32, excerpted in Judy Yung, Gordon Chang, and Him Mark Lai, eds., "Memorial of Chinese Laborers: Rock Springs, Wyoming (1885)," pages 48–54 in idem, *Chinese American Voices from the Gold Rush to the Present* (Berkeley: University of California, 2006); and Craig Storti, *Incident at Bitter Creek: The Story of the Rock Springs Massacre* (Ames, IA: Iowa State University Press, 1991).

[39] Chang, *Ghosts of Gold Mountain*, 232; Nokes, *Massacred for Gold*.

[40] See Chang, *Ghosts of Gold Mountain*, 231–232; and Lew-Williams, *The Chinese Must Go*, 91–165.

[41] Amendments to the Exclusion Act of 1882 were passed in 1884, which forbid Chinese from any place of origin (not just China) from entering, except for teachers, students, diplomats, merchants, and tourists. The Scott Act of 1888 kept Chinese laborers who left the United States from returning, canceling their certificates for re-entry.

[42] See Erika Lee, *At America's Gates: Chinese Immigration during the Exclusion Era, 1882–1943* (Chapel Hill, NC: University of North Carolina Press, 2003), 42. See more on the creation of the bureaucracy, records, and officials needed for these laws in Chap. 4.

[43] The essential themes of Yellow Peril date from long before the existence of the United States and can be identified with the conception of the "Mongol" Other in Europe. The use of Yellow Peril in public discourse, art, and entertainment continues to this day. See John Kuo Wei Tchen and Dylan Yeats, eds., *Yellow Peril! An Archive of Anti-Asian Fear* (London: Verso, 2014).

Revelation and Yellow Peril

As in other moments of American crisis and feverish hate, pundits and politicians made use of the Book of Revelation to construct and illustrate the situation, inverting the metaphor of America as the New Jerusalem to emphasize the existence of its enemies and the need for violent exclusion. Yellow Peril tropes fit easily into the apocalyptic imaginaries and narratives drawn from its text. At the foundation of apocalyptic Yellow Peril imagery and stories used to exclude Chinese from entry and acceptance in the United States lies the belief in a divine, immutable distinction between white Americans and the Chinese "race."

This is at the heart of Senator Bayard's speech against Chinese immigration in 1882, mentioned above, before the passing of the Chinese Exclusion Act. Bayard argued that those against restrictions to Chinese immigration had only profit in mind and did not care about the plight of (white) Americans, and he couched this argument in Christian language:

> [Those creators of the Burlingame Treaty with China] overlooked or disregarded the difference of race, they overlooked the difference between Chinese and Christian civilization … They saw but one thing—a profitable commerce, and they rushed with haste into a treaty that considered Americans and Chinamen as if they were all of the same race, habits, and characteristics—all equally and alike entitled and fitted to become citizens of the Republic of the United States.[44]

However, Bayard argued, "A man cannot faithfully serve two contending governments at the same time." Of course, Bayard meant the United States and China in the immediate context, but he paraphrased a biblical text that served his purposes precisely. The text is found in both the Gospels of Matthew and Luke: "No man can serve two masters; for either he will hate the one, and love the other; or else he will hold to the one, and despise the other. Ye cannot serve God and mammon" (Matt 6:24 KJV).[45]

Bayard alluded to this Christian text to insinuate that his fellow congressmen served either China and greed or the United States and God. And the distinction between Chinese and Americans—implied by Bayard's rhetoric to be white and Christian—is too great to ever allow Chinese to immigrate and live in America, which is something that God never intended:

> [those enabling Chinese immigration] overlooked the great and *manifest* distinctions between these two nations and their population …. Why was there not some mingling of *reverence* in this, why was there not some respect paid to the *finger of the Almighty* when he points out the difference between races of mankind?[46]

---

[44] 47th Congress, First Session, Congressional Record vol. 13.2, 2616, April 5, 1882.

[45] I use the Matthean KJV translation here since it is closest to Bayard's paraphrasing. See also Luke 16:13.

[46] 47th Congress, First Session, Congressional Record vol. 13.2, 2616, April 5, 1882, emphasis added.

The Chinese, in Bayard's view, were a race wholly separate and, more importantly, unchristian and unable to belong to the people of God. That the Chinese were "pagan" and inevitably disloyal to America had already been stated repeatedly by Senators in Congress in decades past.

Thus, for example, Senator William Stewart (R-NV) argued in 1870 against Chinese naturalization: "until they renounce paganism, until they renounce imperialism, which this generation will never do, we should not propose to engraft them upon the body politic."[47] So also Senator George Williams (R-OR) during that same session denounced the idea of Chinese naturalization: "Imagine such an oath administered to Chinamen, ignorant of God, Christ, the Bible, and the Christian religion; ignorant of the Constitution of the country, its laws, its customs, and its habits!"[48] The idea that Chinese should be allowed to acquire American citizenship, introduced in an amendment by Senator Charles Sumner (R-MA), was equivalent to worship and sacrifice at an idol's altar, according to Senator Williams: "Ignorance, idolatry, immorality, vice, disease, and prostitution are the *deities* of [Senator Sumner's] theory; and *to them* he is now ready to *sacrifice* the pride and glory of American citizenship."[49]

It is no coincidence that Senator Williams named "ignorance, idolatry, immorality, vice, disease, and prostitution" as the deities identified with the Chinese and China. These elements have characterized "the East" in European and American Orientalism for centuries. And these imagined features of China and the Chinese play into both their allure and threat in apocalyptic Yellow Peril discourse. Just as the "Chinaman" could be both the exploitable "coolie" and the destroying horde, so also China as the source of status luxuries—silk, tea, porcelain—could also symbolize the decadent and degenerate Babylon of Revelation, the enemy and opposite of the New Jerusalem, the Bride of Christ.[50]

Revelation 17 presents the Whore of Babylon, who represents, in the book's ancient context, the city of Rome, fleshed out and enrobed in lavish, misogynist detail[51]:

---

[47] 41st Congress, 2nd Session, Congressional Globe 5151, July 4, 1870. Also quoted in Gold, *Forbidden Citizens*, §1.30, 14.

[48] 41st Congress, 2nd Session, Congressional Globe 5151, July 4, 1870. Also quoted in Gold, *Forbidden Citizens*, §1.30, 18–19.

[49] 41st Congress, 2nd Session, Congressional Globe 5151, July 4, 1870. Also quoted in Gold, *Forbidden Citizens*, §1.30, 18, emphasis added.

[50] On Chinese luxury goods as status symbols in the nineteenth century, see Kyla Wazana Tompkin, *Racial Indigestion: Eating Bodies in the 19th Century* (New York: New York University Press, 2012), 132; also John Kuo Wei Tchen, *New York before Chinatown: Orientalism and the Shaping of American Culture 1776–1882* (Baltimore: Johns Hopkins University Press, 1999); on the increase of export and trade of tea, silks, porcelain, and other handicrafts from China to America, see Yen-p'ing Hao, *The Commercial Revolution in Nineteenth-Century China: The Rise of Sino-Western Mercantile Capitalism* (Berkeley: University of California Press, 1986).

[51] For more on ancient and current interpretation of the misogyny, tragedy, and power of this figure, see Shanell T. Smith, *The Woman Babylon and the Marks of Empire: Reading Revelation with a Postcolonial Womanist Hermeneutics of Ambiveilence* (Minneapolis: Fortress Press, 2014).

> and I saw a woman sitting on a scarlet beast that was full of blasphemous names, and it had seven heads and ten horns. The woman was clothed in purple and scarlet and adorned with gold and jewels and pearls, holding in her hand a golden cup full of abominations and impurities of her prostitution, and on her forehead was written a name, a mystery: "Babylon the great, mother of whores and of earth's abominations." And I saw that the woman was drunk with the blood of the saints and the blood of the witnesses to Jesus. (Rev 17:3-6)

Here appear all the characterizations of China in the anti-Chinese discourse of the Senate in the 1870s and 1880s: pagan idolatry, decadent dissipation, greed, sexual corruption and prostitution, impurities and filth, and—most of threatening all—the conquering and consumption of Christian peoples, the saints, and witnesses of Jesus.

While the U.S. Senators do not explicitly name China the Whore of Babylon, the likening of China to the apocalyptic Whore and the enemies of God's kingdom is clear. And for cartoonists and novelists of the time, who had more room for poetic license than U.S. Senators, the imagery and horror of Revelation provided a vast resource for anti-Chinese illustrations and literature.

Possibly the first Yellow Peril novel in America,[52] Pierton Dooner's *Last Days of the Republic* (1880) tells the story of continued importation of "coolies" for economic profit and the spread of Chinese populations beyond the American West and into New England and the South. This allows Imperial China to invade slowly until "[t]he coil of the Asiatic serpent was gradually encircling the entire body of the victim, now virtually within its grasp."[53] Soon, Chinese armies march across the nation, in which each Chinese soldier—unlike the "Caucasian" soldier who fights "when military glory is the promised reward"—instead "loves luxury" and "above and beyond all these ... worships gold."[54] This effete and greed-motivated militia overwhelm the American armies by sheer numbers and brutality, finally making its way to Washington, where the novel concludes: "The Republic had fought its last battle; and the Imperial Dragon of China already floated from the dome of the Capitol."[55]

In this fearmongering novel, Babylon-China wins, demonstrating the consequences of the idolatrous worship of mammon rather than God. The final image of the dragon flying above the Capitol Building is the Qing Dynasty flag of China at the time, featuring a Chinese *lóng* (龍). While in Chinese cultural tradition, the *lóng* symbolizes power, blessing, the Emperor, water, and rain, Europeans had, by the nineteenth century, equated the *lóng* with the demonic dragon and serpent of the Bible and of Revelation in particular.[56]

---

[52] H. Bruce Franklin, *War Stars: The Superweapon and the American* Imagination (New York: Oxford University Press, 1988), 33.

[53] P. W Dooner, *The Last Days of the Republic* (San Francisco: Alta California Publishing House, 1880), 96.

[54] Dooner, *The Last Days of the Republic*, 234.

[55] Dooner, *The Last Days of the Republic*, 256.

[56] For a history of European and later Chinese Christian interpretation of the *lóng* with regard to biblical dragons and snakes, see Emily Dunn, "The Big Red Dragon and Indigenizations of Christianity in China," *East Asian History* 36 (2008): 73–85.

In Revelation the dragon first appears in Chap. 12, "a great red dragon, with seven heads and ten horns and seven diadems on his heads" (Rev 12:3). This is the beast threatening to snatch away the child born of the woman clothed in the sun, but he is defeated by an army of angels led by the archangel Michael:

> And war broke out in heaven; Michael and his angels fought against the dragon. The dragon and his angels fought back, but they were defeated, and there was no longer any place for them in heaven. The great dragon was thrown down, that ancient serpent, who is called the devil and Satan, the deceiver of the whole world ... Then the dragon was angry with the woman and went off to wage war on the rest of her children, those who keep the commandments of God and hold the testimony of Jesus. (Rev 12:7-9, 17)

This dragon, along with its various permutations seen in the beast of the sea (Rev 13:1-10) and the beast on which rides the Whore of Babylon (Rev 17), is ultimately destroyed in the Lake of Fire (Rev 19:19-20:3). It is with this draconic Satan that European and American imagination equates the ancient *lóng* of China and Chinese peoples.

Dooner's *Last Days of the Republic* depicts the "Asiatic serpent" and the "Imperial Dragon of China" overtaking the United States, and Robert Wolter's 1882 novel *A Short and Truthful History of the Taking of California and Oregon by the Chinese in the Year A.D. 1899* goes even further, with explicit use of Satan and the text of Revelation.[57] The story begins by depicting Chinese immigrants in much the grossly exaggerated way senators were using in Congress, describing Chinese laborers inundating every business, service industry, mine, shop, and household throughout the West. On the scene appears the Chinese Prince Tsa, who "bore less resemblance to a human being than he did to Milton's Satan."[58]

Prince Tsa is the mastermind behind a nefarious plot, executed by Chinese people up and down the coast. On December 31, 1899, the Chinese of California and Oregon poison their white employers, customers, and communities, and then march to take over the land, while the prince holds state leaders captive. At the conclusion of the novel, the narrator warns that such events had been foretold, stating, "In this liberal-minded age ... we hesitate to draw upon the Apocalypse for quotations in support of these opinions, but those who believe in revelations may find much to support them in prophetic predictions."[59] The author ends the novel by driving home, again, the Satanic forces at work in the immigration of Chinese to San Francisco, declaring that "The Black Dragon has forced the passage of the Golden Gate."[60]

---

[57] Robert Wolter ["A Survivor"], *A Short and Truthful History of the Taking of California and Oregon by the Chinese in the Year A.D. 1899* (San Francisco: A.L. Bancroft and Company, 1882).

[58] Wolter, *A Short and Truthful History of the Taking of California and Oregon by the Chinese in the Year A.D. 1899*, 58.

[59] Wolter, *A Short and Truthful History of the Taking of California and Oregon by the Chinese in the Year A.D. 1899*, 79.

[60] Wolter, *A Short and Truthful History of the Taking of California and Oregon by the Chinese in the Year A.D. 1899*, 79.

Fig. 2.2 W. A. Rogers, "The Dragon's Choice," *Harper's Weekly*, 44 no. 2278 (August 18, 1900): cover image

This is the same Dragon-as-China depicted in political cartoons such as "The Dragon's Choice" (Fig. 2.2), which appeared on the cover of *Harper's Weekly* on August 18, 1900, at the climax of the conflict between the Boxers and the Euro-American alliance.

The image shows the menacing beast, breathing smoke from its mouth, standing over villages on fire—a dragon taking its menacing stand on the seashore (Rev. 12:18). Facing it with calm stoicism is Uncle Sam, white haired, muscular, dressed in sailor whites and adorned with stars, aboard a mighty white ship, a strong bulwark, with canon aimed and ready. The bestial, ravening, dark, and satanic China is challenged by the human, rational, white, and angelic United States and presumably the European countries of the Eight Nations Alliance, its allies in the conflict.

A few years prior to Roger's "The Dragon's Choice," Helmut Knackfuss depicted "The Yellow Peril" (*die Gelbe Gefahr*) (Fig. 2.3) in imagery even more explicitly drawn from Revelation. Knackfuss's illustration circulated first in the *Leipziger Illustrierte Zeitung* in Germany in 1895 and, after gaining popularity throughout

2 America, the New Jerusalem, and Anti-immigrant Discourse

Fig. 2.3 H. Knackfuss, "The Yellow Peril," *Harper's Weekly* 42, no. 2144 (January 22, 1898): 76

Europe, was printed Stateside in *Harper's Weekly* in 1898.[61] Knackfuss based his drawing on a sketch by Kaiser Willhelm II, by whom he had been commissioned.[62] The Kaiser reportedly had a nightmare in which he saw this vision, an apocalyptic warning against the encroachment of Asia—Japan (a rising military threat) and China—upon the European nations.[63] On the right hand side of the illustration looms a colossal Buddha aflame, riding black storm clouds that form a menacing dragon with glowing eyes, like the Whore of Babylon seated on the seven-headed beast (Rev 12:3).

The perspective of the audience is aligned with that of white European nations, represented here as goddesses and women warriors dressed in a mix of nationalist

---

[61] The illustration generated many spin-offs and parodies, and even an illustration purporting to show an Asian perspective. See Peter C. Perdue and Ellen Sebring, "The Boxer Uprising I: The Gathering Storm in North China (1860–1900)," in *MIT Visualizing Cultures*, https://visualizingcultures.mit.edu/boxer_uprising/pdf/bx_essay02.pdf.

[62] Peter Paret, "The Tschudi Affair," *Journal of Modern History* 53.4 (1981), 590.

[63] See Kuo Wei Chen and Yeats, *Yellow Peril!*, 12–13.

and Greco-Roman symbols.[64] They stand in the foreground on a mountain precipice, under a shining white cross, and leading them is the Archangel Michael, portrayed with typical iconography: wings, Romanesque armor, and a flaming sword. He extends one arm in a sweeping gesture toward the battlefield, upon which he will soon lead them to war, as he also does in Revelation against the great dragon, Satan (Rev 12:7-9).[65]

Warning captions in French and English run below the illustration: *Nations Européennes! Défendez vos biens sacrés!* "Nations of Europe! Join us in the defence of your faith and your homes!" The implications of this illustration and other Yellow Peril cartoons and literature are clear: the demonic Orient will seize and destroy lands, white cultures, and white womanhood, unless the Christian West wages holy war against it.

But the dragon does not fight alone. As it says in Revelation, "Michael and his angels fought against the dragon. The dragon *and his angels* fought back" (Rev 12:7). As shown above in both Dooner's and Wolter's novels, Imperial China may be the dragon driving the attack, but it is the "horde" of sneaky, ruthless Chinese who form the terrible army overtaking the land. This is, in fact, the way Chinese immigrants were described in one Oregon newspaper of 1892, on the eve of the ten-year deadline by which the Chinese Exclusion Act had to be renewed. *The Dalles Daily Chronicle*, an Oregon newspaper, describes the threat in apocalyptic terms, playing with the designation of China as "the Celestial Kingdom" (*Tiān cháo*) and the slur of "Celestial" to refer to Chinese people. Under the headline, "A Celestial Horde," it reads:

> The woods are full of Chinese over in Canada. It is said the denizens of the Flowery Kingdom, in large numbers, are dodging behind trees and hiding in sequestered nooks, ready to make a break for the United States the minute the clock strikes 12 on the night of the 3d.[66]

The Chinese lurk just beyond the borders, an evil, angelic host of another realm, ready to descend—literally, from Canada!—to invade at the stroke of midnight of doomsday.

Due in part to apocalyptic rhetoric used in news media, as in this article, in Yellow Peril literature, and in speeches on the Senate floor, legislation from the Page Act to Chinese Exclusion Act to the Geary Act was passed. For white nativists, the boundaries and walls of the New Jerusalem must not be breached, especially not

---

[64] They may be identified as (from right to left): Marianne (France), Germania (Germany), Mother Russia (Russia), Austria (Austria-Hungary), Italia (Italy), Great Britain (Britannia), and Hispania (Spain). See also Asmut Brückmann, *Die europäische Expansion: Kolonialismus und Imperialismus 1492–1918* (Leipzig: Klett, 2005), 79.

[65] The angel Michael also plays the role of battle commander in other Jewish apocalyptic sources, for example, in Daniel 12:1. See Darrell D. Hannah, *Michael and Christ: Michael Traditions and Angel Christology in Early Christianity* WUNT 109 (Tübingen: Mohr Siebeck, 1999).

[66] "A Celestial Horde," *The Dalles Daily Chronicle*, April 30, 1892, vol. 3 (118): front page, https://chroniclingamerica.loc.gov/lccn/sn85042448/1892-04-30/ed-1/seq-1/#words=act+Act+Chinese+exclusion+Exclusion.

by the demonic horde of Chinese. And so, until the Chinese Exclusion Act and its amendments were repealed in 1943, unless a temporary visitor or immediate family of a resident, all Chinese immigrants were denied entry to the United States.

Waiting at the Golden Gate

Nevertheless, Chinese travelers and other sojourners from East and South Asia continued to seek a home in America. In order to "process" travelers that arrived at San Francisco Bay, and to prevent their escape, the government opened a detention center in 1910 at a locale also imbued with apocalyptic overtones: Angel Island in the San Francisco Bay. Ironic happenstance and heavenly ideation would have it that the threatening "celestial horde" must be held back at the mystical *Isla de Los Angeles*.[67] The Angel Island detention center embodied exactly the apocalyptic dichotomy of promise and disaster typical of American immigration. The announcement of its opening regurgitated a national discourse of hospitality toward immigrants, while it simultaneously enacted the national policy of racist exclusion. Thus, the *San Francisco Chronicle* declared in 1909 that when the immigrants arrive at Angel Island, the "newcomers from foreign shores will probably think they have struck *paradise.*"[68]

This language echoes the paradisial expectations of Columbus, but those outside the golden city experienced quite a different reality. From the perspective of Chinese travelers, Angel Island could be understood either as the mythical "Island of Immortals" of Chinese fables[69] or as a hellish jail guarded by devils—called *gwáilóu* in Cantonese and *guǐzi* in Mandarin.

This is the sentiment expressed in one of the many poems carved by detained Chinese men on the walls of the barracks of Angel Island Immigration Station:

> This place is called an island of immortals,
>   When in fact, this mountain wilderness is a prison.[70]

Although San Francisco was *Gāmsāan/Jīnshān*—or "Gold Mountain"—in Chinese imagination (and is even now called *Gauh Gāmsāan/Jiù Jīnshān*, "Old Gold Mountain"), this shining city could also be a symbol of exclusion. Another barracks carving reads:

---

[67] Named *Isla de Los Angeles* by Juan Manuel de Ayala in 1775. See Erwin G. Gudde, *1000 California Place Names: Their Origin and Meaning* (Berkeley: University of California Press, 1947), 3–4.

[68] Louis Stellmann, "San Francisco to Have the Finest Immigration Station in the World," *San Francisco Chronicle*, August 18, 1907, 4.

[69] On the Island of Immortals or Mount Penglai see Wai-Ming Ng, *Imagining China in Tokugawa Japan: Legends, Classics, and Historical Terms* (Albany: SUNY Press, 2019), 190, n. 3.

[70] Poem 23 in Him Mark Lai, Genny Lim, and Judy Yung, eds., *Island: Poetry and History of Chinese Immigrants on Angel Island, 1910–1940* (San Francisco: Hoc Doi, 1986), 60.

> I bought an oar and arrived in the land of the Golden Mountain.
> Who was to know they would banish me to Island?[71]

What Chinese immigrants found on Angel Island were not open doors, free ports, and inclusion in the New Jerusalem. Instead, they found themselves herded into segregated quarters—men from women and Europeans from "Orientals."[72] They were subjected to humiliating physical examinations, because they and other Asians were understood to carry more infectious diseases than other races.[73] Above all, they were subject to hours, days, and sometimes weeks of interrogation in order to prove their identity and claims for the right to enter the country. Every Chinese detainee had to stand trial, guilty until proven innocent, and each case was investigated and analyzed; files and paper trails were sifted.[74]

This rejection, interrogation, inspection, and humiliation stands in sharp contrast to the promise of paradise. This does not signal, however, that America failed as the New Jerusalem, but rather that the metaphor continued (and continues today) to serve the political interests of those using it in immigration discourse—first as immigrants, then as nativists. America as the New Jerusalem, with its gleaming walls and foundation, set as a "shining city on a hill," presents a fresh beginning, moral aspirations, promises of wealth, safety, and stability. But the appearance of the New Jerusalem of Revelation 21–22 comes after a long narrative of violent warfare, plagues, and judgment. Implicit in the purity of those within the city walls is the exclusion of the "impure" without—"Outside are the dogs and sorcerers and fornicators and murderers and idolaters, and everyone who loves and practices falsehood" (Rev 22:15).

Discussion Questions

1. Do you find the promise of a New Jerusalem in the Book of Revelation something redemptive? Why or why not?

---

[71] Poem 36, Lai, Lim, and Yung, *Island*, 86.

[72] See Erika Lee and Judy Yung, *Angel Island: Immigrant Gateway to America* (Oxford: Oxford University Press, 2010), 34.

[73] See Nayan Sha, "Making Medical Borders at Angel Island" in *Contagious Divides: Epidemics and Race in San Francisco's Chinatown* (Berkeley: University of California Press, 2001), 179–203. See also Chap. 2.

[74] See Robert Barde and Gustavo J. Bobonis, "Detention at Angel Island: First Empirical Evidence," *Social Science History* 30 (2006): 103–136. Lee Puey You, who arrived at Angel Island April 13, 1939, was deported back to China November 8, 1940. Lee's case is not straightforward—she was instructed by her family to claim falsely that she was the daughter of a U.S. citizen. Nevertheless, the conditions, treatment, and immigration policies at work in her case remain reprehensible. See Lee and Yung, *Angel Island*, 93–95.

2. Have you encountered descriptions of America (or of another nation) in apocalyptic terms? Was it positive (as in a comparison with paradise or heaven or the New Jerusalem) or negative (as in association with disaster, war, and chaos)?
3. Should the Bible be used in political/national rhetoric? Or if this is inevitable, how should it be used?

Bibliography

Barde, Robert, and Gustavo J. Bobonis. 2006. Detention at Angel Island: First Empirical Evidence. *Social Science History* 30: 103–136.
Bottoms, Michael D. *An Aristocracy of Color: Race and Reconstruction in California and the West: 1850–1890*. Norman, OK: University of Oklahoma Press.
Bremer, Francis J. 2012. *Building a New Jerusalem: John Davenport, a Puritan in Three Worlds*. New Haven: Yale University Press.
Brückmann, Asmut. 2005. *Die europäische Expansion: Kolonialismus und Imperialismus 1492–1918*. Leipzig: Klett.
Byrd, James P. 2013. *Sacred Scripture, Sacred War: The Bible and the American Revolution*. Oxford: Oxford University Press.
Chang, Gordon H. 2019. *Ghosts of Gold Mountain: The Epic Story of the Chinese Who Built the Transcontinental Railroad*. Boston: Houghton Mifflin.
Chang, Gordon H., and Shelly Fisher Fishkin, eds. 2019. *The Chinese and the Iron Road: Building the Transcontinental Railroad*. Stanford, CA: Stanford University Press.
Chung, Sue Fawn, Fred P. Frampton, and Timothy W. Murphy. 2005. Venerate These Bones: Chinese American Funerary Practices as Seen in Carlin, Elko County, Nevada. In *Chinese American Death Rituals: Respecting the Ancestors*, ed. Sue Fawn Chung and Priscilla Wegars, 107–145. Lanham, MD: AltaMira Press.
CPPR.org. FAQs: How Many Died Building the Central Pacific Railroad. Central Pacific Railroad Photographic History Museum. http://cprr.org/Museum/FAQs.html#died.
Davenport, John. 1672. *The Power of the Congregational Churches Asserted and Vindicated*. London: [s.n.] [written ca. 1648].
Delaney, Carol. 2006. Columbus's Ultimate Goal: Jerusalem. *Comparative Studies in Society and History* 48 (2): 260–292.
Denton, Daniel. 1670. *A Brief Description of New-York*. London: John Hancock.
Dooner, P.W. 1880. *The Last Days of the Republic*. San Francisco: Alta California Publishing House.
Dunn, Emily. 2008. The Big Red Dragon and Indigenizations of Christianity in China. *East Asian History* 36: 73–85.
Franklin, Bruce H. 1988. *War Stars: The Superweapon and the American Imagination*. New York: Oxford University Press.
Gold, Martin B. 2012. *Forbidden Citizens: Chinese Exclusion and the U.S. Congress: A Legislative History*. Alexandria, VA: TheCapitol.Net.
Hamdani, Abbas. 1979. Columbus and the Recovery of Jerusalem. *Journal of the American Oriental Society* 99 (1): 39–48.
Hannah, Darrell D. 1999. *Michael and Christ: Michael Traditions and Angel Christology in Early Christianity WUNT 109*. Tübingen: Mohr Siebeck.
Hao, Yen-p'ing. 1986. *The Commercial Revolution in Nineteenth-Century China: The Rise of Sino-Western Mercantile Capitalism*. Berkeley: University of California Press.
Hardesty, Donald L. 2003. Archaeology and the Chinese Experience in Nevada. *South Dakota History, Ethnic Oasis: The Chinese in the Black Hills, Special Historic Preservation Issue* 33 (4): 363–379.

Harrod, Ryan P., and John J. Crandall. 2015. Rails Built of the Ancestors' Bones: The Bioarchaeology of the Overseas Chinese Experience. *Historical Archaeology* 49 (1): 148–161.

Karuka, Manu. 2019. *Empire's Tracks: Indigenous Nations, Chinese Workers, and the Transcontinental Railroad*. Oakland, CA: University of California Press.

Koshy, Susan. 2004. *Sexual Naturalization: Asian Americans and Miscegenation*. Stanford, CA: Stanford University Press.

Lai, Him Mark, Genny Lim, and Judy Yung, eds. 1986. *Island: Poetry and History of Chinese Immigrants on Angel Island, 1910–1940*. San Francisco: Hoc Doi.

Lanman, Jonathan T. 1981. The Religious Symbolism of the T in T-O Maps. *Cartographica* 18 (4): 18–22.

Lee, Erika. 2003. *At America's Gates: Chinese Immigration During the Exclusion Era, 1882–1943*. Chapel Hill: University of North Carolina Press.

Lee, Erika, and Judy Yung. 2010. *Angel Island: Immigrant Gateway to America*. Oxford: Oxford University Press.

Lew-Williams, Beth. 2018. *The Chinese Must Go: Violence, Exclusion, and the Making of the Alien in America*. Cambridge, MA: Harvard University Press.

Mather, Cotton. 1702. *Magnalia Christi Americana or The Ecclesiastical History of New-England from Its First Planting in the Year 1620 unto the Year of our Lord, 1698*. London: Thomas Parkhurst.

Nokes, Gregory R. 2009. *Massacred for Gold: The Chinese in Hells Canyon*. Corvallis, OR: Oregon State University Press.

Peffer, George Anthony. 1986. Forbidden Families: Emigration Experiences of Chinese Women under the Page Law. *Journal of American Ethnic History* 6 (1): 28–46.

Perdue, Peter C. and Ellen Sebring. The Boxer Uprising I: The Gathering Storm in North China (1860–1900). In *MIT Visualizing Cultures*. https://visualizingcultures.mit.edu/boxer_uprising/pdf/bx_essay02.pdf.

Phelan, John Leddy. 1970. *The Millennial Kingdom of the Franciscans in the New World*. 2nd ed. Berkeley: University of California Press.

Roediger, David R., and Elizabeth D. Esch. 2012. *Production of Difference: Race and the Management of Labor in U.S. History*. New York: Oxford University Press.

Saxton, Alexander. 1995. *The Indispensable Enemy: Labor and Anti-Chinese Movement in California*. Berkeley: University of California Press.

Sha, Nyan. 2001. *Contagious Divides: Epidemics and Race in San Francisco's Chinatown*. Berkeley: University of California Press.

Shalev, Eran. 2013. *American Zion: The Old Testament as a Political Text from the Revolution to the Civil War*. New Haven: Yale University Press.

Smith, Shanell T. 2014. *The Woman Babylon and the Marks of Empire: Reading Revelation with a Postcolonial Womanist Hermeneutics of Ambiveilence*. Minneapolis: Fortress Press.

Spickard, Paul. 2007. *Almost All Aliens: Immigration, Race, and Colonialism in American History and Identity*. New York: Routledge.

Storti, Craig. 1991. *Incident at Bitter Creek: The Story of the Rock Springs Massacre*. Ames, IA: Iowa State University Press.

Tchen, John Kuo Wei. 1999. *New York before Chinatown: Orientalism and the Shaping of American Culture 1776–1882*. Baltimore: Johns Hopkins University Press.

Tchen, John Kuo Wei, and Dylan Yeats, eds. 2014. *Yellow Peril! An Archive of Anti-Asian Fear*. London: Verso.

Tompkin, Kyla Wazana. 2012. *Racial Indigestion: Eating Bodies in the 19th Century*. New York: New York University Press.

Tuveson, Ernest Lee. 1968. *Redeemer Nation: The Idea of America's Millennial Role*. Chicago: University of Chicago Press.

Winship, Michael P. 2012. *Godly Republicanism: Puritans, Pilgrims, and a City on a Hill*. Cambridge, MA: Harvard University Press.

Wolter, Robert ["A Survivor"]. 1882. *A Short and Truthful History of the Taking of California and Oregon by the Chinese in the Year A.D. 1899*. San Francisco: A.L. Bancroft and Company.

Woodward, David. 1987. Medieval *Mappaemundi*. In *The History of Cartography*, ed. J.B. Harley and David Woodward, 286–379. Chicago: University of Chicago Press.

Wright, John Kirtland. 1927. *The Geographical Lore of the Time of the Crusades: A Study in the History of Medieval Science and Tradition in Western Europe*. New York: American Geographical Society.

Yung, Judy, Gordon Chang, and Him Mark Lai. 2006. Memorial of Chinese Laborers: Rock Springs, Wyoming (1885). In *Chinese American Voices from the Gold Rush to the Present*, 48–54. Berkeley: University of California.

Zamora, Margarita. 1993. *Reading Columbus*. Berkeley: University of California.

3
Waves of Memory and Possibility: Remembering New Songs, Re-forming Old Ones as Asian Settlers

Sue Jeanne Koh

Introduction

Here I stand, watching the tide go out
So all alone and blue
Just dreaming dreams of you

I watched your ship as it sailed out to sea
Taking all my dreams
And taking all of me

The sighing of the waves
The wailing of the wind
The tears in my eyes burn
Pleading, "My love, return"

Why, oh, why must I go on like this?
Shall I just be a lonely stranger on the shore?

The sighing of the waves
The wailing of the wind
The tears in my eyes burn
Pleading, "My love, return"

Why, oh, why must I go on like this?
Shall I just be a lonely stranger on the shore?

"Stranger on the Shore," Andy Williams (1962)[1]

---

[1] Andy Williams, "Stranger on the Shore," Track 4 on *The Essential Andy Williams*. Columbia Records, 2013, CD.

S. J. Koh (✉)
Humanities Center at the University of California, Irvine, CA, USA

St. Mark and New Hope Presbyterian Churches, Newport Beach and Anaheim, CA, USA

© The Author(s), under exclusive license to Springer Nature Switzerland AG 2023
K. C. Pae, B. Lee (eds.), *Embodying Antiracist Christianity*,
https://doi.org/10.1007/978-3-031-37264-3_3

nos·tal·gia | \ nä-ˈstal-jə , nə- also nȯ-, nō-; nə-ˈstäl- \

1: a wistful or excessively sentimental yearning for return to or of some past period or irrecoverable condition
also : something that evokes nostalgia
2: the state of being homesick : HOMESICKNESS[2]

When my father was nineteen years old, he lay in a hospital bed recovering from an operation that removed half of his stomach. He was hospitalized for a briskly bleeding ulcer, which was likely triggered by the stress and grief of his mother's sudden death from a hemorrhagic stroke. Years later, when listening to a favorite nightly Korean radio show, "My Life's Path" (CBS 93.9FM), which features an eclectic mix of pop, including American oldies, he recalled the longing melodic lines of "Stranger on the Shore" while recuperating.

I always found this side of my dad surprising. He was a patient and loving father but in many ways also inhabited a familiar portrait of an Asian immigrant professional who had emigrated to the United States shortly after the passing of the Immigration Act of 1965. Slim and neat, generally quiet although not shy, he had arrived in the late 1960s to pursue graduate studies in civil engineering. Although his father did not approve of his desire to go, he obtained a full scholarship from the University of Notre Dame to fund his education. He built a life in the United States with our mother, who joined him in 1975, and raised my sister and me in quiet suburban Philadelphia. I understood his devotion to Notre Dame football, but it was sometimes difficult to square his wistfulness for these popular American songs, with their overtly lush instrumentation, vocal harmonies, and, above all, the way they spoke to romantic longing, with my dad's pragmatic personality—songs that portrayed regretful ex-lovers, like Patti Page's "I Went to Your Wedding" or soldiers longing to be reunited with their loved ones, as in "Tie a Yellow Ribbon Round the Ole Oak Tree."

A part of our family's lore was that my father learned the sounds of English by listening to the American Forces Korean Network (AFKN), a ubiquitous presence in South Korea for over four decades.[3] I imagined him by a radio, listening to the day's events, much like we listened to KYW News Radio (1060 AM) on our hour-long commute to and back from our Korean immigrant church. Only more recently, after he died from a year-long struggle with pancreatic cancer, and my sister and I were putting together a playlist for a delayed virtual memorial, did memories of these old songs and our dad's pleasure in them resurface. I realized that his introduction to these songs must have come through AFKN. I imagined my father hearing

---

[2] *Merriam-Webster.com*, s.v. "nostalgia," accessed February 16, 2013, https://www.merriam-webster.com/dictionary/nostalgia.
[3] Kyung Hyun Kim, *Hegemonic Mimicry: Korean Popular Culture of the Twenty-First Century* (Durham, NC: Duke University Press, 2021), 27.

the perambulating tempos of the clarinet and guitar conjuring Andy Williams' dulcet voice through the radio speaker and how this song, along with others like it, stirred a longing to leave post-war Korea for the United States.

The stranger in Williams' song is lonely because his love has left, venturing out across the sea. After hearing the story of this song from my sister, I wondered whether our father secretly saw himself in this song as that melancholic narrator, expressing a hidden longing for something or someone he had lost. But though my initial instinct in hearing this story was to align our father with the protagonist, as I reflected on this story for this essay, I realized that, in fact, our father was the one who had journeyed out across the ocean, leaving the person on the shore. He was loved but had spent many of his adult years away from his own birth family and place of origin, a private man who was respected but not naturally social, focusing his energies on his marriage and family. He enjoyed the geographic expansiveness of the United States, its siren calls of possibility and opportunity.

As a Korean immigrant who was profoundly shaped by the material and psychic losses of post-war Korea, the nostalgic sounds of American popular songs signaled to my father the potential of the United States as both a place of economic opportunity and a new place which he could call home. He sought to settle in the United States; the verb "settle," as in to reside somewhere new, evokes the sense of making a place comfortable or familiar, creating order out of chaos, relaxing in a place that was once strange. To step into these sounds, however, meant also to step into synchronous registers of settler formation in the United States. Inspired by Sara Ahmed's argument that emotions "*do things,* and work to align individuals with collectives,"[4] I offer American popular music as an object lesson for how it guides the listener into a world of immigrant and settler positionalities. Ahmed argues that emotions are not simply expressions of individual psychological states of mind but that they form a collective that "takes shape through the impressions made by bodily others."[5] They work concretely to position individuals with social groups or nation-states and *respond* to others within and without those collectives. "It is not just that we feel for the collective (such as in discourses of fraternity or patriotism), but how we feel about others is what aligns us with a collective, which paradoxically 'takes shape' only as an effect of such alignments."[6] Emotions not only *move* but *attach* themselves to that "which holds us in place, or gives us a dwelling place"[7]; as a result, emotions materially orient us in relation to each other and to the world.

The music that my father heard on the sound waves of AFKN offered possibilities of fulfillment, including socioeconomic mobility and political freedom. A wave, as both water and sound, is characterized by a horizontal, oscillatory movement that both conceals and reveals, and overlaps with and recedes from surfaces. It is a

---

[4] Sara Ahmed, "Collective Feelings: Or, the Impressions Left by Others," *Theory, Culture & Society* 21, no. 2 (April 1, 2004): 26, https://doi.org/10.1177/0263276404042133.
[5] Ahmed, "Collective Feelings," 27.
[6] Ahmed, "Collective Feelings," 27.
[7] Ahmed, "Collective Feelings," 27.

suggestive analogy for the dynamics at play in Asian settler formation, for the music of immigrant possibility was also music that centered white settler emotions.[8] For white settlers, nostalgia can reinforce their positions as the beginning of the American project, a project that depends on narratives of national innocence. In the foregrounding of white settler emotions as desirable ones, the Asian immigrant comes into being through the unwitting erasure of indigenous histories and presence. The immigrant longing to belong merges with the reality that we yearn to belong to stolen land, that fulfillment for one group depends on the erasure of another. Un-obscuring these related dynamics is challenging because, while Asian settler formation on the mainland is connected to U.S. imperialism in the Pacific, the language that it speaks is not of violence or military strikes. Rather, it sings in the registers of personal gratitude and national innocence, making it difficult to know where immigrant desires for belonging and white settler nostalgia begin and end.

Why is it important for Asian American Christians and church communities to understand themselves not only as immigrants but also as Asian settlers? I offer three moral arguments. One, that insofar as Asian Americans understand themselves as *Americans*, they, too, must reckon with the history of the United States as a country built in significant part on eliminating indigenous peoples and sovereignty, an ongoing reality from which many Asian American communities benefit. Two, although the racialization of Americans of *Asian* descent is distinct from the colonizing experiences of indigenous Americans, these two trajectories are part and parcel of strategies of the white settler state in the United States.[9] As a result, even when addressing particular and pressing issues of anti-Asian racism, Asian Americans must also include, as Quyen Nhu Le argues, indigenous reparative struggles in their considerations for justice.[10] Thirdly, as Asian American *Christians*, we must recognize and reckon with how Christian thought and practice has translated to settler relations to the land so that our dreams of home and belonging have become inextricably entangled with territoriality and property.

Overall, in facing the challenge of Asian settler colonialism, Asian American Christians must grapple with questions of complicity and solidarity. By complicity here I do not mean direct responsibility or participation in creating American

---

[8] Admittedly, I have simplified the narrative of musical influences in Korea in order to highlight music's role in immigrant formation by way of white settler emotions. Post-war Korea was open to a mélange of American and Japanese music, such as trot and jazz, even as different genres were censored because of the geopolitical realities associated with them. The influence of black performers, such as Louis Armstrong or Nat King Cole, is complex and beyond the scope of this chapter, and must be considered in relation to the presence of African American soldiers in Korea and the U.S. civil rights movement. However, at least Kyung Hyun Kim points to the imbrication of blackness in the evolution of K-pop and how Korean music is no longer to be found in an "essentialized" ethnic identity but rather must negotiate itself in the context of "global racial subjectivities." Kim, *Hegemonic Mimicry*, 5–6.

[9] See Quynh Nhu Le, *Unsettled Solidarities: Asian and Indigenous Cross-Representations in the Américas* (Philadelphia, PA: Temple University Press, 2019).

[10] Le, *Unsettled Solidarities*, 12.

structural hegemonies, but rather responding to and accepting the emotional pathways that illuminated the United States as the fulfillment of democratic liberalism. American music reinforced the position of the white, Christian settler as a locus of mimetic desire. What might it mean to narrate my father's pleasure in American pop songs as not merely a surprising anomaly or biographical detail, but also as pursuit of the promise of American exceptionalism? What might it mean to remember the Korean immigrant church in which we were raised not only as a place of belonging but as forged from buried and overlapping convergences of settler colonial policies, assimilationist practices, and theological beliefs and practices?

This reframing acknowledges the limits of our knowing but also insists that new knowing presses us to responsibility, even when we did not create the injustices. These limits apply to my own piece; I can only offer reflections that are adjacent to Indigenous experiences and histories. As a second-generation American of Korean descent, I can only say that my critical analysis is adjacent to the multiple pathways that other Americans of Asian descent have traveled. And yet, as someone who was baptized as an infant in a white Presbyterian church in Indiana, whose American 'godmother' lived in Korea as the daughter of Presbyterian missionaries and the granddaughter of Oliver R. Avison[11], I know that I must accept that the settler story of the United States is somehow also my own.

My questions aren't meant to spoil the memories of my father's pleasure in these songs or deny the formative and loving influence of the Korean immigrant church in my own life. It means, first, to unlearn immigrant beliefs in the intertwined narratives of national innocence and transcendence, nostalgic narratives which identify European settlers who arrived on the shores of North America as the originators of what would become heralded as America for all. The goal of my excavation is to consider how our longings for "belonging" have materialized as settler homes and to begin recalibrating our understandings of our histories and futures together.

Settled Accretions

To understand Asian settler formation is to highlight settler colonialism as both a continuing and transnational phenomenon, realities that are not initially captured in familiar definitions, as seen here: settler colonialism is a "distinct type of colonialism that functions through the replacement of indigenous populations with an invasive settler society that, over time, develops a distinctive identity and sovereignty."[12] Patrick Wolfe, an Australian anthropologist and significant voice in establishing settler colonial studies, described settler colonialism as dependent on a "logic of

---

[11] Missionary and philanthropist who established Severance Hospital, the first Western-style hospital in Korea.

[12] "Settler Colonialism," *Global Social Theory* (blog), https://globalsocialtheory.org/concepts/settler-colonialism/. The United States, Australia, Canada, and South Africa are examples of settler states.

elimination"[13] which manifests itself through policies and actions which are directed toward disrupting or destroying indigenous relations to the land and kinship structures. However, it is important to understand that settler colonialism does not simply mean the genocidal removal of indigenous peoples from the land but continues in the form of the extraction of value, or capital, from the land. Real estate and land development depend on certain ontological claims that the land must be *made* productive, consonant with earlier historical and theological claims that indigenous lands were *terra nullius,* or empty land.

Understanding settler colonialism in this way illuminates how it is not simply a structural or governmental event but also one invested in forming the human's desire for the land in particular ways. Specifically, "human relationships to land are restricted to the relationship between owner and property" in such a way that seems natural or obvious.[14] By privileging the white, patriarchal family as the norm, settler colonial laws historically reinforced the convergence between an individualistic, Christian theological anthropology, whiteness, and capitalist orientations to the land. The Dawes Act (1887) was explicitly passed in order to break up tribal ways of relating to each other and to the land and encourage assimilation into white American society. The allotment of land given was in proportion to the size of the family unit; as a result, heads of households (fathers) were given larger plots of land compared to individuals, whose plots of lands were also determined according to their age and marital status. Later alien land laws in California (1913 and 1920) prevented Japanese, Korean, and Chinese immigrant farmers from owning land due to their status as non-citizens (citizenship status being denied to non-white immigrants of Asian descent). Both instances affirm whiteness, as Cheryl Harris notes, by its "right to exclude."[15]

Only later, with the Supreme Court cases of *Oyama v. California* (1948) and *Takahashi v. California Fish and Game Commission* (1948), were these alien land laws struck down and Asians no longer considered ineligible for citizenship. After 1965, immigrants from Latin America, Asia, Africa, and southern Europe began to change the face of the United States. In signing the immigration act, then president Lyndon B. Johnson sought to overturn the quota system established by the Johnson-Reed Act in 1924, which established quotas based on national origins: "It corrects a cruel and enduring wrong in the conduct of the American nation."[16] Johnson's words contained a fundamental optimism regarding the goodness and value of the

---

[13] Patrick Wolfe, "Settler Colonialism and the Elimination of the Native," *Journal of Genocide Research* 8, no. 4 (2006): 387–409, https://doi.org/10.1080/14623520601056240.

[14] Paul Berne Burow, Samara Brock, and Michael R. Dove, "Unsettling the Land: Indigeneity, Ontology, and Hybridity in Settler Colonialism," *Environment and Society* 9, no. 1 (September 1, 2018): 59, https://doi.org/10.3167/ares.2018.090105.

[15] Cheryl I. Harris, "Whiteness as Property," *Harvard Law Review* 106, no. 8 (1993): 1707–91, https://doi.org/10.2307/1341787.

[16] Adam Strom, "President Johnson and the 1965 Immigration Action," *Re-Imagining Migration* (blog), October 11, 2018, https://reimaginingmigration.org/president-johnson-and-the-1965-immigration-action/.

American, democratic project—one that depended on a narrative of national innocence that touted the United States as a "nation of immigrants."[17]

Swirling Sediments: National Innocence and Indigenous Erasure

The word *innocence* evokes several different valences. Perhaps most popularly, *innocence* is descriptive of children's nature, whether in terms of inherent quality, as in being without guile, or a state of being, as in "untainted with, or unacquainted with, evil."[18] In modern philosophy, this sense of the word is also tied closely to John Locke's idea of the *tabula rasa,* referring to the belief that the mind is an unformed, "blank slate" that receives data and constructs rules through sensory experience. The account of Adam and Eve's sin in Genesis 3 is often also narrated as a fall from innocence (although this specific association is closer to John Milton's epic poem, *Paradise Lost,* rather than the scriptural account). In this sense, being innocent also means to be without guilt, or to find someone innocent means the rectification of a wrong or a return to justice.

In all these cases, the term *innocence* evokes the tense of a beginning, of origins. The very characterization of the United States as a nation that upholds liberal democratic ideals of inclusion and equality depends on a particular historical narrative, one that includes John Winthrop's "city on a hill" and the struggle for independence against a tyrannical monarchy, and occludes the elimination of Indigenous peoples, histories, and ways of life. This is not to say that Indigenous peoples do not figure at all in this narration of American history, but they usually do so in ways that frame their presence in terms of accommodation (e.g., the hospitality of the Wampanoag tribe to the Pilgrims at the "first Thanksgiving"), necessary assimilation (e.g., the Dawes Act), or as foils to democratic ideals (e.g., "Custer's Last Stand"). The tenets of American exceptionalism depend on the denial of Indigenous sovereignty through policies of progressive land displacement and genocide in such a way that positions indigenous peoples as backward or pre-modern.

Settler colonialism, then, is a phenomenon that places different racial groups in temporal contrast to each other, which Le articulates through the phrase, "settler racial tense." "Settler racial tense" describes the mutually constitutive racial formations that (white) settlers, Asian (aliens), and indigenous communities occupy in terms of where they are placed along a timeline, so that we can begin thinking about the differences between Asian and indigenous communities in terms of their location in space and time rather than simply racial identity. The term "tense" refers not

---

[17] A reference to then-Senator John F. Kennedy's book, written for the Anti-Defamation League's One Nation Library series. John F. Kennedy, *A Nation of Immigrants*, Harper Perennial Modern Classics (New York: Harper Collins, 2018).

[18] Oxford English Dictionary, s.v. "Innocence, n.," accessed February 16, 2023, https://www.oed.com/view/Entry/96292.

only to the grammatical act of conjugating a verb to indicate its place in time (past, present, future) but also to whether the action is continuing (imperfect) or completed (perfect).[19] In the white settler imagination, Asian figures are both perceived as "technologically advanced" (and so "conditional perfect future tense"), and on the other as wellsprings of exotic and ancient wisdom ("past perfect"). Both tenses cast the Asian as alien, or outside of time, but in a way that is "central to the continual rewriting of the 'normative' time and space of settlement."[20] In contrast, indigenous peoples have often been cast in terms of the past tense as "prior" to colonization and so not part of present-day processes of white settler governance. However, although Asian immigrants and indigenous peoples occupy different temporal positions, Le stresses that the erasure of indigenous peoples from U.S. settler history is connected to, and not separate from, U.S. imperial expansion through the Pacific. The history of Western, and then specifically American music, can help to make this connection clearer.

Sound Waves of Settler Colonialism

Music in Korea (and indeed elsewhere) historically has reflected political and socioeconomic values and positions, rather than being a universally shared source of culture or entertainment, a reality that holds significance for later musical developments. Although John Lie writes that no one exactly knows when Koreans first encountered Western music, what was heard must have been strange, or at least certainly different.[21] The first fundamental differences are in the musical scale used—diatonic (European) versus pentatonic (Korean)—as well as instruments, like the piano or violin, versus the *kayagum* and *komungo*. Korean traditional music reflected class differences; *chongak* ("orthodox music") was employed and enjoyed by the aristocratic classes, reflecting a more austere or formal style, while *minsok umak* (people's music) was more expressive and emotional, accompanied by drums and dancing.

By the late nineteenth century, Western music was a definitive presence in Korea, with Christian missionaries first sharing elements of European musical culture via hymns. Japan's annexation of Korea in 1910 brought mandates for cultural assimilation, including the erasure of the Korean language and names. Korean music was also targeted, but instead of replacing it with traditional Japanese music, the sounds of *modern* Japan were institutionalized. Both Japanese and Korean elites thought that music, especially ceremonial and military, was illustrative of the West's

---

[19] Le, *Unsettled Solidarities*, 12.

[20] Le, *Unsettled Solidarity*, 13.

[21] I cannot do justice to John Lie's sweeping, historical narrative of Korean music during the late nineteenth and twentieth centuries and recommend it to interested readers. John Lie, *K-Pop: Popular Music, Cultural Amnesia, and Economic Innovation in South Korea*, 2014. Ebook Central, http://ebookcentral.proquest.com/lib/uci/detail.action?docID=1711046.

technological might: "belonging more to cultural technology than to traditional culture."²² Moreover, this music—and especially Western choral music—was thought to help form "ethical, loyal subjects." Music reinforced Japan's cultural hegemony, imposing the norms of empire as a language of aspiration and assimilation.

Through the period of Japanese occupation, Western music increasingly dominated the soundscape in urban areas; in Christian missionary schools, Korean children (girls especially) were introduced to singing in choral harmonies. This choral music, also known as *ch'angga*, was an amalgam of genres—European anthems, Christian hymns, Japanese choral music, and American folk tunes—and embraced especially by the educated elite. What was probably not anticipated was how this same demographic, which also led the Korean independence movement, infused *ch'angga* with a different kind of political import than was intended; as Lie describes, "sentiments critical of Japanese rule were often articulated in *ch'angga*, not in Korean folk tunes."²³ The language of Korean independence did not turn to indigenous cultural sources but instead both mimicked and subverted the language of Japanese hegemony.

In the 1920s, *yuhaengga*, or popular songs, became increasingly *de rigeur*, a symbol of sophistication for colonial, urban Koreans who socialized in public venues like the theater, movie theaters, and cafes. Although these popular songs were marked by a mix of Japanese and Western musical influences, their appeal cannot simply be explained as Korean acquiescence to the superior sounds of empire. Rather, these songs resonated with their listeners because the songs freshly adapted familiar elements in Korean traditional songs—for example, the pentatonic scale or three-beat rhythms—and bridged the pre-colonial era with the present-day one, producing old sounds with Western instruments. The themes of these songs often spoke to lost love or evoked rural countryside, offering urban listeners an escape from the realities of colonized existence. Romantic love, then, as expressed in a well-known song, "Tears of Mokpo,"²⁴ could also be understood as a cipher for diaspora or displacement.

After the liberation of Korea from the Japanese at the end of World War II, the nascent government made efforts to eradicate Japanese influences, including in music. American music soon became the dominant force, with its "brighter timbre ... and upbeat lyrics"²⁵ associated with the sounds of democracy and freedom, a connection that became even stronger during, and in the wake of, the Korean War. Although Lie notes that the influence of American music was, at least initially, mainly limited to the army bases and the camp towns that developed around them, Kyung Hyun Kim describes how the demand for Korean performers in American military clubs was high, even starting in the late 1950s. The demand for these

---

²² Lie, *K-Pop: Popular Music, Cultural Amnesia, and Economic Innovation in South Korea*, 9.
²³ Lie, *K-Pop*, 17.
²⁴ *Tears of Mokpo*, 2011, https://www.youtube.com/watch?v=VJFgDKZ5MkA.
²⁵ Lie, *K-Pop*, 38.

performers, who learned and sang American songs at a rapid rate, was so great that the Korean booking agencies established a system of auditions to identify the most talented musicians.[26]

Later, these performers would become the foundation for the Korean entertainment industry, providing the groundwork for the later global success of K-pop.[27] Nevertheless, alongside the drive for education, the English language and American culture became the currencies for progress, and because AFKN was more readily available than Korean programming during the 1970s and 1980s (which was heavily impacted by government censorship), Koreans became familiar with American popular culture: TV, film, and music. All of this is to say that my father was not unique in terms of his fondness for American popular songs. Perhaps these affective attachments to the United States were intensified after the period of Japanese colonization and the threat of communism, with the waves of American music romancing Korean immigrants to the shores of the United States, washing over and providing emotional escape from military devastation and presence.

American popular songs thus expressed future tense possibilities of innocence regained, characterizing Americans as peaceful and happy—as one song described, "gentle people with flowers in their hair."[28] Music does not need the reality of place to be effective; in this sense, the United States itself was conjured out of music, forged through the material, historical, and political conditions of Christian missionary activity, Japanese colonization, and American military presence. My father and others like him began the process of assimilating into the narratives of American exceptionalism and progress even before they stepped foot onto the shining and beautiful shores of the United States.

Settler Colonial Nostalgia

How could we sing the Lord's song in a foreign land? - Ps. 137:4

History reveals that even as Asian immigrants believed that the United States was a land full of promise—"Gold Mountain" or "Beautiful Land"—the question of Asian immigrant belonging has often been answered with incidents of violence, racist rhetoric, and exclusion. The desire to belong, in other words, is not commensurate with actual belonging. America has needed Asian labor but has not always desired Asian immigrants as neighbors and friends. To hear and believe in the sounds of American freedom has not always meant its fulfillment.

To belong in the United States means to live in the emotional register of happiness, what Jeffrey Santa Ana identifies as the "primary feeling [for American

---

[26] Kim, *Hegemonic Mimicry*, 7.

[27] Kim, 8.

[28] *San Francisco (Scott McKenzie)*, 2009, https://www.youtube.com/watch?v=bch1_Ep5M1s.

personhood] in a liberal capitalist society."[29] On an instinctive level, happiness exemplifies individual experiences of success and belonging in American society—the emotional payoff from having a well-paying job, owning a home, and being part of a nuclear, heterosexual family. But Santa Ana notes how achieving such belonging also reinforces the status quo of an American society; to achieve such happiness means accepting structural inequalities and *preserving* the happiness "of those who are privileged enough to live the good life promised by [the American dream]."[30] Happiness in this sense is distinctly enjoyed in the present tense, "the pursuit of happiness" no longer a future aspiration. The American Dream has been a settler one, one that has privileged the white male in a proprietary relationship to the land.

It is when the white settler's present-day happiness is threatened in some way that nostalgia for the past appears and often takes on a racializing cast. During the latter half of the nineteenth century, white Californians, threatened by the Chinese presence and the rapid industrialization of California, organized the Free Soil Movement. Their rhetoric frequently evoked "the freedom, independence, and autonomy that had once been imaginable to them in a premodern capitalist idyll,"[31] what Iyko Day terms "romantic anticapitalism."[32] A popular Gold Rush song, "California As It Was and Is" by John A. Stone (pseudonym "Old Put"), explicitly paints a nostalgic picture of California before the arrival of Chinese laborers:

> *I remember, I remember, when the Yuba used to pay,*
> *With nothing but a rocker, five hundred dollars a day.*
> *We used to think t'would always last, and would, with perfect ease,*
> *If only Uncle Sam had stopped the coming of the Chinese.*

Such songs framed Chinese immigrants as "[containing] the ghostly presence of their departed dreams of freedom, and all that this freedom had promised in terms of acquiring independence, individualism, and acquisitive happiness."[33] Chinese immigrants were valued for their labor, but not for their presence. White settler nostalgia, then, expresses a specific kind of homesickness which naturalizes the white person's relationship to the land in contrast to other (racialized) bodies, the desire to *recover* an idealized type of (white, American) connection to land.

What does it mean to belong? The lament of Psalm 137 expresses the painful and fresh memories of the Babylonian exile, of the Judeans' deportation from their homeland in 586 BCE. It is, as Robert Alter writes, the "spontaneous" expression of "collective emotion," of the feeling and reality of being "there" rather than "here,"

---

[29] Jeffrey Santa Ana, *Racial Feelings: Asian America in a Capitalist Culture of Emotion* (Philadelphia, PA: Temple University Press, 2015), 6.
[30] Santa Ana, *Racial Feelings*, 6.
[31] Santa Ana, *Racial Feelings*, 16.
[32] Iyko Day, *Alien Capital: Asian Racialization and the Logic of Settler Colonial Capitalism* (Durham, NC: Duke University Press, 2016), 10.
[33] Santa Ana, *Racial Feelings*, 17–18.

of the longing to be in one's home.³⁴ Although the psalmist speaks to the specific experiences of the Judeans' historical displacement, early modern European Reformers, as well as contemporary Asian American theologians, have found exile to be a flexible metaphor to reflect the dissonances between feeling at "home" in a given space versus experiences of racialization, migration, and religious conflict. This is to say that the psalm, as part of Scripture, has been able to sing in multiple keys of nostalgia or homesickness in ways distant from its original context. It has spoken in the register of both the colonized and those who became European settler colonialists on Turtle Island.

To speak in the key of nostalgia in the context of the United States, then, is to speak in tones that are ambivalent and fraught. To the extent that Americans of Asian descent have left behind their countries of origin to make new homes in the United States, responses to anti-Asian racism have predominantly focused on highlighting Asian American stories of belonging in the United States. Historical narratives such as Ronald Takaki's *From a Different Shore*³⁵ or Erika Lee's *The Making of Asian America*³⁶ offer stories of dangerous ocean crossings to signify the material and psychic sacrifices of people of Asian descent. Other strategies focus on increasing the representation of Asian Americans in various sectors, as well as uplifting Asian American narratives across media platforms. Stories describe immigrant struggles of adjusting to life in a new country, as well as put multigenerational family realities on display. They depict Asian Americans in diverse work settings, from being parking valets (as in *Shang-Chi*) to high-powered corporate lawyers (e.g., *The Joy Luck Club*). Such strategies are reminiscent of the ethnic histories of Asians in Hawai'i, which mainly "tell the story of Asians' civil rights struggles as one of nation building in order to legitimate Asians' claims to a place for themselves in Hawai'i."³⁷ However, as Candace Fujikane notes, this focus reinforces a "white settler historiography"³⁸ of the Hawai'ian Islands insofar as they highlight the labor and contributions of Asians in developing Hawai'i's economy and infrastructure and so justify belonging by dint of the value their labor has brought to the islands. These representative strategies, while not demonstrating wholesale assimilation to white American values or histories, nevertheless still depend on settler logics.

For my father and others, Asian immigrant churches also have been places of belonging, a place to "sing the Lord's song in a foreign land" and so make the contours, sounds, and cultural practices of the United States less unfamiliar. Such

---

³⁴ Robert Alter, *The Book of Psalms: A Translation with Commentary* (New York: W. W. Norton & Company, 2009), Kindle.

³⁵ Ronald Takaki, *Strangers from a Different Shore: A History of Asian Americans, Updated and Revised Edition* (Boston: Little, Brown and Company, 1998).

³⁶ Erika Lee, *The Making of Asian America: A History* (New York: Simon & Schuster, 2015).

³⁷ Ronald Takaki, *Strangers from a Different Shore: A History of Asian Americans, Updated and Revised Edition*, (Boston: Little, Brown and Company, 1998).

³⁸ Candace Fujikane, "Introduction: Asian Settler Colonialism in the U.S. Colony of Hawai'i," in *Asian Settler Colonialism: From Local Governance to the Habits of Everyday Life in Hawai'i*, ed. Jonathan Y. Okamura and Candace Fujikane (Honolulu: University of Hawaii Press, 2008), 2.

communities, too, have been able to adapt the Western Christian practices and beliefs that they received by blending them with their own cultural sensibilities and heritages, perhaps as much acts of nostalgia as they are expressions of faith. It is also true, however, that many of these church communities depend on settler relationships to the land in ways that do not acknowledge present-day indigenous sovereignty; rather, they continue to relate to Native American populations in ways that reinforce missionary postures so that Native Americans continue to be cast in the past tense. We often still look to white church models to direct our preaching, worship, outreach, and church planting. Are there ways to consider how Asian American narratives of loss and racialization intersect with Indigenous narratives of continued displacement to create new lines of solidarity? Are we willing to advocate for Indigenous sovereignty, even risking the possibility of giving up our own pursuits for the symbols of belonging? There are no easy answers, but my father's story compels me to consider the possibilities.

Discussion Questions

1. Do you know the history of the land on which your church community is situated? Who are the Indigenous communities to which the land belongs?
2. How is the history of your church community narrated? What stories, both personal and communal, might need to be re-told in order to un-obscure our settler identities? What stories of loss and homecoming are described, as related to your cultural heritages?
3. What are some practices that might need to be examined in order to decenter belonging in our church communities and instead focus on bridges of solidarity?

Bibliography

"Settler Colonialism." *Global Social Theory* (blog). https://globalsocialtheory.org/concepts/settler-colonialism/.
Alter, Robert. 2009. *The Book of Psalms: A Translation with Commentary*. New York: W. W. Norton & Company.
Ahmed, Sara. "Collective Feelings: Or, the Impressions Left by Others." Theory, Culture & Society 21, 2 (2004): 25-42. https://doi.org/10.1177/0263276404042133.
Burow, Paul Berne, Samara Brock, and Michael R. Dove. 2018. Unsettling the Land: Indigeneity, Ontology, and Hybridity in Settler Colonialism. *Environment and Society* 9 (1): 57–74. https://doi.org/10.3167/ares.2018.090105.
Day, Iyko. 2016. *Alien Capital: Asian Racialization and the Logic of Settler Colonial Capitalism*. Durham: Duke University Press.
Fujikane, Candace. 2008. Introduction: Asian Settler Colonialism in the U.S. Colony of Hawai'i. In *Asian Settler Colonialism: From Local Governance to the Habits of Everyday Life in Hawai'i*, ed. Jonathan Y. Okamura and Candace Fujikane. Honolulu: University of Hawaii Press.

Harris, Cheryl I. 1993. Whiteness as Property. *Harvard Law Review* 106 (8): 1707–1791. https://doi.org/10.2307/1341787.

Kennedy, John F. 2018. *A Nation of Immigrants. Harper Perennial Modern Classics*. New York: Harper Collins.

Kim, Kyung Hyun. 2021. *Hegemonic Mimicry: Korean Popular Culture of the Twenty-First Century*. Durham, NC: Duke University Press. https://dukeupress.edu/hegemonic-mimicry.

Le, Quynh Nhu. 2019. *Unsettled Solidarities: Asian and Indigenous Cross-Representations in the Américas*. Philadelphia, PA: Temple University Press.

Lee, Erika. 2015. *The Making of Asian America: A History*. New York: Simon & Schuster.

Lie, John. K-Pop: Popular Music, Cultural Amnesia, and Economic Innovation in South Korea, 2014.

Ana, Santa, and Jeffrey. 2015. *Racial Feelings: Asian America in a Capitalist Culture of Emotion*. Philadelphia: Temple University Press. https://www.jstor.org/stable/j.ctt155jm9r.

Strom, Adam. President Johnson and the 1965 Immigration Action. *Re-Imagining Migration* (blog), https://reimaginingmigration.org/president-johnson-and-the-1965-immigration-action/.

Takaki, Ronald. 1998. *Strangers from a Different Shore: A History of Asian Americans, Updated and Revised Edition*. Boston: Little, Brown and Company.

Wolfe, Patrick. 2006. Settler Colonialism and the Elimination of the Native. *Journal of Genocide Research* 8 (4): 387–409. https://doi.org/10.1080/14623520601056240.

4
The Cosmopolitics of Belonging: Model Minority Superheroes and Theological Imagination

B. Yuki Schwartz

The *X-Men* character Jubilee entered my life just at the moment when I needed to imagine the world differently. I was a teenager who had just graduated from high school in the rural Oklahoma town where I had grown up, and where my understanding of myself as Asian American—or "half-Japanese" as I had been taught to describe myself—had been shaped. In my short lifetime of imperfect assimilations that consisted of bullying over my skin and hair color, the shape of my eyes, the food that I ate, and the languages that I could and could not speak, I was constantly searching for belonging that I never could find. As I prepared to leave home for college, the persistent question of "Where are you *really* from?" and its more brutal counterpart, "Why don't you go back to your own country?" became even more unanswerable. I couldn't claim a country where I was "really" from if the country where I was really from refused to claim *me*.

The ability to imagine belonging for me came in the form of *The Uncanny X-Men* #261, which featured Jubilee, a second-generation Chinese American teenager from Southern California who as an Asian American teenager appeared to be everything I was and wasn't. Like me, Jubilee couldn't speak her parents' language, favored McDonald's over traditional Asian foods, and claimed her own histories and experiences against what I thought were stereotypical assumptions. Unlike me, she was bold and outspoken, willing to take chances in order to do what she thought was right. She was my first Asian American comics superhero, and encountering her began my lifelong love of superheroes and comic books. She helped me imagine the world, and myself, differently. Like pop culture writer Jeff Yang, in describing the origins and biographies of popular superheroes as alien(ated) beings who protected communities that rejected them, "I could dream myself into these heroes because

---

B. Y. Schwartz (✉)
Constructive and Political Theologies at Claremont School of Theology, Claremont, CA, USA
e-mail: yschwartz@cst.edu

© The Author(s), under exclusive license to Springer Nature Switzerland AG 2023
K. C. Pae, B. Lee (eds.), *Embodying Antiracist Christianity*, https://doi.org/10.1007/978-3-031-37264-3_4

their origins, as fantastic as they were, were so oddly familiar. Isn't this an Asian American story?"[1] In Jubilee, I began to see my story as an Asian American one, and she has remained for me a nostalgic favorite character.

She is also a problematic favorite. Hers is an "Asian American" story mediated through structures of unrecognized white supremacy that shore up myths about US settler colonialism and global imperialism. Written and illustrated by white USian men, Chris Claremont and Marc Silvestri, respectively (though with a cover drawn by Korean American artist Jim Lee), *X-Men* #261 takes place in Marvel Comics' fictional Asian country of Madripoor.[2] From her beginning, Jubilee's identity, conveniently for her white writers and audiences, lacked history, context, and community, so that she could conform to the white liberal norms of the Marvel Comics universe. Her experiences with grappling with her racialized identity, shown in scenes where people of color chastised her for not matching a stereotyped identity, reflected beliefs about "reverse" racism, making her a token for performative liberal tolerance. Zak Moy articulates the love-hate relationship that I and other Asian American *X-Men* fans have had with Jubilee throughout her publication history: the mixture of gratitude at seeing a character who is meant to represent you, while knowing the harm that such stereotypical representations can do. "The problem is that when, otherwise positive, design choices like these get applied to Asians by non-Asians, it can perpetuate the 'model minority' label. The racial wedge that systemically divides Asians from other BIPOC groups. It's the culprit of the toxic confusion of figuring out how to both rectify and rebel against the system, while simultaneously being placated and pacified by it. Ain't that some shit?"[3] As I learned more about Asian American history and the community's collective and intersectional resistances against racism and US imperialism, I understood how Jubilee and other "Asian American stories" from mainstream comics had foreclosed the parts of my imagination that I needed in order to survive. I eventually stopped reading superhero comics, finding other ways to seed my imagination through narratives, histories, and theologies born out of intersectional struggles for liberation from Asian North American organizers and theologians.

---

[1] Jeff Yang, "Introduction," in *DC Festival of Heroes: The Asian Superhero Collection,* Kindle edition (New York: DC Comics, 2020), location 4.

[2] X-Men writer Chris Claremont was also the inventor of the fictional island of Madripoor, whose imaginary location is said to be somewhere in the real world Strait of Malacca. Appearing in print for the first time in 1983, Madripoor is an orientalized version of Singapore, a modern-day pirate haven where lawlessness, exoticism, and criminal riches exist atop an impoverished underclass. Madripoor most recently appeared in the Marvel Comics University Disney+ television show *The Falcon and the Winter Soldier,* where it was critiqued for being an Asian-imagined location that lacked any visible Asian faces or bodies. See Therese Lacson, "Where are the Asians in *The Falcon and the Winter Soldier*'s Madripoor?" *Comics Beat,* https://www.comicsbeat.com/falcon-and-the-winter-soldier-asians-madripoor/; "Madripoor," *Marvel,* https://www.marvel.com/comics/discover/2072/madripoor.

[3] Zak Moy, "X-Men's Jubilee: An Icon Short of Iconic. #StopAsianHate," *Medium,* March 30, 2021, https://zakmoy.medium.com/x-mens-jubilee-an-icon-short-of-iconic-stopasianhate-3e180714b53a.

However, during the 2020 beginning of the COVID-19 pandemic, I found myself turning back to Jubilee as I sought refuge in my imagination from the sharp increase in physical, verbal, social and social media, and economic attacks on Asian Americans, Asian people residing in the United States, and Pacific Islanders whom attackers mistook for Asian Americans.[4] Violence against Asian Americans, Asian people residing or visiting the United States, and Pacific Islanders is not a new phenomenon, and neither are the struggles of the members of these conjoined communities to mitigate the harm they have experienced within the white supremacist system of the United States. The pandemic, and racist rhetoric issued by former US-President Trump that blamed China and Asian people for its origins and spread, spurred the harm, reckoning, and resistance that were already going on. As I lamented, taught about, contextualized, and critically reflected on this violence, I recognized the familiar longing to imagine belonging in the world differently. I realized how much of what I call my theological imagination had been formed by superhero stories, and how much I needed, as Yang describes, "something, anything, to give us back our dreams."[5]

This essay examines this process of shaping and reshaping my theological imagination through Asian and Asian American comic book superheroes. I first examine comic book superheroes as not merely products of pop culture, but as characters that reveal shifting social, political, and *theological* understandings about individual and national identity, belonging, and power. I also will seek out the ways that Asian and Asian American superheroes participated—or were foreclosed from participating—in the creation, maintenance, and shifting of those theological and political understandings about national belonging and power. I then investigate Asian American superheroes as model minority characters whose narratives sometimes expose minor feelings: affective experiences that are deemed as ugly, unsettled, and unassimilable into structures of white colonial capitalism and imperialism, and how the serial nature of comic book superhero stories participates in this exposure of minor feelings. Finally, I explore how Asian American superhero narratives that dwell within minor feelings—specifically the minor feeling of shame—reveal the contradictions and hybridities, capacities and limitations, and critical choices about identity, power, and care that make communal belonging possible.

---

[4] The organization #StopAAPIHate reported 6603 incidents of violence against Asian-identified people between March 19, 2020 and March 31, 2021, an increase from 3795 in the previous year. See Russell Jeung, Aggie J. Yellow Horse, and Charlene Cayanan, "Stop AAPI Hate National Report: 3/19/20 - 3/31/21," May 6, 2021, #StopAAPIHate.org, https://stopaapihate.org/wp-content/uploads/2021/05/Stop-AAPI-Hate-Report-National-210506.pdf.

[5] Yang, "Introduction."

The Theological Imagination of US Superheroes

Theological imagination is the capacity to create ideas, images, or practices regarding the relationship human beings have with what they consider to be the divine or of ultimate concern, and the relationship they have with one another in light of their relationship with the divine or ultimate concern. Imagination is not a neutral or pure wellspring of creative thinking or dreaming that exists disconnected from the social and political worlds a person is embedded within. As Heike Peckruhn notes, imagination is a process that occurs within and through bodies that are raced, sexed, gendered, classed, and further identified as religious or non-religious, colonizer or colonized, within systems and locations that themselves are raced, sexed, gendered, classed, and further identified as religious or non-religious, colonizer or colonized. Peckruhn writes, "My theological imaginations are in/my bodily experiences, what I imagine as truth about myself and others, how I experience despair and what is aligned with my desire for freedom, what and where I imagine hope and salvation emerge in bodily experiences that is my knowledge of the world."[6] To also paraphrase Catherine Walsh and Walter Mignolo's argument on decolonial thinking, if our thinking is provoked by the histories of the places where our bodies live, so is our imagination, which is shaped by the world-systems of racism, sexism, and coloniality that classify our bodies with meanings created long before we ever arrived into the world.[7] However, those meanings are not the final word. Kwok Pui-lan describes postcolonial theological imagination as an ability to discern the wrongness of coloniality in the world, as well as the ability to search for decolonial or liberative meanings and patterns to interpret the world. Kwok writes, "Without the power of imagination we cannot envision a different past, present, and future. Without interrogating the mind's 'I/eye,' we are left without alternative perspectives to see reality and to chart where we may be going. For what we cannot imagine, we cannot live into and struggle for."[8] This process of post/decolonial theological imagination is not a linear plan toward universal shifts in either imagination or the embodied systems they rest and resist within, but a process in which imaginations are continuously shaped through fraught and contingent encounters, relationships, and negotiations that take place within cracks, fissures, and hybrid spaces.

As a practice of imagination, theology is not separate or immune from the world-systems that shape it, but is produced within intersecting economic, political, and social institutions. In the United States, these institutions exist within structures of white settler colonialism and global imperialism, participating in what Willie James

---

[6] Heike Peckruhn, "Embodied Knowing: Body, Epistemology, Context, and Hermeneutics," in *What Is Constructive Theology?: Histories, Methodologies, and Perspectives,* ed. Marion Grau (London: T&T Clark, 2020), 89.

[7] Catherine E. Walsh and Walter Mignolo, *On Decoloniality: Concepts, Analytics, Praxis* (Durham: Duke University Press, 2018), 2.

[8] Kwok Pui-lan, *Postcolonial Imagination and Feminist Theology* (Louisville, KY: Westminster John Knox, 2005), 30.

Jennings calls a "diseased (sic) social imagination" that prevents inhabitants of that society from being able to recognize the validity of the experiences of people who are living outside of or in resistance to white settler colonialism and imperialism.[9] European and US Christian imaginations under these structures are unable to shift, adapt, or embrace fluidity or uncertainty, especially as they encounter people of non-European races or non-Christian religions. "Other people and their ways of life had to adapt, become fluid, even morph into the colonial order of things, and such a situation drew Christianity and its theologians inside habits of mind and life that internalized and normalized that order of things."[10] Jennings points out that theologies and theological imagination that are constructed and shaped by coloniality are not solely restricted to religious life and liturgies that are organized around private beliefs, nor do they act in opposition to secular life and "order of things." Rather, theological belief and imagination are intimately intertwined with secular beliefs and imagination, mutually and interactively co-constitute colonial orders of things. This co-constitution makes imaginative productions such as concepts, narratives, ideas, figures, and worlds symptomatic carriers of the theological, even and especially when they exist outside of what is traditionally connected to religious life.[11]

This means that the figure of pure imagination that I am exploring in this essay, the US comic book superhero, cannot be separated from this symptomatic colonial theological imagination. Since their beginnings, US mainstream comic books have had a reputation for being a negative influence on children's moral characters,[12] but superhero narratives also act as carriers of theological themes and teachings, including idealizations of theological anthropology, identities of national chosenness, and desires for individual or collective salvation. According to Anthony R. Mills, the individualistic, frontier-shaped monomyth of characters such as Superman and Batman reflected and reified stated values of mainstream identity under US imperialism, with Superman in particular acting as a figure who "personifies the Puritan work ethic and embodies the US ideals of fair play, equal opportunity, and

---

[9] Willie James Jennings, *The Christian Imagination: Theology and the Origins of Race* (New Haven: Yale University Press, 2010), 6.

[10] Jennings, *The Christian Imagination*, 8.

[11] As described by Ranjana Khanna, symptomaticity indicates the co-connectedness and mutual dependence of realms of knowledge, structures, or systems necessary for understanding self, world, and Other. Rather than implying a base or foundation out of which all discourse, politics, or theology might separately grow, Khanna indicates that these structures are necessary to one another, reinforcing each other's ideas, concepts, or imaginings. See Khanna, *Dark Continents: Psychoanalysis and Colonialism* (Durham, NC: Duke University Press, 2003), 34.

[12] The most famous instance in the United States of this belief of comic books' potential for causing degenerate behaviors in children occurred in the 1950s, when psychologist Fredric Wertham led a public crusade against what he claimed was comic books' pathological influence on children, particularly around themes of violence, sex, and homosexuality. The crusade eventually led to a congressional hearing and the moves by the comics industry to self-censor what was considered to be adult content. See Anthony R. Mills, *American Theology, Superhero Comics, and Cinema: The Marvel of Stan Lee and the Revolution of a Genre* (New York: Routledge, 2014), 28.

maximization of one's own potential."[13] As images of extraordinary power or ability, superheroes theologically mimic an ideal of divine ontology where knowledge of good and evil is inherently perfect, and saviors enact this perfection by being selfless, sacrificial "destroyer(s) of evil."[14] Ben Saunders argues that as characters who embody readers' longings for freedom from limitation and the power to satisfy ethical and existential quandaries, superheroes who were created and developed during comics' Golden and Silver Ages have typically reflected popular social, political, and moral concerns.[15] For example, the ways that Superman carried out his calling to support "truth, justice, and the American way" shifted from siding with impoverished US communities and ghettoized people in his earliest iterations during the Depression in the 1930s, to supporting US imperial capitalism during the Cold War. Saunders argues that superheroes are illustrative reflections of readers' moral and theological concerns as they change, stating, it's "not that virtuous action is something of a moving target, but that Superman apparently must move with it. Whatever we collectively imagine 'good' to be at any given time, it seems that Superman must strive to be that, too."[16]

This emphasis on the superheroes' "goodness" was policed by the Comics Code Authority (CCA), which lasted from 1954 to the early 2000s and let comics publishers regulate the content of their own comic books. The CCA required clear demarcations between the ethical hero who upheld the communal status quo and the villains they fought, who were depicted as deviant, immoral, and irredeemably evil, a requirement that, according to Mills, preserved US theological ideals of its own purity and innocence. Especially during the Golden Age, comics participated in the constant reinforcement of the national myth that the United States was "the embodiment of all that is right."[17] At the same time anyone who threatened that innocence were cast as deviant villains who could never quite be vanquished.[18] Formed within the constrained social imagination of white settler colonialism and US imperialism, mainstream US superheroes tend to symbolize and glorify the United States as a chosen, perfect community. "The traditional superhero myth suggests that power in one set of capable hands is the surest way to achieve justice, that democratic systems

---

[13] Mills, *American Theology, Superhero Comics, and Cinema*, 26–27.

[14] Mills, *American Theology, Superhero Comics, and Cinema*, 27.

[15] The Golden Age of Comics in the United States marks the beginning of comic books as popular, mass media publications. This era began in 1938 with the publication of Action Comics #1, featuring the debut of the character Superman, and lasted until the 1950s. This era is known for the creation of some of the most lasting superhero characters, such as Superman, Batman, and Wonder Woman. The Silver Age of Comics followed the Golden Age, and lasted until about the mid-1970s, and featured the expansion of comics to include more superheroes and superhero teams and included more adult themes and stories based in reality. Later "ages" of comics—the Bronze and Modern Ages—continued to diversify and expand upon the work of Silver Age creators.

[16] Ben Saunders, *Do the Gods Wear Capes? Spirituality, Fantasy, and Superheroes* (London: Bloomsbury Academic, 2013), 30.

[17] Max J. Skidmore and Joey Skidmore, "More Than Mere Fantasy: Political Themes in Contemporary Comic Books," *Journal of Popular Culture* 17, no. 1 (Summer 1983): 84.

[18] Mills, *American Theology, Superhero Comics, and Cinema*, 46.

can't be trusted to perform their tasks alone, that the hero would never take advantage of those he serves, and that the world requires American superheroism."[19]

In the Silver and Bronze Ages of US comics, which began in the 1970s and continued toward the end of the twentieth century, the image and the national commitments of US superheroes changed as the mainstream culture shifted. Superheroes, especially those featured in Marvel Comics storylines created by Stan Lee and Jack Kirby, resisted the Manichean binaries of good versus evil that reinforced a national myth of a pure US goodness against external evils that threatened it. Stories depicted both superheroes and supervillains as grounded within historical communities, with complex motivations, relationships, and solidarities that often reflected real world communities' organizing and activism around issues of social justice. Ramzi Fawaz describes US superheroes in the Silver Age and beyond as navigating the tension between the poles of individualistic rightness and communal ethical responsibility, as comic books explored "how various experiences of superhuman transformation might change what it means to be human and, consequently, what kind of community the superhero might affiliate with when the traditional markers of belonging—namely, proper humanity and national citizenship—no longer held true."[20] Mills, too, charts this shift theologically as reflecting the rise of contextual theologies that described human ontologies as dynamic, rather than static, relational rather than autonomous, and vulnerable rather than aggressive. Superheroes no longer were the idealized saviors safeguarding the purity of a chosen community, but imperfect messianic outcasts who "ambivalently fight on behalf of a humanity they deem morally degraded yet capable of redemption."[21] However, these changing theologies, and the superheroes who embodied them, functioned within the economics and politics of US global imperialism, participating in what Christina Klein describes as an "anti-conquest" strategy of affective sentimentality, stressing a narrative of global integration that employed the metaphors of family, togetherness, culture, and community. Themes of tolerance, acceptance, and universalism that began appearing in superhero comics of the Silver Age resisted the US nationalism of the Golden Age but did not depart from US imperial strategies, as comics became part of a "global imaginary of integration (that) generated an inclusive rather than a policing energy."[22]

---

[19] Greg Garrett, *Holy Superheroes!* (Louisville, Ky.: Westminster John Knox, 2008), 47.

[20] Ramzi Fawaz, *The New Mutants: Superheroes and the Radical Imagination of American Comics*, (New York: New York University Press, 2015), 22.

[21] Fawaz, *The New Mutants*, 204.

[22] Christina Klein, *Cold War Orientalism: Asia in the Middlebrow Imagination, 1945-1961* (Berkeley: University of California Press, 2003), 23.

Asian Americans Superheroes in US Theological Imagination

It's important to take note of what structures US superhero stories were asking global imaginaries to integrate themselves within. The primarily white, cis-male, and sexually straight superheroes of the Golden Age, who were created by white, cis-male, and sexually straight creators, embodied comics creator Chris Ware's observation that, "If you treat comics as a visual language and trace their origins, they point back, essentially, to racism."[23] On the one hand, in the Silver Age and beyond, white, cis-male, and sexually straight characters were joined by heroes who were Black, Indigenous, Latinx, Asian, women, and queer, and whose inclusion allowed white creators to include stories centered on themes of political and social justice that these communities faced. [24] On the other hand, Mills notes that for most of the Silver Age, racialized characters continued to be portrayed in stereotyped ways, and that the messages of cosmic justice and universal tolerance primarily were centered on whiteness-informed values.[25] Fawaz argues that these stereotypes were not clearly or directly communicating racist or supremacist agendas, but alongside those agendas also carried possibilities for resisting them. Characters of the Silver Age and beyond had identities, embodiments, and powers that constantly shifted and changed throughout their storylines, a narrative process that Fawaz describes as demonstrating "fluxability, … a state of material and psychic becoming characterized by constant transition or change that consequently orients one toward cultivating skills for negotiating (rather than exploiting) multiple, contradictory identities and affiliations."[26] Racialized and minoritized superheroes' participation within these stories did reflect Cold War, and then later neoliberal, commitments, but their fluxability simultaneously provided opportunities for what Fawaz calls "comic book cosmopolitics," a process of imaginative world-making that expanded belonging beyond the local or national (or earthly) community and de-emphasized assimilation in favor of cross-cultural negotiations with differences. Comic book cosmopolitics also acknowledged the concerns and insights of readers who, through letters to comics publishers, shared their thoughts on storylines and the ways they reflected real world social and political concerns. According to Fawaz, "From the

---

[23] Chris Ware in Jared Gardner, "Same Difference: Graphic Alterity in the Work of Gene Luen Yang, Adrian Tomine, and Derek Kirk Kim," in *Multicultural Comics: From Zap to Blue Beetle*, ed. Frederick Luis Aldama and Derek Parker Royal (Chicago: University of Chicago Press, 2010), 135.

[24] While writers and primary artists of mainstream comics during the Silver Age tended to be white men, Filipino American men worked at Marvel Comics as supporting artists such as inkers, letterers, and cover artists beginning in the 1980s, including Ernie Chan, Rudy Nebres, Tony DeZuniga, Alex Niño, Alfredo Alcala, and Nestor Redondo. See Rina Ayuyang, "Introduction," in *Marvel Voices: Identity* #1, Kindle edition (New York: Marvel Comics, 2021), location 2, and Greg LaRocque, "Now There's Something Different," in *Secret Identities: The Asian American Superhero Anthology* (New York: The New Press, 2009), 81.

[25] Mills, *American Theology, Superhero Comics, and Cinema*, 130.

[26] Fawaz, *The New Mutants*, 24.

late 1950s onward, a new generation of comic book mutants, aliens, and cyborgs encouraged audiences to form deep attachments to figures of deviancy, monstrosity, and marginalization. These fantasy figures spoke to people's desires, 'by identifying bodies, worldviews, and behaviors commonly denigrated by American public culture as both pleasurable and desirable.'"[27]

Asian-identified characters emerged in US mainstream comics as both colonizing stereotypes and participants in comic book cosmopolitics. Golden Age comics depicted Asian characters primarily as "Fu Manchu–style villains, yellow hordes, or bucktoothed Japanese or Vietcong soldiers"[28] that referenced "yellow peril" tropes of nineteenth- and early twentieth-century anti-Asian campaigns in the United States. Asian and Asian American heroes appeared in Silver Age comics "as martial arts masters, mathematical savants, or ancient mystics,"[29] or as variants of what Jane Iwamura describes as the "Oriental Monk." According to Iwamura, the Oriental Monk is

> [A] type of icon … onto which we project our assumptions, fears, and hopes. Although the Oriental Monk has appeared to us through the various media vehicles of American pop culture, we recognize him as the representative of an otherworldly (though perhaps not entirely alien) spirituality that draws from the ancient wellsprings of "Eastern" civilization and culture. And as Americans' current love affair with such figures as the Dalai Lama attests, the representation of this icon has only gained in popularity and impact.[30]

Indeed, the first Asian American hero with super powers in comic books was Shang-Chi, whose creation sought to capitalize on the popularity of Bruce Lee and the martial arts movies of the 1970s.[31] In addition to the literal "Oriental monk" characters with martial arts-based powers such as Shang Chi, Katana, Grace Choi, and Colleen Wing, even Asian and Asian American characters who don't have explicit martial arts abilities still have powers that relate visually, culturally, or aesthetically with stereotypical understandings of Asian history and culture. For example, manifestations of the character Sunfire, a Japanese hero with radiation-based fire powers, referred to the US bombing of Japan during World War II; Jubilee's ability to create "articulate, quasi-animate, transitory plasmoids," which appear as floating, multi-colored fireworks, link her to China's invention of gunpowder and fireworks.[32] These specific powers are manifestations of virtual orientalism, which

---

[27] Fawaz, *The New Mutants*, 47.

[28] Jeffrey A. Brown, *Panthers, Hulks, and Ironhearts: Marvel, Diversity, and the 21st Century Superhero* (New Brunswick, NJ.: Rutgers University Press, 2021), 89.

[29] Brown, *Panthers, Hulks, and Ironhearts*, 89.

[30] Jane Iwamura, *Virtual Orientalism: Asian Religions and American Popular Culture* (New York: Oxford University Press, 2011), 5.

[31] Brown, *Panthers, Hulks, and Ironhearts*, 94; The first Asian American heroic character was government agent Jimmy Woo, who did not have mystical or superhuman powers. Woo appeared first in Marvel's *Yellow Claw* series in the 1950s, and sporadically in Marvel series up to the present day. See Brown, *Panthers, Hulks, and Ironhearts*, 92.

[32] Jubilee explains her powers in her first appearance in *The Uncanny X-Men* #244. See Chris Claremont and Marc Silvestri, "Ladies Night," *The Uncanny X-Men* #244, Kindle edition (New York: Marvel Comics, 2013), location 2.

Iwamura points out does not rely upon the heroes' illustrated *bodies* alone, but requires supporting contextual characteristics such as clothes, hairstyles, and supporting environmental cues such as accents or ritual or social practices—or in this case powers that refer to these things—that affectively activate other senses that add to their virtual legibility. These associations with so-called Oriental aesthetics are not purely secular or cultural, but Oriental Monks, especially as the figure was developed and reified through entertainment media, are spiritualized alongside Western values of tolerance and protection of the vulnerable. Social justice as enacted by the Oriental Monks of US entertainment media became individualized and made cosmic through this specific spirituality. "Under this rubric, it is assumed that changing the hearts of individuals will automatically lead to changing society. To a post-1960s liberal audience who obviously felt sympathy toward the plight of racial minorities but who nevertheless were wary of certain measures taken by these groups toward self-determination and weary from extended conflict, this simple adage proved seductive."[33] Mills observes this trend with racialized superheroes as well, as publishers replaced social justice stories based on the Civil Rights, pacifist, and other political movements with stories focused on superheroes' personal introspection and escapism.[34]

All these factors combine to create what I identify as Asian American model minority superheroes. Culturally and theologically upholding the monomyth of US anti-conquest colonialism and imperialism, Asian American model minority superheroes are a problem. However, Asian American model minority superheroes also offer opportunities for theologically imagining belonging in the United States in resistance to the myriad and conjoined violences Asian and Asian North American people face, in complex and multiple ways, especially as their story arcs and characterizations have been taken up by Asian and Asian North American creators who are consciously working to create narratives that call for imagining the world and belonging otherwise. Rather than being stuck with the Manichean choice of either white, anti-conquest liberal assimilation as Oriental Monks whose depictions sell back individualized spiritualities to audiences, or permanent exclusion as yellow peril villains, Asian American model minority superheroes mirror back the struggles, choices, and fluxable negotiations Asians and Asian North Americans make under the constraints of white US imperialisms and support the work of theologically imagining an otherwise way of collective belonging.

---

[33] Iwamura, *Virtual Orientalism*, 133.
[34] Mills, *American Theology, Superhero Comics, and Cinema*, 99.

Seriality and Model Minority Minor Feelings

> In popular imagination, Asian Americans inhabit a vague, purgatorial status: not white enough nor black enough; distrusted by African Americans, ignored by whites unless we're being used by whites to keep the black man down. We're the carpenter ants of the service industry, the apparatchiks of the corporate world. We are math-crunching middle managers who keep corporate wheels greased but never get promoted since we don't have the right 'face' for leadership. We have a content problem. They think we have no inner resources. But while I may look impressive, I am frantically paddling my feet underwater, always overcompensating to hide by devouring feelings of inadequacy.[35]

Before focusing on the Asian American model minority superhero, I begin with the model minority and the possibilities it has for theological imagination. In her book *Minor Feelings,* Cathy Park Hong describes the model minority dilemma that Asian Americans face, forced by the constrained white settler colonial imagination to assimilate, an act that leads to self-hatred and away from solidarity with other people who make up the racialized global majority. "We were the 'good' ones since we were undemanding, diligent, and never asked for handouts from the government. There's no discrimination, they (US society) assured us, as long as you're compliant and hardworking."[36] However, model minority assimilation does not bring belonging, or security, as evidenced by violence against Asian Americans and Asian-identified people, as well as the minimization of that violence as not brutal enough when compared to violence against Black, Indigenous, and Latinx people in the United States. Park Hong names the affective experience of realizing the double bind of model minority existence, and the racialized gaslighting that accompanies it, as "minor feelings: the racialized range of emotions that are negative, dysphoric, and therefore untelegenic, built from the sediments of everyday racial experience and the irritant of having one's perception of reality constantly questioned or dismissed."[37] Minor feelings include affects such as shame, melancholy, irritation, belligerence, and depression, arising not because of major changes, but structural or systemic inertia that prevents any life-giving or significant personal, political, or social transformation from happening. Minor feelings arise in systems that keep individuals or communities stuck in their place within the structures of white imperial capitalism. "Minor feelings occur when American optimism is enforced upon you, which contradicts your own racialized reality, thereby creating a static of cognitive dissonance."[38] They are cumulative, ongoing, contradictory, and unresolvable, all of which are unwelcome or disruptive within social and institutional contexts that demand purity, binaries, or satisfying resolutions.

Although minor feelings can seem to be part of the mechanism that keeps Asian Americans and other assimilated minoritized people within the static model

---

[35] Cathy Park Hong, *Minor Feelings: An Asian American Reckoning* (New York: One World, 2020), 9–10.
[36] Park Hong, *Minor Feelings,* 22.
[37] Park Hong, *Minor Feelings,* 55.
[38] Park Hong, *Minor Feelings,* 56.

minority position created by white imperial capitalism, Park Hong indicates that they can also lead individuals or communities to recognize and reflect upon the individual or community histories, contexts, or political affiliations that caused them, a process that could create a pathway for shifting or sharing the long-term work of dismantling the systemic binds of assimilation and participation in white settler colonialism. If I dwell in minor feelings, then I am daring to upset or disrupt white contentment by bearing witness and testifying to the violence that US settler colonialism and imperialism has inflicted unevenly across different marginalized communities. In staying rooted in minor feelings, I become an "affect alien" who will not cooperate with the order of things, and who will not take my place in the spot the world has designated for me. To be an affect alien "is to be seen as trouble, as causing discomfort for others."[39] This refusal is not only a negation of an oppressive political or social order, but also a theological one that acts to reshape theological imaginations away from the promises of model minority salvation toward other narratives, possibilities, and practices, with others who also have been foreclosed and violently constrained within the imperialist system. As Karen Bray notes, "To listen for the alienation, whether embodied by our fellows in the present or in the ghosts of the past, is to welcome the prayerful lament of those willing to invest in the damage, to take care of and for the exceptions to redemption, those who had or have become the bad investments."[40]

Park Hong argues that because of their unsettled, continuing, and irredeemable nature, minor feelings appear in literature in works that themselves are unsettled, continuing, and unresolvable, such as serial poems and graphic novels. Ruth Meyer describes the seriality of comic books and other ongoing productions as having less to do with the linear sequencing of narratives over time, than with looping, sprawling, and disjointed unfoldings in which characters, environments, and themes appear repetitively, but with differences, or "'(retelling) the same stories *with endless embellishment'*."[41] This feature of seriality was a theological focus of Golden Age superhero stories, whose idealized, static nature and repetitive storylines left them existing within an "oneiric climate … where what has happened before and what has happened after appear extremely hazy."[42] Meyers argues that in the case of Asian villains such as Fu Manchu, seriality was a mechanism that promoted the limiting propagandas of imperialism, but at the same time created opportunities for comics creators, and readers, to identify and grapple with cultural and political anxieties and affects that are part of life under imperialism. "(Serial figures) register such deviations and try to put them into relation with standards of normality, often falling short of their ambitions and thus demarcating deficits and contradictions of

---

[39] Sara Ahmed, *The Promise of Happiness* (Durham, NC: Duke University Press, 2010), 69.

[40] Karen Bray, *Grave Attending: A Political Theology for the Unredeemed* (New York: Fordham University Press, 2020), 127.

[41] Michael Chabon in Ruth Meyers, *Serial Fu Manchu: The Chinese Supervillain and the Spread of Yellow Peril Ideology* (Philadelphia: Temple University Press, 2014), 124 (emphasis in original).

[42] Umberto Eco, "The Myth of Superman," in *Arguing Comics: Literary Masters on a Popular Medium*, ed. Jeet Heer and Kent Worcester (Jackson: University of Mississippi Press, 2005), 139.

a larger scale."[43] According to Jeffrey A. Brown, these deficits and contradictions were also part of the development of Asian American superheroes who "readdress past (anti-Asian stereotyped) depictions without discounting their influence or importance."[44]

Neither Brown nor Meyers describes past or present-day Asian American superheroes such as Marvel Comics characters agent Jimmy Woo, Shang-Chi, Jubilee, Ms. Marvel, Silk, and Brawn, as well as DC's Batgirl, Katana, and Green Arrow, specifically as model minority heroes (other than Jimmy Woo, who's first appearances in the 1950s marked him as an assimilated "good Asian" counterpoint to the villainous Yellow Claw). However, I am reclaiming the appellation as Park Hong describes it as I read these and other Asian North American superheroes. Jubilee and other comics superheroes, especially as their writing and/or art have been taken over by Asian and Asian North American creators, expose the minor feelings that come from the structures, possibilities, and irredeemability associated with Asian and Asian North American belonging within the mainstream US social, political, and theological imaginaries. Not all Asian and Asian American superheroes participate in this work of exposing minor feelings, even when their creators identify as Asian or Asian American, nor does the presence of minor feelings in a serial tale of model minority pain make it a vehicle for this type of imaginative resistance. Comics and graphic novels have the power to communicate, reify, and legitimize the white imperial systems, structures, and values that generate minor feelings in racialized or minoritized people. What I am noticing is that superhero narratives that do attempt to resist these norms highlight the role of minor feelings in order to offer what Jodi Kim describes as an *"unsettling hermeneutic* that disrupts the constitution of American nationalist ontology."[45] Superhero stories that showcase minor feelings function as unsettling hermeneutics when the feelings connect past atrocities and their tendrils to the present, opening up questions and uncertainties in those policies and identities in order to produce counter-narratives against hegemonic mythologies and theological imaginations.

The Serial Shame of Asian American Model Minority Superheroes

In particular, the minor feeling of shame appears often in these types of unsettling and irredeemable superhero stories that challenge national myths of belonging. Stories of shame often center on Asian American characters, linking them to stereotyped notions about "Asian shame" and collective identity. However, stories that

---

[43] Meyers, *Serial Fu Manchu*, 123.

[44] Brown, *Panthers, Hulks, and Ironhearts*, 89.

[45] Jodi Kim, *Ends of Empire: Asian American Critique and the Cold War* (Minneapolis: University of Minnesota Press, 2010), 30 (italics in original).

feature the minor feeling of shame show how that racialized shame originates within the serial complicities and histories of betrayals required for belonging within the United States under colonialism and imperialist structures. This exposure of shame invites reflection about national identity, and encourages opportunities to imagine national identity and belonging differently. Writing about historic distrust and uneven experiences of racism between Black and Asian communities in the United States, Park Hong lifts up shame as a foundational minor feeling guiding her efforts to dismantle white supremacy and her participation in and assimilation to it. Rather than hide her shame or displace it onto bodies that white imperialist imaginings deem as socially and politically more shameful than her own, Park Hong allows shame to guide her toward recognizing an unsettling reality that is shared multiply across bodies, relationships, and polities. Park Hong describes shame as the "flip side of innocence" that comes when the protective scales of white mythologies fall away from individual or collective understandings about the world.[46] Park Hong's musings on the minor feeling of shame turn away from popularized definitions that describe shame as the neurotic experience of one's own flawed being, or as a stigmatized personal identity reinforced by societal or cultural norms. She especially turns away from the dualistic conceptions of shame as an "Asian" or Confucianist-influenced affect, a definition common in uncritical anthropological writings on shame that divide the world into shame and guilt cultures. Park Hong writes, "My shame is not cultural but political. It is being painfully aware of the power dynamic that pulls at the levers of social interactions and the cringing indignity of where I am in that order either as the afflicted – *or* as the afflicter."[47] Similar to Paul Gilroy's concept of "productive shame," which "arises where identification is complicated by responsibility"[48] and works politically, socially, and culturally to bring to light unresolved or unaddressed injustices and violence that national, economic, political, and military powers seek to bury or hide, the minor feeling of Asian American model minority shame can prompt awareness and attention to the ways in which those injustices and violences are such ingrained parts of the world that individuals or communities cannot participate in them without heroic effort to disaffiliate or dismantle them. Park Hong writes, "By not speaking up, we perpetuate the myth that our shame is caused by our repressive culture and the country we fled, whereas America has given us nothing but opportunity."[49]

Shame as a minor feeling appears primarily in graphic narratives outside of this genre, such as semi-autobiographical and experimental works such as the Hernandez Brothers' series *Love and Rockets*, Lynda Barry's *One! Hundred! Demons!* or Adrian Tomine's illustrated novellas, works that Park Hong specifically cites.[50] Park Hong also notes that minor feelings arise in testimonies that expose the shame of

---

[46] Park Hong, *Minor Feelings*, 75.
[47] Park Hong, *Minor Feelings*, 75, italics in original.
[48] Paul Gilroy, *Postcolonial Melancholia* (New York: Columbia University Press, 2005), 99.
[49] Park Hong, *Minor Feelings*, 78.
[50] Park Hong, *Minor Feelings*, 57.

being racialized, simultaneously with the shame of realizing one's place in the racialized structure of the nation. The minor feeling of shame is the realization that "There is a hole in this country"[51] that pits racialized people against one another in order to secure the prosperity of the white majority. An example of this kind of shameful awakening in the superhero comics genre can be found in the two-volume anthology *Secret Identities*, and *Shattered*, both of which are subtitled *The Asian American Superhero Anthology*. Edited by Jeff Yang, Perry Shen, Keith Chow, and Jerry Ma, these books were the first mainstream comics focused solely on Asian American superheroes.[52]

The short, illustrated stories in the *Secret Identities* anthology highlight the exposures of hidden secrets about that identity that is common in Asian North American experiences and give attention to the enforced forgetting of history that kept both US atrocities against racialized people, and solidarities between Asian-identified people and other racialized communities, out of public consciousness. Rather than finding relief in assimilation into white histories or norms and burying those histories and values that are shamed under that assimilation, some of the stories in *Secret Identities* direct attention to the minor feelings that arise in the process of assimilating to whiteness. For example, the first section of the anthology, "War and Remembrance," focuses on stories about Japanese American internment during World War II. In the story "9066," an unnamed superhero echoes the testimonies of Japanese Americans and Japanese residents in the months after Japan's bombing of Pearl Harbor as the US government classified them as enemy subjects and white neighbors began to regard them with suspicion.[53]

Artist Jerry Ma depicts the unnamed Japanese American superhero standing surrounded by white-appearing superhero colleagues who stand with their fists up against an open, unboxed frame, which I interpret as breaking the temporal pace of reading in order to broaden the sentiment the protagonist voices beyond this moment through internal monologue: "I'm surrounded by the very same people I thought had accepted me."[54] This image is followed by a sharp close-up of the hero's face, his eyes closed behind his mask as he looks down in defeat, humiliation, and/or resignation, again stating through internal monologue, "They tell me that if I don't surrender they will take me by force. I know I can't fight them."[55] The hero then states that the reason he cannot fight them is because he knows that his individual actions fighting the white superheroes will be translated onto others in the Japanese

---

[51] Park Hong, *Minor Feelings*, 63.

[52] Jeff Yang and Jeff Castro, "Preface: In the Beginning," in *Secret Identities: The Asian American Superhero Anthology*, ed. Jeff Yang, Parry Shen, Keith Chow, and Jerry Ma (New York: The New Press, 2009), 10.

[53] This story seems to homage the graphic narrative *Citizen 13660*, in which Miné Okubo includes a scene where her character sits on a bus, surrounded by a sea of white faces, looking at her "with suspicion and distrust," while she looks back at them with her arms crossed defiantly. See Miné Okubo, *Citizen 13660* (Seattle, University of Washington Press, 1983), 12.

[54] Jonathan Tsuei and Jerry Ma, "9066" in *Secret Identities*, 27.

[55] Tsuei and Ma, "9066," 27.

American community in ways that his actions in fighting alongside them will not. The story concludes showing a sequence of the hero allowing himself to be captured and placed in a camp, as he echoes the thoughts that *nisei* young adults who had worked hard to assimilate into US citizenship and culture had during their roundup and incarceration: "I thought that it didn't matter who we were when our masks were off. I thought I proved where my loyalties lie when I consistently put myself in harm's way. The truth is it's not what you do that matters, but what you look like. I was a hero once. Now I'm just another Jap."[56] The final panel depicts the hero entering the camp, looking over his shoulder at his former colleagues who guard the Japanese-identified crowd of men with disillusionment, resentment, and anger. This panel gives expression to the minor feelings reported by former Japanese American incarcerees in the decades following their release, as they realized that assimilation provides no protection from the systems of white supremacy.

What many of the stories in the anthologies offer are reflections about that dynamic of shame and its role in cultivating community or negotiating belonging. In turning away from practices of pure model minority assimilation, and in shattering and exposing shamed "secret" identities and histories, possibilities for future politics and practices emerge. A moving example for me is the one-page story "Miss Moti, Shattered" included under *Shattered*'s "The Alien" section. Kripa Joshi illustrates a brief immigration story depicting the dehumanizing and destructive experience of racism at work in the bureaucracy of US immigration. "The look … the wait … and words that fly like cannonballs. They crack our confidence. They shatter our self-esteem."[57] Joshi illustrates the experience literally, as projectiles shoot out of the immigration agent's mouth to break Miss Moti into tiny pieces. The final panels of the comic show ephemeral spirits rising from the litter of broken pieces and cannonballs, reforming her into multiple bodies of her character that stand defiantly, stating, "But we will rise again … stronger."[58] The final panel holds that hope in suspension as the collective Miss Motis wait together for the next salvo. Her brokenness reforms into communal solidarity, becoming a source of endurance that she will have to continue to draw on for future battles. Paired with other stories that highlight communal support and solidarity across Asian identities, or with other racialized communities made vulnerable under similar conditions of US settler colonialism, the stories in the anthologies attempt to reimagine societal politics and practices outside of the status quo.

While these stories are imperfect, sometimes attempting to glorify formerly shamed identities by casting that shame off through new interpretations grounded in purpose or community or national loyalty, often the serial messiness and unfinishedness remain, as each short story offers only a tiny slice of what future work or imaginings can hold. Theologically, the stories in these anthologies offer avenues for reinterpreting concepts of national or communal belonging along the lines of

---

[56] Tsuei and Ma, "9066" in *Secret Identities,* 27–28.
[57] Kripa Joshi, "Miss Moti, Shattered," in *Shattered*, 131 (ellipses in original).
[58] Joshi, "Miss Moti, Shattered," 131.

Fawaz's description of comic book cosmopolitics. In these stories, neither belonging nor the work of collective action are separate from the experience or memory of shame, which aids in the ability to be "fluxable" as that community changes. The shame and the negotiations around it do not resolve into an easy or unproblematic belonging, but hold its hope suspended and repeated in serial fashion. Against manifestations of human wishes for divine power and authority or hopes for collective redemption, Asian American model minority superheroes exist in this space between the shames of exclusion and the solidarity of belonging, indicating new ways to construct and create mechanisms for both. By focusing on the aspects of Asian North American identity and collective belonging that, under US colonial assimilation, is deemed shameful, critical stories about Asian American model minority superheroes suspend ideas around communal or national belonging, gesturing toward different, and constantly mutating, possibilities.

Imagining Jubilee and Belonging in the Era of Anti-Asian Violence

Throughout her character history, Jubilee has lived a serial life of endless embellishments, as an X-men sidekick and hero, team leader, vampire, depowered pro-mutant activist, mother and mentor to other superheroes, in various universes and worlds. In 2021, she was included in the *Marvel Voices: Identity* #1 anthology that featured stories about Asian and Asian North American Marvel superheroes, including Shang-Chi, Silk and Brawn, and Jimmy Woo. While there's nothing in the issue that indicates the anthology was specifically created in response to the anti-Asian violence of the pandemic era, the stories draw upon Asian and Asian North American experiences of exclusion and violence that preceded and exceed this era. The stories of *Identity*, writes Rina Ayuyang in the introduction, make "people like me – folks who once felt like these stories didn't and couldn't 'belong to me'– get excited by the possibilities and power of the superhero genre as a whole."[59] Jubilee's story, "That One Thing," written and colored by Christina Strain and drawn by Jason Loo, shows Jubilee imperfectly tending to her parents' graves and remembering with some shame, regret, and sadness the times that she had rejected her parents' attempts to connect her with her Hong Kong roots. The story ends with her sharing a meal with her adopted son and partner, bringing them into a new circle of family that includes her lost parents, saying, "We're just glad you're both here." Her story is one of several in the issue in which belonging and the possibilities for community remain connected to the disappointments, hurts, and violence of model minority life, which aren't resolved, but are enfolded into larger stories and bigger connections. As Strain writes in the issues epilogue section, "For those of us who feel like outsiders, having a better understanding of these foundations (family, heritage, or

---

[59] Ayuyang, "Introduction" in *X-Men Voices*, location 2.

culture) helps us understand ourselves in a way that makes us feel less alone. Because it helps us understand that we're part of a bigger whole."[60]

When I began this project, I did not expect to return to Jubilee, a model minority superhero who I love and who shamefully reminds me of the violences of my histories, the constraints of my life under white settler colonialism, and the possibilities of belonging in new and different ways that center justice and collective care. Her story, and other stories of Asian and Asian North American model minority superheroes seed my imagination with the realizations that the struggles of the present moment are not only mine to face, and that the work of resistance and reimagination has always been a repeated collective and communal effort, both within my shared Asian North American spaces and outside it as my communities joined with other racialized people facing similar, intersecting, and different violences under the system of white settler colonialism. Theological imagination requires their close, comforting, but also confrontational and challenging presence as we work toward the worlds we dream of together, because imagination and action depend upon one another. As Richard Delgado and Jean Stafancic point out, "Our social world, with its rules, practices, and assignments of prestige and power, is not fixed; rather, we construct it with words, stories, and silence. But we need not acquiesce in arrangements that are unfair and one-sided. By writing and speaking against them, we may hope to contribute to a better, fairer world."[61] For me, to remain in these stories of model minority superheroes is not to escape into navel-gazing, but to participate in a theological practice of reshaping my imagination away from a one-sided racist assimilation to glimpse a future that is contingent, multiple, and unresolvable, and not quite beyond my imaginations.

Discussion Questions

1. What are your practices for developing and interrogating your theological imagination? How have systemic oppressions constrained your theological imagination?
2. What is the world that you want to create? What sources help you imagine that world? How do you live into that imagination through practices, actions, and daily works of justice?
3. How do you live in the tension between the worlds that constrain imaginations and the worlds that could be?
4. What popular culture characters have helped you develop your theological imagination? How?

---

[60] Christina Strain, "Identity" in *Marvel Voices: Identity* #1, location 44.
[61] Richard Delgado and Jean Stefancic, "Introduction" to *Critical Race Theory: The Cutting Edge* (Philadelphia, PA: Temple University Press, 2013), 3.

Bibliography

Ahmed, Sara. 2010. *The Promise of Happiness*. Durham, NC: Duke University Press.
Ayuyang, Rina. 2021. Introduction. In *Marvel Voices: Identity #1*. New York: Marvel Comics. Kindle.
Bray, Karen. 2020. *Grave Attending: A Political Theology for the Unredeemed*. New York: Fordham University Press.
Brown, Jeffrey A. 2021. *Panthers, Hulks, and Ironhearts: Marvel, Diversity, and the 21st Century Superhero*. New Brunswick, NJ: Rutgers University Press.
Claremont, Chris, and Marc Silvestri. 2013. Ladies Night. In *The Uncanny X-Men #244*. New York: Marvel Comics, Kindle.
Delgado, Richard, and Jean Stefancic. 2013. Introduction. In *Critical Race Theory: The Cutting Edge*, ed. Richard Delgado and Jean Stefancic, 1–3. Philadelphia, PA: Temple University Press.
Eco, Umberto. 2005. The Myth of Superman. In *Arguing Comics: Literary Masters on a Popular Medium*, ed. Jeet Heer and Kent Worcester, 134–147. Jackson: University of Mississippi Press.
Fawaz, Ramzi. 2015. *The New Mutants: Superheroes and the Radical Imagination of American Comics*. Kindle edition. New York and London: New York University Press.
Gardner, Jared. 2010. Same Difference: Graphic Alterity in the Work of Gene Luen Yang, Adrian Tomine, and Derek Kirk Kim. In *Multicultural Comics: From Zap to Blue Beetle*, ed. Frederick Luis Aldama and Derek Parker Royal, 132–147. Chicago, IL: University of Chicago Press.
Gilroy, Paul. 2005. *Postcolonial Melancholia*. New York: Columbia University Press.
Garrett, Greg. 2008. *Holy Superheroes!* Louisville, KY: Westminster John Knox.
Iwamura, Jane. 2011. *Virtual Orientalism: Asian Religions and American Popular Culture*. New York: Oxford University Press.
Jennings, Willie James. 2010. *The Christian Imagination: Theology and the Origins of Race*. New Haven, CT: Yale University Press.
Jeung, Russell, Angie J. Yellow Horse, and Charlene Cayanan. 2021. Stop AAPI Hate National Report: 3/19/20 - 3/31/21, *#StopAAPIHate.org*, May 6. https://stopaapihate.org/wp-content/uploads/2021/05/Stop-AAPI-Hate-Report-National-210506.pdf.
Joshi, Kripa. 2012. Miss Moti, Shattered. In *Shattered: The Asian American Superhero Anthology*, ed. Jeff Yang, Parry Shen, Keith Chow, and Jerry Ma, 131. New York: The New Press.
Khanna, Ranjana. 2003. *Dark Continents: Psychoanalysis and Colonialism*. Durham, NC: Duke University Press.
Kim, Jodi. 2010. *Ends of Empire: Asian American Critique and the Cold War*. Minneapolis: University of Minnesota Press.
Klein, Christina. 2003. *Cold War Orientalism: Asia in the Middlebrow Imagination, 1945–1961*. Berkeley: University of California Press.
Kwok, Pui-lan. 2005. *Postcolonial Imagination and Feminist Theology*. Louisville, KY: Westminster John Knox.
Lacson, Therese. Where are the Asians in *The Falcon and the Winter Soldier*'s Madripoor? Published at Comics Beat. https://www.comicsbeat.com/falcon-and-the-winter-soldier-asians-madripoor/.
LaRocque, Greg. 2009. Now There's Something Different. In *Secret Identities: The Asian American Superhero Anthology*. New York: The New Press.
"Madripoor." *Marvel*. https://www.marvel.com/comics/discover/2072/madripoor.
Meyers, Ruth. 2014. *Serial Fu Manchu: The Chinese Supervillain and the Spread of Yellow Peril Ideology*. Philadelphia, PA: Temple University Press.
Mills, Anthony R. 2014. *American Theology, Superhero Comics, and Cinema: The Marvel of Stan Lee and the Revolution of a Genre*. New York and London: Routledge.
Moy, Zak. 2021. X-Men's Jubilee: An Icon Short of Iconic. #StopAsianHate. *Medium*, March 30, https://zakmoy.medium.com/x-mens-jubilee-an-icon-short-of-iconic-stopasianhate-3e180714b53a.
Okubo, Miné. 1983. *Citizen 13660*. Seattle: University of Washington Press.

Hong, Cathy Park. 2020. *Minor Feelings: An Asian American Reckoning*. New York: One World.
Peckruhn, Heike. 2020. Embodied Knowing: Body, Epistemology, Context, and Hermeneutics. In *What Is Constructive Theology?: Histories, Methodologies, and Perspectives*, ed. Marion Grau, 77–102. London: T&T Clark.
Saunders, Ben. 2013. *Do the Gods Wear Capes? Spirituality, Fantasy, and Superheroes*. London: Bloomsbury Academic.
Skidmore, Max J., and Joey Skidmore. "More Than Mere Fantasy: Political Themes in Contemporary Comic Books." Journal of Popular Culture 17, 1 (Summer, 1983): 83-92.
Strain, Christina. 2021. Identity. In *Marvel Voices: Identity #1*. New York: Marvel Universe. Kindle.
Tsuei, Jonathan, and Jerry Ma. 2009. 9066. In *Secret Identities: The Asian American Superhero Anthology*, ed. Jeff Yang, Parry Shen, Keith Chow, and Jerry Ma, 25–28. New York: The New Press.
Walsh, Catherine E., and Walter Mignolo. 2018. *On Decoloniality: Concepts, Analytics, Praxis*. Durham, NC: Duke University Press.
Yang, Jeff. 2020. Introduction. In *DC Festival of Heroes: The Asian Superhero Collection*. New York: DC Comics. Kindle.
Yang, Jeff, and Jeff Castro. 2009. Preface: In the Beginning. In *Secret Identities: The Asian American Superhero Anthology*, ed. Jeff Yang, Parry Shen, Keith Chow, and Jerry Ma, 7–13. New York: The New Press.

5
An Antiracist and Antiwar Feminist Theology: When the US Military Empire Divides Us

Keun-joo Christine Pae

As historian Erika Lee notes, anti-Asian racism in the United States is entangled with a xenophobia that has perpetuated (color-blind) racism and anti-immigration, reinforced white supremacist politics, generated lucrative profits domestically and internationally, and influenced US foreign policy.[1] The COVID-related resurgence of anti-Asian racism only exasperates this tenacious xenophobic racism against Asian Americans, as we are still seen as "perpetual foreigners" and threats to the United States. Centuries-old systematic anti-Asian racism is codependent on anti-Black racism, anti-Muslim sentiments, white settler colonialism, and homophobia. These intertwined forms of discrimination are ideologically and materially manifested through US bases across the globe. These bases find their origin in frontier forts, that is, hundreds of frontier forts built on American Indian territories from the eighteenth through the nineteenth century.[2] The conquest of Indian nations would strategically connect to the building of the US transpacific empire. For the past two centuries, the United States has aggressively consolidated its power in the Asia Pacific by occupying Pacific islands, opening markets, making wars, and constructing bases. Thus, it is crucial to interrogate "militarized racism and racialized

---

[1] Erika Lee, *America for Americans: A History of Xenophobia in the United States* (New York: Basic Books, 2019), 12–15.
[2] David Vine, *Base Nation: How US Military Bases Abroad Harm America and the World* (New York: Metropolitan Books, 2015), 5.

K. C. Pae (✉)
The Department of Religion and Women's and Gender Studies, Denison University, Granville, OH, USA
e-mail: paec@denison.edu

© The Author(s), under exclusive license to Springer Nature Switzerland AG 2023
K. C. Pae, B. Lee (eds.), *Embodying Antiracist Christianity*, https://doi.org/10.1007/978-3-031-37264-3_5

militarism" in America's domestic and international relations as a first step in dismantling them.[3]

In search of antiracist and antiwar feminist theology, this chapter critically interrogates the role of the US military in consolidating white supremacy and sustaining anti-Black and anti-Asian racism. I argue that antiracist feminist theology is synonymous with antiwar feminist theology, which demands a critical analysis of racial politics from a transnational perspective and cross-border coalition-building for peace and justice. My theological reflection is premised on the belief that US imperial militarism is a persistent cause of xenophobia, racism, and interracial conflict at home and abroad. More specifically, this chapter focuses on America's "hot wars" in Asia during the Cold War, and their impact on anti-Asian and anti-Black racism. A significant portion of this chapter analyzes Afro-Asian relations in Japan and Korea between 1945–1953. In this period, the United States replaced or succeeded the Japanese empire in the Asia Pacific at the cost of incarcerating Japanese Americans in internment camps. Furthermore, the Korean War (1950–1953) enabled the United States to congeal the logic of the Cold War and set patterns of interpretation and intervention in the political conflicts of Third World countries in align with US interests.[4] American wars in Vietnam, Iraq, and Afghanistan followed these improvisational and dangerous war patterns, exacerbating xenophobic anti-Asian racism and interracial conflict not only in the United States but also in those warring countries.[5]

Finally, the chapter proposes an image of a God of interstices who exists in radical interconnectedness of all living beings. This image interweaves Asian American antiracist feminist theologies with the antiwar praxis of the Women's International Democratic Federation at the height of McCarthyism. A theological reading of women's antiwar internationalism may revitalize Christian internationalism for global peace and justice by creating alternative myths of Christianity.

---

[3] Mai-Anh Le Tran, "From My Lai to Ferguson: Collaterality, Grievous Deaths, Militarized Orientalism, Benevolence, and Racism" in *Feminist Praxis against US Militarism*, ed. Nami Kim and Wonhee Anne Joh (Lanham, MD: Lexington Books, 2020), 73; Tran uses the phrase "militarized racism and racialized militarism" in her critical reflection on the anti-Black police violence in Ferguson, Missouri and anti-Asian racism in the Vietnam War.

[4] Jodi Kim, *The Ends of Empire: Asian American Critique and the Cold War* (Minneapolis: University of Minnesota Press, 2010), 150.

[5] James Wright, "What We Learned from the Korean War," *The Atlantic*, July 23, 2013, https://www.theatlantic.com/international/archive/2013/07/what-we-learned-from-the-korean-war/278016/.

Defying the Secrecy of the Cold War

On July 29, 2021, Sunisa Lee, an eighteen-year-old gymnast from St. Paul, Minnesota, won the gold medal in the women's gymnastics all-around competition at the Tokyo 2020 Olympic Games. She wrote a new history of the Olympics, being the first Asian American Olympic gold medalist in gymnastics and the first Hmong who has won any Olympic medal. Mainline US media highlighted Lee's family portraits, coined with a model minority stereotype: a hard-working family, parental love for and dedication to the children's success, and strong family ties. Her stepfather, John Lee, touched many Americans' hearts. He built balance beams for Sunisa in their backyard because he could not afford expensive gymnastic training.[6] Despite his fall from a ladder that paralyzed him from the chest down only two days before the 2019 national championships, John Lee encouraged Sunisa to compete to pave the way for her participation in the Tokyo Olympics. American media did not miss this all-American family story. At the same time, the Lee family story reminded the American public of Hmong Americans and their passage to the United States after "the secret war" at the borders of Laos, Vietnam, and Thailand during the Vietnam War.[7] Sunisa Lee, now the most famous Hmong, rekindled Hmong pride. Lee's odyssey to the Olympic gold medal reveals the multiple dimensions of America's forgotten history beyond one amazingly disciplined gymnast and her family.

Lee's gold medal invokes the secrets of America's anti-communist wars in Asia, just as Native Americans remind the US public of European settler colonialism. Indeed, it is not a secret that the US armed forces have fought various wars and skirmishes in the Asia Pacific and expanded bases or "lily pads" to ensure a more agile and efficient projection of US power not only in the region but also over other parts of the world.[8] However, the violent racial conflict inside the US military and the racialized interactions between American soldiers and local Asians in Japan, Korea, and Vietnam are unknown parts of history—not to mention American soldiers' rape of local Asian women, and imperialist attitudes toward them.

The Cold War consolidated the post-World War II Asian/American identity and the role of the United States in the Asia Pacific. However, the United States still does not comprehend the struggles of newly emancipated Asian countries after World War II, struggles which have shaped and reshaped Asian Americans' self-understanding and relationships with the United States. As anthropologist Heonik Kwon insightfully points out, the Cold War, both as a concept and as a reality, encompassed "plural struggles for the world" rather than implicating the bifurcation

---

[6] Caitlin O'Kane, "Suni Lee's Dad Was Paralyzed Two Years Ago. Now, He's a Model for the Tenacity His Daughter Shares," *CBS News*, July 30, 2021, https://www.cbsnews.com/news/suni-lee-olympic-gymnastics-gold-medal-father-paralyzed/.

[7] Ma Vang, *History on the Run: Secrecy, Fugitivity, and Hmong Refugee Epistemologies* (Durham, NC: Duke University Press, 2021), 5.

[8] Maria Höhn and Seungsook Moon, "Conclusion: Empire at the Crossroads?" in *Over There: Living with the US Military Empire from World War Two to the Present*, ed. Maria Höhn and Seungsook Moon (Durham, NC: Duke University Press, 2010), 400.

of international politics during the second half of the twentieth century.⁹ America's memories of the Cold War are linear and monolithic—rivalry and stalemate with the former Soviet Union and, finally, victory over it. In contrast, Asian Americans' stories of the Cold War consist of multiple temporalities, contradictions, and fragments, as political struggles in their ancestral lands were complex, and Asian Americans still live with the effects of America's Cold War in Asia. Here, Jodi Kim's conceptualization of the end of the Cold War as the "ends of the US empire" is helpful in understanding how the American Cold War has shaped Asian American identity:

> …[T]his protracted Cold War imperialist relation between Asia and America contradictorily configures the "Asian American" subject not only as immigrant, racial (minority) formation, or putative liberal citizen-subject of the US nation-state, but also as postimperial exile or "refugee" who simultaneously is a product of, bears witness to, and critiques imperialist and gendered racial violence.¹⁰

Sunisa Lee's golden medal cannot hide what the United States did in Southeast Asia. Asian Americans, who constantly invoke shameful secrets of the United States, can hardly be considered insiders, but only outsiders, and thus, perpetual foreigners.

Anti-Black Racism and Anti-Asian Racism in the United States and East Asia

One may wonder how Blacks and Asians see each other. Do Asians otherize African Americans due to their blackness? Do African Americans see Asian Americans as perpetual foreigners due to their racial, cultural, and religious differences? Afro-Asian relations are complex and often antagonistic.

Although the primary force in anti-Black and anti-Asian racism is white supremacy, both forms of racism cannot be effective without Blacks and Asian Americans' compliances with structural racism and racialized US overseas military operations. The Cold War enemies of the United States had East Asianized faces. African Americans, whether on battlefields in East and Southeast Asia or in the United States, were influenced by the social construction of anti-Asian racism. African American occupiers in Japan, frontline fighters in Korea and Vietnam, and Civil Rights activists in the United States exhibited politically and emotionally complex attitudes toward Asians. For some, Asians were brothers and sisters of color, enemies of the United States, untrustworthy and cruel communists, or an inferior and squalid species. Asians also developed similar sentiments toward Blacks. In the meantime, North Korea, Communist China, and North Vietnam propagandized state-sanctioned violence against Blacks in the United States to undermine African

---

⁹ Heonik Kwon, *The Other Cold War* (New York: Columbia University Press, 2010), 5–7.
¹⁰ Jodi Kim, *Ends of Empire*, 7.

American soldiers' morale during wars. Asian women and children were often caught in the clash between anti-Black and anti-Asian racism.

Prostitution and Anti-Asian Racism

Black soldiers' encounters with local Asians during the early Cold War were sexualized, because American soldiers could not freely associate with local civilians except female prostitutes or hostesses at bars, dance halls, and restaurants around bases. Prostitution was readily available for American soldiers when they arrived on Japanese shores. Japan already had public brothels throughout the country, as well as the comfort women system for Japanese soldiers during World War II.[11] Although the Supreme Commander for the Allied Powers in Japan and the Japanese government shut off coercive and state-sponsored prostitution, they were not interested in abolishing commercial prostitution, especially around US bases.[12] However, the systemic development of US military prostitution (or the Rest and Recreation business) in Japan was possible owing partially to the Korean War.

A few months after the Korean War had broken out on June 25, 1950, American GIs, including the All-Black 24th Infantry Regiment, arrived in Korea directly from Japan. By 1951, the 215,000 soldiers stationed in Korea outnumbered the 100,000 in Japan.[13] GIs stationed in Korea complained about the lack of sexually available women along with widespread poverty and poor sanitation there.[14] During the war, poverty-stricken women, war widows, and orphans flocked around UN/US bivouacs throughout Korea. These camp followers sold sex to UN/US soldiers for meager economic earnings or for food and daily goods.[15] However, Korea was unattractive to American soldiers beyond what they could tolerate on the battlefield. Many journalists reported the complaints of American soldiers who struggled with extreme weather in summer and winter, the smell of rice paddies fertilized by human excreta, and squalid Koreans.[16] Sex with Korean women in shanty houses, tents, and on

---

[11] Prostitution industries in Korea were first developed while colonized by Japan (1910–1945). The US military government in Korea abolished prostitution in 1948 but was not interested in commercialized prostitution. US military prostitution industries became systematized and sophisticated upon the networks of brothels from the Japanese colonial period. See Keun-joo Christine Pae, "The Prostituted Body of War: U.S. Military Prostitution in South Korea as a Site of Spiritual Activism" in *Transformational Embodiment in Asian Religions: Subtle Bodies, Spatial Bodies*, ed. George Pati and Katherine C. Zubko (New York: Routledge, 2019), 187–205.

[12] Michael Cullen Green, *Black Yanks in the Pacific: Race in the Making of American Military Empire after World War II* (Ithaca, NY: Cornell University Press), 65.

[13] Green, *Black Yanks in the Pacific*, 111.

[14] Green, *Black Yanks in the Pacific*, 67.

[15] Katherine Moon, *Sex among Allies: Military Prostitution in US-Korea Relations* (New York: Columbia University Press, 1997), 28.

[16] Green, *Black Yanks in the Pacific*, 127.

blankets outdoors was a temporary remedy for GIs eager to release their anxiety, stress, fear, and anger in a war that was meaningless other than for economic gains.

The prolonged stalemate of the Korean War and the end of America's occupation of mainland Japan in 1951 enabled Japanese entrepreneurs to develop the R&R business. Beer halls, bars, red-light resorts, and strip-tease shows were available to American servicemen who flew from Korea to Japan for a vacation from the war. American combat personnel could (theoretically) earn a five-day leave in Japan for every six weeks of frontline service.[17] The San Francisco Treaty of 1951 established the bilateral relationship between Japan and the United States. Japan regained its sovereignty, while the United States could station its military in Okinawa indefinitely. Since its occupation of Japan, the United States pushed the construction of military bases in Okinawa due to the Island's strategic importance in the Pacific. The San Francisco Treaty allowed the United States to control lands, seas, and even the people of Okinawa. During the Korean War, "B-29 and B-26 bombers flew sorties out of Okinawa's Kadena airfields to the Korean Peninsula."[18] Since the Korean War ended as a truce in 1953, US bases in Okinawa have served the US military empire in containing communist China and the former Soviet Union while consolidating US global power. The United States strategically constructed bases in Okinawa by using Japanese companies from the mainland and hiring Okinawans to "spur the rapid growth of Okinawa's economy" and eventually make it dependent on jobs and business generated by the bases.[19] The R&R system is an integral part of the Okinawan economy, dependent on the US war economy.

Anti-Black Racism in Japan and Korea

African American soldiers' encounters with local women in Japan and Korea, whether they were prostitutes or civilian workers around US bases, often ended up in romantic relationships. However, their romantic interests toward Asian women faced many political and cultural challenges—anti-Black racism, anti-Asian racism, US immigration laws, US military policy, and so forth.

The arrival of African American soldiers in Japan and Korea after World War II reinforced anti-Black racism in those countries. More specifically, a discourse of eugenics shaped Japanese people's self-understanding of their race and racial superiority over their colonized counterparts. As Francis Galton's *Hereditary Genius* was translated into Japanese shortly after its publication in England in 1869, imperial Japan adapted the European version of racist eugenics while developing its own

---

[17] Green, *Black Yanks in the Pacific*, 69.
[18] Etsuko Takushi Crissey, *Okinawa's GI Brides: Their Lives in America*, trans. Steve Rabson (Honolulu: University of Hawaii Press, 2017), 15.
[19] Crissey, *Okinawa's GI Brides: Their Lives in America*, 16.

version.[20] Semantic and semiotic inventions around eugenics "were part of the ideological agenda of the Meiji Restoration (1868) and were incorporated into the postwar (and current) constitution of 1947."[21] Japan's constitution defines nationality and citizenship "as a matter of blood, or *jus sanguinis* (as opposed to citizenship determined by place of birth, or *jus solis*)."[22] Imperial Japan's project of improving the Japanese race was either by associating it with the Aryan race or by representing it as the "amalgam of Asians and Pacific Islanders."[23] Thus, the Japanese were scientifically suitable to rule over the Asia Pacific. In contrast, postwar Japan emphasized the "homogeneity" of the Japanese race over the ethnically hybrid Pan-Asian empire narrative. Thus, in contemporary Japanese society, lighter skin is still preferred, and white is "a common symbol of culturally valued 'purity' and 'cleanliness.'"[24]

Besides the native anti-Black prejudice of Japanese society, white soldiers spread horror stories among Japanese civilians purported African American behaviors such as rape, violence, pillage, and murder.[25] To be sure, these rumors reflected racist rhetoric in Jim Crow America. Since African American occupiers were not welcomed in Japan, Japanese women associated with them had to justify their involvement with these unwelcomed soldiers. Economic gain might be the most important reason for those Japanese women, particularly for prostitutes. Nevertheless, they pointed out the gentle characters and manners of Black soldiers as the significant reasons to date, co-habit with, and cater to them.

Whether an economically necessary union or true love, Afro-Japanese romance was scrutinized by multiple constituencies—Japanese society, the US military and government, and African American communities. The US military was not interested in controlling military prostitution but merely warned soldiers about the consequences of their serious relationships with Japanese women. American politicians and military leaders were concerned about interracial romance, especially between Black men and white women inside the United States and overseas bases. Sexual relations between African American soldiers and white women in post-World War II Europe led to a reduction in the number of African American soldiers in the United Kingdom and Germany. Afro-Asian romance did not get attention from the authorities until African American soldiers wanted to make families with Japanese women. Although the 1947 revision of the War Brides Act allowed American servicemen to bring their foreign wives to the United States, the Asian Exclusion Act of 1924 was repealed only in 1952 with the McCarran-Walter Act, which removed

---

[20] Jennifer Robertson, "Eugenics in Japan: Sanguinous Repair" in *The Oxford Handbook of the History of Eugenics*, ed. Allison Bashford and Philippa Levine (London: Oxford University Press, 2010), 432.
[21] Robertson, "Eugenics in Japan," 433.
[22] Robertson, "Eugenics in Japan," 433.
[23] Debito Arudou, *Embedded Racism: Japan's Visible Minorities and Racial Discrimination* (Lanham, MD: Lexington Books, 2015), 18.
[24] Arudou, *Embedded Racism*, 16; 21.
[25] Green, *Black Yanks in Pacific*, 63.

race as a criterion for granting permanent residence.[26] The McCarran-Walter Act opened only a narrow door for Black servicemen to bring their Asian wives until President Lyndon Johnson signed the New Immigration Act in 1965, which finally removed the national origin formula from the law of immigration and naturalization. Furthermore, forty-one states had laws banning interracial marriage at one time or another. Sixteen states still prohibited interracial marriage in 1967, when the Supreme Court finally abolished interracial marriage bans (i.e., Loving v. Virginia).[27] Black-Japanese couples faced social confusion in racially polarized American society when they arrived in the early 1950s since Japanese could be considered white, for instance, in Oklahoma.[28]

The Convergence of International and Domestic Racial Politics

Before World War II, Asian Americans, African Americans, and other racial minorities on the West Coast lived in the same neighborhoods, but the socioeconomic trajectories of Black and Asian Americans started diverging in the early Cold War.[29] Christina Klein critically analyzes the Cold War Orientalism of the US mainstream media, which portrayed Asians as a model minority, supporters of US democracy and moral values, and victims of communism who could be fully assimilated with American culture and society.[30] Far from being the enemies of the United States, these images of Asians were crucial in order for the United States to maintain public support for its (anti-communist) wars and occupations in the Asia Pacific. However, changing socio-political attitudes toward Asians evoked resentment among African Americans, as structural racism continued to threaten their livelihood. Historian Michael Cullen Green analytically summarizes Afro-Asian relations in the United States. The Cold War struggle for hearts and minds appeared to favor Asians, but not as of yet the interests of Black people.[31]

Japanese internment camps during World War II represent the most horrendous form of xenophobic anti-Asian violence. For the US government, the Japanese internment camp was a "military necessity," but in reality, the camp was the acme of many-decade-accumulated anti-Japanese racism.[32] When President Roosevelt signed Executive Order 9066 on February 19, 1942, which gave the military the power to "round up and expel entire communities without compensation, due

---

[26] Crissey, *Okinawa's GI Brides*, 7.

[27] Phyl Newbeck, *Virginia Hasn't Always Been for Lovers: Interracial Marriage Bans and the Case of Richard and Mildred Loving* (Carbondale: Southern Illinois University Press, 2008), 3.

[28] Green, *Black Yanks in the Pacific*, 82.

[29] Green, *Black Yanks in the Pacific*, 83.

[30] Christina Klein, *Cold War Orientalism: Asia in the Middlebrow Imagination, 1945–1961* (Berkeley: University of California Press, 2003), 19–60.

[31] Green, *Black Yanks in the Pacific*, 84.

[32] Lee, *America for Americans*, 183.

process, or proof of wrongdoing," Japanese Americans made up less than 0.1% of the entire American population.[33] Nevertheless, Japanese Americans were considered a threat to US national security and sent to designated concentration camps without due process. The incarceration of Japanese Americans ironically enabled African Americans and other racial minorities to buy affordable houses and stores left behind by Japanese Americans. For instance, Los Angeles's Little Tokyo was metaphorically renamed by Bronzeville as African Americans and their families settled into one of the few neighborhoods available to them.[34] The African American magazine *Ebony* predicted the "betrothing" of Japanese American returnees from concentration camps and African Americans or the wedding of Little Tokyo and Bronzeville because both groups were victimized by racism and shared the same political interests. Afro-Asian amity at home and abroad indulged in intimate and gendered rhetoric that pictured Asians as subordinate partners.[35] Although African Americans were hopeful for coalition-building with Asian Americans, the US military empire undermined their hope for political solidarity with other racial minorities.

Black GIs' Japanese wives were caught in the US racial politics, Japanese anti-Black racism, and US Cold War militarism. American society generally considered Asian women married to GIs as wild prostitutes who tempted innocent young American men. African American communities suspected these women's intentions to marry their men. In addition, the Japanese media portrayed the Japanese wives of Black GIs as the world's unhappiest brides.[36] These military brides were isolated from Japanese American communities, the Japanese brides of white GIs, and African American communities. Black GI-Japanese couples were forced to socialize exclusively with one another.[37] The social condition of the Korean wives of Black GIs was similar, if not worse. Between 1945–1952, the Japanese and Korean lovers of African American soldiers faced unique challenges caused by US immigration laws and military policy. Black GIs experienced legal difficulties in having the US government and military recognize their unions with Asian women as well as economic challenges in flying their wives and children to the United States. Moreover, the Korean War separated Black GIs from their Japanese families. Some of them were even killed in the war, as the frontline fighters in Korea were predominantly soldiers of color.[38] Subsequently, a significant number of women were left behind with bi-racial children after the departures of Black GIs. The so-called brown baby crisis in East Asia and Europe after World War II was the predictable result of racist US immigration laws and racial politics in the US military and in countries where US soldiers were stationed.[39]

---

[33] Lee, *America for Americans*, 203.
[34] Green, *Black Yanks in the Pacific*, 62.
[35] Green, *Black Yanks in the Pacific*, 62.
[36] Green, *Black Yanks in the Pacific*, 86.
[37] Green, *Black Yanks in the Pacific*, 85.
[38] Green, *Black Yanks in the Pacific*, 78–80.
[39] Green, *Black Yanks in the Pacific*, 87–89.

Anti-Communism and Racism: Korea-US Relations

In Korea, six thousand miles from the United States, racist McCarthyism brought bloody forms of violence, from genocide to rape. Atrocities committed by American soldiers against Korean civilians stemmed from the quasi-racist, anti-communist justification of the Korean War.[40] American politicians and military authorities generally viewed Koreans as (potential) communists or "reds," whether they were refugees, civilians, soldiers, or children. Racial slurs such as gooks were regularly used to ignite enmity toward Koreans among American soldiers. For American soldiers and politicians, Koreans and their land were not subjects to be defended from communists but were enemies to be destroyed. Korea was not a battlefield or land to be liberated but an "arena" to hunt down red gooks.[41]

During the Korean War, racial politics was unfolded in a complicated manner. Black intellectuals and activists, such as Paul Robeson and W. E. B. Du Bois, argued that the Korean War was a race war where poor young Black men were allured into America's imperialist fascism fight against the yellow race.[42] In contrast, Black soldiers and some leading African American magazines such as *Ebony* praised American soldiers for patriotically fighting against "slant-eyed" Korean enemies, unshaken by North Korea's racial propaganda.[43] The celebration of Black soldiers' accomplishments in Korea further dehumanized the North Korean Army and Koreans while congealing the US power in the Asia Pacific. Blacks' celebratory voices were reactionary to rampant racism in the US military stationed in Korea. White servicemen attacked Black soldiers' military performance, calling the 24th Infantry Regiment of all Black soldiers "the Bugout Boogie."[44] For Black soldiers, one way to fight against anti-Black racism in the US military was to show their courage and advanced skills to kill inferior, sneaky, and evil Korean communists.

Racism in the US military, interwoven with Koreans' xenophobia and anti-Black racism, has complicated local racial politics in at least three ways. First, the hierarchical dichotomy between white soldiers and soldiers of color created a racial hierarchy among the Korean prostitutes, who catered to American soldiers. Korean women who entertained white soldiers had racial privilege compared to those associated with Black soldiers as women's racial location in the R&R business has been determined by the skin color of their GI customers. The invisible but firm racial line still exists in entertaining camptowns around US bases in Korea.

Second, Korea's xenophobia discriminated (and still discriminates) against bi-racial children, especially Black children, born of US/UN soldiers and Korean

---

[40] Dong Choon Kim, "Forgotten War, Forgotten Massacres—the Korean War (1950–1953) as Licensed Mass Killings," *Journal of Genocide Research* 6, no. 4 (2004): 531.

[41] Green, *Black Yanks in the Pacific*, 118.

[42] Christine Hong, *A Violent Peace: Race, US Militarism, and Cultures of Democratization in Cold War Asia and the Pacific* (Stanford, CA: Stanford University Press, 2020), 4–5.

[43] Green, *Black Yanks in the Pacific*, 126.

[44] Green, *Black Yanks in the Pacific*, 126.

women. The Korean War initiated transnational adoption due to the overwhelming number of orphaned and abandoned children, including bi-racial children. Children were relinquished on the streets and at orphanages for many reasons: They might have been born outside wedlock, their families might have been too poor, and so on. The adoption of Korean children by American families continues until now. At the early stage of transnational Korean adoption, the system seemed to be the byproduct of the war, and the US military created the conditions for it. However, as scholar SooJin Pate argues, Korean adoption did not start merely with the war but with neocolonial conditions between the United States and South Korea after World War II. The system continues owing to "the interminable nature of US imperialist and geopolitical investments regarding South Korea."[45]

Black children in postwar Korea caught the attention of African American women activists. They were invested in adopting Black Korean children just as their white middle-class counterparts adopted children from Korea. These women desired to adopt or find proper Black families for Black Korean children because (1) the children were "culturally" African Americans while their mothers were Asian, and (2) unlike white men who abandoned their children mothered by non-white women, African Americans should take "communal" responsibility to raise their children.[46] However, Jim Crow America discouraged African Americans from adopting Black Korean children while middle-class whites (mostly Christians) came to "rescue" Korean children of any color. Structural racism and poverty did not give African American families enough legal outlets to adopt Korean children transnationally.[47] In addition, the Korean government did not allow African American families to adopt white Korean children or so-called full-blood Korean children, arguing that the children would be further marginalized if adopted by racial minorities. As a result, only a small number of Black Korean children could find homes among African American families.[48]

Third, post-Korean War society used the Black body to reclaim its national pride after Japanese colonialism and the unending Korean War. The war allowed the US military to stay in South Korea for an indefinite time which would further undermine Koreans' national pride. In the 1960s and 70s, the camptown literature, which dealt with people's lives around US camps in South Korea, portrayed the white, Asian (Korean), and Black bodies differently. Since the Korean woman's body represented the Korean nation, her raped and prostituted body symbolized the nation controlled by the United States after Japanese colonialism. In the camptown literature, the United States exhibited its power over Korea through the idealized

---

[45] SooJin Pate, *From Orphan to Adoptee: US Empire and Genealogies of Korean Adoption* (Minneapolis: University of Minnesota Press, 2014), 3.

[46] Kori Graves, *A War Born Family: African American Adoption in the Wake of the Korean War* (New York: New York University Press, 2020), 11–17.

[47] Graves, *A War Born Family*, 17–18.

[48] Susie Woo, *Framed by War: Korean Children and Women at the Crossroads of US Empire* (New York, 2019; online edition, NYU Press Scholarship Online, 2020), https://doi.org/10.18574/nyu/9781479889914.001.0001.

muscular white body (i.e., white soldier) and his (forced) intercourse with a Korean woman (prostitute). In contrast, the Black body would masturbate out of barbaric excitement while observing a white man penetrating a Korean woman.[49] Hence, the masturbating Black body was Koreans' interpretation of Blacks' mimicry of unattainable white power. The literature often used the Black body to deny the legitimacy of the American power in Korea, mock American barbarianism and savageness, or underscore Korea's moral superiority over the Black race.[50]

Racialized militarism and militarized racism are intimately intertwined in American wars in Asia. Heterosexual romance, interracial marriage, childbearing and rearing, and conjugal relations affect and are affected by racialized militarism and militarized racism. Simultaneously, as historian Simeon Man convincingly argues, the value of Asian Americans and African Americans depends on their participation in the war economy which recruits some of them to kill others. In other words, "national inclusion was premised on the very notion that their lives were expendable in order to safeguard the freedoms promised by the nation-state."[51]

Antiwar/Antiracist Feminism When Christianity Matters

What feminist theological discourse would emanate from the Asia Pacific? How would Christian theology help inspire antiracist and antiwar feminism? Or is Christianity relevant to international movements for peace and justice? To answer these questions, let us first consider the definition of antiwar feminism. According to feminist sociologist Cynthia Cockburn,

> [A]ntimilitarist and antiwar feminism is by definition multi-dimensional, taking as its core not just 'body politics' but a far wider range of concerns. For a start, it cannot fail to have *a critique of capitalism*, and new forms of imperialism and colonization, class exploitation and the thrust for global markets, since these are visibly implicated among the causes and motors of militarism and war. Next, since many wars involve intra-state and inter-state nationalisms, this feminism also has that cluster of *race/culture/religion/ethnicity* in view. In these two significant relational fields of class and race, this feminism perceives the working of gender relations and is alert to how they intersect.[52]

Cockburn's definition of antiwar feminism is similar to that of Radical Black Peace Activism in the early Cold War period. "Radical Black Peace Activists" such as W. E. B. Du Bois and Paul Robeson were internationalists who penned antiracist,

---

[49] Jee Hyun An, "A Strange Encounter: 'Blackness' and Postcoloniality in Korean Military Camptown Literature," *English Language and Literature* 64, no. 1 (2018): 39–60. https://doi.org/10.15794/jell.2018.64.1.003.

[50] See An, "A Strange Encounter," 39-60.

[51] Simeon Man, "Anti-Asian Violence and US Imperialism," *Race & Class* 16, no. 2 (2020): 28, https://journals.sagepub.com/doi/10.1177/0306396820949779.

[52] Cynthia Cockburn, *From Where We Stand: War, Women's Activism, and Feminist Analysis* (New York: Zed Books, 2008), 228.

anti-imperialist, and antiwar traditions.[53] In addition, radical Black women activists, including Beulah (Beah) Richardson and Yvonne Gregory, crafted a political analysis to broaden the scope of civil rights activism, working through the Civil Rights Congress, the Women's Committee for Equal Justice, and the all-Black women's organization Sojourners for Truth and Justice.[54] Articulating interconnected forms of oppression, these women asserted Black women's right to self-defense and control over their bodies. The women situated their activism in the postwar context and, simultaneously, the long history of sexualized violence against Black women.[55] However, McCarthyist America surveilled Black internationalists (and any revolutionary or radical activists outside white hetero-patriarchal norms), depicting Radical Black Peace Activism as a quintessentially anti-American and communist threat to internal stability. Nonetheless, Radical Black Peace Activists delivered a persistent message that peace is "inextricable from international solidarity and the end of all forms of racialized exploitation."[56] Like Radical Black women activists, antiwar feminists in our time emphasize intersectional analysis, as war cannot be separated from racial capitalism.

Christian theology does not always register in antiracist and antiwar feminism. Instead, many scholars understand Christianity as an ideological force behind European imperialism, patriarchal militarism, exploitative capitalism, and racial hierarchy. For instance, Cockburn argues that "the church and the military" are the two institutions that have assisted patriarchy in sustaining "the ascendency of men with striking success" by ideology and by hardware, respectively.[57] Feminist theologians have also extensively debunked the ideological marriage between Christianity and patriarchy consolidating anti-Black racism and white supremacy. Christianity has not simply perpetuated racism in its institution and society but also created social realities that exploit and demoralize people of color.

According to womanist ethicist Rima Vesely-Flad, state-sanctioned police violence against Blacks and their mass incarceration are the materialization of "the symbolic constructs of racialized and polluted bodies."[58] Christianity has aided in constructing Black bodies as symbolically polluted bodies.[59] The impoverishment and mass incarceration of Blacks always go hand in hand with the social, cultural, and religious constructs of Blacks as polluted and sinful bodies. Asian American theologian Jessica Wai-Fong Wong would agree with Vesely-Flad's analysis of the intimate connection between the material and the symbolic in Christianity's

---

[53] Charisse Burden-Stelly, "In Battle for Peace during 'Scoundrel Time': W. E. B. Du Bois and United States Repression of Radical Black Peace Activism," *Du Bois Review* 16, no. 2 (2019): 556.

[54] Dayo Gore, *Radicalism at the Crossroads: African American Women Activists in the Cold War* (New York: New York University Press, 2011), 13.

[55] Gore, *Radicalism at the Crossroads*, 13.

[56] Burden-Stelly, "In Battle for Peace during 'Scoundrel Time,'" 558.

[57] Cockburn, *From Where We Stand*, 243.

[58] Rima Vesely-Flad, *Racial Purity and Dangerous Bodies: Moral Pollution, Black Lives and the Struggle for Justice* (Minneapolis, MN: Fortress Press, 2017), xvi–xvii.

[59] Vesely-Flad, *Racial Purity and Dangerous Bodies*, xvii.

racialization of humans supposedly created in the image of God. Through the lens of icon theology, Wong persuasively argues that whiteness has been constructed as an image of purity, similar to God, while blackness has been considered "disordered."[60] Thus, the material depravity and subjugation of people of color are the ideal realities of Christian supremacy. Wong's analysis of Christianity's role in creating racial hierarchy through images of the sacred is instrumental. One's skin color on medieval paintings, icons, and texts signifies their spiritual state. For instance, dark pigments associated with Jews symbolize that Jews joined the devil's disorder of denying and crucifying Jesus.[61] In the United States, the exclusion of Asians from naturalization and immigration is based not only on race but also on religion.[62] It might be exhausting to list the cases of political exclusion of diverse groups of people based on both religion and race. The non-white body does not simply mean skin color but indicates moral corruption and spiritual disorders, just as Black soldiers were labeled cowardly barbarians while all Koreans were untrustworthy communists.

Religion in general, and Christianity in particular, matter in thinking about antiwar feminism. A rigorous analysis of religion's role in making wars and sustaining racial hierarchy must be incorporated into crafting antiracist and antiwar feminism. Simultaneously, we feminist theologians and ethicists must rediscover the forgotten legacy of people's movements for peace and justice in Christianity and recuperate the liberative images of God.

Renewing Christian Internationalism: A Theological Reflection on the Women's International Democratic Federation

Antiwar and antiracist feminism in conversation with Black and Asian American feminist theologies may revitalize Christian internationalism. The term internationalism is often misunderstood in the United States, where the anti-communist legacy falsifies it as un-American, if not anti-American. Although any definition of internationalism would be insufficient, the core of internationalism lies in *anti-imperialism, antiwar, and radical equality at every level of human society*. Indeed, these values are congruent with the Christian moral values of love, justice, and liberation with special concerns for the marginalized.

---

[60] Jessica Wai-Fong Wong, *Disordered: The Holy Icon and Racial Myths* (Waco, TX: Baylor University Press, 2021), 6–8.

[61] Wong, *Disordered*, 44–45.

[62] The US government's series of denaturalizing naturalized South Asian immigrants and South Asian exclusion in the early 1900s are the good examples of anti-Asian hate based on both religion (Hinduism) and race. See Erika Lee, *The Making of Asian America: A History* (New York: Simon and Schuster, 2015), 151–173.

When US McCarthyism valorized anti-communist racist war in Korea, the Women's International Democratic Federation (WIDF) strenuously networked among women across all continents. From the WIDF's beginning in 1945, African American women, Asian and African women from colonized countries, Latin American women, and European and North American white women shared governance based on the principle of equality.[63] According to historian Suzy Kim, the WIDF had four interrelated principles that appealed to diverse global members: (1) anti-fascism, peace, women's rights, and children's rights advanced the right to self-determination and democratic freedoms, with calls for an end to war and militarism, (2) equality between the sexes through equal pay for equal work and equal opportunities in education and professional training, (3) social services for women, and (4) the protection of mothers irrespective of marital status.[64]

As the Korean War became a globalized anti-communist war, the Federation recognized the increase in military expenditures across the globe. Increased military budget in many countries reinforced global war capitalism, and, as a result, class, race, and gender equality deteriorated. For example, the United Kingdom sacrificed its nascent welfare system to send troops and weapons to Korea.[65] Western European and North American countries that had barely escaped World War II engaged in another war in Korea by forcing poor people and racial minorities to sacrifice for the war economy. The United States saw a whopping 52.5 billion dollars in military spending due to the Korean War, which led 350 women to demand that the United Nations immediately withdraw US forces from Korea.[66] US representative to the WIDF Betty Millard reported to the WIDF Council meeting in February 1951 that the Women for Peace group emerged from the women's march to the United Nations. The group, consisting of "eighty organizations from forty states and forty-six cities," brought 1000 women pilgrims to Washington D. C. and demanded a ban on atomic weapons and an end to the Korean War.[67] Leftist feminists in the United States took the early Cold War era as a significant moment to sophisticate their radical theories and praxis based on intersectionality analysis. One of them was radical Black feminist Beulah Richardson, whose 1951 poem, "A Black Woman Speaks of White Womanhood, of White Supremacy, of Peace," connected racial and gender justice with global peace and popularized antiwar and antiracist feminist messages at the height of the Korean War.[68]

The WDIF's work had been generally forgotten until recently, when a group of feminist scholars and historians started rediscovering this critical piece of global

---

[63] Taewoo Kim, *Witches of the Cold War: The Korean War and Women's Peace Activism* (Paju, Republic of Korea: Changbi, 2021), 14. [Naengjeon-eoi Manyeodeul, Korean].

[64] The WIDF's First Congress in 1945 represented forty countries and by 1985, 135 member organizations from 117 countries. See Suzy Kim, "The Origins of Cold War Feminism during the Korean War," *Gender and History* 31 no. 2 (July 2019): 464.

[65] Kim, *Witches of the Cold War*, 34.

[66] Kim, "The Origins of Cold War Feminism during the Korean War," 466.

[67] Kim, "The Origins of Cold War Feminism during the Korean War," 466.

[68] Kim, "The Origins of Cold War Feminism during the Korean War," 466.

feminist history. One of the WDIF's notable works is their report on the Korean War. The North Korean women, affiliated with the WIDF, invited its delegates to investigate the US and Korean military's total destruction of cities on the Korean Peninsula through saturation bombing, mass killings of civilians, systematic rape of women, and other war crimes. Twenty-one delegates from eighteen countries, including the United Kingdom, Denmark, Cuba, Vietnam, China, and the USSR, visited North Korea through China in 1951. They produced a report on the bloody realities of the Korean War as objectively as possible.[69] The report showed the number of farm animals, schools, houses, and hospitals destroyed by the US military and the number of women raped and children killed.[70] When the delegates returned to their respective countries, the United States and Western countries whose troops fought against North Korea and China vehemently denied the validity of the WDIF report. While some delegates were accused of complying with the Soviet Union and betraying their countries, none of them denied the recorded facts on the report. In fact, the delegates sent to North Korean exhibited various ideological positions. Some of them were leftists, and some others liberal feminists who were skeptical of the communist propaganda.[71] Despite their racial and ideological differences, the WDIF delegates were truthful to their report, accountable to Korean women, and committed to global peace and justice.

To be sure, the WDIF's history does not hint at Christianity, although Monica Pelton, an English commissioner, grew up in a devout Anglican family.[72] However, the WDFI's Cold War activism gives me ideas about how to read Christian peace activism and rediscover Christian internationalism. For instance, Asian American Christian women have a long history of international solidarity work. Asian/American feminist theologians Rita Nakashima Brock and Nami Kim retell the story of Asian American Protestant women internationalists in the early twentieth century. When the Asian Exclusion Act threatened the livelihood of Asian Americans, Asian American women faithfully worked for racial justice in the United States and anti-imperialist work in their countries of origin colonized by Western and Japanese empires.[73] We should rediscover and retell the stories of Asian American and Black Christian women's transnational solidarity work— Christianity not as these women's identities but as active tools in connecting diverse people for peace and justice.

Furthermore, Brock articulates a feminist theological concept of "interstitial integrity." The notion suggests the construction of the self in radical relationality to others—including non-human beings, peoples, multiple cultures, social systems, religions, and spiritualities. Brock's interstitial integrity highlights Asian/American

---

[69] Kim, "The Origins of Cold War Feminism during the Korean War," 467.

[70] Kim, "The Origins of Cold War Feminism during the Korean War," 469.

[71] Kim, *Witches of the Cold War*, 8–9.

[72] Kim, *Witches of the Cold War*, 8–9.

[73] Rita Nakashima Brock and Nami Kim, "Asian Pacific American Protestant Women" in *Encyclopedia of Women and Religion in North America,* vol. 1, ed. Rosemary Skinner Keller and Rosemary Radford Ruether (Bloomington: Indiana University Press, 2006), 499–500.

women's embodied identity grounded betwixt and between engaged relationships and the feminist theological praxis of decolonization.[74] Emphasizing the indispensability of a transnational analysis in feminist theology, Kwok Pui-lan also presents an image of God, "a God of the interstices" that rises from the mobilization of transnational networks that stand in solidarity with victims of violence, war, and oppression.[75] The WDIF's antiwar and anti-imperialist activism resonates with a God of the interstices and interstitial integrity. A God of interstices is not a new image reflected from the contemporary context of the US transpacific empire. Instead, this God has existed since the creation of the world and reverberated again and again when people of faith embody transnational work for peace and justice.

Finally, as Religious Studies scholar Laurie Patton argues, to create a new material reality, we need a new story, a new "myth." Myth is not a fabricated story but the story that gives new symbols, meanings, and wisdom for life and human society.[76] To be sure, myth is based upon our deep appreciation of life, critical reflection on interconnectedness among all forms of lives, and deep yarning for the Divine, wholeness, and the fullness of life. We need a myth to reconstruct Christian internationalism from an antiracist and antiwar feminist perspective.

The beginning of Christian internationalism is usually considered to be the early twentieth-century Euro-American Protestant missionary movement. During this interwar period, Christian internationalists refused to endorse any nationalist claims through religious languages. Moreover, realists and pacifists worked together, distancing themselves from institutional and legalistic relations between nation-states while emphasizing the importance of interpersonal and intercultural relations. In this way, modern Christian internationalists were antiracists, anti-imperialists, and antimilitarists who saw the domestic in the international and the vice versa.[77] We should rediscover stories like modern Christian internationalists especially written from a feminist theological perspective so that we can create new Christian symbols, ideologies, stories, and realities, namely, myth. The true meaning of Christian internationalism is not to proselytize so-called heathens but to convert our hearts and minds to Jesus' praxis for radical peace, justice, and equality just as Asian liberation theologian Aloysius Pieris defines the meaning of true conversion to be converted to liberation of all human beings.[78]

---

[74] Rita Nakashima Brock, "Cooking without Recipes: Interstitial Integrity" in *Off the Menu: Asian and Asian American North American Women's Religion and Theology*, eds. Rita Nakashima Brock, et al., (Louisville, KY: Westminster John Knox Press, 2007), 136.

[75] Kwok Pui-lan, "Fishing the Asia Pacific: Transnationalism and Feminist Theology" in *Off the Menu: Asian and Asian American North American Women's Religion and Theology*, eds. Rita Nakashima Brock, et al., (Louisville, KY: Westminster John Knox Press, 2007), 18–19.

[76] Laurie Patton and Eboo Patel, "Plural America Needs Myths: An Essay in Foundational Narratives in Response to Eboo Patel" in *Out of Many Faiths: Religious Diversity and the American Promise* (Princeton, NJ: Princeton University Press, 2018), 151–80, https://doi.org/10.2307/j.ctvd58sn2.14.

[77] Michael Thompson, *Christian Internationalism in the United States between the Great War and the Cold War* (Ithaca, NY: Cornell University Press, 2015), 4–5.

[78] Aloysius Pieris, *An Asian Theology of Liberation* (Edinburgh, UK: T&T Clark, 1988), 41.

Conclusion

Taking American wars and occupations in the Cold War Asia Pacific as cases to analyze the complex entanglement of anti-Black and anti-Asian racism home and abroad, this chapter accentuates the inseparability between antiracist feminism and antiwar feminism. To dismantle militarized racism and racialized militarism, we need alternative stories and myths—not racial and class struggles in the war economy but cross-racial and cross-border solidarity work for race, class, and gender justice. As alternative stories, I first critically reflected on Christianity's ideological and material construction of racism, second engaged with feminist internationalism (i.e., The Women's Democratic International Federation) in the early Cold War period, and third delineated a God of interstices.

Now I imagine early Christians who diligently walked through deserts, towns, and villages and crossed seas to deliver "good news" about the coming Kin-dom of God, full of peace and justice. The WDIF's delegates of the Korean War could be compared to early Christians. Both groups were faithful to what they witnessed and envisioned for a world of peace and justice, while many people did not see political economic oppression against the racialized and gendered poor. What good news would we embody in times of war, racist violence, and COVID-19?

Discussion Questions

1. This chapter argues that the United States still lives with the legacy of anti-Asian and anti-Black racism caused by American wars in Cold War Asia. How have diverse armed conflicts in Korea, Vietnam, Syria, Iraq, Ukraine, Israel/Palestine, and many other places shaped racial relations in the American church and society?
2. What kind of movements do you consider as Christian internationalism for peace and justice? How can Christians reimagine Christian internationalism through a God of the interstices rather than the evangelical missionary movement?
3. What role can religion play in supporting Afro-Asian solidarity for peace and justice? Share some examples of the Afro-Asian solidarity.

Bibliography

An, Jee Hyun. 2018. A Strange Encounter: 'Blackness' and Postcoloniality in Korean Military Camptown Literature. *English Language and Literature* 64 (1): 39–60. https://doi.org/10.15794/jell.2018.64.1.003.

Arudou, Debito. 2015. *Embedded Racism: Japan's Visible Minorities and Racial Discrimination*. Lanham, MD: Lexington Books.

Brock, Rita Nakashima, and Nami Kim. 2006. Asian Pacific American Protestant Women. In *Encyclopedia of Women and Religion in North America*, ed. Rosemary Skinner Keller and Rosemary Radford Ruether, vol. 1, 498–505. Bloomington: Indiana University Press.

Brock, Rita Nakashima. 2007. Cooking without Recipes: Interstitial Integrity. In *Off the Menu: Asian and Asian American North American Women's Religion and Theology*, ed. Rita Nakashima Brock, Jung Ha Kim, Kwok Pui-lan, and Seung Ai Yang, 125–143. Louisville, KY: Westminster John Knox Press.

Burden-Stelly, Charisse. 2019. In Battle for Peace during 'Scoundrel Time': W. E. B. Du Bois and United States Repression of Radical Black Peace Activism. *Du Bois Review* 16 (2): 555–574. https://doi.org/10.1017/S1742058X19000213.

Cockburn, Cynthia. 2008. *From Where We Stand: War, Women's Activism, and Feminist Analysis*. New York: Zed Books.

Crissey, Etsuko Takushi. 2017. *Okinawa's GI Brides: Their Lives in America*. Translated by Steve Rabson. Honolulu: University of Hawaii Press.

Gore, Dayo. 2011. *Radicalism at the Crossroads: African American Women Activists in the Cold War*. New York: New York University Press.

Graves, Kori. 2020. *A War Born Family: African American Adoption in the Wake of the Korean War*. New York: New York University Press.

Green, Michael Cullen. 2010. *Black Yanks in the Pacific: Race in the Making of American Military Empire After World War II*. Ithaca, NY: Cornell University Press.

Höhn, Maria, and Seungsook Moon. 2010. Conclusion: Empire at the Crossroads? In *Over There: Living with the US Military Empire from World War Two to the Present*, ed. Maria Höhn and Seungsook Moon, 397–408. Durham, NC: Duke University Press.

Hong, Christine. 2020. *A Violent Peace: Race, US Militarism, and Cultures of Democratization in Cold War Asia and the Pacific*. Stanford, CA: Stanford University Press.

Kim, Jodi. 2010. *The Ends of Empire: Asian American Critique and the Cold War*. Minneapolis: University of Minnesota Press.

Kim, Dong Choon. 2004. Forgotten War, Forgotten Massacres—the Korean War (1950–1953) as Licensed Mass Killings. *Journal of Genocide Research* 6 (4): 523–544.

Kim, Suzy. 2019. The Origins of Cold War Feminism during the Korean War. *Gender and History* 31 (2): 460–479.

Kim, Taewoo. 2021. *Witches of the Cold War: The Korean War and Women's Peace Activism*. Chang Bi: Paju, Republic of Korea. (*Naengjeon-eoi Manyeodeul*, Korean).

Klein, Christina. 2003. *Cold War Orientalism: Asia in the Middlebrow Imagination, 1945–1961*. Berkeley: University of California Press.

Kwok, Pui-lan. 2007. Fishing the Asia Pacific: Transnationalism and Feminist Theology. In *Off the Menu: Asian and Asian American North American Women's Religion and Theology*, ed. Rita Nakashima Brock, Jung Ha Kim, Kwok Pui-lan, and Seung Ai Yang, 3–22. Louisville: Westminster John Knox Press.

Kwon, Heonik. 2010. *The Other Cold War*. New York: Columbia University Press.

Lee, Erika. 2019. *America for Americans: A History of Xenophobia in the United States*. New York: Basic Books.

———. 2015. *The Making of Asian America: A History*. New York: Simon and Schuster.

Man, Simeon. 2020. Anti-Asian Violence and US Imperialism. *Race & Class* 16 (2): 24–33. https://journals.sagepub.com/doi/10.1177/0306396820949779.

Moon, Katherine. 1997. *Sex Among Allies: Military Prostitution in US-Korea Relations*. New York: Columbia University Press.

Newbeck, Phyl. 2008. *Virginia Hasn't Always Been for Lovers: Interracial Marriage Bans and the Case of Richard and Mildred Loving*. Carbondale: Southern Illinois University Press.

O'Kane, Caitlin. 2021. Suni Lee's Dad Was Paralyzed Two Years Ago. Now, He's a Model for the Tenacity His Daughter Shares. *CBS News*, July 30, https://www.cbsnews.com/news/suni-lee-olympic-gymnastics-gold-medal-father-paralyzed/.

Pae, Keun-joo Christine. 2019. The Prostituted Body of War: U.S. Military Prostitution in South Korea as a Site of Spiritual Activism. In *Transformational Embodiment in Asian Religions: Subtle Bodies, Spatial Bodies*, ed. George Pati and Katherine C. Zubko, 187–205. New York: Routledge.

Pate, SooJin. 2014. *From Orphan to Adoptee: US Empire and Genealogies of Korean Adoption*. Minneapolis, MN: University of Minnesota Press.

Patton, Laurie L., and Eboo Patel. 2018. Plural America Needs Myths: An Essay in Foundational Narratives in Response to Eboo Patel. In *Out of Many Faiths: Religious Diversity and the American Promise*. NED-New edition, vol 6, 151–80. Princeton University Press. https://doi.org/10.2307/j.ctvd58sn2.14.

Pieris, Aloysius. 1988. *An Asian Theology of Liberation*. Edinburgh, UK: T&T Clark.

Robertson, Jennifer. 2010. Eugenics in Japan: Sanguinous Repair. In *The Oxford Handbook of the History of Eugenics*, ed. Allison Bashford and Philippa Levine, 430–448. London: Oxford University Press.

Le Tran, Mai-Anh. 2020. From My Lai to Ferguson: Collaterality, Grievous Deaths, Militarized Orientalism, Benevolence, and Racism. In *Feminist Praxis against US Militarism*, ed. Nami Kim and Wonhee Anne Joh, 63–83. Lanham, MD: Lexington Books.

Vang, Ma. 2021. *History on the Run: Secrecy, Fugitivity, and Hmong Refugee Epistemologies*. Durham, NC: Duke University Press.

Vesely-Flad, Rima. 2017. *Racial Purity and Dangerous Bodies: Moral Pollution, Black Lives and the Struggle for Justice*. Minneapolis, MN: Fortress Press.

Vine, David. 2015. *Base Nation: How US Military Bases Abroad Harm America and the World*. New York: Metropolitan Books.

Wong, Jessica Wai-Fong. 2021. *Disordered: The Holy Icon and Racial Myths*. Waco, TX: Baylor University Press.

Woo, Susie. 2019. *Framed by War: Korean Children and Women at the Crossroads of US Empire*. Online Edition. New York: New York University Press. NYU Press Scholarship Online, 2020. https://doi.org/10.18574/nyu/9781479889914.001.0001.

Wright, James. 2013. What We Learned from the Korean War. *The Atlantic*, July 23. https://www.theatlantic.com/international/archive/2013/07/what-we-learned-from-the-korean-war/278016/.

Part II
Cross-Racial and Cross-Border Solidarity

6
Intimate Encounters at the Unhomely Home: Reading Morrison's *Home* and the Gospel of John's Homecoming Story

Jin Young Choi

The Korean War, the Black Soldier, and Home

My positionality in the diaspora, as well as my upbringing and socialization in the divided country of Korea, has shaped my subjectivity and reading of the Bible. Living in the diaspora means continuously searching for a home. Home for a diasporic subject is not an either/or place, but somewhere she longs to belong when being othered. The experience of being othered helps me see other others who are estranged from and in their homes. This encounter is personal and collective, as our subjectivities emerge from shared historical experiences of oppression and resistance where different cultures are in contact. Seeking a home in the diaspora is, thus, to cross the paths of other histories. My journey in the diaspora is a process of seeing my own cultural history from the outside and its intimacies with other histories.[1] More specifically, my "homing desire" in the diaspora leads my memory back to the forgotten but intimate history of the Korean War.[2]

The Korean translation of this essay appears in *Beyond War: Post-Cold War Discourse for Peace in Theology and Humanities*, ed. Kyeongil Jung (Seoul: Interhouse, 2023).

[1] See Heonik Kwon, *After the Korean War: An Intimate History* (New York: Cambridge University Press, 2020); Lisa Lowe, *The Intimacies of Four Continents* (Durham, NC: Duke University Press, 2015).

[2] For the difference between home and homing desire, see Avtar Brah, *Cartographies of Diaspora: Contesting Identities* (London: Routledge, 1996), 187–194.

J. Y. Choi (✉)
Professor of New Testament and Christian Origins and the Baptist
Missionary Training School Professorial Chair in Biblical Studies at Colgate Rochester Crozer Divinity School, Rochester, NY, USA
e-mail: jchoi@crcds.edu

Growing up in a rural town near the DMZ in South Korea two decades after the Korean War, I still saw armed vehicles and soldiers—both Black and White—riding on trucks on the narrow street just in front of my house. American soldiers were viewed as the protector and savior of my nation. In my aunt's graphic storytelling, I often confused these scenes of the 1970s with the situations of Japanese colonization and the Korean War. I was warned not to enter the mountain near our home because, allegedly, some spies from North Korea were there. Leaflets with Kim Il Sung's portrait were easily found on the hill and elsewhere in town. Our homework asked us to produce drawings showing our animalized enemies knocked down with a thorned club.

My parents wanted their children to receive a better education, so I moved with my grandmother and siblings to a neighborhood in the northern part of Seoul at age eleven. At that time, I felt the distance of about twenty miles between the two homes was enormous, though we often visited our parents on weekends. The scariest part was passing the checkpoint, where military police officers stopped the bus and checked everyone on it. The bus also passed a military construction through the hidden halves of an automatic iron gate. I was in fear whenever I passed through that space, imagining that the iron blockade would close the road if a war broke out. My parents would be caught between North Korea and Seoul and then be sacrificed. The very idea I would not see them again made me frightened and deeply saddened. The checkpoint and obstructions generated anxiety and fear—fear of a potential separation and loss of family and the fear of another war. The imagined war never ended in my psyche until I became an adult.

Kuan-Hsing Chen argues in his book *Asia as Method* that, "colonialism and the cold war have produced different affective experiences of East Asian people." He continues, "the complex effects of the war, mediated through our bodies, have been inscribed into our national, family, and personal histories."[3] The Korean War was a product of the Cold War and produced the wall that has torn the country and families apart. Even as a child of the so-called post-war period, the war memories were passed down to my body and affected the formation of my subjectivity. There was the figure of a stranger—the Black soldier sitting insidiously in my memory. I often overheard neighbors calling him with a racial slur, which generated a mixed sense of gratitude and dread, of shunning and pity. I forgot this complex figure, whose embodiment of a savior was suspect until I read Toni Morrison's 2012 novel *Home*. *Home* tells the story of African American man named Frank Money, who suffered racial violence and trauma in the American South before the end of Jim Crow and fled to serve in the desegregated troops of the Korean War.[4]

Home, Morrison's poignantly imaginative historical fiction, is a mediator for me to engage those historical connections, as it reveals such a visceral contact of histories and subjectivities. She describes the reality in which African Americans were dehumanized in the segregated South, the traumas caused by racism and war, and

---

[3] Kuan-Hsing Chen, *Asia as Method: Toward Deimperialization* (Durham, NC: Duke University Press: 2010), 118, 214.

[4] Toni Morrison, *Home* (New York: Vintage, 2012).

healing within the community. But the war Morrison depicts is historically particular, and thus the injustices Black people have experienced are closely related to the history of the Other, in this case, Korean people.[5] Some scholars in transnational Asian American studies have discussed how White supremacy and anti-Black racism are intertwined with the expansion of the US empire across the Asia-Pacific region.[6] Morrison's *Home* tells a story of the global trauma of colonial and racialized violence that African Americans have endured. I explore how the Other in this story conjures up the violent scenes clandestinely witnessed by members of African American and Asian diaspora communities so that they can revisit those scenes and, if even possible, heal one another's wounds.

Additionally, I will read the biblical text, juxtaposing its themes of home, haunting, and healing with the haunting scenes of global violence in the present time. My reading of John's Gospel sees Jesus as a victim of state-sponsored violence backed by the Roman Empire. After his death on the cross, he visits his disciples as a ghost in his wounded body. I read the story of Jesus' return home to Galilee as a homecoming story.[7] It is an unhomely home in which remembering and healing can take place.

As described, I employ an intertextual reading of the haunting stories to explore linkages between and among texts to colonial, racialized subjects' encounters across time and geography through the medium of haunting. Just as interrelationships among and across texts produce meanings, engaging the Other's history generates intersubjectivity. This intertextual reading begins with listening to stories of trauma and healing in ancient and contemporary texts and aims to provide a space for global engagement through collective mourning and restoration among minoritized communities.

Morrison on Home

Toni Morrison identifies two prevailing and closely related motifs of her fiction writing: race and home. As "an already-and always-raced writer" living in a "racial house," she nonetheless tries to rebuild it from a "windowless prison" into a

---

[5] I use the "Other" in terms of the self-other relation in historical or cultural encounters, which also have phenomenological and psychological dimensions. While the Other can be collective (e.g., a community, people, or nation), I highlight the singularity of an encounter between the Self and the Other, which requires an ethical response.

[6] See Nadia Y. Kim, *Imperial Citizens: Koreans and Race from Seoul to LA* (Stanford, CA: Stanford University Press, 2008); and Nami Kim and Wonhee Anne Joh, ed., *Critical Theology against US Militarism in Asia* (New York: Palgrave Macmillan, 2016).

[7] For the full version of my interpretation, see my essay, "Epistemology of Intimacy and Haunting Diaspora: Rereading the Johannine Jesus' Journey Home," in *A Pact of Love with Criticism, A Pact of Blood with the World: Towards Geopolitical Biblical Criticism, Essays in Honor of Fernando F. Segovia*, ed. Amy L. Allen, Francisco Lozada, Jr., and Yak-hwee Tan (Atlanta, GA: Society of Biblical Literature Press, forthcoming).

"race-specific yet nonracist home."[8] Yet Morrison's *Home* presents more than a physical place where those wounded subjects finally find a home. The racial house has been built in the Black man's psyche, and thus he must be released from the imprisoned mind. Thus, Morrison often interweaves the theme of masculinity into stories of racial trauma.

Morrison employs a literary technique to illustrate the psychic impact of racism by putting Frank Money's narration in odd-numbered chapters, while the third-person narrator continues in even-numbered chapters.[9] In Chap. 1, Frank begins his story with the brutal scene of fighting horses that he and his younger sister Cee (Ycidra) secretly saw in Lotus, Georgia. The description that the horses "stood like men" or "rose up like men" is repeated four times in the first chapter. Yet, what they saw is not only this brutal scene but a human body buried by some men: "*a black foot with its creamy pink and mud-streaked sole being whacked into the grave.*"[10] Critics observe that such violent memories are inscribed in Frank's masculine identity, but simultaneously contradicted by his instinct to protect his sister as a brother as he tries to "*pull her trembling into my* [his] *own bones.*"[11] This short chapter ends with his narration:

> *Since you're set on telling my story, whatever you think and whatever you write down, know this: I really forgot about the burial. I only remembered the horses. They were so beautiful. So brutal. And they stood like men.*

Frank's narration here implies that someone listens to him and continues to tell his story, particularly what he cannot remember and how traumas are implicated in his racial and masculine identity. Morrison not only is the implied author-narrator but also walks inside the text, as if she sits with him and listens to his stories.[12]

In the second chapter, the narrator's story starts with twenty-four-year-old veteran Frank escaping barefoot from a Seattle mental institution, where he has been confined by the police, to the house of a pastor, named Rev. John Locke, six blocks away. Frank is determined to head to Georgia as he has received a message that his sister is in critical condition. The narrator then tells the story of an earlier escape from his Texas home at the age of four. His parents, along with fourteen other families, were forced by a racist mob's death threat to vacate their homes within twenty-four hours. An older man, who refused to leave, got blinded and lynched. Frank's family took on a long journey to Lotus, Georgia, where her mother delivered her

---

[8] Toni Morrison, "Home," in *The House That Race Built: Black Americans, U.S. Terrain*, ed. Wahneema Lubiano (New York: Pantheon, 1997), 4–5.

[9] She structures the plot by alternating Frank's first-person retrospective view (italicized) and the third-person narrator perspective (nonitalicized) chapter by chapter.

[10] Morrison, *Home*, 4. The contents cited in italics here and afterward are Frank's testimony.

[11] Morrison, *Home*, 4.

[12] For a discussion of this literary technique using Frank's "dual-voiced narrative" and its "psychological effects of war and racial violence on masculine self-identity in 1950s America," see Jan Furman, "Telling Stories: Evolving Narrative Identity in Toni Morrison's *Home*," in *Toni Morrison: Memory and Meaning*, ed. Adrienne Lanier Seward and Justine Tally (Jackson: University Press of Mississippi, 2014), 231.

baby Cee in a church basement. The family moved into the house of the siblings' grandparents, but their step-grandmother abused them while their parents worked all day in the field. Frank played the role of the protector of his baby sister.

When Lotus becomes an unbearable place for the teenaged Frank, he joins the desegregated army in Korea with his hometown friends, Mike and Stuff. While the desegregated military could have been an exit from racism, as Rev. Locke describes, an "integrated army is an integrated misery. You all go fight, come back, they treat you like dogs. Change that. They treat dogs better."[13] For my purposes, I will fast-forward to Chap. 9, where Frank's first-person narration tells of his encounter with a Korean girl sneaking to scavenge for food during his guard duty. He recounts, "*[M]y relief guard comes over, see her hand and shakes his head smiling ... says something in Korean. Sounds like 'Yum-yum.' She smiles, reaches for the soldier's crotch, touches it. It surprises him.*" When Frank sees "*the two missing teeth*" in her face, the guard blows her head off.[14] Frank narrates that the guard killed the girl, feeling disgusted with his arousal.

In Chap. 10, the third-person narrator continues the story of the returning veteran Frank on his journey to rescue his endangered sister in Georgia, the journey mentioned in Chap. 2. The racial violence he encounters during his journey southward overlaps with his guilt over the failure to save his friend Mike during the war. Meanwhile, Cee becomes a victim of a White supremacist doctor's illegal eugenic experiment and is close to death when Frank arrives at the doctor's house. Frank rescues her in a "markedly nonviolent" manner, and this action transforms his childhood heroic self—"*strong good me tied to the* [violent] *memory of those horses and the burial of a stranger.*"[15] Since he can take his sister home, he finally "stand[s] like a man."[16] Some argue that this is the way Morrison's work always brings gender and race together, constructing "authentic masculinity" or "African American heroism" as "not achieved by victory in battle but by courage without violence."[17]

However, the rediscovery of his manhood does not mean his recovery from trauma. In order for his childhood home, Lotus, "*the worst place in the world, worse than any battlefield,*" to be a new home for the siblings, belonging and healing are necessary.[18] He brings his declining sister to the community of women in Lotus. The communal care, sharing, and support that the women practice is in stark contrast to the racializing medical industry of "antiblack misogyny."[19] Miss Ethel and the women in the community provide Cee with cure and protection to the extent that

---

[13] Morrison, *Home*, 18.

[14] Morrison, *Home*, 95.

[15] Morrison, *Home*, 104, 114.

[16] Irene Visser, "Fairy Tale and Trauma in Toni Morrison's *Home*," *Melus* 41, no. 1 (2016): 13–54.

[17] Linda Krumholz, "Dead Teachers: Rituals of Manhood and Rituals of Reading in *Song of Solomon*," in *Toni Morrison's Song of Solomon: A Casebook*, ed. Jan Furman (Oxford: Oxford University Press, 2003), 220; cited in Visser, "Fairy Tale and Trauma," 155.

[18] Morrison, *Home*, 83.

[19] A. J. Yumi Lee, "Repairing Police Action after the Korean War in Toni Morrison's *Home*," *Radical History Review* 137 (2020): 119.

even her brother is not allowed to visit her because "his maleness would worsen her condition."[20] As in her other writings, Morrison depicts such collective care of the women's community as distinctively African American.[21] Miss Ethel convinces Cee, "Now you back home," and goes on to say nobody can decide who she is because "[T]hat's slavery." Cee's response demonstrates what home means: "I ain't going nowhere, Miss Ethel. This is where I belong."[22]

Cee has gained physical and emotional strength and reunites with her brother in their rebuilt house. She speaks to Frank about her infertility, but she is strong enough to mourn without her brother's emotional support. She tells Frank that she sees a baby girl's smile everywhere in the house. The little girl might be her unborn child, killed by the White supremacist doctor. While responding, "Who would do that to a young girl? And a doctor?", Frank is deeply troubled by Cee's visions of a baby girl. It triggers his repressed memory, and now he must speak the truth (to the narrator in Chap. 14).

> Then Cee told me about seeing a baby girl smile …. It hit me. Maybe that little girl wasn't waiting around to be born to her. Maybe it was already dead, waiting for me to step up and say how.
> I shot the Korean girl in her face.
> I am the one she touched.
> I am the one who saw her smile.
> I am the one she said "Yum-yum" to.
> I am the one she aroused.[23]

His inability to remember his killing of the Korean girl after his arousal and shame may be understood as a symptom of post-traumatic stress disorder (PTSD).[24] According to trauma theory, a person who has directly experienced a violent event can negate what happened, and a realization of the incident comes later with much pain. Thus, Frank "belatedly" remembers the truth regarding the murder of the girl through "the therapeutic process of narrating his story," and his shame and guilt are overcome by confronting "what constitutes his most profoundly traumatic memory."[25] However, some critics argue that *Home* is not just the narrative of an individual's trauma but "fully engages African Americans' history of enslavement,

---

[20] Morrison, *Home*, 119.

[21] Gay Wilentz, "Civilizations Underneath: African Heritage as Cultural Discourse in Toni Morrison's *Song of Solomon*," *African American Review* 26, no. 1 (1992): 61–76; cited in Visser, "Fairy Tale and Trauma," 158.

[22] Morrison, *Home*, 125–126.

[23] Morrison, *Home*, 134.

[24] Manuela Lopez Ramírez, "The Shell-Shocked Veteran in Toni Morrison's *Sula* and *Home*," *Atlantis* 38, no. 1 (2016): 129–147.

[25] Visser, "Fairy Tale and Trauma," 156–157. Alternatively, Frank's symptoms can be regarded as moral injury because, with the alleviation of his traumatizing symptoms of PTSD, he can now "construct a coherent memory" of his experience and feel shame and guilt. See Rita Nakashima Brock and Gabriella Lettini, eds., *Soul Repair: Recovering from Moral Injury After War* (Boston: Beacon Press, 2013), xiii. But to my knowledge, no critics relate Frank's trauma and violation of consciousness to moral injury.

disenfranchisement, and continuing oppression and discrimination."[26] Maxine L. Montgomery also contends that the Black body, particularly in Cee's disfigurement, is "a potent site of trauma" and functions as a symbol of "the fractured history owing to the devastation of the transatlantic slave trade."[27] What is required for healing and restoration is remembering or "re-memory," which is a "psychic return to the past."[28] At the closing of *Home*, Frank and Cee revisit the place of their violent childhood memory and rebury the bones of the long-ago lynching victim in a quilt she made. This ritual is necessary for the siblings to consummate their re-membering of the past and finally finding a home as a place of healing and belonging.

This conclusion, signifying what home means, leads critics, like Mark A. Tabone, to define home as "an arrival rather than an origin."[29] Home is Morrison's version of a utopia that is achieved by the "endless work" of collective labor "down here" in this world, not in an imaginary or ahistorical place.[30] In this sense, Morrison's vision of "world-as-home that we are working for" offers "a hopeful resolution to the suffering on the part of a global community of marginalized subjects."[31] Morrison's conceptualization of home, along with her historical specificity, ethical praxis, and global vision, opens a space in which diasporic subjects can also find a meaningful, even if temporary, home.

However, I want to critically consider the tensions in these ideas of home. First, I inquire if many critics' view of home, as globally imagined, is not still caught up in American exceptionalism. Such a reading may not be what Morrison intends, as she narrates in Frank's voice: "They knew about Korea but not understanding what it was about didn't give it the respect—the seriousness—Frank thought it deserved."[32] Indeed, she makes an authorial effort to "rip the scab off of the 1950s" by excavating "obscure moments in our national history, re-constructing them from the vantage point of the marginalized subjects who witnessed those events firsthand."[33] The integrated US troops could exhibit "the 'liberal' renovation of the US war machine,"

---

[26] Irene Visser, "Entanglements of Trauma: Relationality and Toni Morrison's *Home*," *Postcolonial Text* 9, no. 2 (2014): 6.

[27] Maxine L. Montgomery, "Re-membering the Forgotten War: Memory, History, and the Body in Toni Morrison's "Home," *College Language Association Journal* 55, no. 4 (2012): 333.

[28] Montgomery, "Re-membering the Forgotten War," 324. Visser elaborates the term 're-memory' in Morrison's work as the "deliberate act of revisiting a memory." Such a memory is collective because of its continuity through generational transmission. Thus, re-memory, as a relational concept, involves body memory. Visser, "Entanglements of Trauma," 11–14. Similarly, I will use "re-membering" interchangeably with remembering to imply an act of revisiting traumatic body memories.

[29] Mark A. Tabone, "Dystopia, Utopia, and 'Home' in Toni Morrison's *Home*," *Utopian Studies* 29, no. 3 (2018): 295.

[30] Tabone, "Dystopia, Utopia, and 'Home'," 292–293.

[31] Tabone, "Dystopia, Utopia, and 'Home'," 293; Montgomery, "Re-membering the Forgotten War," 332.

[32] Morrison, *Home*, 136.

[33] Montgomery, 322; Lisa Shea, "Toni Morrison on 'Home'," *Elle*, June 15, 2012. https://www.elle.com/culture/books/interviews/a14216/toni-morrisonon- home-655249/.

expanding the US empire across the Asia-Pacific region by providing the military with newly recruited soldiers.[34] Black veterans, like Frank Money, returned with trauma to the brutal reality of racism at home.

Moreover, buried in the US historical moments were the tragedies that this US-involved war brought to another nation. The war was not declared a war, though it destroyed cities and the countryside and resulted in four million casualties, including two million civilians and over three million refugees.[35] More importantly, this war without an end is forgotten in Americans' national consciousness.[36] Veterans with PTSD are rightly regarded as war victims, but as Mimi Thi Nguyen notes, their role as perpetrators is concealed. Instead, "their pain is narrated in order to rescue liberal empire from the criminality of its wartime conduct."[37] If there is a figure who remains obscured in the fractured history, it is the disfigured Korean girl, a victim of an African American soldier. In a talk on *Home* at Oberlin College, Morrison says, "write about something you don't know. And don't be scared, ever."[38] In her writing as "travel[ing] into the haunted American history, and legacy, of slavery," she encounters the Other—another shattered history. This history is disclosed through the ghost of Cee's unborn child, which conjures another fragmented figure. What does it mean for the Korean girl, who is lost at home, to be re-membered or return home?

This reading leads me to ask another question concerning the cultural nationalist concept of home as arrival. David L. Eng problematizes home as the point of arrival in which such a home is equated with an American dream that is attainable. He notes Asians' migration to the United States is closely related to the latter's hegemonic expansion in the Asia-Pacific region.[39] Feeling "suspended between departure and arrival, Asian Americans remain permanently disenfranchised from home, relegated to a nostalgic sense of its loss or an optative sense of its unattainability."[40] Such a diasporic understanding of home is expressed as a "perpetually deferred

---

[34] Lee, "Repairing Police Action," 124–125; citing Christine Hong, "The Unending Korean War," in *The Unending Korean War*, ed. Christine Hong and Henry Em, special issue, *positions: asia critique* 23, no. 4 (2015): 606.

[35] Gary Y. Okihiro, *The Columbia Guide to Asian American History* (New York: Columbia University Press, 2001), 26.

[36] See Dong-Choon Kim, *The Unending Korean War: A Social History* (Honolulu: University of Hawaii Press, 2009).

[37] Nguyen, Mimi Thi, *The Gift of Freedom: War, Debt, and Other Refugee Passages* (Durham, NC: Duke University Press, 2012), 113. Lee also cites Nguyen's discussion of the "diagnosis of PTSD—a phenomenon peculiarly tied to wars of American empire," in "Repairing Police Action," 131.

[38] Joanna Connors, "Nobel laureate Toni Morrison, a Lorain native, talks at Oberlin College about New Book, 'Home'," *Cleveland.com*, March 15, 2012, https://www.cleveland.com/metro/2012/03/nobel_laureate_toni_morrison_a.html.

[39] David L. Eng, "Out Here and Over There: Queerness and Diaspora in Asian American Studies," *Social Text* 15, no. 3–4 (1997): 31–52.

[40] Eng, "Out Here and Over There," 31; also cited in Choi, "Epistemology of Intimacy and Haunting Diaspora."

state of achievement, an uninhabitable domain."[41] While Frank and Cee, the racially wounded, marginalized subjects, arrive home, the murdered Korean girl migrates as a ghostly figure through Frank's traumatic memory of racism and war and his witness to and participation in gendered violence. Whether or not the girl was symbolically buried in the sibling's reburial of the murdered man,[42] a diasporic reading of *Home* hauntingly searches for a site where racialized Americans and transnational subjects together re-member the victims of US imperialist and racist projects.

John's Homecoming Story[43]

While there is no exact correlation between Morrison's *Home* and John's Gospel, I observe some overlapping motifs in both texts. As *Home* depicts an African American veteran's journey home, John describes Jesus' life as consisting of multiple journeys—journeys into this world (1:1–18), within this world (1:19–17:26), and departing this world (18:1–21:25). Jesus' death on the cross is not the end of his journey. Instead, just as Frank and Cee return to their childhood home, the Gospel narrative ends with his return to Galilee, the hometown of Jesus and his disciples. Whereas Lotus is the place of trauma and healing for the siblings, Galilee is a home where Jesus' followers re-member the traumatic past and are healed. Most interestingly, Morrison alludes to a passage in John in her article, "Home."

> I prefer to think of a-world-in-which-race-does-not-matter as something other than a theme park, or a failed and always-failing dream, or as the father's house of many rooms. I am thinking of it as home.[44]

In John 14:2, Jesus says, "My Father's house has many rooms" (NIV).[45] The father's house is a prime example of "abiding" (*menei*), a technical term in John to describe belonging or the kinship bonds between Jesus and the father God. This father-son relationship is of foremost importance in the Gospel from the beginning: Jesus is with his father and close to his father's bosom (1:2, 18). But the son does not remain

---

[41] Eng, "Out Here and Over There," 32.
[42] Lee states, "In giving the anonymous man a proper burial, they are also symbolically laying to rest the ghosts of three apparently disconnected incidents of extrajudicial violence—Cee's forced sterilization, Frank's killing of the Korean girl, and their joint childhood witnessing of the aftermath of a murder." Lee, "Repairing Police Action," 133. Wall argues that Frank's ritual that reburies the bones of a victim whom he does not know is an "act of atonement" through which he makes amends to his victim. Only then can they "turn the home that has been a source of pain and suffering into a place of redemption and love." Cheryl A. Wall, "Trying to Get Home: Place and Memory in Toni Morrison's Fiction," in *Toni Morrison: Memory and Meaning*, ed. Adrienne Lanier Seward and Justine Tally (Jackson: University Press of Mississippi, 2014), 64.
[43] While some interpretive arguments are found in my essay, "Epistemology of Intimacy and Haunting Diaspora," here I attempt to connect the points to Morrison's ideas of home.
[44] Morrison, "Home," 3.
[45] NRSV translates, "In my Father's house there are many dwelling places."

in this physically intimate relationship and leaves home for the world (v. 9). In this new home where he lives among people, Jesus still "abides" in the father. This affectionate relationship is extended to others who love Jesus so that they abide in him and thus in his father. Jesus will finally return to his original home, the father's house, after his public life in the world. Most important of all, it will not be an eternal home exclusively for the father and his son (8:35) but a home with "many rooms (*monai*)" for anyone who loves Jesus (14:2): "My father will love them, and we will come to them and make our home (*monēn*) with them" (v. 23).[46]

"The father's house with many rooms" sounds inclusive, but why does Morrison disclaim such an image of home? It is primarily because she makes a "radical distinction between the metaphor of house and the metaphor of home."[47] Her consciousness as a raced writer living in a racial house leads her to imagine this house as ruled by the father: "I knew from the very beginning that I could not, would not, reproduce the master's voice and its assumptions of the all-knowing law of the white father."[48] As pointed out, making home is thus enduring work, the "job of unmattering race," while "the father's house with many rooms" may be viewed as an "impossible future" of the "race-free world."[49] As I reread John's Gospel deconstructing the heteropatriarchal language of "father and son," my reading of "the father's house" resonates with Morrison's reception of the image.

Jesus' words envision an ideal home to return to—the father's house in heaven, which is transcendent and welcoming, but it is not the destination of his journey in the Gospel narrative. His death on the cross is depicted as the consummation of his journey: "'It is finished.' With that, he bowed his head and gave up his spirit (*pneuma*)" (19:30). John 20:31, which explains the purpose of the writer, would have been a reasonable conclusion.[50] In the final scene in John 21, however, the risen Jesus returns to his disciples, who lock themselves in a house full of fear. This time he breathes *pneuma* unto them (20:22). Like the ghostly figures in haunted houses in Morrison's fictions, which invoke traumatic memories, Jesus appears as a ghost, nonetheless, embodied with physical wounds and scars.

In place of telling such stories as Jesus' ascension to his heavenly home, or the disciples' proclamation of the risen Christ, John ends the Gospel with a poignant homecoming story. Their Galilean home may be a place of failure, estrangement, and unfulfillment. When Jesus visits them and invites them to eat fish and bread together, it simultaneously becomes an intimate but unsettling place. Jesus' repeated questions to Simon Peter, "Do you love me?", not only evoke the painful memories

---

[46] The Greek word, *monē*, is used only twice (John 14:2, 23) in the New Testament.

[47] Morrison, "Home," 3. My discussion of the term "own" as a family language in relation to "home" in John's Gospel (cf. 1:11; 10:3-4; 13:1; 16:32, translated as "home") may help in understanding the distinction between house and home. See Choi, "Epistemology of Intimacy and Haunting Diaspora."

[48] Morrison, "Home," 4.

[49] Morrison, "Home," 3–4.

[50] John 20:31 "But these are written so that you may come to believe that Jesus is the Messiah, the Son of God, and that through believing, you may have life in his name."

of Peter's betrayal when law enforcement agencies arrested and bound his beloved teacher (18:18; 21:15–19),[51] but while "Peter felt hurt" (21:17), through re-membering and the communal ritual, he is also restored. Answering, "You know that I love you," he now knows what these words mean. Not only Peter, but whoever will follow the crucified Jesus, listens to his haunting voice: "Do you love me? Tend my people," though it may risk your life. Tabone reads the conclusion of *Home* as describing "an affirmative 'beloved community' that enables healing, belonging, and self-determination."[52] Similarly, responding to the beloved, who died an unjust death and can return nowhere other than home, demands from the living an affective bond to the haunting presence and the "ethical praxis" of caring.[53] If Morrison undertakes the "endless work" of "unmattering race," Jesus' homecoming story leads us to the "interminable and unforeclosable work of mourning" for those living only a "bare life" in the death zone of imperial sovereignty.[54] In these contexts, communal care means persistent resistance.

In both Morrison's *Home* and John's Gospel, home is not necessarily either an origin or an arrival, but where, as well as desiring and making a home together, people re-member, mourn, and recover—even if it may be painful. John's story of Jesus' homecoming (or his perpetually suspended return) describes an intimate and unsettling encounter which makes re-membering and healing possible. It is an open ending in which Jesus' ghostly apparition in the wounded body continuously haunts his followers, asking what home means in historical moments affected by imperial, racial, and sexual violence and traumas.

Conclusion: Haunting for Cross-racial Solidarity

Morrison invites the reader to witness "the body as consummate home," that is, "the estranged body, the legislated body, the violated, rejected, deprived body" in the context of globalism or transnationalism.[55] Grace M. Cho searches for this kind of body—the ghostly figure of *yanggongju* (GI bride; literally, Western princess), who portends familial and geopolitical secrets and wounds for the Korean diaspora. This figure is "a body assembled to transmit traumatic memory" of the "forgotten" war

---

[51] John highlights the presence of the overwhelming military forces, such as the Roman military cohort (*he speira*), its commander (*ho chiliarchos*), and the Judean police (*hoi hypēretai*, 18:12).

[52] Tabone, "Dystopia, Utopia, and 'Home'," 292.

[53] Tabone, "Dystopia, Utopia, and 'Home'," 303; citing Shari Evans, "Programmed Space, Themed Space, and the Ethics of Home in Toni Morrison's *Paradise*," *African American Review* 46, no. 2–3 (2013): 381–396.

[54] Tat-siong Benny Liew, "The Word of Bare Life: Workings of Death and Dream in the Fourth Gospel," in *Anatomies of Narrative Criticism: The Past, Present, and Futures of the Fourth Gospel as Literature*, ed. Tom Thatcher and Stephen D. Moore (Atlanta, GA: Society of Biblical Literature Press, 2008), 175.

[55] Morrison, "Home," 5.

and sexual violence.⁵⁶ Cho argues that the "migration of trauma across both generational and geographic borders" produces "new forms of kinship and new kinds of bodies."⁵⁷

What I see through the hauntings expressed in the writings of John, Morrison, and Cho is the assemblage of wounded bodies with traumatic memories. If Avery F. Gordon describes hauntings as "those singular yet repetitive instances when home becomes unfamiliar,"⁵⁸ my intertextual reading of the haunting stories reveals that racialized colonial histories are entangled. In this case, haunting is transhistorical, cross-cultural, and transnational. Moreover, the singularity of this haunting that is incessant and intricate requires a response, which Spivak calls an "ethical relationship."⁵⁹ Hence, haunting is different from trauma in that haunting produces "a something-to-be-done" for restoration or healing.⁶⁰

In my diasporic journey, constantly longing for home, I have witnessed ghosts both proleptically and belatedly. The image of the Black soldier as an Other in my early formation of nationalist (and subconsciously racist) consciousness was incorporated into my inherited war memories. Reading Morrison's *Home*, that enigmatic figure emerges in the character of Frank Money as the one who embodies the arduous journey across the Transatlantic Ocean to the deep South of America and then to the Korean War across the Pacific Ocean—to an unforgettable "forgotten" war. This traumatized figure embodies the historical complexity of "being policed at home" and simultaneously carrying out a "police action" against racialized others overseas.⁶¹ Synchronously, I am haunted by the ghost of the Korean girl migrating through the repressed truth of the racialized veteran, just as the ghosts of the *yanggongju*, who arrived on American soil as GI brides, haunt the Korean diaspora. Frank Money would tell ongoing stories beyond the 1950s of the military technologies deployed to expand US hegemony in the Asia-Pacific region, which were also used to suppress Black people through policing and mass incarceration.⁶²

We are continually haunted by Black lives killed by police brutality. On March 23, 2020, the singular event of the killing of another Black man, named Daniel

---

⁵⁶ Grace M. Cho, *Haunting the Korean Diaspora: Shame, Secrecy, and the Forgotten War* (Minneapolis: University of Minnesota Press, 2008), 40–41.

⁵⁷ Cho, *Haunting the Korean Diaspora*, 39.

⁵⁸ Avery Gordon, *Ghostly Matters: Haunting and the Sociological Imagination* (Minneapolis: University of Minnesota Press, 1997), xvi; cf. Jacques Derrida, *Specters of Marx: The State of the Debt, the Work of Mourning and the New International* (New York and London: Routledge, 2011), 10.

⁵⁹ Gayatri Chakravorty Spivak, *A Critique of Postcolonial Reason* (Cambridge, MA: Harvard University Press, 1999), 383–384.

⁶⁰ Gordon, *Ghostly Matters*, xvi.

⁶¹ Lee, "Repairing Police Action," 126–127.

⁶² Jian Neo Chen, "#Blacklivesmatter and the State of Asian/America," *Journal of Asian American Studies* 20, no. 2 (2017): 269, https://muse.jhu.edu/pub/1/article/662565. President Harry Truman called US intervention in the Korean conflict the "police action." Lee reads *Home* in the way Morrison "depicts policing and militarism as linked forces that protect and propel racism and liberal empire." Lee, "Repairing Police Action," 119–120.

Prude from Chicago, at the hands of law enforcement took place on a deserted street of Rochester, New York, where I currently live. Having a mental illness, he ran out of his brother's home into the night. The police handcuffed him, pinned his face down on the pavement, and covered his head with a hood. The haunting image of this Black man running shoeless (and naked) overlaps again with Frank Money, who escaped shoeless in the middle of the night from the mental hospital to the home of the pastor, who assisted him in heading through Chicago down to Georgia.

Witnessing the intimate—and often conflictual and discomforting—histories and subjectivities of African Americans and of a people from a war-torn country, I also choose to reread John's Gospel, which illustrates Jesus as executed by state power in Roman-occupied Palestine. Just as in *Home,* the story of Jesus' homecoming at the end of the Gospel portrays an unhomely home where re-membering and healing, through haunting, can take place. This intertextual reading of haunting stories, including my memories, invites minoritized communities to listen to an Other's unspoken history and find links with one's own story of going against global injustices promoted by liberal imperialism and White supremacist racism.

While there must be many ways of pursuing cross-racial solidarity, I, following Morrison, dare to be haunted by the Other, that is, other histories. When the official history obscures the unjust past and instead memorializes the glory of oppressive powers (e.g., US military intervention as a "police action" or the desegregated Korean War as a "successful racial revolution" or "a living example of democracy in action"),[63] alternative knowledge of history comes when the dead returns home. Even literature produced by colonized and raced writers like John and Morrison can be read from a single dominant or formalist viewpoint. As Cho suggests, reading with the ghosts "calls into existence new listening and speaking bodies that the ghost requires as witnesses to its own exorcism."[64] When attending to the violent past of global injustices, in which we and others, ancestors and possibly future children, are involved, marginalized subjects across the globe mourn and heal together. Returning home is like that new form of kinship that emerges amid coalitional work for anti-racism and decolonization.

Discussion Questions

1. Some readers understand that Morrison indirectly shows how White supremacy and anti-Black racism are interrelated with the exercise of US post-war hegemonic power in the Asia-Pacific. While this essay cannot provide comprehensive illustrations of anti-Black racism and the Korean War, it focuses on how one's history is interrelated to another's. In discussing multiple encounters or repeated

---

[63] Lee Nichols, *Breakthrough on the Color Front* (New York: Random House, 1954), 53, 144; cited in Hong, "The Unending Korean War," 606.

[64] Cho, *Haunting the Korean Diaspora,* 41.

histories of oppression, what surprises you? If any subject or event needs to be remembered, what may it be?
2. There are different ways of remembering. On the dedication stone at the Korean War Memorial in Washington, DC, the following words are inscribed: "Our nation honors her sons and daughters who answered the call to defend a country they never knew and a people they never met."[65] In contrast, Morrison's protagonist says, "They knew about Korea but not understanding what it was about." How can we better understand other racialized community's history or experiences beyond what has been publicly claimed or taught?
3. Discuss which concepts of home presented by Morrison and in this essay are helpful or challenging. Consider intersectional aspects of race, gender, sexuality, religion, nation, and empire. For example, should care work be limited to a particular gendered or racialized community? In what ways can the ideas of home or home-making practices contribute to the work of justice and healing across racial lines?

Bibliography

Brah, Avtar. 1996. *Cartographies of Diaspora: Contesting Identities*. London: Routledge.

Chen, Jian Neo. 2017. #Blacklivesmatter and the State of Asian/America. *Journal of Asian American Studies* 20 (2): 265–271.

Chen, Kuan-Hsing. 2010. *Asia as Method: Toward Deimperialization*. Durham: NC: Duke University Press.

Cho, Grace M. 2008. *Haunting the Korean Diaspora: Shame, Secrecy, and the Forgotten War*. Minneapolis: The University of Minnesota Press.

Choi, Jin Young. forthcoming. Epistemology of Intimacy and Haunting Diaspora: Rereading the Johannine Jesus' Journey Home. In *A Pact of Love with Criticism, A Pact of Blood with the World: Towards Geopolitical Biblical Criticism, Essays in Honor of Fernando F. Segovia*, ed. Amy L. Allen, Francisco Lozada, Jr., and Yak-hwee Tan. Atlanta, GA: Society of Biblical Literature Press.

Connors, Joanna. 2012. Nobel Laureate Toni Morrison, a Lorain Native, Talks at Oberlin College about New Book, 'Home'. *Cleveland.com*, March 15, https://www.cleveland.com/metro/2012/03/nobel_laureate_toni_morrison_a.html.

Derrida, Jacques. 2011. *Specters of Marx: The State of the Debt, the Work of Mourning and the New International*. New York and London: Routledge.

Eng, David L. 1997. Out Here and Over There: Queerness and Diaspora in Asian American Studies. *Social Text* 15 (3–4): 31–52.

Evans, Shari. 2013. Programmed Space, Themed Space, and the Ethics of Home in Toni Morrison's *Paradise*. *African American Review* 46 (2–3): 381–396.

Furman, Jan. 2014. Telling Stories: Evolving Narrative Identity in Toni Morrison's *Home*. In *Toni Morrison: Memory and Meaning*, ed. Adrienne Lanier Seward and Justine Tally, 231–242. Jackson: University Press of Mississippi.

Gordon, Avery. 1997. *Ghostly Matters: Haunting and the Sociological Imagination*. Minneapolis: University of Minnesota Press.

Hong, Christine. 2015. The Unending Korean War. *positions: asia critique* 23 (4): 597–616.

---

[65] Visit: https://www.defense.gov/Multimedia/Experience/Korean-War-Memorial/.

Kim, Dong-Choon. 2009. *The Unending Korean War: A Social History*. Honolulu: The University of Hawaii Press.

Kim, Nadia Y. 2008. *Imperial Citizens: Koreans and Race from Seoul to LA*. Stanford, CA: Stanford University Press.

Kim, Nami, and Wonhee Anne Joh, eds. 2016. *Critical Theology Against US Militarism in Asia*. New York: Palgrave Macmillan.

Krumholz, Linda. 2003. Dead Teachers: Rituals of Manhood and Rituals of Reading in *Song of Solomon*. In *Toni Morrison's Song of Solomon: A Casebook*, ed. Jan Furman, 201–232. Oxford: Oxford University Press.

Kwon, Heonik. 2020. *After the Korean War: An Intimate History*. New York: Cambridge University Press.

Lee, A. J. Yumi. 2020. Repairing Police Action After the Korean War in Toni Morrison's *Home*. *Radical History Review* 137: 119–139.

Lee, Nichols. 1954. *Breakthrough on the Color Front*. New York: Random House.

Liew, Tat-siong Benny. 2008. The Word of Bare Life: Workings of Death and Dream in the Fourth Gospel. In *Anatomies of Narrative Criticism: The Past, Present, and Futures of the Fourth Gospel as Literature*, ed. Tom Thatcher and Stephen D. Moore, 167–193. Atlanta, GA: Society of Biblical Literature Press.

Lowe, Lisa. 2015. *The Intimacies of Four Continents*. Durham, NC: Duke University Press.

Montgomery, Maxine L. 2012. Re-membering the Forgotten War: Memory, History, and the Body in Toni Morrison's "Home". *College Language Association Journal* 55 (4): 320–334.

Morrison, Toni. 1997. Home. In *The House That Race Built: Black Americans, U.S. Terrain*, ed. Wahneema Lubiano, 3–12. New York: Pantheon.

———. 2012. *Home*. New York: Vintage.

Brock, Rita Nakashima, and Gabriella Lettini, eds. 2012. *Soul Repair: Recovering from Moral Injury After War*. Boston, MA: Beacon Press.

Nguyen, Mimi Thi. 2012. *The Gift of Freedom: War, Debt, and Other Refugee Passages*. Durham, NC: Duke University Press.

Okihiro, Gary Y. 2001. *The Columbia Guide to Asian American History*. New York: Columbia University Press.

Ramírez, Manuela Lopez. 2016. The Shell-Shocked Veteran in Toni Morrison's *Sula* and *Home*. *Atlantis* 38 (1): 129–147.

Seward, Adrienne Lanier, and Justine Tally, eds. 2014. *Toni Morrison: Memory and Meaning*. Jackson: University Press of Mississippi.

Shea, Lisa. 2012. Toni Morrison on 'Home'. *Elle*, June 15, https://www.elle.com/culture/books/interviews/a14216/toni-morrisonon- home-655249/.

Spivak, Gayatri Chakravorty. 1999. *A Critique of Postcolonial Reason*. Cambridge, MA: Harvard University Press.

Tabone, Mark A. 2018. Dystopia, Utopia, and 'Home' in Toni Morrison's *Home*. *Utopian Studies* 29 (3): 291–308.

Visser, Irene. 2014. Entanglements of Trauma: Relationality and Toni Morrison's *Home*. *Postcolonial Text* 9 (2): 6–21.

———. 2016. Fairy Tale and Trauma in Toni Morrison's *Home*. *Melus* 41 (1): 141–164.

Wilentz, Gay. 1992. Civilizations Underneath: African Heritage as Cultural Discourse in Toni Morrison's *Song of Solomon*. *African American Review* 26 (1): 61–76.

Wall, Cheryl A. 2014. Trying to Get Home: Place and Memory in Toni Morrison's Fiction. In *Toni Morrison: Memory and Meaning*, ed. Adrienne Lanier Seward and Justine Tally, 53–65. Jackson: University Press of Mississippi.

7
Beyond Siloed Solidarity: The Place of Asian Americans in the Struggle for Racial Justice

Jessica Wai-Fong Wong

Following the murder of George Floyd, America was plunged into a period of racial reckoning during which Asian Americans began voicing a line of questioning that had, to that point, remained largely taboo. Is there a place in today's racial justice movement for Asian Americans to voice their stories of suffering alongside those of Black Americans? Is there a place beyond Asian-specific circles for the Asian American to engage fully in the work of justice in a way that allows her to be both seen and heard? Is there a place for her voice in the larger racial discourse? In the United States, questions about Asian American voice and place in the wider conversation about race and in the work of anti-racism have often been answered in one of two ways: Either the Asian American is welcomed into racial justice circles, but relegated to a background, supportive role akin to that of the White ally; or she is encouraged to take on a leadership position in the fight for justice, but directed to focus her attention on organizing the Asian American community for AAPI rights. Put simply, Asian Americans who are fighting for racial justice in the United States have regularly been either denied full agency as activists or pushed into Asian-focused siloes and toward exclusively Asian American-centered concerns.[1] Why is

---

[1] There have been efforts in U.S. history wherein racial groups have worked side-by-side in the fight for greater liberation; the Civil Rights movement with its Poor People's Campaign is one notable example. To recognize the degree to which racial division is present within social justice circles is not to dismiss instances of true solidarity and collaboration. Instead, recognizing the presence of such division within racial justice work is to acknowledge the seemingly inevitable influence of our racially divided society upon groups that are very much located within that society. For more on the history of Asian American participation in the Civil Rights Movement and the way in which the Black/White paradigm undercuts such efforts, see Janine Young Kim, "Are Asians Black?: The Asian-American Civil Rights Agenda and the Contemporary Significance of the Black/White Paradigm," *The Yale Law Journal* 108, no. 8 (June 1999): 2385.

J. W.-F. Wong (✉)
Systematic Theology at Azusa Pacific University, Azusa, CA, USA
e-mail: jessicawong@apu.edu

© The Author(s), under exclusive license to Springer Nature Switzerland AG 2023
K. C. Pae, B. Lee (eds.), *Embodying Antiracist Christianity*, https://doi.org/10.1007/978-3-031-37264-3_7

this the case? Why does it seem as though the practice of silencing and functionally erasing Asian Americans, which is so prevalent in the wider culture, has been replicated within certain racial justice circles? And how might Christian theology offer insight into possible ways forward?

It is important to note from the beginning that this line of inquiry is not intended to challenge the Black struggle for justice. It is not one that advances a "generic intersectional" critique against racially specific justice organizations in an attempt to decenter concerns about racial injustice or to mute the voices of other people of color.[2] It is not one that aims to pit justice for Asian Americans over against that of Black Americans. In fact, quite the opposite. By considering how the dominant logic of race has found its way into aspects of the social justice movement in the United States, this essay seeks to challenge the ways in which the pursuit of racial justice has too often been treated as a competition between racial groups for resources and recognition.

While this preamble may strike some as unnecessary, akin to Jennifer Nash in her investigative critique of intersectionality and Black feminism, I recognize that my analysis of racial justice efforts in the United States is "deeply uncomfortable terrain" that runs the risk of my being labeled a traitor to the Black community, if not to all people of color.[3] If not engaged carefully, the argument that I am making may either be misidentified as an iteration of the well-meaning but attenuating position that has come to be associated with White liberals or, alternatively, misused by conservatives to delegitimize the place of identity politics and the important work of racial justice organizations. Both misreadings would be unfortunate, for my goal is not to attenuate or delegitimize existing justice efforts but to issue an analysis that prompts healthy introspection, so that an even more powerful, communal undertaking of the work is made possible.

The System of Race and Pursuit of Justice

With that said, we return to our original question: Why does it seem as though the practice of silencing and functionally erasing Asian Americans, which is so prevalent in the wider culture, has been replicated within certain racial justice circles? In an effort to answer this question, we must begin with the concept of *race*. Unlike ethnicity, race is a social construct. It is not innate. It is not biological. It is

---

[2] For more on how intersectionality has been used to undermine racial justice efforts, see Ashlee Christoffersen, "Is Intersectional Racial Justice Organizing Possible? Confronting Generic Intersectionality," *Ethnic and Racial Studies* 45, no. 3 (2021): 407–430, https://doi.org/10.1080/01419870.2021.1928254.

[3] Jennifer C. Nash, *Black Feminism Reimagined: After Intersectionality* (Durham, NC: Duke University Press, 2019), 33.

something that society has imagined into existence.[4] And yet, despite being socially constructed, racial categories have real material, economic, and psychological consequences. This way of seeing the world has justified not only colonial conquest, but it has also prompted more subtle injustices related to evaluations of intelligence, job opportunities, judicial sentencing, and housing. Moreover, it has become an essential aspect of how people understand themselves, read power, navigate the world, and experience belonging.

Thanks to all of these very real effects, race, in spite of its imaginative beginnings, has come to occupy a key place in identity politics and, consequently, a key place in identitarian racial justice circles. What follows is that the concept of race that sits at the center of the racial logic dominating Western modernity remains a powerful organizing idea within the very groups aimed at challenging said logic. It is the presence of this concept, with its definitive and organizing power, that produces notable parallels between the given racial system and these anti-racist efforts, especially along the lines of *kinship and belonging*, *purity*, and *power*.

By recognizing these parallels, I am not suggesting that the ideologies at work within these two contexts are one and the same. However, acknowledging the conceptual similarities that exist between them is important if we are to try to understand why the siloing and marginalization that Asian Americans experience within society at large seems to be replicated in certain ways within certain antiracist communities.

Kinship and Belonging

The parallels that exist between the given system of race and a number of racial justice organizations is somewhat unavoidable, for both recognize *race* as an essential category for making sense of the world. Describing this overlap as "somewhat unavoidable" is my attempt to acknowledge the significant impact that the idea of race has on the modern world. It is somewhat unavoidable insofar as Americans have been habituated from an early age to see themselves and the people around them through the lens of race; to assess and categorize people along racial lines.[5] By

---

[4] Jessica Wai-Fong Wong, *Disordered: The Holy Icon and Racial Myths* (Waco, TX: Baylor University, 2021), 5.

[5] Elsewhere, I describe this process of entering into racial sight as follows: "Through various social apparatuses, the uninitiated are trained to see and engage the world in a proper, ideologically informed way. They are taught to see in a manner consistent with the dominant understanding of racial and gendered order, the order that has colonized the landscape of our modern Western social imaginary. Seemingly benign images and narratives from television, children's bedtime stories, and history textbooks paint a certain picture of the world. These recurring stories, concepts, images, and ideas inculcate children into a coherent vision of reality—one that celebrates the goodness of whiteness and warns of the evils of blackness. Each iteration of this storyline, though differing in its details, champions the same racialized logic. These frequently repeated narratives form what Fanon recognizes as 'a series of propositions that slowly and subtly—with the help of books, newspapers, schools and their texts, advertisements, films, radio—work their way into one's mind and shape one's view of the world of the group to which one belongs.' This racialized vision of the world, with its attending network of meaning, is the 'reality' into which the modern subject is indoctrinated." See Wong, *Disordered*, 18-19.

accepting the given racial categories as normative and even inevitable, race is allowed to continue functioning as a dominant means of establishing both identity and belonging.

Communities fighting for racial justice are not exempt from this racialized way of viewing kinship.[6] Even within certain justice circles, race continues to be seen as key to one's identity and, in turn, an important means of affiliation and coalition building.[7] Political philosopher Nancy Fraser notes how, in the United States in the late twentieth century, a split between the pursuit of justice as "social politics of equality" and the pursuit of justice as "cultural politics of difference" became increasingly pronounced.[8] While the former remained primarily concerned with redistributive justice and equity, the latter became focused on the societal recognition of cultural differences, often manifest along racial lines. It is this focus on racial difference that makes its way into identity politics, prompting a number of justice groups to recognize race as a primary means of identification and affiliation, thereby further entrenching the identitarian concept of race within the American sociopolitical landscape. This privileging of identitarian, racially-based kinship comes with a variety of advantages. It offers a space of potential belonging, "participatory parity," and activism.[9] However, it can also produce a zero-sum mentality, a perspective that has the effect of weakening inter-racial solidarity and strengthening resistance to social change.[10] Zero-sum thinking is tied to feelings of fear that there is not enough to go around, which makes people, especially those who see

---

[6] Michael Omi and Howard Winant, "The Theory of Racial Formation," in *Racial Formation in the United States*, 3rd ed. (New York: Routledge, 2014), 107. Jonathan Tran also speaks about the way in which the concept of race entails a black/white binary thinking. Insofar as this concept is the definitive framework utilized not only within our racialized society but also within antiracist circles, it is inevitable that the same logic that rules racialized society will also infect antiracist justice circles. See Jonathan Tran, *Asian Americans and the Spirit of Racial Capitalism* (Oxford: Oxford University Press, 2021), 8.

[7] Within Asian American justice groups, the focus on race as the primary means of coalition building tends to be complicated. Part of the complication can be traced to the distinct role that ethnicity plays in intra-Asian relationships. Factors including diverse and at times antagonistic relational histories, linguistic and cultural differences, and unique immigrant experiences in the United States all contribute to coalition building among Asian Americans depending heavily on factors beyond race. See Dina G. Okomato, "Organizing Across Ethnic Boundaries in the Post-Civil Rights Era: Asian American Panethnic Coalitions" in *Strategic Alliances: Coalition Building and Social Movements*, ed. Nella Van Dyke and Holly J. McCammon (Minneapolis: University of Minnesota Press, 2010), 147.

[8] Nancy Fraser, "Social Justice in the Age of Identity Politics: Redistribution, Recognition, Participation,," in *WZB Discussion Paper*, FS I 98-108 (Berlin, 1998), 1.

[9] Fraser, "Social Justice in the Age of Identity Politics," 5.

[10] Anna Stefaniak, "Zero-sum Beliefs Shape Advantaged Allies' Support for Collective Action," *European Journal of Social Psychology* 50, no. 3 (April 26, 2020): 13.

themselves as somehow advantaged by the given system, less inclined to join efforts to challenge it.

Even among people of color, this mentality can lead to apathy toward inter-racial solidarity work. Pitting one's own people's liberation over against that of others, one's primary concern becomes the liberation of one's own racial or ethnic community. Evident in the struggle over affirmative action, this zero-sum approach to justice positions the well-being of Asian Americans over against that of Black Americans. Such racially myopic thinking reinforces the established system of oppression, but it does so under the guise of progress.[11] Convinced that we are fighting for justice for our own people, we can unwittingly participate in and, thereby, reinforce larger systems of oppression. While appearing natural and even inevitable, efforts to dismantle the current system by way of this racially siloed approach can have the unintentional consequence of further fortifying it.

Pure and Impure

A similar observation can be made about boundary-setting practices present in both the given racial system and identitarian racial justice circles. As has been well established, boundaries play an important part in the constitution and safeguarding of a community. By marking who is in and who is out, who is good and who is bad, who is orderly and who is disorderly, who is pure and who is impure, communal identity can be strengthened. Boundary setting aims to protect a group from the threat posed by others. By providing a means of differentiating those who are properly ordered

---

[11] David L. Eng and Shinhee Han, *Racial Melancholia, Racial Dissociation: On the Social and Psychic Lives of Asian Americans* (Durham, NC: Duke University Press, 2018), 41. Also see Michael Omi and Dana Takagi, "Situating Asian Americans in the Political Discourse on Affirmative Action," *Representations*, no. 55 (1996), 155-162. Even assuming that striking affirmative action would prove beneficial to Asian American applicants (a claim that is certainly contested), the question of whether such a move should be considered "progress" in the Asian American struggle against institutional racism remains. Even if one grants that a ban on affirmative action would produce an uptick in the number of Asian American students admitted to certain universities, it is also true to say that the inevitable decrease in other non-White racial groups would have a detrimental impact upon the student body. One study shows that a ban on affirmative action impacted campus climate in ways that were "'critical' to the success of students of color." The study states that these changes "silenced conversations about race and racism, made it more difficult for community members to vocalize support for racial diversity initiatives, and made administrators feel 'disempowered' to resolve issues related to race." In many ways, these consequences are a byproduct of the colorblindness central to the argument for anti-affirmative action and, relatedly, to its denial of the problem of White privilege. The very argument that denies the problem of whiteness as a means dismantling affirmative action leaves in its wake a campus where problems related to race and the hegemony of whiteness go unrecognized. See Katie Reilly, "As the Harvard Admissions Case Nears a Decision, Hear From 2 Asian-American Students on Opposite Sides," *Time*, March 2, 2019, https://time.com/5546463/harvard-admissions-trial-asian-american-students/.

(us) from those who are disordered (them), the community is better prepared to protect itself.[12]

At the heart of the modern logic of race is the pursuit of proper order, a sense of order rendered even more significant through implicit ties to God's divine will.[13] Theologically weighted binaries of good and bad, ordered and disordered, pure and impure, saved and damned have been attached to categories of race, making *whiteness* and *blackness* into more than assessments of skin pigmentation and cultural norms. Beyond aesthetics and culture, they have been reimagined as descriptors that capture a person's moral, intellectual, social, and even spiritual state.[14] They have been made into ontological categories.

It would be naïve to assume that these conceptions of blackness and whiteness apply only to those racially categorized as Black or White. Instead, this way of seeing and organizing impacts everyone. Willie Jennings describes the all-encompassing process by which people are drawn into the evaluative power of race, noting how "these body differences will be articulated through white and black in such a powerful way that their similitude will extend to all people. These bodies, black and white, become almost spectral, more precisely, conceptually able to be superimposed over all other bodies."[15] The significance of blackness and whiteness extends beyond Black and White people. Everyone is located on the spectrum between blackness and whiteness; no one escapes the constraints of the modern racial optic's imaginative ordering or its real-world consequences. The question is not whether one is impacted by this way of imagining the world but to what extent one is imagined to embody the chaos of blackness or the holy order of whiteness.

This all-encompassing, theologically charged racial distinction stands at the heart of the modern racial logic's power and the exclusionary tendencies of the current conception of race alive in the United States.[16] And the bifurcated theological concepts of in and out, pure and impure, saved and damned, orderly and disorderly,

---

[12] This boundary setting entails discernment between those who are orderly from those who are disorderly, all of which is part of modernity's *panopticon* at work. See Michel Foucault, *Discipline & Punish: The Birth of the Prison*, trans. Alan Sheridan (New York: Vintage Books, 1995), 300.

[13] In the colonial and modern eras, *blackness* becomes imbued with notions of impurity; demonic intellectual, physical, and social disorder; societal chaos; and damnation of both one's soul and one's humanity. While *whiteness* comes to encapsulate the opposite. Whiteness signifies purity, intellectual acuity, physical beauty, the accomplishments of Western civilization, and even spiritual salvation. (Wong, *Disordered*, 53-56.) As early as the fourteenth century, there is evidence of such a strong correlation between whiteness and Christian salvation that in one fictional travelogue the author tells the story of his party's surprising encounter with a group of Black Christians from Africa. It is in spite of their being "black as pitch" that they identified as Christians; see Nancy F. Marino, *El libro del conoscimiento de todos los reinos [The book of knowledge of all kingdoms]* (Tempe, AZ: Arizona Center for Medieval and Renaissance Studies, 1999), 61; see also Willie James Jennings, *The Christian Imagination: Theology and the Origins of Race* (New Haven, CT: Yale University Press, 2010), 23.

[14] Wong, *Disordered*, 56-59.

[15] Jennings, *The Christian Imagination*, 31.

[16] Jennings, *The Christian Imagination*, 31.

and friend and foe further undergird this racialized framework through which those within Western modernity are evaluated. Driven by a fear of blackness and its disordering effects on what is assumed to be God-ordained, properly ordered (i.e., White), Western civilization, the existence of disorderly (non-White) people within American society must be addressed, for their unmitigated presence threatens to corrupt civilized society's proper order.[17] It is the ontological disorder, impurity, corruption, and damnation of those associated with blackness that renders people of color, in general, and the Black population, in particular, a threat to the well-being of White Western society.

And while antiracist efforts in the United States seek to challenge this established logic, echoes of the same racial order and racialized conception of belonging remain present within justice groups that build their coalition along racial lines. Though functioning with a distinct sense of right or proper order, all those living and working within the modern Western context have, to one degree or another, been shaped by its dominant racial vision. It is therefore unsurprising that racially organized antiracist communities tend to reflect a dynamic of inclusion and exclusion similar to that which characterizes the given racial logic.[18] This dynamic is not only present in the construction of a group through the distinction of racist from antiracist but also through internal divisions within the antiracist coalition.[19]

Within identitarian antiracist groups, race continues to be treated as a key means of assessing threat and trustworthiness, for race continues to hold an essentialized significance. The only difference is the meaning ascribed to each racial identity. Instead of those who are Black being seen as untrustworthy, within Black identitarian racial justice groups, it is those who identify as White who are treated with greater suspicion and who need to prove themselves. Driven by a strongly essentialized conception of race that is particularly poignant in the United States and by memory of past betrayal, identitarian racial justice groups like Black Lives Matter are intentional in organizing their multicultural coalition into members and allies along racial lines, with only Black participants able to become members and all others designated as allies.[20] At their monthly meetings, BLM LA directs attendees to temporarily separate into four groups according to race—Blacks, Blacks who are participating for the first time, other people of color, and Whites—so that each

---

[17] Wong, *Disordered*, 22-24.; More on the connection between whiteness and American identity can be found in Peter McLaren, "Unthinking Whiteness, Rethinking Democracy: Or Farewell to the Blonde Beast; Towards a Revolutionary Multiculturalism," *Educational Foundations* 11, no. 2 (1997): 26.

[18] Jonathan Tran, *Asian Americans and the Spirit of Racial Capitalism* (Oxford: Oxford University Press, 2021), 156.

[19] Clément Petitjean and Julien Talpin discuss this particular form of "group style" in "Tweets and Doorknocks: Differentiation and Cooperation between Black Lives Matter and Community Organizing," *Perspectives on Politics* 20, no. 4 (December 2022): 1277. For a picture of how the United States racial group style differs from that of Brazil, see Michèle Lamont et al., "Brazil," in *Getting Respect*, Responding to Stigma and Discrimination in the United States, Brazil, and Israel (Princeton, NJ: Princeton University Press, 2016), 122-191.

[20] Petitjean and Talpin, "Tweets and Doorknocks," 1280.

group can discuss how they might best contribute to the movement. Black people must be the ones who lead the fight for Black liberation, with all others positioned in a supportive role.[21] As James Cone puts it in *God of the Oppressed*, "To those whites who continually proclaim their goodwill, despite the long history of racism, the most blacks can say is: 'There may be a place for you, but you will have to do what we say, without suggesting that you know what is best for our liberation.'"[22] Potential White allies may be included in a supportive capacity in the struggle for Black liberation, but only after serious examination and with great caution. And, though less explicitly stated, this same logic applies to other people of color as well.

On the one hand, such boundary setting is understandable. The history of the Civil Rights Movement has given the Black community ample reason to distrust those claiming to be White allies. The threat that the ally, in particular the unproven ally, poses within identitarian antiracist circles today is similar to the threat that the mulatto posed to the racial order of things in the nineteenth and twentieth centuries. In both cases, the danger is that of *passing* and the attending risk of *contamination*. Speaking to this, early twentieth-century Jamaican-American author Claude McKay describes why White folks in the United States seemed to have a bigger issue with mulatto Americans than Black Americans. "For they're never sure about us, they can't place us," McKay writes.[23] Passing is particularly dangerous because it threatens to introduce, without detection, a fundamental disorderliness into properly ordered society. Within identitarian antiracist groups, this same anxiety is present around the untested ally, especially one belonging to another race.

It is also true to say that, although a social construct, race has real-life consequences. One's life experiences are impacted by one's social location. Race is a part of this equation. It follows that because of these racially determined experiences, people of a certain race are perhaps able to understand an organization's mission and vision in ways that those belonging to a different race, with different experiences, cannot. Thus, central to the practice of differentiating belonging and responsibility along racial lines is the assumption that race is essential to one's commitment to the cause and ability to lead in ways keeping with the organization's vision. Put differently, in part, the distinctions of inclusion and exclusion present within identitarian antiracist groups stems from a fear of what will happen if those of another race are permitted into the inner circle, into positions of leadership and voice.

This fear of the threat of disorderly people within one's own ranks has made participation in the work of justice into something closely guarded. Those securely positioned within the inner circles of identitarian antiracist communities have functioned as gatekeepers, carefully assessing the purity of the intentions of those who wish to participate in the work of liberation. And while there is ample room to critique the history of allyship within the racial justice movement in the United States, an overabundance of caution leading to thresholds of belonging organized

---

[21] Petitjean and Talpin, "Tweets and Doorknocks," 1279.

[22] James Cone, *God of the Oppressed*, revised edition (Maryknoll, NY: Orbis Books, 1997), 199.

[23] Claude McKay, "NearWhite," *Gingertown*, (New York: Harper and Brother, 1932), 95-96.

according to racial identity can have the consequence of closing groups off from the creative potential present in moments of unexpected encounter.[24] In our attempt to protect ourselves, we must be careful not to unintentionally obstruct our own path to transformational justice.

My argument, here, is not against all practices of gatekeeping. There is a certain degree of guardedness that is both merited and necessary. Instead, my argument is simply that we must be careful about how we go about this practice of gatekeeping. While necessary at times, if left unchecked, our impulse to protect ourselves can cut us off from potential partners and friends, leading us to hamstring the very movement we wish to champion. It follows that our primary question is not whether it is wise to practice gatekeeping when building coalitions; the concern is not a practical one. Our question is how the fundamental logic driving identitarian antiracist groups today, the logic that allows and even encourages this form of gatekeeping, coincides with the established racial logic. Are our antiracist efforts driven by an order that is truly distinct from the established racial logic? Or is the same logic simply being manifest within distinct contexts?

Power

The practice of gatekeeping is ultimately an exercise in power, an effort to shift established dynamics of power. Opposed to a system aimed at securing White (male) supremacy, America's current racial justice movement focuses on the empowerment of people of color, most overtly, the Black population. Due to America's long history of anti-Black racism and the way in which Black populations have been treated as largely disposable, if not entirely eliminable, Black voices and concerns are now rightly being privileged in the overarching push for justice today. In an attempt to correct the injustices of the established system, Black voices and issues must be centered in conversations concerning racial justice in the United States.

There is, however, an unintended consequence to the current implementation of this corrective. Because justice is largely imagined to be and, therefore, treated as a zero-sum game, the movement suffers from the mistaken and perhaps unconscious belief that in order to elevate Black voices, others must be silenced.[25] This, of course, is an unintentional byproduct of our current form of identity politics. As Jonathan Tran writes, "Coalition solidary premised on racial identity turns the degree of one's racial suffering into the basis for one's belonging, with predictable results – only

---

[24] For more on the troubled history of White allyship, see Matt R. Jantzen, "Neither Ally, Nor Accomplice: James Cone and the Theological Ethics of White Conversion," *Journal of the Society of Christian Ethics*, December 8, 2020.

[25] For more on how zero-sum thinking is inherent to the given racial logic, see Heather McGhee, *The Sum of Us: What Racism Costs Everyone and How We Can Prosper Together* (New York: One World, 2021).

certain races count. When race (e.g., "whiteness") serves as the common enemy around which a coalition is built, then racial identity (i.e., one's suffering owing to one's race) becomes the criterion for participation. Just as race narrows what counts as suffering, so it narrows pathways for shared forms of life."[26] Based on the assumption that there is only so much empathy, only so many resources, and only so much power to go around, there is a tendency to limit voice and presence to those who have suffered the greatest degree of trauma. This means that Asian Americans, among other racial groups, frequently find themselves pressed into either passive and largely voiceless support of the Black struggle for justice or into racially isolationist pursuits of progress.

Approaching the work of racial justice by way of identitarian comparative suffering is, once again, a byproduct of seeing justice as a competition for limited resources and fearing that there is not enough. Comparative suffering is predicated upon the assumption that we are functioning within an economy of scarcity. And yet, for those who identify as Christian, this is not how power and resources work within the divine economy of God, for God's economy is marked by radical abundance.[27]

The Order of God

The Christian story offers us an altogether different order. It is neither the order of our racialized world nor, perhaps to our surprise, the order of racial justice, at least not in its current form. While the work of justice communities certainly gestures toward the order that defines God's kingdom, the two are not equivalent. The order of God is distinct and often paradoxical.

Power

God's order challenges established conceptions of power. There is a more expansive, truer power that exists beyond the given logic, beyond the disciples fighting about who gets to sit next to Jesus in his glory.[28] Contradicting the dominant system, power and honor are no longer located in the privileging of self but in service and humility. Power, within this context, is expressed in giving oneself for the other. It

---

[26] McGhee, *The Sum of Us*, 13-14.
[27] Matthew 14:13-21, *New Testament, Revised Standard Version*.
[28] Mark 10:35-45; Scripture will be from the *New Revised Standard Version* unless otherwise noted.

is a power that is not predicated upon staking out room for oneself and one's own people but being bound to the other.[29]

As previously noted, the manifestation of power within identitarian racial justice groups today is regularly shaped by the impulse to protect oneself and one's own people—a people frequently imagined along racial lines. Yet, the exercise of power to which Christians are being called is not marked by an exclusivity born out of a desire for self-protection but by a posture of vulnerability. Of course, there are some who will object to this critique of power. They will argue that the posture I am prescribing opens up those who are already vulnerable to experiences of violence inconsistent with the will of God.[30] There is validity to this concern. It is important to recognize that the vulnerability I am suggesting is not appropriate for everyone at all times. We are not always ready for a step like this. And yet, it is also true that God has and continues to call us toward this open-handed way of being with others, a way of being that leads to unexpected communion and expansive kinship.

Kinship and Belonging

The order of God draws us not only into deeper communion with our "own people" but also into communion with those who are outside of our racially and ethnically established circles. This way of being with others is grounded in the reality of the Trinity. Social Trinitarians have long argued that we are created and called to be in a relationship in a manner that is rooted in the reality of Godself. As the three persons of the Trinity are with and for one another, not collapsing the other into the self but still bound to the other in *perichoretic* love, so are we to be with and for others.[31]

This divinely ordered way of relating is, of course, most profoundly realized in the person of Jesus.[32] As fully God and fully human, Jesus is the clearest manifesta-

---

[29] Dietrich Bonhoeffer, *Creation and Fall: A Theological Exposition of Genesis 1-3* (Minneapolis, MN: Fortress Press, 2004), 63.

[30] For Black women who have historically been forced into the oppressive role of surrogate, the cross is no longer a symbol of redemption and hope but of systemic violence. See Dolores Williams, "Black Women's Surrogacy Experience and the Christian Notion of Redemption" in *After Patriarchy: Feminist Transformations of the World Religions*, eds. Paula M. Cooey, William R. Eakin, and Jay B. McDaniel (Maryknoll, NY: Orbis Books, 1991), 11.

[31] For a focused treatment of the internal order of the immanent Trinity and its implications for the social relationality to which we are called, see Jessica Wai-Fong Wong, "Social Trinitarianism Through Iconic Participation," in *Companion to Political Theology*, ed. Rubén Rosario-Rodriguez (London: T&T Clark, 2019), 900-902.

[32] Kathryn Tanner rightfully recognizes that the fundamental weakness of social trinitarianism lies in the ontological distinction that exists between the Creator and creation. How can social trinitarians suggest that human beings embody a certain way of being that mirrors that of God when God is wholly other from creation? In response to this question, Tanner points to Jesus. See Kathryn Tanner, *Christ the Key*, Current Issues in Theology (Cambridge, UK: Cambridge University Press, 2010), 244-245.

tion of this divine sociality. His behavior toward us is an indication of how we should be with one another.[33] Considering scriptural accounts of Jesus' life, we recognize the ways in which he draws near to those who are considered impure. Both Jewish Levitical law (Lev.15) and its Priestly counterpart (Num. 5:1-4), for example, are clear about the unclean nature of women with abnormal genital discharge (*zabah*, זבח). For the sake of society—its health as well as its sociopolitical and spiritual order—such women are to follow specific protocols which, in more stringent cases, includes separating themselves from the community for seven days following their last day of discharge.[34] They are considered impure while afflicted in this manner and believed to have a contaminating effect on any person or object with whom they come into contact. As such, during this time, they are excluded from aspects of social and religious life, if not altogether barred from participation.[35]

It is in this state of seemingly perpetual defilement due to unnatural genital discharge that the gospels' hemorrhaging woman finds herself.[36] And while there is disagreement among biblical scholars as to the extent of the woman's exclusion in the Second Temple Period, what is clear is that her persistent physical condition signals a state of impurity that, to one degree or another, impacts her capacity to participate within properly ordered society and religious life.[37] What is striking about her encounter with Jesus is that when she touches him, he does not grow angry. He does not send her away. Instead, he loudly and publicly inquires after the person who touched his cloak. He wants to encounter her in the presence of the crowd. In doing so, he openly defies the established practice of excluding certain people for the sake of maintaining personal and societal purity. Whether by way of washing rituals or association with prostitutes, Jesus challenges given protocol surrounding purity and, in this manner, subtly defies the established conception of "right order," thereby inviting the faithful into an altogether different sensibility.

Yet, participation in God's divine order occurs not only through imitation of Christ. Jesus does more than model this sacred sociality. His very body functions as an entry point into the holy order of God wherein we are prompted to live with and for others in a manner consistent with God's triune relationality.[38] As we experience the grace of entering Christ's body through baptism, we are welcomed into an altogether different order. His is an order wherein *power* is not something found in

---

[33] Tanner, *Christ the Key*, 236-237.

[34] Numbers 5:1-4.; Leviticus 15:25-30.

[35] Susan Haber, "A Woman's Touch: Feminist Encounters with the Hemorrhaging Woman in Mark 5.24-34," *Journal for the Study of the New Testament* 26, no. 2 (December 2003): 175-177.

[36] Haber, "A Woman's Touch," 174. Mark 5:25-34; Luke 8:43-48.

[37] See Susan Haber's analysis of the different interpretations of the implications attending the hemorrhaging woman's condition. Haber, "A Woman's Touch," 177–78. While some scholars argue that the woman's impurity is only an issue within the Temple setting in Jerusalem, Haber notes that such a reading misses the ritual of purification (*mikvaot*) that archeological evidence suggests was a common practice among the Jewish people outside of Jerusalem and its Temple.

[38] Wong, "Social Trinitarianism Through Iconic Participation," 902-904.

assertions of strength or the exclusion of others but in humility and the welcoming of strangers. It is an order wherein the bonds of blood are superseded by the bonds found within the body of Christ.[39] Within the context of Christian social justice circles, this means that the intimate bonds of kinship must extend beyond the connections afforded by race.

Pure and Impure

This order, found in Christ, is the same order that marks the radical movement of the Spirit, which challenges our established conceptions of *purity*. As previously noted, distinctions of pure and impure, of in and out, serve as a means of self-protection. Maintaining these strict categories creates the illusion that we have the capacity to protect ourselves from those we have deemed inherently disordered, from those who pose a threat to our civilized, properly ordered society. Yet, as I have been suggesting, God's order appears to be far less about maintaining what we understand as pure or proper and far more about the act of joining, marked by a kind of *productive contamination*.

In the Book of Acts, the Spirit is described as pressing the Jewish Christian community toward believing Gentiles who have long been considered unclean.[40] According to the scriptural narrative, Peter—faithful Jew that he is—receives a vision from God. Three times a sheet containing unclean food is lowered and set before him. Each time, God directs Peter to "get up… kill and eat." Each time, Peter refuses: "By no means, Lord; for I have never eaten anything that is profane or unclean." To which God replies, "What God has made clean, you must not call profane."[41] Following this vision, Peter hears a knock at the door, and the Spirit directs him to go with the Gentile Cornelius's men. He is to share with them the good news of the Gospel.[42] The Spirit directs this devout Jewish man toward those once considered unclean, toward those previously thought to be profane, toward those whose presence was once believed to have a corrupting influence on God's holy people. Even Peter, upon entering Cornelius' house, acknowledges the profound shift that God has initiated. "You yourselves know that it is unlawful for a Jew to associate with or to visit a Gentile, but God has shown me that I should not call anyone profane or unclean."[43] The Spirit is pressing God's people to join those once regarded as impure.

---

[39] Willie James Jennings, "Being Baptized: Race," in *The Blackwell Companion to Christian Ethics*, ed. Stanley Hauerwas and Samuel Wells, 2nd ed. (Malden, MA: Wiley-Blackwell, 2011), 286-288.
[40] Willie James Jennings, *Acts*, First edition, Belief: A Theological Commentary on the Bible (Louisville, KY.: Westminster John Knox Press, 2017), 111-118.
[41] Acts 10:9-16
[42] Acts 10:17-23
[43] Acts 10:28

The discomfort and disorientation that Peter experiences is an important, though often overlooked, aspect of Christian discipleship, for it reminds us of our limited capacity as human creatures to grasp the proper order of God. While we frequently deceive ourselves into thinking that we fully understand and, therefore, should function as arbiters of God's holy order, the unexpected promptings of the Spirit serve to remind us otherwise. In this way, the Spirit's actions help to inculcate within us a posture of humility, for we are forced to acknowledge that we can neither predict nor control God's movements.[44]

Purity of the Plantation and Freedom of the Spirit

The Spirit is an agent of the *productive contamination* that characterizes God's holy economy. Marked by unpredictable freedom, her movement through the world stands in stark contrast with the purity-obsessed, compartmentalized plantation logic that drives the established racial order. Anthropologist Anna Tsing notes the way in which plantation logic seeks to maximize efficiency for the sake of scalability.[45] Everything must be simplified to be made scalable. Toward this end, the order that characterizes the plantation alienates people from the things they produce and denudes workers of their particular identities by reimagining them as discrete units of labor.[46] "Techniques of alienation" are used to "turn both humans and other beings into resources," which has the effect of "segregat[ing] humans," "polic[ing] identities," and "obscuring collaborative survival."[47] Meant to maximize efficiency and productivity, this approach has the effect of stripping people of their particularity, severing relational connections, and disabling efforts aimed at communal wellbeing.

When applied to the project of whiteness upon which American citizenship is founded, this plantation logic helped to give birth to the social reform movement at the turn of the century.[48] As non-White immigrants flooded American shores in the late-nineteenth and early-twentieth centuries, social and political leaders began thinking about how (White) American citizenship might be made scalable. How are

---

[44] Dietrich Bonhoeffer recognizes limitations as essential to freedom. God gifts one human being to another to function as a reminder of their limitations and, in turn, as a reminder that they are creatures and not God. Being kept in proper relationship with God, such limits function as gifts. See Dietrich Bonhoeffer, *Creation and Fall: A Theological Interpretation of Genesis 1-3*, fifth edition (New York: Macmillan Pub. Co., 1969), 61. Similarly, the Spirit's radical and unexpected movement functions to remind us of the natural limitations of our creaturely condition, once again, a limitation that is ultimately a blessing.

[45] Anna Lowenhaupt Tsing, *The Mushroom at the End of the World: On the Possibility of Life in Capitalist Ruins* (Princeton, NJ: Princeton University Press, 2015), 37-40.

[46] Tsing, *The Mushroom at the End of the World*, 5-6.

[47] Tsing, *The Mushroom at the End of the World*, 19.

[48] Wong, *Disordered*, 4. Also see, Ruth Frankenberg, *White Women, Race Matters: The Social Construction of Whiteness* (Minneapolis: University of Minnesota Press, 1993), 233.

these non-White immigrants to be made into real American citizens? Social reformers like Jane Addams concluded that only insofar as immigrants can be removed (i.e., alienated) from their particular, non-uniform cultural customs can they be readied for American identity. She asserted that the immigrant must shift "from the region of the uncultivated person into the possibility of the cultivated person."[49] Or, put in the even more forthright language of Richard Henry Pratt, a social reformer dedicated to the assimilation of Amerindian children, the state must "kill the Indian in him, [in order to] save the man."[50] The immigrant or indigenous person is imagined within this context as a discrete unit that, when alienated from the messiness of his culture and past relationships, can be made into the sought-after commodity that is proper White American citizenry.

The fact that the modern system of race, with its alienating assimilationist trajectory, is built upon plantation logic feels matter of course. However, what is perhaps surprising, and what I have been suggesting throughout this essay, is that traces of this logic can be found within aspects of identitarian racial justice efforts today. In both contexts—within the established racial system and within certain antiracist efforts to combat said system—plantation logic has turned people into resources by "segregat[ing] humans" and "polic[ing] identities" in a manner that ultimately "obscur[es] collaborative survival."[51]

Yet, the Spirit invites us into an altogether different logic and, with it, another way of being in relationship. Her order is nothing like that of the plantation. Instead of separating people into antiseptically organized, efficiency-driven categories, the Spirit's movements tend to be wild and unpredictable, drawing together different peoples, places, stories, histories, and objects in ways that are unexpected and sometimes even seemingly chaotic. Instead of being marked by the rigid boundedness of purity, the Spirit of God is marked by *freedom* leading to productive contamination. The Spirit draws us into a divine state of mycelial blooming that invites mingling and overflow. And it is out of these messy, divinely prompted encounters that something new emerges. It is from this space of meeting that we are given the gift of new creation, of new humanity, and of an altogether new socio-political reality.[52]

It is important to note that the Spirit's overflowing, unpredictable, connective, and, in this sense, contaminated order does not always appear to us as orderly. Her

---

[49] Jane Addams, *Twenty Years at Hull House* (New York: Macmillan Pub. Co., 1938), 232, cited in James B. Salazar, *Bodies of Reform: The Rhetoric of Character in Gilded Age America*, America and the Long 19th Century (New York: New York University Press, 2010), 234.

[50] Henry Pratt, "The Advantages of Mingling Indians with Whites," in *Nineteenth Annual Session* (The National Conference of Charities and Correction, Boston: Press of Geo. H. Ellis, 1892), 46, cited in Salazar, *Bodies of Reform*, 230.

[51] Tsing, *The Mushroom at the End of the World*, 19.

[52] This gifting is true of God's transgressive encounter with creation in the incarnation of Jesus, as God chose to enter the messy reality of our existence and, in doing so, to extend to us the gift of new humanity and, through Christ's body, entry into a new social order. And it is true of the Spirit's movement today.

movement lacks the control and precision, the rigid boundary setting and subsequent alienation that attends the plantation logic dominating our society, for she calls us into that vulnerable and unpredictable space of encounter with others. During Pentecost, the Galilean disciples not only witness to other Galileans, but, by the power of the Spirit, they speak to people from Mesopotamia, Judea, Cappadocia, Asia, Egypt, and Rome. The Spirit falls upon Jews as well as Gentiles. And, as their ministry continues, the Spirit presses the apostles further. She presses them outward, moving them toward new lands and peoples. This account in Acts reveals the Spirit's proclivity for expansion, one that transgresses established boundaries and, in the process, forms a new community. Within this new order, people are no longer separated according to land, language, or lineage. There is no place for nationalist or ethnocentric aspirations here.

The order established by the Spirit is radically different from the order to which we are accustomed. And because her order is different, because it is unexpected, when the movement of the Spirit is evaluated through the lens of our given conception of order, it can at times appear to us not as order at all but as a disorder, for it flouts our prevailing structures and ways of understanding the world. In fact, the Book of Acts describes how some who witness Pentecost fail to recognize it as a miracle but, instead, believe it to be the unruly behavior of people who have had too much to drink.[53] Bound to our own vision of order, we have a tendency to mistake the movement of the Spirit for something else. We struggle to recognize it for what it is. Yet, according to scripture, it is this seemingly disordered, messy gathering of diverse peoples at Pentecost who most profoundly manifests the holy order of God's kingdom.

Transgressing established boundaries and clean categories, this holy order, characterized by precarity and contamination, is the space wherein connectivity and new life emerges. "Precarity," Tsing writes, "is the condition of being vulnerable to others. Unpredictable encounters transform us; we are not in control, even of ourselves.... we are thrown into shifting assemblages, which remake us as well as our others."[54] It is toward such spaces of transformative meeting that Christians seeking racial justice must journey. And we must do so without the expectations and safeguards that, in an attempt to protect ourselves, precludes true encounter. "A precarious world is a world without teleology," Tsing notes. "Indeterminacy... is frightening, but... [it is] also what makes life possible." Encounter is precarious; it threatens the idea of the pure self and even throws into question the assurance of our survival. However, the precarity of encounter is also essential to our survival, for it is needed in the production of new life and identity.[55] This move into precarious contamination is difficult to make, especially given the *de facto* privileging of order—both within the church and outside of it, both on the side of racism and on the side of justice. Safeguarding the orderliness of our social body by carefully

---

[53] Acts 2:13.
[54] Tsing, *The Mushroom at the End of the World*, 20.
[55] Ibid., 29.

evaluating who belongs and who does not is a means of protecting our community from the threat of those who we fear to be fundamentally incompatible. By doing so, both parties believe they are protecting what they see as right or proper order.

However, scripture tells a different story. It reveals to us that at the heart of right order, which in this case is God's holy order, is the delight-filled work of the Spirit, which is always moving us toward others, not simply for the purpose of joining, but with the goal of creating something new. Spirit-led encounters culminate in the act of creation. What does it look like for Christians fighting for justice to loosen their grip on their conception of "right" or "proper" order and, instead, to open themselves up to the even more radical work of the Spirit? What categories will the Spirit collapse? To whom will the Spirit bind us? What will family look like in her wake?

Previously, we noted that the order of God is profoundly present within the body of Christ. What we did not acknowledge at the time is the way in which the union established through baptism is also the work of the Spirit. It is the Spirit that binds in love to one another.[56] The Spirit forms bonds of kinship that transcend blood. And it is the logic of this holy community that offers a liberative correction to our siloed thinking. For Christians fighting for greater justice in the world, making room for the Spirit's movement means allowing any anxiety and fear over whose vision of justice or whose theological voice will prevail to give way to the productive space of encounter. The goal is no longer to stake out room for the preeminence of one's own ideas or sociopolitical influence. The primary posture is no longer that of gatekeeping or self-preservation. Instead, the holy space of authentic encounter is one wherein something entirely new is allowed to emerge, even when we are unsure what shape and form it will take. What results is not a detraction from the cultural specificity of any of our ethnically or racially distinct communities or ways of thinking, but the cultivation of a vision of the world and relationship marked by the overflow and abundance of the Spirit.

And while certainly not equivalent to the Kingdom of God, it is interesting to consider the ways in which the coalition building within community organizing might be seen as a gesture toward the movement of the Spirit. As with identitarian antiracist activists, dismantling racial injustice is a core commitment for community organizers. However, race is not central to the group's self-conception, organization, or approach to enacting change. Driven by a desire for redistributive justice over the politics of representation, community organizers pursue change through building coalitions around issues that impact people of all races.[57] This distinction in vision is then reflected in their approach to the work. Relying less heavily on social media and street demonstrations, community organizers utilize door-to-door canvassing techniques, "a practice that symbolizes crossing social barriers beyond the social spaces [to which] one belongs."[58]

---

[56] Augustine of Hippo, *On the Trinity*, ed. Philip Schaff, trans. Arthur West Haddan, vol. 3, Nicene and Post-Nicene Fathers (Buffalo, NY: Christian Literature Publishing Co., 1887), XV.17.27.

[57] Petitjean and Talpin, "Tweets and Doorknocks," 1276. Also see Cedric G. Johnson, "The Panthers Can't Save Us Now: Anti-Policing Struggles & the Limits of Black Power," 2017.

[58] Petitjean and Talpin, "Tweets and Doorknocks," 1281.

So, too, with the Spirit, it is in this risky and frightening space of crossing barriers, this space of encounter, this unpredictable space that, due to its unfamiliarity, may even appear to us as disordered, that we are met by God's expansive and creative Spirit. Here, in this holy place—between you and me—that the economy of scarcity characterizing plantation thinking is replaced by the economy of abundance that marks the order of God. No longer is my articulation of suffering curtailed by yours. No longer are we in competition with one another. Instead, your lamentations and expressions of joy function to bolster mine; just as my efforts toward your liberation is a struggle for my own freedom. In this holy space of encounter, we are met by the possibility of something new; we are met by the possibility of living into the promise of our becoming, which is the promise of "new creation." And yet, this possibility can only become a reality if we learn to open ourselves up to a way of being beyond the safety of our siloed existence, which is beyond even our siloed solidarity.[59]

Discussion Questions

1. Why do you think that we, as human beings, so often succumb to *zero-sum thinking* and behavior? Do you think that this manner of thinking is manifest within your racial community? If so, in what ways? Do you think that zero-sum thinking corresponds with the teachings of Christ and the call of Christian discipleship? Why or why not?
2. What is it about clearly defined categories of in/out, pure/impure, and good/bad that humans find so compelling? Why do you think that we have this impulse when it comes to race? Are there other areas in which your community tends toward this way of thinking?
3. If it is true to say that the Spirit's movement is one of "productive contamination" that results in the creation of a new community, what might this mean for how God is calling us to understand and engage the world? How might this manifest along racial lines?
4. According to the author, scripture speaks of God's profound care and provision for all of creation (Matthew 6:26-33). Within the context of our efforts to bring about greater racial justice, in what situations are we being called to cease worrying about shoring up our own security (i.e., stop tending to our immediate self-interest and the interest of our own ethnic or racial group) and, instead, to work toward the larger goal of actualizing the "kingdom of God," here, on earth?

---

[59] 2 Corinthians 5:17; Galatians 6:15.

Bibliography

Addams, Jane. 1938. *Twenty Years at Hull House*. New York: Macmillan Pub. Co.
Anderson, Benedict. 2006. *Imagined Communities: Reflections on the Origin and Spread of Nationalism*. New York: Verso.
Augustine of Hippo. 1887. On the Trinity. In *Nicene and Post-Nicene Fathers*. Edited by Philip Schaff. Trans. A.W. Haddan. 3. Buffalo, NY: Christian Literature Publishing Co. http://www.newadvent.org/fathers/130115.htm.
Bonhoeffer, Dietrich. 2004. *Creation and Fall: A Theological Exposition of Genesis 1-3*. Minneapolis, MN: Fortress Press.
Christoffersen, Ashlee. 2022. Is Intersectional Racial Justice Organizing Possible? Confronting Generic Intersectionality. *Ethnic and Racial Studies* 45 (3): 407–430. https://doi.org/10.1080/01419870.2021.1928254.
Cone, James. 1997. *God of the Oppressed*. Revised ed. Maryknoll, N.Y.: Orbis Books.
Eng, David L., and Shinhee Han. 2018. *Racial Melancholia, Racial Dissociation: On the Social and Psychic Lives of Asian Americans*. Durham, NC: Duke University Press.
Foucault, Michel. 1995. Discipline & Punish: The Birth of the Prison. Trans. A. Sheridan. New York: Vintage Books.
Frankenberg, Ruth. 1993. *White Women, Race Matters: The Social Construction of Whiteness*. Minneapolis: University of Minnesota Press.
Fraser, Nancy. 1998. Social Justice in the Age of Identity Politics: Redistribution, Recognition, Participation. In *WZB Discussion Paper*, 29. FS I 98-108. Berlin. http://hdl.handle.net/10419/44061.
Haber, Susan. 2003. A Woman's Touch: Feminist Encounters with the Hemorrhaging Woman in Mark 5.24-34. *Journal for the Study of the New Testament* 26 (2): 171–192.
Jantzen, Matt R. 2020. Neither Ally, Nor Accomplice: James Cone and the Theological Ethics of White Conversion. *Journal of the Society of Christian Ethics*. https://doi.org/10.5840/jsce202012731.
Jennings, Willie James. 2017. *Acts*. First edition. Belief: A Theological Commentary on the Bible. Louisville, KY: Westminster John Knox Press.
———. 2011. Being Baptized: Race. In *The Blackwell Companion to Christian Ethics*, ed. Stanley Hauerwas and Samuel Wells, 2nd ed., 277–289. Malden, MA: Wiley-Blackwell.
———. 2010. *The Christian Imagination: Theology and the Origins of Race*. New Haven, CT: Yale University Press.
Johnson, Cedric G. 2017. The Panthers Can't Save Us Now: Anti-Policing Struggles & the Limits of Black Power.
Kim, Janine Young. 1999. Are Asians Black?: The Asian-American Civil Rights Agenda and the Contemporary Significance of the Black/White Paradigm. *The Yale Law Journal* 108 (8): 2385. https://doi.org/10.2307/797390.
Lamont, Michèle, Graziella Moraes Silva, Jessica S. Welburn, Joshua Guetzkow, Nissim Mizrachi, Hanna Herzog, and Elisa Reis. 2016. Brazil. In *Getting Respect: Responding to Stigma and Discrimination in the United States, Brazil, and Israel*, 122–191. Princeton, NJ: Princeton University Press. https://www.jstor.org/stable/j.ctv346qr9.8.
Marino, Nancy F. 1999. *El Libro del Conoscimiento de Todos los Reinos [The Book of Knowledge of All Kingdoms]*. Tempe, AZ: Arizona Center for Medieval and Renaissance Studies.
McGhee, Heather. 2021. *The Sum of Us: What Racism Costs Everyone and How We Can Prosper Together*. New York: One World.
McKay, Claude. 1932. NearWhite. In *Gingertown*. New York: Harper & Brother.
McLaren, Peter. 1997. Unthinking Whiteness, Rethinking Democracy: Or Farewell to the Blonde Beast; Towards a Revolutionary Multiculturalism. *Educational Foundations* 11 (2): 5–39.
Nash, Jennifer C. 2019. *Black Feminism Reimagined: After Intersectionality*. Durham, NC: Duke University Press Books.

Okomato, Dina G. 2010. Organizing Across Ethnic Boundaries in the Post-Civil Rights Era: Asian American Panethnic Coalitions. In *Strategic Alliances: Coalition Building and Social Movements*, ed. Nella Van Dyke and Holly J. McCammon, 143–169. Minneapolis: University of Minnesota Press.

Omi, Michael, and Dana Takagi. 1996. Situating Asian Americans in the Political Discourse on Affirmative Action. *Representations* 55: 155–162.

Omi, Michael, and Howard Winant. 2014. The Theory of Racial Formation. In *Racial Formation in the United States*, 3rd ed., 105–136. New York: Routledge.

Petitjean, Clément, and Julien Talpin. 2022. Tweets and Doorknocks: Differentiation and Cooperation between Black Lives Matter and Community Organizing. *Perspectives on Politics* 20 (4): 1275–1289. https://doi.org/10.1017/S1537592722001049.

Reilly, Katie. 2019. As the Harvard Admissions Case Nears a Decision, Hear From 2 Asian-American Students on Opposite Sides. *Time*, March 2. https://time.com/5546463/harvard-admissions-trial-asian-american-students/.

Salazar, James B. 2010. *Bodies of Reform: The Rhetoric of Character in Gilded Age America*. America and the Long 19th Century. New York: New York University Press.

Stefaniak, Anna. 2020. Zero-sum Beliefs Shape Advantaged Allies' Support for Collective Action. *European Journal of Social Psychology* 50 (3). https://doi.org/10.1002/ejsp.2674.

Tanner, Kathryn. 2010. *Christ the Key*. Cambridge, UK: Cambridge University Press.

Tran, Jonathan. 2021. *Asian Americans and the Spirit of Racial Capitalism*. Oxford, UK: Oxford University Press.

Tsing, Anna Lowenhaupt. 2015. *The Mushroom at the End of the World: On the Possibility of Life in Capitalist Ruins*. Princeton, NJ: Princeton University Press.

Williams, Dolores. 1991. Black Women's Surrogacy Experience and the Christian Notion of Redemption. In *After Patriarchy: Feminist Transformations of the World Religions*, ed. Paula M. Cooey, William R. Eakin, and Jay B. McDaniel, 1–14. Maryknoll, NY: Orbis Books.

Wong, Jessica Wai-Fong. 2021. *Disordered: The Holy Icon and Racial Myths*. Waco, TX: Baylor University Press.

———. 2019. Social Trinitarianism Through Iconic Participation. In *T&T Clark Handbook of Political Theology*, ed. Rubén Rosario Rodríguez, 513–525. London: T&T Clark.

8
The Confines of "Antiracism" Work in the Intersectional Realities of "Anti-Asian" Violence

Nami Kim

The Questions We Are Asking

Five feminist theologians, including myself, participated in a virtual roundtable in June 2021 on the topic of anti-Asian violence, particularly the Atlanta mass shooting that took place on March 16, 2021. Robert Aaron Long, a 21-year-old self-proclaimed evangelical Christian white man, purchased a gun hours before shooting and killed eight people, including six Asian women, four of whom were of Korean descent, at three massage spas in the Atlanta area. At this roundtable, the moderator posed a series of guiding questions for conversation. Included among the questions were the following: *Can we talk about the way the AAPI community is often not even in solidarity within its own body? As you've watched AAPI Christians respond to the sudden visibility of the anti-Asian racism and violence of the past year, what have been your reactions? How has the current and ongoing work towards solidarity across the AAPI community and across racializations been necessary and/or problematic? Are there some forms of advocacy in the AAPI Christian community that have been further invisibilizing parts of our community?*[1] We could not respond to all of the questions posed by the moderator, not only due to time constraints but also because of the heaviness we all felt deriving from our proximity to the topic that we were discussing. Not only were six of the shooting victims Asian women, but four of them were Korean women. Five of us on the roundtable were Asian/

---

[1] I thank Christine Hong for asking such thought-provoking questions during our webinar held on June 16, 2021. "Building Solidarities: A Conversation with Korean Feminist Theologians." Iliff School of Theology. Denver, CO, June 16, 2021.

N. Kim (✉)
Department of Philosophy and Religious Studies, Spelman College, Atlanta, GA, USA

American[2] women and, more specifically, women of Korean descent. We shared gender and ethnic identities with four victims. Was that why we were constantly called on and invited to talk about our thoughts and feelings about the Atlanta mass shooting? What else did we share with four victims, as well as with all six Asian women victims? And did it matter—or not?

Drawing from these lingering questions and the roundtable questions, in this essay, I discuss some of the challenges posed by the antiracism work engaged in by Korean Christian pastors and leaders in response to the Atlanta mass shooting. Minority nationalism, which stems from the singularity of race as an operating principle, is the underlying logic of their antiracism work. Such minority nationalism is frequently conjoined with the notion of "national belonging" or "inclusion," which is concomitant with the binary of deserving and undeserving persons. This binary is also a constitutive part of the "theology of decency," a theology that sanctions gender and sexual normativity and conformity, thereby reinforcing "structural and social inequalities under the guise of some normal and natural order to life."[3] In this essay, I propose that rejecting this theology of decency is a needed step for a Christian praxis of solidarity across differences. My aim is not to simply criticize the antiracism work engaged in by Korean Christian leaders in the Korean ethnic churches as well as in the larger Korean diaspora in the United States.[4] Instead, I seek to probe how the call to combat racism becomes inadequate when it is understood and carried out primarily based on common racial identity without addressing real material conditions and other intersecting structures of oppression and exploitation that produce differences. Through the examination of the Atlanta spa shootings from an intersectional, transnational feminist perspective, I argue that antiracism work solely based on shared racial identity cannot end or prevent violent incidents like the Atlanta mass shootings. Instead, the combined issues of racialized misogyny and class hierarchy, US foreign policy, and wars in Asia among others must also be considered.

Focusing on the Atlanta mass shootings is not to center a "spectacular" incident of violence over other varying forms of violence that have targeted Asian/American women. As much as the murder of six Asian/American women became a "moment of awakening" for some people within Asian American communities, prompting them

---

[2] Regarding the use of the signifier slash "/" between "Asian" and "American," see David Palumbo-Liu, *Asian/American: Historical Crossings* (Stanford, CA: Stanford University Press, 1999), 1.

[3] Cathy J. Cohen, "Deviance as Resistance: A New Research Agenda for the Study of Black Politics." *Du Bois Review: Social Science Research on Race* 1, no. 1 (March 2004): 33.

[4] I use the terms "Korean ethnic church" and "Korean immigrant community" based on how its Korean translations ("Han-in kyohoe" and "Han-in imin sahoe," respectively) are used in the larger Korean diaspora in the United States. As Korean American scholars have noted, however, there are marginalized diasporas within the larger Korean diaspora, such as the diaspora of Korean adoptees and what Grace M. Cho calls a "diaspora of camptown." See Grace M. Cho, "Diaspora of Camptown: The Forgotten War's Monstrous Family," *Women's Studies Quarterly* 34, nos. 1-2 (2006): 309-331. See also Jodi Kim, "'The Ending Is Not an Ending at All': On the Militarized and Gendered Diasporas of Korean Transnational Adoption and the Korean War," *Positions: Asia Critique* 23, no. 4 (Fall 2015): 807-835.

to contest the anti-Asian racism that has often not been taken seriously, it also exposed that the antiracism work that is grounded in minority nationalism and its proposed solutions cannot make substantial changes in the lives of Asian/American women, particularly those who work in the low-wage service industry. The white gunman's actions further revealed multiple intersecting issues relating to racialization, gender, class, labor, (im)migration, gun violence, US militarism in Asia, and evangelical theological emphasis on "purity." The indispensability of an intersectional feminist framework that is transnational, materialist antiracist, anti-heteropatriarchal, and anti-imperialist has become clearer in our attempts to make sense of complexly and complicatedly interrelated violences that are committed against minoritized people, including Asian/American women amid intersecting social, political, economic, and religious realities. Intersectional analysis, as Angela Y. Davis and many other feminists have reminded, helps us to "move beyond individual identities and single-issue politics" when we seek to forge solidarity across differences.[5]

The Atlanta Mass Shooting: "An Awakening Moment" for Who?

In spite of the increased reports of bullying, harassment, and verbal and physical assaults against Asian/Americans, particularly "East" Asian/Americans, since the outbreak of the Corona virus, largely due to its politicization as the "Chinese virus," "Wuhan virus," or "Kung flu," it was the Atlanta spa shootings on March 16, 2021, that finally made people see the gravity of violence against Asian/Americans, particularly Asian/American women. Included among those who at last realized the seriousness of anti-Asian violence are evangelical Korean pastors and church leaders who have nationally and transnationally joined the chorus of calling for the fight against racism in general and anti-Asian racism in particular. For instance, a Christian organization in Korea extended sympathies to the victims and their families, condemning anti-Asian racism. The moderator of the National Caucus of Korean Presbyterian Churches (NCKPC) in the United States issued a statement on "hate crimes against people of Asian descent."[6] The president of the Korean United Methodist churches also issued a statement, condemning "hate crimes."[7]

---

[5] Linda E. Carty and Chandra Talpade Mohanty, "Introduction: An Archive of Feminist Activism-Conversations with Margo Okazawa-Rey, Angela Y. Davis, Himani Bannerji, Minnie Bruce Pratt, Amina Mama, Aida Hernandez-Castillo, and Zillah Eisenstein," in *Feminist Freedom Warriors: Genealogies, Justice Politics and Hope*, eds. Chandra Talpade Mohanty and Linda E. Carty (Chicago, IL: Heymarket Books, 2018), 10.

[6] Byeong-Ho Choi, "Urgent Message Regarding the Recent Hate Crimes Against People of Asian Descent," *Columbus Korean Presbyterian Church*, March 21, 2021, https://www.kpccoh.org/nanum/17988.

[7] Eungsun Kim, "Asian American United Methodists Issue a Statement Condemning Hate Crimes against Asians in the United States." *UMC News*, March 18, 2021, https://www.umnews.org/ko/news/asians-united-methodists-condemn-the-rise-of-anti-asian-violence-in-us.

Some Korean pastors in the Atlanta area stressed that churches can no longer stay silent about racism and "hate crimes" against Asian/Americans, urging coalitional work against racism. Seeing the urgency of addressing racism as part of Christian ministry, a prominent Korean pastor organized a vigil service for the victims in the city with other religious leaders to collectively grieve and to condemn anti-Asian violence. Another pastor in Atlanta also stressed that Koreans and Asian Americans can no longer ignore the importance of antiracism work, which is crucial not only for this generation but also for their children.[8] In their sermons and speeches, some pastors also emphasized the importance of taking responsibility as American citizens. As such, this brutal incident was condemned as a racially motivated "hate crime" that pointed up the need for increased law enforcement in Korean/Asian-owned business areas and even around Korean ethnic churches.[9] This, however, has alarmed some people who don't consider more policing as a suitable response to anti-Asian violence.

It is confounding that these pastors and Christian leaders had not realized the severity of anti-Asian violence nor considered speaking up against racism whether in the public or in the pulpit earlier, when in fact neither anti-Asian violence nor violence against other racialized people in the United States is a new phenomenon.[10] Anti-Asian racism, more specifically racist violence against Asian/Americans (read "East" Asian/American), is far from a "recent" phenomenon. While its long history includes the mass murder of nineteen Chinese immigrants in Los Angeles in 1871, it has become more visible and palpable during the COVID-19 pandemic, largely due to increased reports, documentation, and media attention.[11] Asian/Americans who are Muslim or who "look Muslim" have long faced and endured multi-dimensional anti-Muslim racism, particularly since 9/11. Furthermore, there are activists, faith leaders, scholars, and concerned people in Asian American communities who have long engaged in antiracism work in connection to other anti-oppression work.

---

[8] Anderson Kim, "After the Atlanta Shootings, Korean Ethnic Churches Say It is Now Our Work to Combat Racial Discrimination," *Christian Today*, March 22, 2021, https://www.christiantoday.co.kr/news/338895.

[9] In May 2021, the Biden administration signed the COVID-19 Hate Crimes Act into law.

[10] As history teaches us, some Korean churches have not been silent through their solidarity work with African American Churches, for example, after the LA Uprising or the 4.29 (Sa-I-Gu). It cannot be presumed that any antiracism work has only started in 2021 by evangelical pastors who had a moment of "awakening." See Jane Hong, "The L.A. Uprisings Sparked an Evangelical Racial Reckoning," *The Washington Post*, April 29, 2022, https://www.washingtonpost.com/outlook/2022/04/29/la-uprisings-sparked-an-evangelical-racial-reckoning.

[11] *Stop AAPI Hate* has insistently condemned and documented the cases of anti-Asian violence, harassment, and discrimination during the COVID-19 pandemic. See https://stopaapihate.org.

See also Janelle Wong and Karthick Ramakrishinan, "Anti-Asian Hate Incidents and the Broader Landscape of Racial Bias," *AAPI Data*, March 30, 2021, https://aapidata.com/blog/cross-racial-march2021-survey/?fbclid=IwAR0mEtADeTLNWjVblNObrVmvEoxmoFLOpJovWmLPU9wLTEWmD9q843j8YrY.

According to their survey, similar rates of reported experience with hate incidents were shown among different communities of color in 2021.

Given the persistent significance of church in the larger Korean diaspora in the United States, it is nonetheless assuring to see some self-proclaimed evangelical pastors and church leaders finally raising their collective voices against racism as a matter of faith. This can be considered an encouraging sign when many Christian leaders still keep silent or take a bystander stance on racism because they consider engaging in conversations on racism "too political," let alone considering antiracism work as part of ministry. This is particularly so when leaders of a mainline Korean megachurch in the Atlanta area decided not to participate in the ecumenical vigil service for the victims of the Atlanta mass shooting, because the Asian women victims worked at "massage spas"[12] insinuating that they were sex workers. Given that less than twenty out of the approximately two-hundred Korean ethnic churches in the Atlanta area joined the ecumenical vigil service or publicly condemned this atrocious incident, this megachurch must not be alone in its reasoning. Though not entirely surprising, it is profoundly disheartening and disturbing that prominent church leaders refused to publicly grieve the victims' deaths due to their alleged profession as sex workers. The victims of the brutal murder were deemed *ungrievable* lives.

While the context in which grieving is discussed in Judith Butler's *Frames of War* is "conventional" warfare, her take on "ungrievable lives" helps us to understand the rendering of the Atlanta mass shooting victims as publicly ungrievable. Ungrievable lives, Butler argues, are "those that cannot be lost, and cannot be destroyed, because they already inhabit a lost and destroyed zone."[13] In the context of war, when ungrievable lives are "destroyed," "nothing is destroyed," because they are "ontologically, and from the start, already lost and destroyed."[14] Like ungrievable lives lost and destroyed in war, when Asian women's lives were lost and destroyed by horrific violence, there is nothing to grieve because they were "already lost and destroyed." This resonates with what Hye-Kyung Kang says about Asian women victims being treated only as "sex workers, or even immoral temptresses, devoid of humanity" in news headlines and reports.[15] In the eyes of the Korean megachurch leaders, they were already without humanity. Thus, their humanity was not lost by the shootings. Their lives were not publicly grievable because grievability is "a presupposition for the life that matters."[16] To put it differently, their lives did not matter and therefore their lives were ungrievable. When Korean church leaders refused to publicly grieve the victims of the Atlanta spa shootings because of their perceived profession, they rejected seeing them as persons whose lives mattered. They refused to mourn their deaths. The victims were not considered worthy of

---

[12] This information was shared by a member of the said Korean megachurch, who attended in the meeting that decided not to attend the vigil service for the stated reason.

[13] Judith Butler, *Frames of War* (New York: Verso Books, 2016), Introduction, Kindle.

[14] Butler, *Frames of War*, Introduction, Kindle.

[15] Hye-Kyung Kang, "Racist, Colonialist and Misogynist Narrative Abets Violence Against Asian Women," *The Seattle Times*, March 18, 2021, https://www.seattletimes.com/opinion/racist-colonialist-and-misogynist-narrative-abets-violence-against-asian-women.

[16] Butler, *Frames of War*, Introduction, Kindle.

being considered victims of anti-Asian violence because their lives did not matter to the church leaders.

It is necessary to note, however, that the stance taken by the evangelical Korean pastors and church leaders after having an "awakening moment" is evidently different from that of the megachurch that decided not to attend the vigil service. At the same time, it is ironic and unsettling: While they stand together in their condemnation of racist violence and discrimination, most of them have not denounced other forms of oppression, exploitation, and discrimination that affect women of Asian descent. Most evangelical pastors and church leaders have rarely spoken against sexism, heteropatriarchy, homophobia, classism, and state violence that have affected Asian/American women, particularly those in the low wage service sector, as well as sexual and gender minorities. Some of them have been bystanders, remaining silent about these systemic matters, and others have inflicted harms through words and actions that harbor prejudice and discrimination. For instance, a Christian organization in Korea that has spoken against LGBTQI people issued a statement denouncing racism as a "challenge to God," expressing condolences to the victims of the Atlanta mass shooting and Koreans living in the United States. This organization has deplored racism saying that "the Bible prohibits the killing and commands no discrimination against people," while opposing the passing of an anti-discrimination bill in Korea and condemning homosexuality as a sin against God.[17] As such, the self-contradictory, dubious positions taken by some evangelical Christian leaders cannot be unnoticed. Although they say they care about the victims of discrimination and violence, they only address racism as if it is neatly separated from other forms of oppression. Korean pastors and church leaders who say they condemn racism without denouncing misogyny, heteropatriarchy, homophobia, "whorephobia," and class hierarchy can only engender harm in the lives of women in the Korean diaspora. They cannot dismantle anti-Asian racism while disempowering marginalized members within their own community. If Korean ethnic churches are to work against anti-Asian racism, they should not pick and choose which "Koreans" or "Asians" they want to protect from violence and racism, as if a person is affected by different forms of oppression in a compartmentalized way. This has further implications for building solidarity across differences because we must ask what kind of solidarity work we are seeking to forge and for who and for what.

---

[17] Daewoong Lee, "Deep Condolences to the Victims of Atlanta Shootings and to Korean Americans," *Christian Today,* March 19, 2021, https://www.christiantoday.co.kr/news/338864.

The Confines of Antiracism Work: Minority Nationalism and "National Belonging" in a Settler Colonial Nation-State

The kind of antiracism work recently advocated and engaged in by evangelical Korean Christians resonates with the antiracism work grounded in minority nationalism. In the midst of social movements of the 1960s and 1970s in the United States, minority nationalism emerged as a "part of the epistemological challenge to racist and colonial legacies of Western thought."[18] This minority nationalism is based on the "internal colonial model" that provided a "comparative analytic that linked the various nationalist movements in the United States."[19] According to this model, differentially racialized groups are deemed as "internally colonized people," similar to discrete and comparable nation-states. As Grace Kyungwon Hong and Roderick Ferguson state, this internal colonial model provided nationalists of color both "a broad narrative for how the United States produced racial divisions and inequalities," and "a comparative framework for understanding those divisions and inequalities at the same time as it furnished a blueprint for coalition."[20] The minority nationalists' view of coalition is, then, based on the understanding of different yet equivalent violence against minority groups sanctioned by the United States. Like the nationalism that served as a force to overthrow colonial powers in the nineteenth and twentieth centuries, minority nationalism can forcefully rally people based on common "racial" or "ethnic" identity to fight against racism in the United States. It does not, however, challenge "patriarchy, nationalism, and capitalism as normative systems."[21] Nor does it take into account differences along the lines of gender, sexuality, and racialized class hierarchies that exist within racialized communities, therefore further rendering those who are most vulnerable and precarious within respective communities invisible.[22] Accordingly, a racial coalition built on minority nationalism can be limited in that it is driven by "a fraternal politics across race, ethnicity, and nation aimed at heteropatriarchal retrieval."[23] Some of the antiracism work that has gained a momentum in Asian American communities, including the larger Korean diaspora during the COVID-19 pandemic, echoes the idea of minority nationalism that stresses singular racial identity as mobilizing force and its corresponding notion of national belonging. One common thread that runs through the notion of "national belonging" as a strategy to combat anti-Asian racism is the

---

[18] Grace Kyungwon Hong and Roderick A. Ferguson, "Introduction," in *Strange Affinities: The Gender and Sexual Politics of Comparative Racialization*, eds. Grace Kyungwon Hong and Roderick A. Ferguson (Durha, NC; London: Duke University Press, 2011), 6.

[19] Hong and Ferguson, "Introduction," 7.

[20] Hong and Ferguson, "Introduction," 8.

[21] Hong and Ferguson, "Introduction," 3.

[22] Gayatri Gopinath's discussion of minority nationalism in the Indian diasporic community in New York City also shows the continuation of this dynamic well. See Gayatri Gopinath, "Nostalgia, Desire, and Diaspora," *Positions: East Asia Cultures Critique* 5, no. 2 (Fall 1997): 467-489.

[23] Hong and Ferguson, "Introduction," 8.

grand narrative of the United States as the country of immigrants and its accompanying myth of Asians as a model minority. In such a narrative, the trans-Atlantic slave trade, the genocide of the Indigenous people, US wars and military involvement in Asia, and "Islamophobia" as anti-Muslim racism and hostility against Islam are erased.

While claiming national belonging or being American in the work of antiracism can be a "direct reaction to the American tendency to see Asian Americans as perpetual foreigners," it helps maintain "the importance of national borders" and the dominance of "America."[24] Such emphasis on national belonging as a strategy to combat anti-Asian racism aligns with what is called official, or state-recognized US antiracism. Discussing three successive state-recognized US antiracisms—"racial liberalism (1940s to 1960s), liberal multiculturalism (1980s to 1990s), and neoliberal multiculturalism (2000s)"—Jodi Melamed argues that official antiracisms generate "conditions that have required the health and the security of the U.S. state to be one of the primary goals of antiracism."[25] State-recognized antiracisms focus on the symbolic and ideological as sites of politics precisely because such official antiracism protects, rather than threatens, "material inequality." The current "neoliberal multiculturalism" era reinforces "the abstraction of both wealthy and poor Asian North Americans,"[26] erasing critical differences among them. While disconnected from material reality and other anti-oppression work, antiracism work within the frame of neoliberal multiculturalism may still bring "symbolic" changes in representation and visibility, but it does so without bringing about substantial changes to the existing material conditions, let alone transforming them. Enhancing visibility and representation is important but inadequate if it is detached from the material reality under which many Asian/Americans, particularly women who are in the low wage service sector and those who are undocumented, struggle daily to survive while being exposed to often demeaning and violent working conditions. As Melamed has aptly put it, what is needed is "a persistent critique of representations of difference that make no difference."[27] Simply calling for state-recognized antiracism work can further serve those who are already privileged in the racialized class hierarchy without making any meaningful changes in the lives of those who fall outside the confines of such privileged normativity and conformity. As such, disconnecting anti-Asian racism neatly from other forms of exploitation and oppression does not help underprivileged Asian/Americans who are at the bottom of a racialized class hierarchy, including those who are undocumented as well as gender and

---

[24] Janet Hoskins and Viet Thanh Nguyen discuss such a "domestic focus" in claiming America and its implications in the context of Asian American Studies and its relation to American Studies. See Janet Hoskins and Viet Thanh Nguyen, *Transpacific Studies: Framing an Emerging Field* (Intersections: Asian and Pacific American Transcultural Studies) (Honolulu: University of Hawai'i Press, 2014), Introduction, Kindle.

[25] Jodi Melamed, *Represent and Destroy: Rationalizing Violence in the New Racial Capitalism* (Minneapolis, MN: University of Minnesota Press, 2011), Introduction, Kindle.

[26] Iyko Day, *Alien Capital* (Durham, NC: Duke University Press, 2016), chap. 4, Kindle.

[27] Melamed, *Represent and Destroy*, Epilogue, Kindle.

sexual minorities in the larger Asian American communities. Rather, it can be harmful, for it can blame them as "undeserving" victims of anti-Asian violence for being who they are and what they do or not do. Combating anti-Asian racism solely based on shared racial identity also affects solidarity work. A solidarity or coalitional work that is formed based on racial or ethnic identity benefits those who are deemed "respectable, model" Asians and therefore "deserving" victims of racism while leaving unattended "undeserving" people whose identities and lives fall outside the normative activities and behaviors prescribed by society. Such solidarity work only strengthens the official antiracism work while concealing the real work ahead of us that needs to be done in order to change the material conditions of the majority of people who are precarious and vulnerable in a white supremacist, ableist, neoliberal capitalist heteropatriarchal society.

The claim to Americanness through the notion of national belonging is also based on the assumption that one becomes American through the process of Americanization. Insistence on national belonging as "American" as a primary way to increase visibility or to combat anti-Asian racism can function inadvertently, if not intentionally, to affirm that an "American" is a "white American," since "whiteness" is entrenched in "Americanness." Taking on belonging as (white) American means participating in anti-blackness, settler colonialism, and imperialist violence, regardless of one's "intention." As Deepa Iyer argues, Americanization takes place through anti-blackness. What she means is that Americanization entails "accepting, internalizing, perpetuating the racist images and narratives about Blacks…"[28] It also means that, whether one intends to or not, one becomes a member of a settler colonial state. Reflecting on the Atlanta spa shootings in relation to US wars in Asia and European colonization, Viet Thanh Nguyen shares the story of the Cherokee people being expelled from Georgia in 1838 and the Trail of Tears. Then, he poignantly says, the Asian victims "may or may not have known of this history. But when Asian immigrants and refugees come to claim our share of the American Dream, this history is also what we claim. And sometimes this history claims us."[29] Asian/American claims of national belonging as "American" and as "responsible citizens" require a difficult yet necessary conversation on settler colonialism in relation to racialization of Asian/Americans in the United States, non-Native racialized people acquiring citizenship, having a "good" job, and reproducing next generations have direct and indirect implications for Indigenous people's ongoing struggles against settler colonialism and their work for sovereignty and self-determination. As Quynh Nhu Le

---

[28] Deepa Iyer, *We Too Sing America: South Asian, Arab, Muslim, and Sikh Immigrants Shape Our Multiracial Future* (New York: The New Press, 2015), 104. Nadia Kim also discusses the process of Americanization for Asian/Americans, including Korean/Americans, taking place even before their arrival in the U.S. during the cold war era due to U.S. imperialism's role in "immigrants' transnational understandings of 'race' and their related identities." See Nadia Y. Kim, *Imperial Citizens: Koreans and Race from Seoul to LA* (Stanford: Stanford University Press, 2008).

[29] Viet Thanh Nguyen, "From Colonialism to Covid: Viet Thanh Nguyen on the Rise of Anti-Asian Violence," *The Guardian*, April 3, 2021, https://www.theguardian.com/books/2021/apr/03/from-colonialism-to-covid-viet-thanh-nguyen-on-the-rise-of-anti-asian-violence.

aptly asks, we need to probe "how to register and theorize the role of non-Native racialized communities within the processes of settlement."[30]

In the following, I will briefly mention some differing perspectives on Asian/Americans' relation to settler colonialism offered by Asian American studies scholars as a first step to engage such critical probing, which is much needed for solidarity work. One perspective defines Asian/Americans as settlers of color who benefit from and are invested in settler colonialism by delineating a clear binary of settlers and natives. For instance, by defining Asian migrants in Hawai'i as "settlers of color," Candace Fujikane argues that while Asian migrants did not migrate to become settlers, it is important to acknowledge "the ways that they [Asian migrants and their descendants] are beneficiaries of US settler colonialism," and how "early Asian settlers were both active agents in the making of their own histories and unwitting recruits swept into the service of empire."[31] For Fujikane, what defines "the status of Asians as settlers" is not "colonial intent" but rather "the historical context of U.S. colonialism of which they unknowingly became a part."[32]

In their powerful critique of the "metaphorization" of decolonization as an effort to decenter settler perspective in educational settings, Eve Tuck and Wayne Yang argue that the decolonial desires of different groups of people can "similarly be entangled in resettlement, reoccupation, and reinhabitation that actually further settler colonialism," since this structure is built on the settler-native-slave triad.[33] They point out how those who enter or are brought into the settler colonial nation-state through "colonial pathways," commonly described as "immigration," are "invited to be a settler" in some cases or are rendered an "illegal, criminal presence" in other cases.[34] Tuck and Yang continue by saying that "the attainment of equal legal and cultural entitlements is actually an investment in settler colonialism."[35] If "becoming white" is not an option for people of color, they can "become a brown settler," or a "subordinate settler."[36] Sunera Thobani also argues that "the expansion of the institution of citizenship to incorporate Asian Americans more fully can simultaneously deepen the practices that organize the destruction of Indigenous sovereignty."[37]

---

[30] Quynh Nhu Le, *Unsettled Solidarities: Asian and Indigenous Cross-Representations in the Americas* (Philadelphia, PA: Temple University Press, 2019), 9.

[31] Candace Fujikane, "Introduction: Asian Settler Colonialism in the US Colony of Hawai'i," in *Asian Settler Colonialism: From Local Governance to the Habits of Everyday Life in Hawai'i*, eds. Candace Fujikane and Jonathan Y. Okamura (Honolulu: University of Hawai'i Press, 2008), 7.

[32] Fujikane, "Introduction," 20.

[33] Eve Tuck and K. Wayne Yang, "Decolonization Is Not a Metaphor," *Decolonization: Indigeneity, Education, and Society* 1, no. 1 (2012): 1.

[34] Tuck and Yang, "Decolonization Is Not a Metaphor," 17.

[35] Tuck and Yang, "Decolonization Is Not a Metaphor," 18.

[36] Tuck and Yang, "Decolonization Is Not a Metaphor," 18.

[37] Sunera Thobani, "Navigating Colonial Pitfalls: Race, Citizenship, and the Politics of 'South Asian Canadian' Feminism," in *Asian American Feminisms and Women of Color Politics*, eds. Lynn Fujiwara and Shireen Roshanravan (Seattle: University of Washington Press, 2018), 159.

In a different vein, contending that it is unclear if a settler identity or a status can be attributed to racialized migrants including Asian immigrants outside Hawai'i, Iyko Day argues that "for slaves and racialized migrants, the degree of forced or voluntary migration or level of complicity with the settler state is ultimately secondary to their subordination under a settler colonial mode of production driven by the proprietorial logics of whiteness."[38] Paying attention to varied processes of settler colonial racialization, Day maintains that "highly differentiated populations of African slaves and Asian migrants historically represented alien rather than settler migrations."[39] Both groups were alien laborers in a settler colonial context that relied on such labor. As she makes clear, however, this shared status of being "alien" does not imply "an equivalence in the heterogeneous racial experience of African slaves and Asian migrants."[40] Instead, their "unsovereign alien status was a precondition of their exploitation and intersects with the multiple economic logics that require and reproduce alien-ness in settler colonies."[41] In the more recent context of immigration reforms in which both the upsurge of skilled and affluent migrants from Asia and the similar increase of undocumented migrants have taken place, neoliberal multiculturalism, which is one of the official antiracisms discussed by Melamed, "facilitates the fulfillment of settler colonial capitalism through the migrant labor system."[42] As Day argues, such a "sexualized and racialized migrant system" is central to the settler colonial mode of capitalist reproduction.[43]

A further perspective is found in Sunaina Maira and Magid Shihade's efforts to address the experiences of Asian immigrants in relation to Indigenous peoples both in the United States and overseas in the context of Asian American studies' core debates on citizenship and social movements. Drawing from Mahmood Mamdani's arguments on settler colonialism in South Africa, Maira and Shihade pay attention to the logics of the colonial-settler state rather than heavily emphasizing settler identity. According to Maira and Shihade, Mamdani differentiates the "conservative nationalist approach" that defines every immigrant as a settler from "radical nationalism," which distinguishes between "settlers whose privileges were legally guaranteed by the settler state, and immigrants who had varying degrees of racialized privilege."[44] For Maira and Shihade, what Mamdani suggests is that the problem is not really the settler, but "the settler state, the legal setup that guaranteed settler privilege. . . . The enemy from this point of view was everyone who defended the

---

[38] Day, *Alien Capital*, Introduction, Kindle.

[39] Day, *Alien Capital*, Introduction, Kindle.

[40] Day, *Alien Capital*, Introduction, Kindle.

[41] Day, *Alien Capital*, Introduction, Kindle.

[42] Day, *Alien Capital*, chap. 4, Kindle. See also John Park, "Emergent Divides: Class and Position among Asian Americans." *CR: The New Centennial Review* 6, no. 2 (2006): 57–72. Cited in Day, *Alien Capital*, Kindle.

[43] Day, *Alien Capital*, Epilogue, Kindle.

[44] Mahmood Mamdani, *Good Muslim, Bad Muslim*, 228. Quoted in Sunaina Maira, Magid Shihade, "Meeting Asian/Arab American Studies: Thinking Race, Empire, and Zionism in the U.S.," *Journal of Asian American Studies* 9, no. 2 (June 2006): 134.

power of the settler state."⁴⁵ As Maira and Shihade argue, considering settler colonialism as "part of U.S. imperial culture deepens the critique of multiculturalism within Asian American studies and challenges not just the construction of the 'model minority' but the very notion of inclusion within, rather than opposition to, a settler state built on genocide and slavery."⁴⁶ As Maira and Shihade underscore, Mamdani's analysis of settler colonialism further helps us to understand Zionism as a settler colonialist ideology by connecting it to the United States's role in supporting settler colonialism overseas, which has to do with the formation of United States as a settler colonial nation-state.

These perspectives on settler colonialism in relation to the experiences and racialization of Asian/Americans help us to ask about the implications of claiming "Americanness" through "national belonging" to a settler colonial nation-state as well as the challenges that arise in the solidarity work. Though further discussion of this issue is beyond the confines of this essay, such interrogation also requires us to critically interrogate the theological underpinnings of settler colonialism, such as the notions of chosenness and divine providence that are frequently proclaimed and invoked through sermons, Bible studies, and everyday usage of languages and metaphors in ecclesiastical context.

Intersectional Realities of "Anti-Asian" Violence

The Atlanta spa shooting spree shook Asian American communities including the Korean diasporic community, alarming them about the enormity of anti-Asian violence, particularly ones that target Asian/American women. At the same time, the limits of antiracism work based on common racial identity within Asian American communities including the Korean diaspora have been revealed. As racial justice advocates have rightly spoken and written, the brutal murders of six Asian women at massage spas showed how Orientalism, gendered racism, racialized misogyny, racialized class hierarchy, US wars and militarism in Asia, and anti-sex-work sentiment are interwoven. It was racialized gendered violence that took place in a workplace that is stigmatized in the Korean diaspora in the United States. It has become indisputable that we cannot talk about anti-Asian racism and violence without mentioning other intersecting forms of exploitation and oppression, including necropolitical labor such as sex work, which is "the extraction of labor" premised on "the possibilities of death, rather than the ultimate event of death itself."⁴⁷ The treatment of Asian women as "prostitutes" in the United States, especially women from China, goes back to the late nineteenth century. The Page Act of 1875 was the first federal

---

⁴⁵ Sunaina Maira and Magid Shihade, "Meeting Asian/Arab American Studies: Thinking Race, Empire, and Zionism in the U.S." *Journal of Asian American Studies* 9, no. 2 (June 2006): 135.
⁴⁶ Maira and Shihade, "Meeting Asian/Arab American Studies," 135.
⁴⁷ Jin-Kyung Lee, *Service Economies: Militarism, Sex Work, and Migrant Labor in South Korea* (Minneapolis: University of Minnesota Press, 2010), 7.

immigration law in the United States that was created to ban Chinese women from entering the United States based on their alleged sexual immorality. The ways in which Asian women are viewed and treated particularly as "sex workers" by the white male gaze also has to do with US foreign policy in Asia as illustrated by wars and the presence of military bases across Asia.[48] In other words, the Atlanta mass shooting and other cases of anti-Asian violence, especially those that target Asian women, show that the workings of insidious racialized misogyny and anti-sex-work sentiment are related to the long-standing history of US wars in Asia in conjunction with US-led capitalist globalization. These military actions and wars foreground and perpetuate anti-Asian racism and particularly racialized gendered violence through the pernicious stereotypes of Asian women as prostitutes, mail-order brides, or factory workers with nimble fingers, perpetuating hypersexualization, sexual objectification, and fetishization of Asian women. Without addressing the links between anti-Asian misogyny, US immigration and foreign policies, and US military presence in Asia, calls to stop anti-Asian racism will only have a limited impact. In other words, the goals of dismantling anti-Asian racism cannot be pursued discretely from other forms of struggles because oppressive powers have always joined their forces against marginalized people. This indicates that opposing anti-Asian racism necessitates an approach that recognizes how these struggles are intertwined and that requires solutions that are also multifaceted. As Audre Lorde so aptly put it, "There is no such thing as a single-issue struggle because we do not live single-issue lives."[49]

Furthermore, Asian women who are sex workers are ostracized, alienated, shamed, and shunned in their own ethnic communities. As I mentioned earlier, they are considered disposable and publicly ungrievable lives. What we need to ask is, as Grace Cho says, why "sex workers are treated as disposable"?[50] As Jin-Kyung Lee argues, sex workers' disposability is "an integral element of prostitution as an occupation."[51] As part of necropolitical labor, sex work and the sex worker are one of the "most disposable (labor) commodities."[52] Both the white gunman who targeted Asian women specifically working at massage spas and leaders of a Korean

---

[48] See Christine Ahn, Terry K. Park, and Kathleen Richards, "Anti-Asian Violence is Rooted in US Empire," *The Nation*, March 19, 2021, https://www.thenation.com/article/world/anti-asian-violence-empire/.

[49] Audre Lorde, "Learning from the '60s," in *Sister Outsider: Essays and Speeches* (New York: Ten Speed Press, 1984), 138.

[50] In relation to this question, Grace Cho is also asking, "why so many immigrant women and women of color have jobs that put them at greater risk of sexual violence," jobs that include not only the "overtly sexualized, like massage-parlor work, but also domestic work and food industry work." See "WORDS UNSPOKEN: Grace M. Cho on anti-Asian violence, mental health, and the livingness of trauma," *Artforum*, May 25, 2021, https://www.artforum.com/interviews/grace-m-cho-on-anti-asian-violence-mental-illness-and-the-livingness-of-trauma-85778.

[51] Lee, *Service Economies*, 6.

[52] Lee, *Service Economies*, 7.

megachurch conflated "massage workers" with "sex workers."[53] As Esther K, a co-director of Red Canary Song, says, such conflation "without any nuance is very specific to anti-Asian racism against Asian women."[54] She says that Asian women who work in spas face "the sexism and whorephobia" interwoven with anti-Asian racism and anti-immigrant sentiments.[55] The victims were targeted based on the conflation of massage workers with sex workers "without any nuance." This also raises the question of why there are so many attempts to not name or acknowledge sex work. Grace M. Cho attributes this distancing to "the fear that acknowledging a person's status as a sex worker will deny them their victimhood," as well as having to do with the shame and stigma attached to sex work.[56] Horrifying incidents like the Atlanta spa killings cannot be adequately discussed without interrogating this stigma and shame as well as, verbal, physical and sexual violence in the workplace, police intimidation and violence against sex workers, and the discrimination that Asian spa workers face whether they participate in sex work or not.[57]

Rejecting a Theology of Decency

While the "purity culture" prevalent in evangelical Christianity was scrutinized in relation to the white gunman's presumed motivation and background, a theology of decency prevailing in Korean ethnic churches has not been critically interrogated. The victims of the mass shooting were further victimized by a theology of decency that justified some churches' refusal to publicly grieve them. Such theology contributes to either reinforcing the idea that the victims of the shootings don't deserve proper grieving in public due to their alleged labor as sex workers or excessively stressing the point that the victims are "Asian" and that they sacrificed for families as grandmothers, mothers, daughters, aunts, and sisters. The latter position refrains from mentioning the victims' work but highlights them as sacrificial mothers, filial daughters and sisters, and hardworking immigrants. It might be a position with good intentions, but its effects include the reinscription of the respectability narrative, which in turn reinforces the theology of decency. In order for the victims to

---

[53] See Kang, "Racist, colonialist and misogynist narrative abets violence against Asian women." https://www.seattletimes.com/opinion/racist-colonialist-and-misogynist-narrative-abets-violence-against-asian-women/?fbclid=IwAR2V4t6ErPaTwQyV_U6DK6thzdXQ8lmq5wLfVqjUTVdLG7lqMdV5obsVUdI.

[54] Marie Solis, "'A specific kind of racism': Atlanta shootings fuel fears over anti-sex-work ideology," *The Guardian*, March 18, 2021, https://www.theguardian.com/us-news/2021/mar/18/atlanta-spa-shootings-anti-sex-worker-racism-sexism.

[55] Angelina Chapin, "Every Day, Massage-Parlor Workers Face Violence," *The Cut*, March 19, 2021, https://www.thecut.com/2021/03/every-day-massage-parlor-workers-face-violence.html.

[56] "Words Unspoken: Grace M. Cho on anti-Asian violence, mental health, and the livingness of trauma," *Artforum*, May 25, 2021, https://www.artforum.com/interviews/grace-m-cho-on-anti-asian-violence-mental-illness-and-the-livingness-of-trauma-85778.

[57] See "Words Unspoken."

"fit" the narrative of deserving oppressed peoples, connections to the heteropatriarchal family must somehow be made to illustrate respectability and deservingness. To fall into "indecency," as the late feminist theologian Marcella Althaus-Reid said, is "to fall outside the tenuous definition of men respecting women's lives, a dangerous development, especially for poor women."[58] Such a focus on respectability is in tandem with the binary of "virgin and whore," also a characteristic of theology of decency. Theology of decency reinforces and is underpinned by sexual mores, legal status, and the model minority myth and path. If "decency" or "respectability" is a condition for a public form of grievability or the condition required to qualify as a human being, more specifically as a "woman," a theology that warrants it must be rejected by Christians, for it renders some people ungrievable, distinguished from other grievable lives.

Whether or not women fit with such gender and sexual normativity and conformity, the theology of decency is harmful to them, for it disciplines and regulates women's lives, further determining if their lives are publicly grievable or not. Any theology that engenders and perpetuates stigma and shame in the name of decency, holiness, or normalcy is discursive violence, which has material effects, for it justifies and reinforces material inequality by rationalizing that indecent or deviant women deserve to be destitute. She alone is solely responsible for her indigent life, although she does not have a way out in a racist, ableist, heteropatriarchal capitalist society. Furthermore, her "indecent" life is considered a threat to the church, to the family, and even to the nation for what M. Jacqui Alexander calls "irresponsible citizenship."[59] Antiracism work grounded in minority nationalism supports the theology of decency by undergirding respectability narratives such as "we are hardworking immigrant families," "we are law abiding and responsible citizens or legal residents," "we too are American," "we are faithful fellow Christian." In such respectability narratives, the stories of diasporic people are narrowed down to one grand narrative that idealizes "the American dream" in the "land of opportunity" as if all co-ethnic people can toss out their differences as soon as they land in the United States.

Rejecting a theology of decency is an indispensable step in forging Christian praxis of solidarity across differences. It means standing in solidarity with sex workers and hearing what they need, which may go against what the dominant Korean diasporic community upholds as worthy and respectable. It also necessitates supporting policies that assist instead of further harming them. For instance, supporting decriminalization of sex work, not relying on law enforcement, investing in affordable healthcare and housing, advocating gun control, and challenging respectability narratives that are consumed and promoted in faith communities can be part of such work. Rejecting a theology of decency also entails refusal to accept or

---

[58] Marcella Althaus-Reid, "On Wearing Skirts Without Underwear: 'Indecent Theology Challenging the Liberation Theology of the Pueblo'. Poor Women Contesting Christ," *Feminist Theology* 20 (1999): 42.

[59] M. Jacqui Alexander, *Pedagogies of Crossing: Meditations on Feminism, Sexual Politics, Memory, and the Sacred* (Durham, NC: Duke University Press, 2006), 23.

perpetuate the heteropatriarchal family with its binary gender ideology, in conjunction with refusal to serve as a model minority in the white supremacist heteropatriarchal capitalist society. Rejecting a theology of decency also means engaging in a critical examination of what it means to "belong" or "be included" in a settler colonial nation-state as a presumed model minority, while challenging the settler state that continues to exploit alien labor. Rejecting such theology also helps to imagine a world that is not predicated on the necropolitical labor of the expendable population. Most of all, by rejecting a theology of decency, Christians make an option for the God who sides with those who are deemed undeserving and who are most precarious. In making an option for such God, we also participate in mourning the loss of someone not because we share the same gender and/or ethnic identity nor because our lives are in proximity. Instead, we participate in mourning to collectively grieve for "the life cut short, the life that should have had a chance to live more, the value that person has carried now in the lives of others, the wound that permanently transforms those who live on."[60] Such collective work of grief in the face of unrelenting violence is an integral part of the Christian praxis of solidarity in our real, messy, interdependent, and interconnected world.

Discussion Questions

As this chapter opened with a series of questions, I want to close it by posing a set of questions for further discussion that can lead to praxis, because the work of solidarity to end multiple, intersecting forms of oppression, exploitation, and discrimination needs to continue both inside and outside of Christian faith communities.

1. What are the ways in which antiracism work that is solely based on common racial identity is stressed in Christian ministry (in various forms) in which you are involved? In such a ministry, who is included, and who may be excluded?
2. What respectability narratives within ecclesiastical context reinforce and are reinforced by a "theology of decency"? How can Christians resist such theology?
3. What does "belonging" mean to you? What nation-state, faith community, diasporic community, etc., do you feel you belong to—or are distanced or excluded from? How important is "belonging," and why? In what ways does "national belonging" empower or exclude people?
4. This essay argues that the antiracism work that is primarily based on common racial identity cannot adequately address anti-Asian violence. What kind of "antiracism" work, then, should be advocated and practiced in and beyond the Christian faith community?

---

[60] George Yancy, "Judith Butler: Mourning Is a Political Act Amid the Pandemic and Its Disparities," *Truthout*, April 30, 2020, https://truthout.org/articles/judith-butler-mourning-is-a-political-act-amid-the-pandemic-and-its-disparities/.

Bibliography

Ahn, Christine, Terry K. Park, and Kathleen Richards. 2021. Anti-Asian Violence is Rooted in US Empire. *The Nation*, April 1. https://www.thenation.com/article/world/anti-asian-violence-empire/.

Althaus-Reid, Marcella. 1999. On Wearing Skirts Without Underwear: 'Indecent Theology Challenging the Liberation Theology of the Pueblo'. Poor Women Contesting Christ. *Feminist Theology* 7 (20): 39–51. https://doi.org/10.1177/096673509900702004.

Alexander, M. Jacqui. 2006. *Pedagogies of Crossing: Meditations on Feminism, Sexual Politics, Memory, and the Sacred*. Durham, NC: Duke University Press.

Butler, Judith. 2016. *Frames of War: When Is Life Grievable?* New York: Verso Books.

Carty, Linda E., and Chandra Talpade Mohanty. 2018. Introduction: An Archive of Feminist Activism Conversations with Margo Okazawa-Rey, Angela Y. Davis, Himani Bannerji, Minnie Bruce Pratt, Amina Mama, Aida Hernandez-Castillo, and Zillah Eisenstein. In *Feminist Freedom Warriors: Genealogies, Justice Politics, and Hope*, ed. Chandra Talpade Mohanty and Linda E. Carty, 1–14. Chicago: Haymarket Books.

Chapin, Angelina. 2021. Every Day, Massage-Parlor Workers Face Violence. *The Cut*, March 19. https://www.thecut.com/2021/03/every-day-massage-parlor-workers-face-violence.html.

Choi, Byeong-Ho. 2021. Urgent Message Regarding the Recent Hate Crimes Against People of Asian Descent. *Columbus Korean Presbyterian Church*, March 21. https://www.kpccoh.org/nanum/17988.

Cho, Grace M. 2006. Diaspora of Camptown: The Forgotten War's Monstrous Family. *Women's Studies Quarterly* 34 (1-2): 309–331.

WORDS UNSPOKEN: Grace M. 2021. Cho on anti-Asian violence, mental health, and the livingness of trauma. *Artforum*, May 25. https://www.artforum.com/interviews/grace-m-cho-on-anti-asian-violence-mental-illness-and-the-livingness-of-trauma-85778.

Cohen, Cathy J. 2004. Deviance as Resistance: A New Research Agenda for the Study of Black Politics. *Du Bois Review: Social Science Research on Race* 1 (1): 27–45.

Day, Iyko. 2016. *Alien Capital*. Durham, NC: Duke University Press. Kindle.

Fujikane, Candace. 2008. Introduction: Asian Settler Colonialism in the US Colony of Hawai'i. In *Asian Settler Colonialism: From Local Governance to the Habits of Everyday Life in Hawai'i*, ed. Candace Fujikane and Jonathan Y. Okamura, 1–42. Honolulu: University of Hawai'i Press.

Gopinath, Gayatri. 1997. Nostalgia, Desire, and Diaspora. *Positions: East Asia Cultures Critique* 5 (2): 467–489.

Hong, Jane. 2022. The L.A. Uprisings Sparked an Evangelical Racial Reckoning. *The Washington Post*, April 29. https://www.washingtonpost.com/outlook/2022/04/29/la-uprisings-sparked-an-evangelical-racial-reckoning.

Iyer, Deepa. 2015. *We Too Sing America: South Asian, Arab, Muslim, and Sikh Immigrants Shape Our Multiracial Future*. New York: The New Press.

Lee, Jin-Kyung. 2010. *Service Economies: Militarism, Sex Work, and Migrant Labor in South Korea*. Minneapolis: University of Minnesota Press.

Kang, Hye-Kyung. 2021. Racist, Colonialist and Misogynist Narrative Abets Violence Against Asian Women. *The Seattle Times*, March 18. https://www.seattletimes.com/opinion/racist-colonialist-and-misogynist-narrative-abets-violence-against-asian-women/?fbclid=IwAR2V4t6ErPaTwQyV_U6DK6thzdXQ8lmq5wLfVqjUTVdLG7lqMdV5obsVUdI.

Kim, Anderson. 2021a. After the Atlanta Shootings, Korean Ethnic Churches Say It is Now Our Work to Combat Racial Discrimination. *Christian Today*, March 22. https://www.christiantoday.co.kr/news/338895.

Kim, Eungsun. 2021b. Asian American United Methodists Issue a Statement Condemning Hate Crimes against Asians in the United States. *UMC News*, March 18. https://www.umnews.org/ko/news/asians-united-methodists-condemn-the-rise-of-anti-asian-violence-in-us.

Kim, Jodi. 2015. The Ending Is Not an Ending at All: On the Militarized and Gendered Diasporas of Korean Transnational Adoption and the Korean War. *Positions: Asia Critique* 23 (4): 807–835.

Kim, Nadia Y. 2008. *Imperial Citizens: Koreans and Race from Seoul to LA*. Stanford, CA: Stanford University Press.

Hong, Grace Kyungwon, and Roderick A. Ferguson. 2011. Introduction. In *Strange Affinities: The Gender and Sexual Politics of Comparative Racialization*, ed. Grace Kyungwon Hong and Roderick A. Ferguson, 1–22. Durham, NC: Duke University.

Hoskins, Janet, and Viet Thanh Nguyen. 2014. *Transpacific Studies: Framing an Emerging Field (Intersections: Asian and Pacific American Transcultural Studies)*. Honolulu: University of Hawaii Press. Kindle.

Le, Quynh Nhu. 2019. *Unsettled Solidarities: Asian and Indigenous Cross-Representations in the Americas*. Philadelphia, PA: Temple University Press.

Lee, Daewoong. 2021. Deep Condolences to the Victims of Atlanta Shootings and to Korean Americans. *Christian Today*, March 19. https://www.christiantoday.co.kr/news/338864.

Lorde, Audre. 1984. Learning from the '60s. In *Sister Outsider: Essays and Speeches*. New York: Ten Speed Press.

Maira, Sunaina, and Magid Shihade. 2006. Meeting Asian/Arab American Studies: Thinking Race, Empire, and Zionism in the U.S. *Journal of Asian American Studies* 9 (2): 117–140.

Mamdani, Mahmood, Good Muslim, Bad Muslim, 228. Quoted in, Sunaina Maira, and Magid Shihade. 2006. Meeting Asian/Arab American Studies: Thinking Race, Empire, and Zionism in the U.S. *Journal of Asian American Studies* 9 (2): 134.

Melamed, Jodi. 2011. *Represent and Destroy: Rationalizing Violence in the New Racial Capitalism*. Minneapolis: University of Minnesota Press. Kindle.

Nguyen, Viet Thanh. 2021. From Colonialism to Covid: Viet Thanh Nguyen on the Rise of Anti-Asian Violence. *The Guardian*, April 3. https://www.theguardian.com/books/2021/apr/03/from-colonialism-to-covid-viet-thanh-nguyen-on-the-rise-of-anti-asian-violence.

Palumbo-Liu, David. 1999. *Asian/American: Historical Crossings*. Stanford, CA: Stanford University Press.

Park, John. 2006. Emergent Divides: Class and Position among Asian Americans. *CR: The New Centennial Review* 6 (2): 57–72.

Solis, Marie. 2021. "A Specific Kind of Racism": Atlanta Shootings Fuel Fears Over Anti-Sex-Work Ideology. *The Guardian*, March 18. https://www.theguardian.com/us-news/2021/mar/18/atlanta-spa-shootings-anti-sex-worker-racism-sexism.

Thobani, Sunera. 2018. Navigating Colonial Pitfalls: Race, Citizenship, and the Politics of 'South Asian Canadian' Feminism. In *Asian American Feminisms and Women of Color Politics*, ed. Lynn Fujiwara and Shireen Roshanravan, 155–178. Seattle: University of Washington Press.

Tuck, Eve, and K. Wayne Yang. 2012. Decolonization Is Not a Metaphor. *Decolonization: Indigeneity, Education, and Society* 1 (1): 1–40.

Yancy, George. 2020. Judith Butler: Mourning Is a Political Act Amid the Pandemic and Its Disparities. *Truthout*, April 30. https://truthout.org/articles/judith-butler-mourning-is-a-political-act-amid-the-pandemic-nd-its-disparities/.

Wong, Janelle and Karthick Ramakrishnan. 2021. Anti-Asian Hate Incidents and the Broader Landscape of Racial Bias. *AAPI Data*, March 30. https://aapidata.com/blog/cross-racial-march2021-survey/?fbclid=IwAR0mEtADeTLNWjVblNObrVmvEoxmoFLOpJovWmLPU9wLTEWmD9q843j8YrY.

Part III
Rereading Memories and Creative Activism

9
Tasting Me/You: Sensory-Affective Multiracial Identity Formations

Heike Peckruhn

In this chapter, I analyze the experiences of Thainess in the United States, specifically through exploring the production and consumption of Thai food as a sensory-affective experience through which Thai racial identity is shaped and experienced.[1] *"How does it feel to be a problem?"*[2] W.E.B. DuBois stirringly asked in his exploration of blackness in the United States. Thainess in the United States is at once a problem, a felt problem for those bearing it and those encountering it. And Thainess as an embodied facet of Asianness in US racial discourse is marked by the felt particular problem of racist love, as Leslie Bow explores: *"[E]xpressed attraction has become a potent form of anti-Asian bias, reinforcing, if camouflaging, racist hate. […] racist love highlights Asian American racialization as marked by a delight that forestalls repulsion."*[3] To be, to become, to embody Thainess in the United States is

---

[1] I am grateful to the group of authors and editors in this volume, who have provided me with a most hospitable and constructive space to explore the ideas of this essay. Their suggestions made this essay stronger. The radical welcome I experienced in this space and in the larger umbrella group PANAAWTM (Pacific, Asian, and North American Asian Women in Theology and Ministry) enlivens and refreshes me. I owe a big Thank You to Kurt Blankschaen for his very generous and excellent feedback, discussion suggestions, and unconditional support, and to Debbie Creamer, for her always reliably constructive and diligent reading and insights.

[2] W.E.B. DuBois, *The Souls of Black Folk* (New York: Knopf, 1993), 7. W.E.B. DuBois's famous question frames the condition of being racially subordinated, of being socially and politically produced as problem, and points to the continuous emotional labor of being of an other-than-white race and being subjected to the violent reading practices of the other's gaze.

[3] Leslie Bow, *Racist Love: Asian Abstraction and the Pleasures of Fantasy* (Durham: Duke University Press, 2022), 7-8. Leslie Bow explores the particular "problem" of Asian Americans, who are freely adored as objects of desire, an attraction that is not the opposite, but the source and force of anti-Asian racism and violence.

H. Peckruhn (✉)
Religious Studies, Eastern Mennonite University, Harrisonburg, VA, USA
e-mail: heike.peckruhn@emu.edu

© The Author(s), under exclusive license to Springer Nature Switzerland AG 2023
K. C. Pae, B. Lee (eds.), *Embodying Antiracist Christianity*,
https://doi.org/10.1007/978-3-031-37264-3_9

living out an affective question that demands the resolve of attraction, desire, hate, repulsion, and delight. To explore this question, I am leaning on Jin Haritaworn's concept of multiracialization as the processes of bodily categorization, of belonging and racialization; processes that are ambivalent and continuous. Bodies with racial meanings emerge in social power relations that entitle some to make sense of others, to have racial knowledge of others, *and* to express and resolve their feelings. Haritaworn focuses specifically on the mixed-race body and reveals its ambiguity to be *not* a biological reality, but a socially and affectively produced knowledge.[4] Haritaworn focuses on bodies with differentially racialized parentage; I extend and appropriate their exploration of the unlearning and repeatedly re-learning of what it means to be embodied in specific racialized ways. I will look at racialization as a sensory-affective process that is continuous and multiple in the formation of variously (and sometimes strategically) employed racial identities and racial feelings in multiple, overlapping contexts.

The social, political, and economic behaviors, limits, and possibilities that materialize race for/through us are imbued with feelings—desires, cravings, repulsion, anxieties—as Frantz Fanon began framing for us.[5] Race and racism exist because our bodies are entangled in socio-political economies that make them feel real, feel significant, and mobilize us towards action.[6] And significantly, if we follow the trajectories laid out by social constructionism and affect theorists, race is *not* a biological reality, but race is something our bodies *do together to feel ourselves racially*.[7] We have feelings about race, our racialization effects and is effected through emotions, and feelings are racialized: Our emotional life is not autonomous.[8] Rather,

---

[4] Jin Haritaworn, *The Biopolitics of Mixing: Thai Multiracialities and Haunted Ascendancies* (London: Routledge, 2016).

[5] Frantz Fanon, *Black Skin, White Masks* (New York: Grove Weidenfeld, 1962).

[6] Patricia Ticineto Clough and Jean O'Malley Halley, *The Affective Turn: Theorizing the Social*. (Durham, NC: Duke University Press, 2007).

[7] Tamar Blickstein, "Affects of Racialization," in *Affective Societies: Key Concepts,* eds. Jan Slaby and Christian von Scheve (New York: Routledge, 2019), 152-166.

[8] For example, "shame" is often constructed as a generic Asian emotion in popular discourse and mental health textbooks. David H. Kim explores the nuances in "shame" and the differentiation of affect in dynamic assimilation/resistance experiences in Asian-American communities in David Haekwon Kim, "Shame and Self-Revision in Asian American Assimilation," in *Living Alterities: Phenomenology, Embodiment, and Race*, ed. Emily S. Lee (Albany: SUNY Press, 2015), 103-132. And David Eng and Shinhee Han complexify Asian-American affective life under the opaque violence of multiculturalism in David L. Eng and Shinhee Han, *Racial Melancholia, Racial Dissociation: On the Social and Psychic Lives of Asian Americans* (Durham, NC: Duke University Press, 2019). See also Cathy Park Hong, *Minor Feelings: An Asian American Reckoning* (New York: One World, 2021) for an investigation into the complexities of Asian-American affect and identity. Ann Cvetkovich also explores how affect travels along racial lines, and how feelings are racialized contextually, how the meaning of feelings, the experience of feelings, can take on particular racial group-specific dimensions (e.g., sadness among African Americans). See Ann Cvetkovich, *Depression: A Public Feeling* (Durham, NC: Duke University Press, 2012). And Berg and Ramos-Zayas explore how feelings are relationally racialized by being attributed to certain people groups according to stereotype, e.g. Andean provincial mestizos materialize in the whitened elite imagination as despotic, vulgar, servile (Ulla D. Berg and Ramos-Zayas, "Racializing Affect: A Theoretical Proposition," *Current Anthropology,* 56, no.5 (2015): 657).

affect/emotions/feelings are forces that shape our bodies and move our bodies together to do something—with, against, along, towards, and away from each other—in specific contexts. Changes in racial identities and feelings of racial belonging are contingent on available practices, language, symbols, and objects.[9]

Growing up in Germany, I did not have a "race." It was not that my brown body did not raise questions and demand labeling of its difference.[10] I grew up with socially acceptable/usable and perceivable categories that sorted national or ethnic hyphenations, assigning labels like "migrant" or "guestworker," "foreign co-citizen" or "passport-German" over against "Bio-Germans."[11] *"But what are you!?!"* Like for many others of various non-white, racially mixed, and racially othered groups, that violent demand of identification and explanation posed to me by others was also quickly internalized, leaving me perpetually unsettled in my search for belonging wherever I moved. When I first arrived in the United States, disorienting multiracializing dynamics continued—learning new vocabularies, sounds, sights, and affects, grouping me and others in different contexts.[12] The racial categories of the United States were foreign to me and were not in my linguistic and emotional repertoire, and I faced continuous encounters of dealing with the feelings of others

---

[9] Scholars theorizing affect often make distinctions between affect, emotions, and feelings, delineating various conceptual differences for their philosophical ends (e.g., to differentiate between preconscious affects and conscious emotions or intensity of feelings). These distinctions matter when affect is considered foundational in a "presocial" or "precognitive" way. It may leave a gap between affect and judgment/cognition, and certain racial feelings and associated practices could be framed unconscious, based in ignorance or lack of awareness, or a racist disposition based in culture or familial upbringing that is simply *there* (and therefore, excusable and "simply" in need of awareness and/or education, an open mind, or moments of reflection). In my chapter, I am mostly interested in the force and reinforcement of feeling race and feelings about race, and will use affect, emotion, and feeling interchangeably for readability, but want to acknowledge here the importance of recognizing affect for its biological aspects and impact on our visceral experiences and identity narratives. For theoretical distinctions and their impact, see Donovan O. Schaefer, *The Evolution of Affect Theory: The Humanities, the Sciences, and the Study of Power* (Cambridge: Cambridge University Press, 2019), and Melissa Gregg and Gregory J. Seigworth, *The Affect Theory Reader* (Durham, NC: Duke University Press, 2011). For an excellent exploration of shame and affective shaping of bodily identity, see Stephanie N. Arel, *Affect Theory, Shame, and Christian Formation* (New York: Palgrave Macmillan, 2016).

[10] Over time, there was a switching from explicitly racial coding in Nazi Germany (though still with labels and taxonomies different from the current US context) to a post-WW2 national/ethnic coded taxonomy to escape the veneer of German racism in a neo-liberal multicultural world. Racial thinking did not disappear though, even if public discourse changed the terms of the debate. See Rita Chin et al., *After the Nazi Racial State: Difference and Democracy in Germany and Europe* (Ann Arbor: University of Michigan Press, 2009).

[11] "Migrant" is an empty term—who counts as having migrant background is neither clearly defined, nor useful—except the term has power in social and political discourse and decision making. "Bio-German" and other terms emerged from comedic use by migrants to refer to non-migrant Germans and were later used as ironic self-reference by Germans, even utilized by right wing groups as a political battle term. See Mohamed Amjahid, *Unter Weissen: Was es heisst, privilegiert zu sein* (München: Hanser Berlin, 2017).

[12] The first racial categories I encountered were on various immigration and registration checklists. I was required to select for myself labels like white, black, Native American, Asian and Pacific Islander, and Hispanic origin. *"But what am I?"* Having grown up in Germany, none of those historically contextualized categories caught me in their net, nor were they part of my self-identification or experience.

who experienced me as racially ambiguous. Everyday encounters are structured by unequal power relations and enlivened by these kinds of affective legacies of imperial knowledges, creating the colonized other. I learned that the reaction of the other—the innocently presented surprise, well-meaningly staged confusion, entitled curiosity ("*I thought you were Latina/Native/Swedish*")—is the normalized reaction of the monoracial white other, the racial subject matter expert, who is entitled to not feel confused, whose sense of secured knowledge had been upset, whose feelings need to be soothed[13] ("*Ah, now I can see it in your hair/eyes/skin.*").

Race is communicated in multiple ways, though in most accounts, the visual is privileged as a technology of racialized recognition. Yet other embodied perceptions like scents, tastes, and sounds can create sensory racialized combinations that evoke visceral racialized emotions and knowledges of self/other in powerfully felt ways. Racial categories are embodied and made effective in constructing and maintaining racial dividing lines through multi-sensory processes—touch, sound, smell, and taste interrelate with and complicate visual markers of race.[14] Daily, we are immersed in specific sensory and emotional experiences that have context-specific meanings attached to them, playing a learning and disciplining game with our bodily movements, and reinforcing our experiencing ourselves as racial beings. In this continuous sensory learning, our affective attachments emerge, so we feel things about race and are made to see, touch, hear, and smell objects and others along racial lines. Creating spaces of belonging, in actual physical places, in group identities, and in personal and institutional relationships, is something we do to carve out moments and spaces that feel good, feel comforting and comfortable. How we feel about ourselves and others in specific contexts is intrinsically linked to how we are made to feel about our placement within a particular racialized group constellation and our recognition as such.[15] *Technologies* of affect are the ways in which "feeling something" is also a subject formation process that can be operationalized to differentiate: Feelings are also "doings" with material consequences, creating visceral boundaries and forceful social arrangements.[16] Our emotions are dynamic and move

---

[13] Jin Haritaworn, "Hybrid Border Crossers? Towards a Radical Socialisation of 'Mixed Race'," *Journal of Ethnic and Migration Studies* 35, no.1 (2009): 116.

[14] See, for example, Mark Smith's exploration of how race is perceived powerfully beyond/despite the visual. Mark Smith, *How Race Is Made: Slavery, Segregation, and the Senses* (Chapel Hill: University of North Carolina Press, 2006).

[15] See Sara Ahmed, *Queer Phenomenology: Orientations, Objects, Others* (Durham, NC: Duke University Press, 2008).

[16] Derek Hook, "Affecting Whiteness: Racism as Technology of Affect," *International Journal of Critical Psychology* 16 (2005): 9-11. "Technologies of affect" are the ways in which "feeling something" is also a subject formation process that can be operationalized to differentiate—feelings are also "doings" with material consequences, creating visceral boundaries and forceful social arrangements. "Technologies" (based in Michel Foucault's work) describes practices, knowledges, discourses (e.g. science, taxonomies, laws, policies, education systems, health care structures, social localized practices, etc.) that produce humans as specific kinds of beings, with specific kinds of differences, ordered in specific kinds of ways. That "we" (those shaped by Western colonial imagination) feel it is common sense that humans "obviously" exist as different kinds of races, belonging to different kinds of places, exhibiting different kinds of traits, etc., and also therefore "obviously" we have different kinds of feelings in specific situations, with different kinds of power relations—that is the power of technologies of affect.

us, and emotions become attached to us, to objects, to symbols, and the intensity and energy of that move us in relation to and with each other. What my body means as body-with-race only materializes and makes sense in relations where certain kinds of race categories are already meaningful and charged with emotion. Those emotions stick to bodies as they move and are moved through space in ways that fix them into certain categories through fear, repulsion, attraction, and admiration of this racial subject as which you are felt and perceived.[17] Thus racial affect and various feelings we have about our racial identity or that of others are neither simply of internal origin nor solely produced and given to us from the outside. It then seems less important to figure out if someone *believes* in racial hierarchies or in a "truth" of race and/or racial supremacies as a material reality, but rather, it is crucial to understand how we come to *feel* our race and that of others, how we instinctively, on a "gut level" respond to others near us. How is it that we may declare non-racist, tolerant convictions, and yet our bodily actions in proximity to racial others embody anxiousness (racialized fright about crime), desire (racialized fetishes of the exotic other), disgust (racialized flavors or smells that feel revolting), fear (racialized terror in the face of policing), or pre-emptive weariness (racialized fatigue and exhaustion in the presence of well-meaning whites)?[18]

To have "Asian" as part of one's racial becoming includes navigating multiple and shifting categories, depending on context and local availability of meaningful ethnic labels, or simplifying stereotypical stand-ins. And being "Asian" also often means that one is both hypervisible *and* invisible in highly affective dimensions of embodied life, such as food and sex. For example, for Asian American women, it often means being hypervisible in terms of sexuality or parenting (the Lotus Blossom, Tiger Moms), but being invisible in terms of labor in industry and affective care work (nannies, maids, sex workers), and being invisible in their roles in political activism and popular movements.[19] Asian-Americanness is a racialized

---

[17] Sara Ahmed, *The Cultural Politics of Emotion* (Edinburgh: Edinburgh University Press, 2004).

[18] Michalinos Zembylas, "Rethinking Race and Racism As Technologies of Affect: Theorizing the Implications for Anti-Racist Politics and Practice in Education," *Race, Ethnicity and Education* 18, no. 2 (2015): 148.

[19] See Kaori Mori Want, "Hypervisibility and Invisibility of Female Haafu Models in Japan's Beauty Culture," in *Red and Yellow, Black and Brown: Decentering Whiteness in Mixed Race Studies,* eds. Joanne L. Rondilla, Rudy P. Guevarra Jr., and Paul R. Spickard (New Brunswick, NJ: Rutgers University Press, 2017); Judy Tzu-Chu Wu, "Hypervisibility and Invisibility: Asian/American Women, Radical Orientalism, and the Revisioning of Global Feminism," in *The Rising Tide of Color: Race, State Violence, and Radical Movements Across the Pacific*, ed. Moon-Ho Jung (Seattle: University of Washington Press, 2014).

identity (not simply an ethnic cultural identity[20]), and food is deeply embedded in this racialization.

Once my specific parental origins are known, I can almost always count on hearing the very sensual declaration of *"I looooove Thai food!"*.[21] I do too. It is my comfort food, the taste and smell and all-around coziness of being with my mother and being cared for by being stuffed with rice, noodles, or curries. Looking for connections to home is a search for the closest Asian grocery store—not even the "best," since options outside of major metropolitan areas can be limited. What an "Asian" food market offers depends on the owners and local demand and might carry products from a diversity of cultural and culinary regions. Whenever I can find the items, spices, and supplies needed to cook Thai food, I can find myself and recreate home. Finding, holding, buying, and consuming the "right" rice, fish sauce, or Tom Yum paste of brands used by my mother can make me smile and cry for joy on some days. Sometimes I won't find everything I need for a dish and make do with what is available or substitute an ingredient. Food—the tastes, smells, and sensations of cooking—is my connection to home and myself, something to cultivate as I check with my mother on the phone to clarify some recipes, speaking with each other in German.

Food makes visceral how racial formations are sensory and affective formations that draw boundaries around food, people, and spaces and inscribe power onto plates and into bodies.[22] That Thainess is a distinguishable racialized flavor (I will elaborate more on this below) illustrates the relational and intersubjective force of affect embedded in and even driving politico-economic dynamics and projects. To be racialized in our embodiment is to be affectively produced: We come to mean some*thing* as some*body* already within a power structure that produces racialized categories of beings, racialized sets of feeling rules, and rules of feeling race.[23] And food also gives us a taste of gendered economic and political structures that give rise to racial formations. We need to trace these structures to understand within which compliances, as well as resistances and challenges to racial knowledges and pressures, take place. Food production and consumption are sensory emotional experiences, sometimes overwhelmingly so. And they are inescapably political and racialized: Who has access to what kind of variety, who can make economic choices over qualities and quantities, what are the costs of agency in food, valuations of healthy vs. junk foods, compensation of labor in the food industries, what kinds of foods can be tasted, seen, and smelled in which/whose communal spaces, who has

---

[20] See Ki Joo Choi, *Disciplined by Race: Theological Ethics and the Problem of Asian American Identity* (Eugene, OR: Cascade Books, 2019).

[21] My Germanness also often triggers assumptions that I love beer (gross) and chocolate (absolutely), though without the sensual intonation that Thainess elicits. I never had anyone moaning *"I just adore Bratwurst sooooo much!"*

[22] Mark Padoongpatt, *Flavors of Empire*, 4.

[23] Berg and Ramos-Zaya, "Racializing Affect," 655.

sovereignty over cuisines and their culinary resourcing—these are highly contentious public issues.[24]

Tracing the affective materiality of racism and racialized identities, especially in Asian-American communities, provides us also with specifically Asian-American feminist theological resources for mobilization. The affective ways in which racialized categories manifest materially—e.g., bodily, economically, spatially—alerts us to the dynamic potential of food and other viscerally felt experiences for transformation into new kinds of acting and aligning bodily differences. Tracing the construction of felt Thainess through culinary histories and productions will help us understand the unrelenting process of multiracialization and differentiation in social interactions. Thainess has always been a racialized identity produced, consumed, and represented largely through food and culinary spaces since there are very few visible Thai communities that take up space geographically and in the social imagination. Our exploration of the intensity with which sensory-affective racial differentiation can occur can illustrate how meaning and judgment emerge in bodily encounters and press bodies into identities, pushing them towards actions that reinforce us/them, in/out, belonging here/there. Below, I will provide a sketch of the history of Thainess in the United States, which was and is most immediately available and curated through global food ways and their cultural and political colonization. I am leaning on the excellent work on the history of Thai racial formation provided by Mark Padoongpatt in *Flavors of Empire*.[25] He shows that the dominant way in which white Americans' knowledge of Thais, and Thai self-knowledge as specific racial other was constructed, consumed, and perpetuated was the sensory space of Thai culinary consumption. Examples of moments and key dynamics presented in his work will be useful here to explore sensory-affective multiracialization in culinary encounters.

Eating Thai Food, Consuming Race: Thai(ness) in America

Thainess in the United States was first mainly available as culinary experience and still often is the only encounter non-Thais may have with it.[26] Whereas other "older" Asian-American communities often have specific histories of discrimination and trauma linked to specific ethnic origins, e.g., Chinese, Japanese, or Korean

---

[24] Alice Julier, Carole Counihan, and Penny Van Esterik, "Introduction: The Continuing Salience of Food and Culture," in *Food and Culture: A Reader*, 4th ed., eds. Carole Counihan, Penny Van Esterik, and Alice Julier (New York: Routledge, 2019), 6.

[25] Padoongpatt, *Flavors of Empire*.

[26] Comparing ethnic restaurants with population size, Thai restaurants have a much higher ratio of population-to-restaurant, e.g. ten times that of Mexican-American restaurants to Mexican-American population. Myles Karp, "The Surprising Reason that there are so many Thai Restaurants in America," *Vice*, March 29, 2018, https://www.vice.com/en/article/paxadz/the-surprising-reason-that-there-are-so-many-thai-restaurants-in-america

experiences, Thai persons largely entered the United States at a time of budding multicultural celebration, when an effort to create a common Asian American culture was already on the way.[27] Simultaneously, white America experienced fear *and* elation over the increasing racial and ethnic diversity: Anti-immigrant and anti-Asian sentiment was on the rise, triggered by perceptions of a foreign invasion destroying opportunities for white workers, *and* celebrations of cosmopolitan diversity became popular, generated by the desire to create the image of a benevolent postwar post-civil-rights US empire.

The few waves of Thai immigrants to the United States in the late 1960s and 1970s were small in comparison to other Asian groups and actually *followed* the emergence of Thainess through culinary culture migrating post WW2. "Thai" was first tasted by Americans as exotic dishes curated mostly by (white) American women. The increase in US military presence globally, and specifically the militarization and occupation of Vietnam and beyond, had propelled the interest of white American housewives in various "exotic" Asian foods.[28] Post WW2, the US-Asian entanglement through military and business infrastructure was one of the (main) transnational conduits for white Americans to "discover" exotic cuisines and introduce them to family and friends at home. White culinary tourists to Thailand during the 1960s—Peace Corps volunteers, military wives, tourists—were smitten with the tastes and smells of their culinary encounters and established their Thai food expertise through translations of recipes and representations of cooking styles to their families and friends. Through their books and classes, they became authorities on "oriental" cuisine, defining "authentic" Thai food through distributing measurable recipes and, with it, a homogenous, palatable image of Thai culture to the US context.[29] For white American women, in a time of a cultural crackdown in society that consolidated whiteness through mass consumption of sameness, Asian foods—their tastes, smells, stories—helped American white women to feel and appear as more interesting, worldly, and cultured individuals. The experienced pleasure of a safe and romantic colonial fantasy (being served and catered to abroad) turned into the appropriation of exotic foods through dinner parties at home and established the hierarchy of status and power of suburban women as culinary adventurers who could spice up their whiteness, and the subordinated race and class position of the Thai other who had yet to be bodily materialize in these spaces.[30]

---

[27] The Asian American Movement of the 1960s and 70s was an effort at historicizing common experiences among subordinated groups and gathering disjunct ethnic cultures for political solidarity and ethical connection. David Haekwon Kim, *Shame*, 106

[28] The other side of the coin is the increase in interest of American men in "exotic" sex workers in Thailand (Thai and migrant workers of other ethnicities) linked to the US military presence during the war in Vietnam. Abel Brodeur, Warn N. Lekfuangfu and Yanos Zylberberg, 'War, Migration, and the Origins of the Thai Sex Industry,' *Journal of the European Economic Association* 16, no.5 (2017):1540-1576.

[29] Padoongpatt, *Flavors of Empire*, 42-53.

[30] Mark Padoonpatt, "Oriental Cookery," in *Eating Asian America: A Food Studies Reader*, ed. Robert Ji-Song Ku (New York: NYU Press, 2013), 186-197, 192, 203.

What passed as "authentic" Thai food in the United States though was in part already an imperial translation, a Thai domestic effort to stave off colonial consumption of national identity. For example, Pad Thai (the ubiquitous and popular dish made with stir-fried rice noodles, vegetables, peanuts, and eggs) was the invention of a twentieth-century nation building project in a heavily militarized Thailand (bolstered by US support). A WW2 rice shortage and the need to manufacture a homogenous citizenry and national culture to create an anticommunist global image prompted the dissemination of food carts, food propaganda, and Pad Thai recipes distributed through the Welfare Department in a two-for effort to increase patriotism and a cheap nutrition supply in the population. "Foreigners" and "foreign" foods were banned from this culinary marketplace, as citizens were encouraged to eat only Thai food with Thai-sourced ingredients to create a distinct national, consumable, and desired feeling of Thainess.[31] Exorcised from the iconic wok-fried "authentically Thai" dish were the Chinese origins of rice noodles, cooking methods, and local ingredients that would have been unpalatable to Western tastes. Pad Thai was part of a sensory-affective cultural identity construction designed to protect Thailand against undesirable foreign and communist influences. Post-WW2 Thailand's economic development plans invested heavily in tourism, which depended on encouraging (or better: coercing) the preservation of "authentic" (read: dominant) Thai culture in order to commercialize it. The increase in tourism required an increase in food palatable to tourists and created a taste for Thai food back in the United States—a discernable, constructed flavor of Thainess shaped by nationalistic policies in Thailand and curated in the United States by white American women. When Pad Thai reached the shores of the United States, it was again (re)structured by transnational trade and the limits of what could be acquired on the marketplace in terms of actual foodstuffs to create flavors of Thailand.[32]

What presents as authentic Thai cuisine, a distinctive and original ethnic flavor, is the sensory-affective labor of excising intermingled origins of Thai regional dishes, of political interventions (domestic and global) creating desire for palatable East-West encounters, and the invisibilizing of actual bodies cooking Thai food in restaurant kitchens, bodies that may carry various Asian and other ethnic labels.[33]

---

[31] Some food historians trace the choice of this particular dish to the influence of the female Chinese housekeeper in the household of the Prime Minister Plaek Phibunsongkhram. Other components of Phibunsongkhram's nation building project were Cultural Mandates, creating a representation of Thainess (legitimized through Thai scholars) including greetings analog to English customs, reshaping dress codes to include gendered distinctions, and European style fashion (Van Esterik 2000, 102-103).

[32] Padoongpatt, *Flavors of Empire,* 48-49.

[33] Authenticity is not self-contained, but culturally negotiated. Authenticity of food and those who can authentically cook is determined by those who get to expertly judge it and have the power to be positioned as experts. When culinary culture and ethnically marked bodies become tightly linked, then authenticity of flavor is linked to authentic, "original" ethnic bodies naturally being able to produce such authentic flavors. Yet it all depends on the expert tongue discerning the level of authenticity, the expert who may be confounded by e.g. non-Thai bodies cooking what passes (or even surpasses!) authentic foods. Choi, *Disciplined by Race,* 42-44.

As Ki Joo Choi explored in relation to Asian-Americanness, defining what is culturally authentic is confounding because it is always already a relational, dynamic, intermingling affair. Authenticity is often a process of selecting what is appealing and desirable in specific contexts, and this relational construction of cultural authenticity-as-identity takes place in a specific social reality that is already constrained by white affective norms in/and what is available and desirable.[34] What makes Thainess appear authentically Thai is not the appearance of some pre-existing original-authentic flavor that is retrieved from exotic places. Thai food permeated and saturated what was available to feel, understand, and authentically represent embodied Thai racial identity. What feels Thai to Thais (and non-Thais) is what is already desirable: specific Thai flavors and culinary experiences, produced with locally available ingredients procured within a web of global political and trade power relations.

Sensory racial grouping and classifications signify difference and create visceral desires within power structures. Dining out had become a trend in the 1970s and 1980s, and white consumers could now safely ingest the previously economically and physically segregated racial/ethnic other—on their culinary terms, maintaining the power differential inherent in whiteness and shedding the semblance of overt hostile racism. Thais coming to the United States during those decades were largely students who entered a world in which Thainess was already an object for consumption. They formed communities to feed themselves with tastes of home where they attended schools (initially in Los Angeles, California, then Illinois, Michigan, Texas, and DC), often cooking with substituted Chinese ingredients (e.g., soy sauce for fish sauce). With the first Thai markets opening, esp. Bangkok Market in the 1970s, Thais were able to switch from substituted Chinese ingredients to cooking with "real" imported Thai produce and goods such as fish sauce, lime leaves, and Thai curries.[35] Due to global tariffs and import restrictions, production zones for Thai ingredients were moved by the growing conglomerate of the Bangkok Market to California and Mexico, making Thai produce widely available throughout certain regions. Thai grocery stores were social networks for Thais to create spaces of belonging, and they also fueled the emergence of a distinguishable Thai food scene.[36]

Initially, Thai communities recruited other Thais to open restaurants to feed Thai communities. But once previously redlined neighborhoods became available to non-whites, food was the gateway for Thais (who had not experienced being zoned out in the first place) to emerge in white neighborhoods. They opened Thai restaurants and nurtured the desire for Thai cuisine in the US consumer who already

---

[34] Choi, *Disciplined by Race*, 46, 55-56.

[35] Bangkok Market represents a pivotal moment for procuring Thai ingredients and through it, Thai American community and identity formation. Opening in East Hollywood, it was the first of its kind, enabling Thai food production beyond substituted ingredients and aiding in food and people emerging with distinct flavor/identity profiles, and promoting economic and communal developments in the Thai community, and sidestepping heightened trade barriers to secure and increase the availability of Thai food ingredients. Padoongpatt, *Flavors of Empire,* 57, 73-77.

[36] Padoongpatt, *Flavors of Empire,* 80-83.

had tasted it here and there.[37] Emerging "Foodie" culture created a white, bourgeois urban subject that constructed itself through the consumption and informational mastery of foreign foods.[38] And white eaters' knowledge of Thainess was heavily constructed through foodie feelings, at the cost of making invisible actual Thai bodies (and Thai history, economic and cultural dynamics, and internally diverse race, gendered, and classed complexities). Gustatory boundaries around Thai identity wafted into other discourses. Reading biological-cultural traits into Thai bodies via food, culinary critics celebrated the integrity and superiority of Thai food, linking it to Thailand's avoidance of colonization.[39] At a time when the US nation-state had no official classification for "Thai," it was white food critics who constructed Thais as a separate group in the US race structure, using food practices to draw distinct lines between other Asian groups (mainly Chinese) and reading opinions on culinary traits and skills back into Thai bodies. The consumption of Thai foods and the affection of white expert tongues tightened the link between Thai bodies and a distinct culinary ethnic-racial identity. Positing a natural ability of Thais to thrive in food service naturalized cooking as a bodily-ethnic property and maintained Thai bodies in a subordinate place in the US service economy.[40] And Thais were prone to pridefully agree. This fixedness of Thainess was embraced by Thais in order to become distinguishable from other Asian groups—to others and themselves. The taste of Thai food drew boundaries between Thais and other Asian groups, and food production and consumption were a way to feel ethnic and national pride and avoid experiences of internal and external anti-Asian hostility. Becoming Thai was a process of making oneself palatable, adjusting, adapting, and changing to a constructed authentic, original flavor. Food was now more than a taste of home, a sense of belonging; it also was a sensory formation and expression of positive national-racial identity. Thainess was a felt superiority, more authentic and savvier than other colonized Asian cultures and historically/presently oppressed Asian-American communities. The embodied collective fear of being seen as too foreign, too exotic (and thereby sharing the experience of hostility directed against other Asian subgroups), and the mindfulness of the inextricable linking of Thai food and Thai bodies had Thai-Americans carefully position themselves always closer to "Thai-Americanness"

---

[37] Padoongpatt, *Flavors of Empire*, 92.

[38] Kyla Wazana Tompkins, *Racial Indigestion: Eating Bodies in the 19th Century* (New York: New York University Press, 2012), 2 and 184.

[39] Casting Thailand and Thainess as anti-colonial or "despite"-colonial country, to construct the image of a superior, advanced, developed culture that withstood imperialism when other countries crumbled, rewrites history and belies Thailand's complicity in US militarism pre- and post-WW2. For an overview of Thai-American relations, Thai and US foreign policy during the Cold War's anti-communist efforts, see Arne Kislenko, "A Not So Silent Partner: Thailand's Role in Covert Operations, Counter-Insurgency, and the Wars in Indochina," *Journal of Conflict Studies* 24, no. 1 (2004): 65-96.

[40] Padoongpatt, *Flavors of Empire*, 105-7.

and further from "Thai-Foreignness" by producing themselves with flavors and ingredients at once exotic and pleasurably non-threatening.[41]

Thai food experienced a boom in the 1980s, emerging out of the popular restaurants in LA Thai Town and a rising celebrity culture. Los Angeles, at this time, was the hub of a global economy that oriented itself towards Asia and the Pacific and had become a top immigration destination, with increasing newcomers from Asia and Latin America to fill labor shortages, leading to intense social disruptions. In the face of anti-Asian and anti-immigrant hostility, restaurants made Thai racial identity discernable and palatable—producing, representing, and consuming Thai flavors and scents made sense of a distinct Thainess that was not only non-threatening but delicious, even craveable. Thai food was marketed as healthier than other Asian options (esp. Chinese and Southeast Asian). Where early restaurants had emphasized Thai-Chinese cooking to appeal to the white consumer's gustatory familiarities, Thai food now emerged as original and distinctly *yum*: the combination of salty, sweet, sour, and spicy. The search for yumness itself had already been present in the desires and yearnings of Thai immigrants, creating a sense of belonging and home in their private kitchens, but Thai yum now was the novelty and marketing strategy aimed at the American consumer. This racialized Thai cuisine attached Thais and non-Thais to a restricted, palatable culinary identity.[42] The sensory differentiation of Thais from other Asian groups created and reinforced racial knowledges and categorizations. Thai food stood in for the complexities and contradictions of actual Thai people and the small Thai American communities who had formed around creating a sense of belonging through cooking familiar foods together.[43] The demand for assimilation put to the racial other was not replaced by, but rather morphed with time into neoliberal multiculturalism, which only strengthened the role of food and restaurants in the formation of Thai-American identity.

Because multiculturalism demands that different Asian communities be distinct, pure, and authentic in order to be a part of the American fabric and evade hostility and discrimination, Thais and non-Thais connected flavor and racial-ethnic labels to differentiate and market themselves. Multiculturalism as a (white) consumer-oriented configuration dissects a disjunctly formed Asian American solidarity and reshapes the conditional acceptance of Asianess in the process of white legitimation of others.[44] In culinary affects, multiculturalism reveals itself not as the response or solution to the increasing anti-Asian hostility, but the *more pleasant flavor* of violence against others. Multiculturalism demands consumable, fun, unthreatening, exotic but still palatable, distinct ethnic identities to be mixed into American society. This social safety-as-recognition promised to an "authentic" American subject

---

[41] Padoongpatt, *Flavors of Empire*, 110.

[42] Padoongpatt, *Flavors of Empire*, 102-104.

[43] Tommy Tang and other celebrity chefs and their foods illustrate how an externalized Thai-American identity emerged through cooking/eating: Tang's food was a fusion type cuisine catering to the American palate, matching his views that Thais should make themselves as palatable to the American taste as possible. Padoongpatt, *Flavors of Empire*, 110.

[44] David Haekwon Kim, *Shame*, 107.

is arranged and coded by whiteness as economic racialized order. It requires the ethnic other to be distinguishable as non-white other, as *specific* other, and to stay within the sensory boundaries of what looks, smells, tastes, and sounds acceptable and acceptably authentic to whiteness.[45] Thai multiracialization is a combination of linking ambiguous and contradictory feelings of bodies in space in relations of power, in which some get to decide who gets to evoke visceral experiences and what kind of feelings are valid (and when, where, how). Desiring and enjoying authentic Thai food is intimately linked to anti-Asian affect: It's ok to be Thai/Asian, as long as it's sensorily confined: not too smelly, not too loudly Asian, not bodily overwhelming in numbers, not too visually ambiguously other, not to creatively challenging in flavor. Everything that is not confined within multiculturalism's limits risks disposal and/or disposability in a globalized marketplace.

At a time when immigration increased and felt social disruptions swelled racial hostilities in cities like Los Angeles, Thais had become recognizable through food, and white Americans established their own racial belonging through affective and sensory connections and consumptions of distinct others. The multiracialization of Thai bodies through food was/is also a heteronormative gendered and classed dynamic. Thai restaurants increasingly used feminized labels connected to a traditional ethnic reference (Siamese Princess, Flower of Siam), using tropes familiar to white consumers to signal authenticity in a gendered, racialized, and sexualized fashion. Artwork and outfits of (female) servers marked the experience of Thai food in specific sensual, submissive, pleasant ways, creating what is heralded as traditional Thai culture. For the food to taste authentic, it had to be presented in other sensorily "authentic" ways. This produced gender and class divisions; Thai women serving customers are often supposed to stage an original Thai restaurant experience in exotic, sensual ways, and they become fetishized ornamental objects.[46] The front rooms and back rooms exposed women to objectification and exploitation and were also places for women (of Thai and other ethnicities) to form networks of support, though it could also exploit and widen class distinctions between them. Relying heavily on underpaid or unpaid labor from undocumented Thais or families, Thai workers and restaurant owners perpetuated class and gender inequalities and white heteronormativity in their culinary racialization dynamics.[47] And in this affective-sensory relational dynamic, a sophisticated, bourgeoise whiteness emerged: The

---

[45] See Padoongpatt's chapter on the Wat Thai in suburban Los Angeles. White neighbors attempted to expel Wat Thai once the community trespassed acceptable boundaries of "quiet Buddhist religious practice" and "safe, pleasant" food consumption. Padoongpatt, *Flavors of Empire*, 143.

[46] Anne Anlin Cheng conceptualizes the femininity of yellow as an abstraction that materializes ornamentally, a particular female objectification in which Asian women exist in perihumanity, the fusion of thingliness and personness, through ornamental personhood. See Anne Anlin Cheng, *Ornamentalism* (New York: Oxford University Press, 2019).

[47] Padoongpatt, *Flavors of Empire*, 112.

pleasurable feeling of tasting the exotic but palatable otherness in public, and then safely returning home.[48]

Thai food locates both Thai bodies and their consumers in proximity to feelings of respectability, while maintaining a carefully controlled intimacy that left white consumers satisfied. The figure of the Thai as natural cook and the figure of the Thai as sex worker are both hetero-racialized constructions of Thai bodies as those with a "natural" proclivity and skill for convivial and intimate labor that can satisfy sensory desires. The restaurant industry as place is structured to render female workers vulnerable to sexual harassment. Thainess and the restaurant setting, rather than allowing for a shedding of the prostitute stereotype, reinforce the sensory consumption of Thai bodies. And it allows the white male consumer to be reconfigured as a sophisticated cosmopolitan in a tolerant multicultural world (over against the figure of the older, "unattractive" working-class consumer of sex work or husband of an Asian mail-order bride).[49]

Thainess became a recognizable racial identity through being taste-able to the white eater. Linking cuisine to place and to human differences, Thais utilized a narrow gustatory image linked with reinforced race-gender stereotypes to forge and feel their Thai selves and became empowered cultural ambassadors who safely interact with Americans consuming their products and identity. And Thai food created places for Thai people, procuring and consuming Thai foods in place-making activities within a dominant racial imaginary that challenge it as well. When the so-called "race riots" took place in 1992, Los Angeles was (and still is) the location of the largest Thai community in the United States. But while Thainess loomed large on the food scene, many Thais increasingly felt ignored on issues such as economic exploitation and lack of access to social services, precisely because they were not visible as bodies, as an (Asian) minority with legal recognition (e.g., in comparison to South East Asian communities recognized as refugees). Koreans were the majority of Asians affected in the riots, and because the conflict was cast as Black-Korean tension, the affected Thai bodies and businesses went unnoticed and increased the need to create a more felt presence as residents and minority community. Out of the hypervisibility of Thai food and the hyperinvisibility of Thai people, Thais had positioned themselves within a neoliberal multicultural society as consumable product, on the social and political margins of US hierarchical racialized structures. The sensory and affective experience of the riots and their aftermath made it viscerally obvious that the distinct flavor of Thai food did not draw boundaries around Thai people that kept them safe from anti-Asian/racist violence. Palatability to white tastes had created a sensory-affective racial alliance based in consumption that was neither reciprocated materially or politically by white Americans nor imbued with the power of white-adjacent safety from racism.

---

[48] Jennifer Jensen Wallach, *How America Eats: A Social History of US Food and Culture* (Lanham, MD: Rowman & Littlefield Publishers, 2013), 174-175.

[49] Haritaworn, *Biopolitics of Mixing*, 139-40.

The dilemma of Asian American identity is that it confines agency within the boundaries and entrapments of whiteness, risking either conforming to stereotypes of Asian Americanness (e.g., in the case of Thais, being natural cooks) or perpetuating whiteness through upholding racialized hierarchical values over against other racialized groups and intra-Asian ethnic group relations, asserting a superior flavor profile over against other ethnic Asian cuisines. Choi proposes critical self-love, a response that is a social protest, made up of acts of defiance that destabilize and transform how Asian Americans are perceived and expected to be.[50] The conditions that create the limitations of racial identity formation for Asian bodies and our experiences of racism in its multitude of embodiments not only maintain white tastes and tastes for whiteness as dominant and domineering force. Within them also lies potential for undoing white supremacist affectivity. That is in part because (as Choi frames it) there is no "outside" origin or innocent relational activity that is not already defined within a racial matrix. But ingredients for resistance need not be resourced only from within and for white palatability and consumption. In the wake of the LA riots, local Thais and Thai organizations attempted to increase political power either through fighting for more resources by increasing visibility as Thais (thereby further distinguishing Thainess over against other Asian identities), or by maintaining political and social invisibility and avoiding anti-(specific)-Asian violence by supporting other Asian political groups representing Thai interests. One of the strategies employed by the Thai Community Development Center was to join other Asian organizations in organizing around labor rights for ethnic minorities (Asian/Thai and others),[51] particularly minoritized low-wage workers, in order to gain political power as a Thai community and increase pan-Asian coalition building. Thai racial identity formation as a nuanced ethnic identity formation had not left the culinary realm but tapped into the labor aspects of food production and consumption. The feeling of being Thai in this contextual, local multiracialization process needed and now could include the feeling of being part of a diverse Asian community with a sense of economic solidarity.

---

[50] The tragedy, as Choi frames it, of Asian American life is precariousness in self-determination, because the relationality within which Asian Americans form their identities and self-understanding is already malformed by whiteness. To love oneself as Asian American, to create spaces of belonging and flourishing as oneself carries the risk of falling into morally dubious patterns, conforming with white notions of what is valuable and meaningful, and/or emulating abusive relationships with others (imitating patriarchal, misogynistic, cis-heteronormative patterns). To discover oneself, and to defiantly defend one's own interests as a racialized being also ought to be an act of solidarity with others who are similarly situated under white oppressive structures, and to love oneself and the other outside of terms set by the white racial imagination. Choi urges us to pause before emphasizing the possibilities and potential of resistance in critical self-love but maintains that hope that resisting oppressive racialized identity formations through critical self-love is possible. Choi, *Disciplined by Race,* 109-110; 167-72.

[51] This was an organization opposed to California's Proposition 187, an anti-immigrant bill that would have disallowed education, health, and social services to be used for "illegal" immigrants. Padoongpatt, *Flavors of Empire,* 150-151.

It was "culinary contact zones" that largely shaped early Thai American multiracialized identity formation within a relation and responses to white perception of Thais—as exotic other, as naturally gifted culinary workers, as consumable cultural palate item. Authenticity—of food, of Thai identity, of Thai gender performance—is often linked to particular essentializing manifestations of the product, the body, and the perception of it all, as judged by the other to whom it appears authentic to. In the relational space of culinary contact zones, authentic Thainess is in that moment and recognition of emotive success, the matching of an inward feeling and contextualized expectations for expression—for whites and Thais alike. Through food and culinary production, Thais in the United States (who were and are often scattered and fragmented, dispersed, migrating and settling with very few visible/feel-able communities) found ways to satisfactorily participate in the US multicultural racial project. Thais who migrated to the United States found value in the various ways to participate—by tracking down "authentic" ingredients (or at least passable substitutes) for their own consumption and that of others in the culinary contact zones that created racial relations. Thai food was and is a way for Thais to represent and differentiate themselves from a general "Asian" identity, to safely belong (i.e., to not confuse the other nor to be without a sense of self). To express Thai identity is a sensory project through food, connected cultural memories, and nostalgia. Yet these feelings about self are reinforced and maintained within a white affective structure that fixes Thai food within a multicultural diversity landscape that produces the racial other based on what they eat and maintains the limits of what is palatable and tolerable.

At the turn of the millennium, as East Hollywood's Thai Town in Los Angeles became nationally known as culinary tourist destination, marketing and selling Thai cuisine was a way to emerge as a specific kind of Asian ethnic group, a desirable one, and this racial, economic, and political strategy reverberated globally. The Thai government recognized the booming popularity of Thai food and established the "Thai Kitchen of the World" campaign, bolstering Thailand's position as global food exporters and promoting ingredients sourced in Thailand for export. Thai cuisine, "authentically" trained exported chefs, and Thai restaurants as Thai information centers were the national economic development strategy.[52] Everyone everywhere loooooves Thai food. The specific dynamic shaped in the US-Thai relationship of sensory-affective multiracialization of Thainess in the United States has gone global and multiplies through localized racial flavors and feelings.

---

[52] Padoongpatt, *Flavors of Empire*, 171-173.

Sensory-Affective Multiracialization as Theological Process and Mobilization

Writing this chapter, I repeatedly asked myself: Why would anyone care about a racial/ethnic minority within a minority? Thais or people with Thai origins make up little more than 300,000 people in the United States (barely 0.1% of the total US population, compared to almost 21 million Asian Americans, which make up almost 6% together).[53] Most of them identify as Buddhist/other, and not as Christian, so why bother exploring Thainess and its sensory-affective multiracialization in search for anti-racist Christian theological resources? Part of my quest was to connect to an embodied knowledge about race, racism, and anti-racism that may come from a specific community but may have resonances for other racialized groups, small or large. And part of it was also a journey of self-discovery to make sense of myself. As a person of German-Thai parentage, butch, queer, Mennonite, now living as an immigrant in the United States, I often felt and still feel like there is no one like me, that there is no community where I could belong—and if there is, it is too small, too fragmented, and too dispersed to give me a home here and now. Sometimes it felt like I was just writing this for myself to explain myself to me. This is the affective power of the US multicultural project: That it offers racial salvation in the process of shaping group belonging and freedom from identity confusion by inscribing palatable identities as satisfactory and desirably authentic. Yet here I am, writing not to retrieve a "real" origin story, but to create felt meaning and increase connection out of the loss of racial belongings and into the heterogeneity of Asianness in the United States and elsewhere.

My own sensory-affective multiracialization includes always having my own sense of self and identity put under question. Claims to a white-framed citizenship by itself are never enough. *"Are you sure you are German? My housekeeper looks just like you, and she is Lebanese!"* is not just an intellectual exercise, but an emotional disruption and sensory categorization into locally available racial groups.[54] *"Ah! You're German-Thai! So that's why you look like you do!"* The investigator is saved from the embarrassment of confusion. I am strategically dissecting myself into my parents' national origins, managing the other's feelings with a legible composite, and managing my own feelings by attempting to cut short the racial investigation to save myself from further scrutiny. In return, my mother's nationality, culture, and ethnicity is now fixed onto my body as a racial identity embedded in my current context in the United States (Asianness in the United States and Asian-

---

[53] US Census Bureau, "Selected Population Profile in the United States," accessed June 1, 2021, https://data.census.gov/cedsci/.

[54] Because "German" is marked white and blond, imagined perhaps holding a stein of beer and wearing leather pants – which by the way is Bavarian, NOT German, as any "real" German would be happy to point out—the question *"You are German and......??!!!"* is a constant refrain. My skin color and other bodily markers are read as non-German, or at least only in hyphenation as White-German-Other. I quickly learned to blame the anxious quest of the other to read my bodily on my own failing to clearly fit an existing label.

Americanness), an identity and context to which I had not experienced a personal historical or experiential connection while growing up.[55] Sometimes, the follow-up on the German-Thai self-identification is to expertly label my bodily features in racialized heteronormative ways. *"You look so much more masculine than the Asian girls I know. That must be the German in you."* The colonial-orientalist legacy makes Thai women only permissible as hyper-feminine servile figures, which renders my masculine, butch, and queer body inauthentically Asian/Thai. [56] With my gender performance read through racialized lenses, and my body opened up to all things romantic and sexual, it is often only a short moment until the need to figure out *"How did your parents meet?"* arises in the other. The very short of the story—that my father went on vacation, met my mother, they fell in love, and got married—invokes layers of Western-Asian interpersonal dynamics and colonial exploitation. Answering racial origin questions is already emotionally laboring in an economy pre-structured by transnational gendered exploitations; it is negotiating and counteracting the prevailing assumptions that bodies like mine are the result of prostitution,

---

[55] My learning of social codes that mark and maintain racial categories in the US pointed me towards learning about Asian immigrants and Asian-American experiences. I loved reading and scoured the library for stories and histories. I caught up to the US racial landscape by learning about the Asian American story within the context of immigration law, nativist dynamics, racial coding and quotas, US imperialism abroad, and more. And on the personal level, it was initially up to Amy Tan to teach me about Chinese mothers and their daughters, because apparently when it came to my understanding the personal dimensions of being (part) Asian in the US, at least during that time, the *Joy Luck Club* was THE go-to in the public imagination and public libraries. I ate up all the Amy Tan novels I could get a hand on, and many times it helped me put my own experiences of being raised by an Asian mother into understandable dynamics. There was nothing comparable to that kind of (autobiographical) fiction in Germany when I grew up, so reading Tan opened up a whole new window into my own world. However useful Tan's novels were to me, her success combined with the scarcity of other published writers also contributed to the fixed and static image of "Asianness" and "Asian mothers" in my own imagination. Today, multiple voices are available to contribute to the heterogenization of Asian-Americanness. Two authors I would like to highlight for their use of food in the construction of identity are Grace M. Cho, *Tastes Like War: A Memoir* (New York: The Feminist Press at the City University of New York, 2021), and Michelle Zauner, *Crying in H Mart: A Memoir* (New York: Alfred A. Knopf, 2021). To me, savoring and discovering a Thai-American autobiographical work is still a rare delight, as with Ira Sukrungruang, *Talk Thai: The Adventures of Buddhist Boy* (Columbia: University of Missouri Press, 2010).

[56] The construction of Thai/Asian femininity through heterosexism (hyperfeminine, hypersexual, subordinate, straight) is in line with the construction of Thai/Asian masculinity through homosexism (effeminate, less masculine, gay), and renders invisible Asian queer femmes and butches. This link, as Haritaworn demonstrates, is an interracial matrix that positions Asians sexually and otherwise at the service of straight and gay whites. Jin Haritaworn, "Queer Mixed Race? Interrogating Homonormativity through Thai Interraciality," in *Geographies of Sexualities: Theory, Practices, and Politics*, 2nd ed., eds. Kath Browne, Jason Lim, and Gavin Brown (London: Ashgate, 2009), 115-126. For a differentiated investigation of Thai gendered subjectivities, and how Western linguistic and gendered hegemonies impact localized expressions and native gender identities, see Megan Sinnott, "Gender Subjectivity: Dees and Toms in Thailand,", *Women's Sexualities and Masculinities in a Globalizing Asia*, eds. Saskia E. Wieringa, Evelyn Blackwood, and Abha Bhaiya (New York: Palgrave Macmillan, 2007), 119-138.

sex tourism, or international interracial agency arrangements.⁵⁷ Do I tell a love story that brackets dynamics of transnational exploitation? Do I gift the story of their relationship, my mother's trauma and grief, and search for belonging against the odds, for the other to consume and absorb into the salvific narrative of neoliberal multiculturalism? At what cost? For what ends? The voyeuristic impulse to know my origin story, my family, is an intrusion into my mother's body more than my father's, with the stereotypes of sex work/tourism and procurement of Thai wives for German husbands lurking in the other's imagination— it is just another violent dissecting reading practice.⁵⁸ It makes me cautious, but with practices comes the skill of utilizing existing ideas, labels, stereotypes to navigate, circumvent, and carve out and claw back some agency in this intrusive dissection now reaching into my parents' racial and gendered bodies.

"*Which is your favorite Thai restaurant?*" often hides a quest for the most authentic flavors to be revealed by me as a native-ish expert. "*Oh, we have a really nice kitchen, why don't you come and cook Thai food for us and some other folks?*" asked the mother of a new acquaintance minutes after having just met me. She already "knew" I would be excellent in procuring Thai food (I am mediocre at best) and did not hesitate in attempting to put my perceived naturally giftedness to the service of her and her white friends. In the absence of Germans who are brown like me, and in the absence of Thai communities that would provide me with a familial and diversified racial group, Thai food in the form of Thai restaurants and ingredients sourced in "Oriental" grocery stores oversignifies how I can become myself within the US racial frame that poses the salvific promise of recognition and participation in the multicultural project.⁵⁹ My own entry point into racial subjectivity, to learn about or connect to Thai-ness—as for other Thais AND non-Thais—remains through the intimate experience of food consumption.

Thai food, US-Thai and Intra-Asian culinary contact, and consumption of "authentic" flavors are all ways in which Thainess has been constructed and represented. And because of the power of food and cooking to make us *feel* things— about ourselves, others, the event itself, places, past-present-futures—it also has the power to move us, to bodily respond. Sometimes I can taste it and can tap into how it feels. In cooking—for myself, for my family, for my friends, with my mother—I get a taste of cooking at the interstices: places of intervention and agency into

---

⁵⁷ Haritaworn, *Biopolitics of Mixing*, 135-6. See also *Haritaworn, Hybrid Border Crossers*, 119.

⁵⁸ This is another layer and facet of creating the figure of the sensual Asian figure that services the appetites of white consumers, here as the desired hypersexual and hyperfeminized Asian prostitute; a figure created as natural in repetitive performative acts as this one in which the figure lurks in the imagination and is reinforced in the effort to disprove it. See *Haritaworn, Biopolitics of Mixing*, 138.

⁵⁹ The boxes to check for racial identity still stump me, though I am more comfortable checking White/Asian and Other than I was 20 years ago. The simple act of checking a box is a way of conforming to the histories of race relation and creation that shaped those boxes in the first place (histories of which I am only very marginally a part) and it also is a way of rebelling, claiming the umbrella of Asianness as an act of defiance to define for myself what being Asian in America can possibly mean.

getting a taste of myself, appreciate the complexity and fullness of life in community, and feeling like I belong.[60] For me, these spaces are often the home kitchen. I make Tom Yum for our Besties Thursday supper club. We share our foods, creating intimacies amongst us who are not kin, who are from different racialized groups, and together we feel like family, finding love and nourishment together in the tastes and flavors we procure of/for each other. In our sensory food connections, this affectivity to share a taste of each other and taste community in the midst of structures of racial (non)belonging is the potential to intimacy, to find recognition of each other in our multitudes. Eating together was our starting point towards being together and finding radical fulfillment in (not despite) our differences.[61]

So can you cook your way out of white supremacist racial codes? Can you eat up and fill a space, so it feels productively affirming of more complex and varied experiences outside of US racial codes? None of the dynamics/encounters explored here are inherently anti-racist. But since food is an essential part of producing racial differentiation and racial knowledge through culinary subject formation, it can also offer a tool for organizing and mobilizing across people groups towards greater social justice. This makes *food work theological work*: It utilizes the ingredients available to us in our contexts, it is the life blood of relationship and community building, value asserting, and boundary casting. Food work, our everyday sensory production and consumption, is purposeful in its acts of self-definition. It mobilizes emotions and identities in rituals of meaning making, meaning deconstruction, and meaning consumption. It creates and sometimes denies cultural fusions and creative mixing, and it connects ideas, senses, feelings, and memories to build relational bonds in the present and to nourish us and our sense of self for another day. The informal communications and interactions that come with food work and consumption are some of the visceral experiences that create spaces for the formation of moral communities, however temporary. Food work structures intimate and social relationships and produces bodies, real and imaginary, in ways that (re)conceptualize and intertwine race, religion, culture, gender, sexuality, and nationality.

Thainess is pre-structured within a multicultural code of salvific social recognition, and just eating Thai food in a restaurant or in the presence of other Thais does not magically make Thainess fully and complexly human. But culinary zones are central to our experience of what more equal and just forms of belonging could be and do. Eating with others, and eating with the Other, can uncover our complicities in maintaining the hierarchical multiraciality that ingests others (however appreciatively), and it can also destabilize how we think of what is sacred in our everyday.

---

[60] I am invoking here Rita Nakashima Brock's concept of interstitial integrity, seeking to understand complex relationships of life that are shaped by racism, sexism, and colonialism, whilst also seeking out life and nourishment in ever-changing patterns of life. Rita Nakashima Brook, "Cooking Without Recipes: Interstitial Integrity," *Off the Menu: Asian and Asian North American Women's Religion & Theology,* eds. Rita Nakashima Brock et al., (Louisville, KY: Westminster John Knox, 2007), 125-143.

[61] Anita Mannur, *Intimate Eating: Racialized Spaces and Radical Futures* (Durham, NC: Duke University Press, 2022), ix, 8-10.

Mom is coming to visit this summer, she will bring with her from Germany some Thai food items procured in Vietnamese owned grocery stores. We will talk, and I will try to pry more stories of her past from her, knowing she will avoid anything to do with her Chinese father, whom I did not learn about until I was an adult. He had abandoned my grandmother and her children when my mother was young, and with that personal experience together with her growing up during established Thai government efforts to construct a pure Thai identity, my mother to herself is "100% Thai" and loves "real" Thai food (meaning the food she cooks herself). And so that makes me half-Thai. How I feel about myself and my racialization has less to do with a discovery of my biological-ethnic DNA makeup and much more with how I come to feel myself when I cook and eat with my mother, or when I go shopping for lemongrass and lime leaves.[62] Mom and I will cook together and conjure up new flavors of ourselves. We will eat together with my American spouse and German father, two interracial couples creating intergenerational community, tasting home within and beyond imperial flavor profiles. *"You make Thai food with what you have. If you don't have Taro, you use potato. Or apples! Apples make good Gaeng Nua."* What mom declares authentically Thai is sourced from local sources around her, on her own terms, challenging sensory-affective norms of comfort and belonging. These everyday experiences shape us, make us human, and give us social and moral orientation. We find dignity in producing and sharing meals together, whilst we are also challenged to provincialize our own taste preferences for who the other can be and become.

Culinary everyday practices are existential resources that can foster resilience to harm and resistance to violence—though fraught, precarious, and complicit. In food work, we imagine ourselves and others, and our contributions towards the flourishing and makings of belonging, yet there are cracks that can give us a taste of our specific vulnerabilities to racializing capitalism and consumptions masked as social salvation. The source for undoing white supremacist affectivity, I am coming to understand somewhere in my bones, is to keep layering our different stories, our particularities into dis-comforting experiences when bridging our heterogenous identities through our bodies.[63] Critically investigating our practices and dispositions towards food, culinary production, and encounter can create possibilities of new patterns of relating to one another, to ourselves, and to the shaping of humanness in difference in our everyday. It can open space to acknowledge the limits of our imaginations, the ways we create gustatory idols of others, and how we are all vulnerable to the ways in which we inscribe identities through our everyday

---

[62] It seems to me that the increasingly popular testing revealing percentages of racial-national-geographic in one's DNA is a technology of white affect to imbue whiteness with positive racial feelings, countering the emptiness of whiteness that is only meaningful in opposition to constructed racial others. Now white people can find joy in discovering 17% of Swedishness or 8% Egyptian in them, even in the absence of meaningful social connection to people/places.

[63] Sue Jeanne Koh, "Interstitial Integrity: Looking Forward, Radical Imagining" (presentation, Annual Conference of Pacific, Asian, and North American Asian Women in Theology and Ministry, Virtual, April 16-18, 2021).

practices. And it can alert us to the ways in which power functions to prescribe boundaries of race, cultural tastes, and what makes sense within an established meaning system.

Since racial identities and felt belonging emerge in contextual affective-sensory multiracialization processes, our anti-racist action and mobilization need to be contextual and specific to location and community. Understanding race as something people do—constantly, repeatedly—in specific contexts with various tools and affective dynamics allows us to understand that many kinds of human (inter)actions, experiences, and productions can potentially contribute to racializing events. And therefore, the possibility to engage in new kinds of relationships, affective movements, and bonds that can resist, transform, or even move beyond racist feelings and identify constructions is also present and inherent in our humanness. What this means for anti-racist mobilization, then, is that changing attitudes and material realities about race do *not* begin with changing minds about recognized identities or rational discourse about the material conditions as attached to racialized identities. Rather, anti-racist social change, or perhaps better put, change towards greater belonging for different kinds of bodies, emerges out of the interwoven movement and complex actions of bodies doing things together, including spaces like dining rooms, home kitchens, and public food festivals. This could propel us to focus less on constraining or regulating racist thought or speech and put more emphasis on: increasing our capacities to interpret and communicate our messy emotional experiences in new ways; being with others in amicable, even intimate relationships beyond what we already assume about self/others and our feelings about us/them, relationships that nonetheless may remain layered with tensions; communally investigating our visceral responses in the everyday and their implications in our mutual racializations.

Multiculturalism promises salvation in/as the recognition of one's identity and self, and culinary productions have become one kind of path to achieve this. Food work is complicit *and* has the potential for subverting this recognition, for being encountered on one's own culinary terms and to locate belonging in our own bodies and sensory relationships. Mark Padoongpatt observes that *"America love[s] our food but not our people. [...] food is at least one nexus where our histories converge to offer a basis for interracial and interethnic solidarity across gender, class, and citizenship [...] to help build and sustain collective challenges against the existing neoliberal racial order."*[64] Anti-racist struggles need to make use of affective forces, the dynamics that draw or repel bodies in a context, to open new conditions of action and being together beyond what has historically been aligned for them. Food, its production, consumption, and innovative creation is one of the fraught potential avenues that connect us to structural, political, and economic realities and racialized embodiment. Anti-racist mobilization can tap into foodways as affective efforts to

---

[64] Mark Padoongpatt, *Flavors of Empire: Food and the Making of Thai America* (Oakland: University of California Press, 2017), 190. Mark Padoonpatt explores the racial formation of Thais in the United States through food ways and food culture, showing how the practices of everyday life are critical in how people make sense of themselves, of others, of the world.

provide radical intimate spaces of flourishing, to affectively shape a more heterogenous, diversified multiraciality that defies, perhaps even ridicules, the fixed categories of white tastes.

Discussion Questions

1. Can you think of experiences when you had to negotiate to enjoy stereotypical foods of your own racial/ethnic group or that of others? How do you navigate such "guilty pleasures"?
2. What are some personal examples of how food shapes how you have learned about yourself and your racial belonging? How is gender interrelated with your experience with racialized foods? Socio-economic class?
3. How do specific racialized foods and food practices connect to your religious/spiritual experiences? What might it teach us about how our experiences of the divine, of flourishing, are connected through food and race?
4. What makes food authentic in your community? Who gets to decide if food or other cultural expression is authentic or not? Why is this decision important?
5. When does the label "authentic" limit an individual's or a community's diversity? What might be situations in which claims of authenticity perpetuate harmful racial stereotypes? What happens when members of a community dispute authenticity?

Bibliography

Ahmed, Sara. 2004. *The Cultural Politics of Emotion*. Edinburgh, UK: Edinburgh University Press.
———. 2008. *Queer Phenomenology: Orientations, Objects, Others*. Durham, NC: Duke University Press.
Amjahid, Mohamed. 2017. *Unter Weissen: Was es heisst, privilegiert zu sein*. München: Hanser Berlin.
Arel, Stephanie N. 2016. *Affect Theory, Shame, and Christian Formation*. New York: Palgrave Macmillan.
Berg, Ulla D., and Ana Y. Ramos-Zayas. 2015. Racializing Affect: A theoretical proposition. *Current Anthropology* 56 (5): 654–677.
Blickstein, Tamar. 2019. Affects of Racialization. In *Affective Societies—Key Concepts*, ed. Jan Slaby and Christian von Scheve, 152–166. New York: Routledge.
Bow, Leslie. 2022. *Racist Love: Asian Abstraction and the Pleasures of Fantasy*. Durham, NC: Duke University Press.
Brock, Rita Nakashima. 2007. Cooking without Recipes: Interstitial Integrity. In *Off the Menu: Asian and Asian North American Women's Religion & Theology*, ed. Rita Nakashima Brock, Jung Ha Kim, Kwok Pui-Lan, and Seung Ai Yang, 125–143. Louisville, KY: Westminster John Knox.
Brodeur, Abel, Warn N. Lekfuangfu, and Yanos Zylberberg. 2017. War, Migration, and the Origins of the Thai Sex Industry. *Journal of the European Economic Association* 16 (5): 1540–1576.
Cheng, Anne Anlin. 2019. *Ornamentalism*. New York: Oxford University Press.

Chin, Rita, Heide Fehrenbach, Geoff Eley, and Atina Grossmann. 2009. *After the Nazi Racial State: Difference and Democracy in Germany and Europe*. Ann Arbor: University of Michigan Press.

Cho, Grace M. 2021. *Tastes Like War: A Memoir*. New York: The Feminist Press at the City University of New York.

Choi, Ki Joo. 2019. *Disciplined by Race: Theological Ethics and the Problem of Asian American Identity*. Eugene, OR: Cascade Books.

Clough, Patricia Ticineto, and Jean O'Malley Halley. 2007. *The Affective Turn: Theorizing the Social*. Durham, NC: Duke University Press.

Cvetkovich, Ann. 2012. *Depression: A Public Feeling*. Durham, NC: Duke University Press.

DuBois, W.E.B. 1993. *The Souls of Black Folk*. New York: Knopf.

Eng, David L., and Shinhee Han. 2019. *Racial Melancholia, Racial Dissociation: On the Social and Psychic Lives of Asian Americans*. Durham, NC: Duke University Press.

Fanon, Frantz. 1962. *Black Skin, White Masks*. New York: Grove Weidenfeld.

Gregg, Melissa, and Gregory J. Seigworth. 2011. *The Affect Theory Reader*. Durham, NC: Duke University Press.

Haritaworn, Jin. 2009a. Hybrid Border Crossers? Towards a Radical Socialisation of 'Mixed Race'. *Journal of Ethnic and Migration Studies* 35 (1): 115–132.

———. 2009b. Queer Mixed Race? Interrogating Homonormativity through Thai Interraciality. In *Geographies of Sexualities: Theory, Practices, and Politics*, ed. Kath Browne, Jason Lim, and Gavin Brown, 2nd ed., 115–126. London: Ashgate.

———. 2016. *The Biopolitics of Mixing: Thai Multiracialities and Haunted Ascendancies*. London: Routledge.

Hook, Derek. 2005. Affecting Whiteness: Racism as Technology of Affect. *International Journal of Critical Psychology* 16: 74–99.

Julier, Alice, Carole Counihan, and Penny Van Esterik. 2019. Introduction: The Continuing Salience of Food and Culture. In *Food and Culture: A Reader*, ed. Carole Counihan, Penny Van Esterik, and Alice Julier, 4th ed., 1–9. New York: Routledge.

Karp, Myles. 2018. The Surprising Reason that There Are So Many Thai Restaurants in America. *Vice*, March 29. https://www.vice.com/en/article/paxadz/the-surprising-reason-that-there-are-so-many-thai-restaurants-in-america.

Kim, David Haekwon. 2015. Shame and Self-Revision in Asian American Assimilation. In *Living Alterities: Phenomenology, Embodiment, and Race*, ed. Emily S. Lee, 103–132. Albany: SUNY Press.

Kislenko, Arne. 2004. A Not So Silent Partner: Thailand's Role in Covert Operations, Counter-Insurgency, and the Wars in Indochina. *Journal of Conflict Studies* 24 (1): 65–96.

Koh, SueJeanne. Interstitial Integrity: Looking Forward, Radical Imagining. Presentation at the Annual Conference of Pacific, Asian, and North American Asian Women in Theology and Ministry, Virtual, April 16–18, 2021.

Mannur, Anita. 2022. *Intimate Eating: Racialized Spaces and Radical Futures*. Durham, NC: Duke University Press.

Padoongpatt, Mark. 2017. *Flavors of Empire: Food and the Making of Thai America*. Oakland: The University of California Press.

Padoonpatt, Mark. 2013. Oriental Cookery. In *Eating Asian America: A Food Studies Reader*, ed. Ku Robert Ji-Song, 186–207. New York: NYU Press.

Park Hong, Cathy. 2021. *Minor Feelings: An Asian American Reckoning*. New York: One World.

Schaefer, Donovan O. 2019. *The Evolution of Affect Theory: The Humanities, the Sciences, and the Study of Power*. Cambridge: Cambridge University Press.

Sinnott, Megan. 2007. Gender Subjectivity: Dees and Toms in Thailand. In *Women's Sexualities and Masculinities in a Globalizing Asia*, ed. Saskia E. Wieringa, Evelyn Blackwood, and Abha Bhaiya, 119–138. New York: Palgrave Macmillan.

Smith, Mark. 2006. *How Race Is Made: Slavery, Segregation, and the Senses*. Chapel Hill: University of North Carolina Press.

Sukrungruang, Ira. 2010. *Talk Thai: The Adventures of Buddhist Boy*. Columbia, MO: University of Missouri Press.

Tompkins, Kyla Wazana. 2012. *Racial Indigestion: Eating Bodies in the 19th Century*. New York: New York University Press.

US Census Bureau. Selected Population Profile in the United States. https://data.census.gov/cedsci. Accessed 1 June 2021.

Wallach, Jennifer Jensen. 2013. *How America Eats: A Social History of US Food and Culture*. Lanham, MD: Rowman & Littlefield Publishers, Inc.

Want, Kaori Mori. 2017. Hypervisibility and Invisibility of Female Haafu Models in Japan's Beauty Culture. In *Red and Yellow, Black and Brown: Decentering Whiteness in Mixed Race Studies*, ed. Joanne L. Rondilla, Rudy P. Guevarra Jr., and Paul R. Spickard, 163–177. New Brunswick, NJ: Rutgers University Press.

Wu, Judy Tzu-Chu. 2014. Hypervisibility and Invisibility: Asian/American Women, Radical Orientalism, and the Revisioning of Global Feminism. In *The Rising Tide of Color: Race, State Violence, and Radical Movements Across the Pacific*, ed. Moon-Ho Jung, 238–265. Seattle: The University of Washington Press.

Zauner, Michelle. 2021. *Crying in H Mart: A Memoir*. New York: Alfred A. Knopf.

Zembylas, Michalinos. 2015. Rethinking Race and Racism As Technologies of Affect: Theorizing the Implications for Anti- Racist Politics and Practice in Education. *Race, Ethnicity and Education* 18 (2): 145–162.

10
Toward Solidarity-Creating Narratives: Anti-Racist Identity Formation in Korean Immigrant Churches

Boyung Lee

Introduction

The current COVID-19 pandemic brought out discrimination that Asian/Americans have experienced for centuries on the US media and social discourse centers. Mainstream media competitively cover the increasing hate crimes against Asian/Americans with specific data and percentages compiled by various organizations, such as #StopAAPIHate and the Center for the Study of Hate and Extremism at California State University in San Bernardino. Often, this media coverage includes detailed descriptions of brutal attacks that different individual Asian/Americans have experienced, the racist motivations of perpetrators, and the racial consciousness the victims have developed because of the experience. Ironically, as such stories are covered almost daily in various news outlets, public awareness of anti-Asian racism is gaining momentum. For example, movements to include Asian/American histories and contributions in textbooks have been initiated by both Asian/American and other racial justice advocacy groups. In some cases, discussions and actions are happening at state government levels, such as the mandates to teach Asian/American studies at schools in New Jersey and Illinois.[1]

Changes are also occurring in Asian/American immigrant churches, where issues like racial justice have been implicitly but strongly regarded as political and social matters that should be separated from the spiritual focus of the church. In Asian/American churches I have been associated with, for instance, I now see pastors and

---

[1] Marian Chia-Ming Liu, "States are Mandating Asian American History Lessons to Stop Bigotry," *The Washington Post*, May 20, 2022, https://www.washingtonpost.com/education/2022/05/20/asian-american-history-schools-aapi/.

B. Lee (✉)
Iliff School of Theology, Denver, CO, USA
e-mail: blee@iliff.edu

lay leaders pray for the struggles and safety of Asian/Americans. Comments about anti-Asian hate crimes and strategies to "overcome" them are also made on various levels. Despite these positive changes, I am concerned about how Asian/American racial justice work is framed and taught at many immigrant churches. In most Asian/American churches, talks about current Asian/American struggles are done in ahistorical contexts without connecting to the long history and presence of Asian/Americans in the United States. Also, most of them exclusively focus on Asian/American struggles and rights while being silent on racism that other minoritized people experience, particularly anti-black racism prevalent in US history and society, including in Asian/American communities. Another concern is that even when solidarity with the Black, Indigenous, and People of Color (BIPOC) communities are mentioned, a dominant framework is what Elizabeth Hanna Rubio calls the "how-to-ism" of racial liberalism that settles anti-racism into a repertoire of predetermined steps, and thus contributes to maintaining white supremacy and racist social ordering.[2]

In this essay, I interrogate these dominant approaches through the lens of narrative identity formation in Korean immigrant church contexts. Cultural psychologists and critical pedagogy scholars argue that group and individual identities are formed, reproduced, or repudiated through the dialectic interaction between society's meta-narrative and individual stories anchored in the social story.[3] Meta-narratives about a group's history, ethnicity, religion, and politics shape the personal stories its members live by, which is called the individual identity formation process. That process serves as the primary tool to maintain the cultural accounts that serve the interests of the powerful of a given society. Minoritized communities have embraced narrative identity formation theory to challenge white supremacy and colonialist meta-narratives. However, I agree with Rubio and others like Benjamin Chang[4] that even within disempowered communities, examining how a group's histories are narrated is critical. Those historical narratives shape their identity and form the framework for racial justice work they do or do not engage in.

Locating myself in the Korean/American immigrant church, I review how each approach I named earlier has shaped Korean/American identity narratives. David Yoo, a Korean American historian, argues that Protestant Christianity has shaped the ideological foundation for Korean/American identity and perspectives, including their views on race and colonialism.[5] Thus, analyzing the Protestant church's ideological and historical narrative is critical to understanding Korean/American

---

[2] Elizabeth Hanna Rubio, "Black-Asian Solidarities and the Impasses of 'How-To' Anti-racisms," *Journal for the Anthropology of North America* 24, no. 1 (2021): 16–31.

[3] Dan P. McAdams and Kate C. McLean, "Narrative Identity," *Current Directions in Psychological Science* 22, no. 3 (June 2013): 236.

[4] Benjamin Chang, "From 'Illmatic' to 'Kung Flu': Black and Asian Solidarity, Activism, and Pedagogies in the Covid-19 Era," *Postdigital Science and Education* (2020) 2:741–756, https://doi.org/10.1007/s42438-020-00183-8.

[5] David K. Yoo, *Contentious Spirits: Religion in Korean American History, 1903–1945* (Stanford, CA: Stanford University Press, 2010).

racial formation and its framework. Through this review, I explore ways for the Korean immigrant Christians to contribute to building an anti-racist church and world in solidarity with other BIOPC communities. I particularly examine how Korean/American Christians can respond to anti-black racism while fighting against anti-Asian hate.

Narrating Our Histories and Forming Our Identities

According to narrative psychologists, human beings construct their identities with stories of what they believe is true and meaningful by internalizing and negotiating normative narratives of their community. People's identity is formed gradually over time as they tell stories about their experiences to and with others. "Through repeated interactions with others, stories about personal experiences are processed, edited, reinterpreted, retold, and subjected to a range of social and discursive influences, as the storyteller gradually develops a broader and more integrative narrative identity."[6] According to Dan P. McAdams and Kate C. McLean, "different cultures offer different menus of images, themes, and plots for the construction of narrative identity, and individuals within these cultures appropriate, sustain and modify these narrative forms as they tell their own stories."[7] In other words, people learn to tell stories fittingly for their cultural group through interactions and conversations with their parents and caregivers early in life and then with peers and primary formation institutions, such as schools and religious communities, as they grow old. A group's stories which include its identity, history, struggles, suffering, and resilience, become a person's stories as s/he/they construct personal narratives by combining their personal experiences with the group's accounts reflected in the meta-narrative.[8]

According to Phillip Hammack, who conducted comparative ethnographical research about the identity development of Israeli and Palestinian youths, communities at odds often teach opposite meta-narratives of related experiences to their members. He found that both Israeli and Palestinian youth appropriate master narratives of their cultural history and reproduce them in their personal stories. Even though they know about problematic elements of the master narratives, both groups still develop competitive identities rooted in their incompatible master narratives.[9] Hammack argues that people who live in conflict-ridden regions and contexts, like Israel and the occupied Palestinian territory, have a much higher tendency to identify with the cultural group at all costs. A person's identity is for the sustenance of

---

[6] McAdams and McLean, "Narrative Identity," 235.
[7] McAdams and McLean, "Narrative Identity," 235.
[8] Phillip L. Hammack, "Narrative and the Cultural Psychology of Identity," *Personality and Social Psychology Review* 12, no. 3 (August 2008): 233, https://doi.org/10.1177/1088868308316892.
[9] Hammack, "Narrative and the Cultural Psychology of Identity," 222–247.

group identity, which faces external threats. Hammack further observes that the connection between master narratives and personal identity narratives is even stronger among historically minoritized and oppressed groups. In this sense, Hammack insists that identity is truly an ideological matter and defines it as the "ideology cognized through the individual engagement with discourse, made manifest in a personal narrative constructed and reconstructed across the life course and scripted in and through social interaction and social practice."[10] In sum, human identity, which takes a form of a narrative filled with ideological content, only works when individual stories are coherent with an available discourse in a specific society with various stances toward other groups, "be that group a rival of equal status, a subordinate group, or an oppressor."[11]

Hammack's definition of identity challenges Korean immigrant Christians to critically examine the familiar ideological narratives they share. Borrowing religious educator Mai-Anh Le Tran's words, we should review "*why* [we] say what [we] say; what is at stake in such narration; what meaning or purpose is derived; what raw materials contribute to how relations and connections are created and sustained through the narrative act."[12] Particularly, what and how do we narrate our history? What's our point of reference for our presence in the United States? What does our historical narrative imply for our stance toward other groups, particularly BIPOC communities? What do our meta-narratives teach about anti-black racism in our society and communities? Who is benefited or is disadvantaged by our narratives? These questions invite Korean immigrant Christians to interrogate racial ideologies and the framework embedded in their identity narratives. Based on the work of several Asian/American studies scholars who have investigated these questions, I will focus on the three concerned issues I mentioned in the introduction. Specifically, I examine each approach's implication for how Korean/Americans respond or do not respond to anti-black racism.

Korean/American Identity Narratives and Anti-black Racism in Churches

In 2021 and 2022, with a Korean/American artist, a Japanese American Ethnic Studies scholar, and a Korean/American philosopher, I co-curated an art exhibit, *inVISIBLE/hyperVISIBLE*, which featured sixteen different artists of Asian heritage from various ethnic and cultural backgrounds.[13] After experiencing a traumatic

---

[10] Hammack, "Narrative and the Cultural Psychology of Identity," 223.

[11] Hammack, "Narrative and the Cultural Psychology of Identity," 232.

[12] Mai-Anh Le Tran, "Narrating Lives, Narrating Faith: "Organic Hybridity" for Contemporary Christian Religious Education," *Religious Education*, 105, no. 2 (2010): 195, DOI: 10.1080/00344081003645186.

[13] For the 2021 exhibit at the Red Line Contemporary Art Center in Denver, CO, see https://www.redlineart.org/invisible-hypervisible. For the 2022 expanded exhibit at the Dairy Arts Center in Boulder, CO, see https://thedairy.org/invisible-hypervisible/.

racist attack from a white man with anti-Asian slurs near my house, which confined me in my house for about eight months[14]. I was personally determined to bring theologically informed education on Asian/Americans to the public through arts. The quote below from the 2022 curatorial statement, written on May 13, the day when the Dallas Korean hair salon shooting happened, states the purpose of this exhibit:

> We, artists and academics, also came together to intervene against heightening violence targeting people of Asian descent, which increased by 340% during the pandemic, by offering a solidarity-building platform through arts among diverse Asian/Americans, BIPOC (Black, Indigenous, and people of color) people, and allies…As we hear news about violence against Asian/Americans, the immediate reaction people often have is fear and indifference. However, we refuse to dwell in that space. Instead, we choose to build a beloved community for ALL people and invite you to join us in (re)imagining a better future together.[15]

A press release that includes the entire curatorial statement was made multiple times for different newspapers, TV, and radio stations, including various Asian language media with the translated statement. I also reached out to the Korean pastors holding weekly meetings for the joint Vacation Bible School (VBS) of the Korean churches in the greater Denver area. The first response from a young Korean pastor's spouse was whether I was developing a new hobby in arts as I was doing nontheological and -church work. I explained to her the situations that Asian/Korean/Americans are facing and the Buffalo Supermarket shooting that happened that day, a tragic example of prevailing anti-black racism and the danger of white supremacy and Christian nationalism that frames discrimination against BIOPC communities. I pleaded the urgency of our time, which calls for Korean Christians' actions with further explanation about anti-Asian/Korean racism and its connection to anti-black racism. However, her simple response was, "I am a recent immigrant, and anti-racism work is for someone like you."

While I was frustrated by her response, another person in the group, a Korean/American male pastor whose theological training was done both in Korea and the United States, joined our conversation. After hearing about our conversation, he said he would strongly support my efforts. These days, Korean and Asian/Americans are the main target of racially motivated hate crimes, including those committed by African Americans. He continued ranting about how unfair it was for Asian/Americans as the US discussions on racism were only about black and white. He declared, "it's the time for us, Asian/Korean/Americans, to claim our equal rights and demand an Asian/American-centered anti-racism education and movement." I still vividly remember the feeling of dismay from these two responses. I felt even more pain because they are not unique but prevail in Korean/American immigrant

---

[14] For a detailed description of my experience and motivation, please watch ABC News coverage, "Turning Anti-Asian Trauma into Power" at https://rb.gy/2n1r1a.

[15] Sammy Seung-min Lee, Boyung Lee, Chad Shomura, and Boram Jeong, "A Curatorial Statement for inVISIBLE | hyperVISIBE: Art Exhibit, Public Lecture & Workshop on Asian America," May 20-July 16, 2022. The Dairy Arts Center. Boulder, CO, https://thedairy.org/invisible-hypervisible/.

churches. They serve as explicit and implicit ideologies that provide foundational narratives for Korean/American immigrants' identity.

1. *"I am a recent immigrant, and Anti-racism work is for someone like you."*

This response I got from the Korean/American pastor's spouse, unfortunately, is not a rare one among Korean/Americans. It is understandable why many of them think like that, as they did most of their schooling in Asia/Korea, and thus they would not have had a chance to learn about Asian/American history. Even if one went to school in the United States, they would have had minimal exposure to Asian/American issues due to the omission of Asian/American history in US education. Notwithstanding, this attitude of indifference or self-excuse harms Korean/Americans and other BIPOC people. Moreover, it creates and perpetuates false ideologies for Korean/American identity formation for the coming generations beyond themselves, which intentionally and unintentionally support the United States' current racial and social hierarchy and the omnipresent white supremacy. I identify two main reasons for this self-excuse and indifference among many Korean/American Christians, namely, Korean/American church's nationalist history and orientation toward Korea, and their connection to the colonial view of the United States as God's benevolent land.

Compared to other Asian/American ethnic groups, the percentage of Christians among Korean/Americans is very high. According to the last Pew Research Foundation survey on America's religious landscape in 2012, while 42% of Asian/Americans are Christians, 71% of Korean/Americans identify as churched Christians. It is the second highest rate among Asian/Americans after Filipino Americans.[16] About this, David Yoo concludes that Protestant Christianity has provided the most crucial entry point to Korean/American history. Churches gave an institutional structure for community and everyday life beyond religious formation.[17] From the beginning, Korean/American churches have served multiple purposes, such as places of worship, social gathering places, employment centers, Korean language school, centers of local and transnational politics, etc. The Korean/American churches have "provided the means by which Koreans carved out and sustained their own identity as a people" and how they have to live in the United States with perspectives on the world shaped by their religion.[18] This tradition is rooted in the early Korean/American's "positive" view of Christianity shaped by American missionaries in Korea, who also significantly recruited the first Korean migrant workers to Hawai'i.

In most Asian countries, Christianity was the religion of European and American colonizers. But in Korea, where the colonizing power was Japan, it

---

[16] The Pew Research Center, "Religious Affiliation, Beliefs and Practices," in *The Rise of Asian Americans* (Washington, D.C.: The Pew Research Center, 2012), 172–173. Also available at https://www.pewresearch.org/social-trends/2012/06/19/chapter-7-religious-affiliation-beliefs-and-practices/.

[17] Yoo, *Contentious Spirits*, 3–4.

[18] Yoo, *Contentious Spirits*, 5.

was Protestant missionaries who brought the nineteenth-century American civil religion of independence and freedom as a Christian message[19] and took the side of the Korean people in their struggles against Japanese imperialism. The American civil religion framed in Protestant Christianity embodied the American colonial project. Protestant missionaries defined and taught proper Christian behavior as acting in accord with white American customs and manners to Koreans. They worked hard and took pride in creating a "miniature America" as a core part of their mission work. For example, in her letter to her American colleague, Ella Appenzeller, Henry Appenzeller's wife, writes, "We, with the Presbyterians and the Legations, are making this end of the city a miniature America. We can show thousands what a home is like, and have made ours as pleasant as possible."[20] However, it appeared to many Koreans of the time that Christianity, presented in the language and forms of American civil religion, condemned their enemy, Japanese imperialism. It gave them spiritual and moral justification for their fights, thus encouraging them to rapidly convert to the Protestant Christianity of American missionaries.[21]

These missionaries were also the leading recruiters of cheap Korean laborers for their home country, America. After the abolition of slavery, American companies needed bargain workers and hired Protestant missionaries in Korea as their recruiters. The missionaries introduced America, particularly Hawai'i, as a paradise and a land of God's benevolence to their young male Korean parishioners.[22] As a result, the first Koreans came to the US territory between 1902 and 1905 to work on Hawaiian plantations. According to David Yoo and Ruth Chung, forty percent of those workers were Christians.[23] Soon after their arrival, they spread out across North America and formed churches in Honolulu (1903), Los Angeles (1904), and other parts of the country.[24] Among many early migrants, there were elite leaders of the Korean independence movement, including Syngman Rhee, who became the first president of South Korea, and others like Ahn Chang-ho and Pak Yong-Man. They considered themselves exiled Christians devoted to their homeland's freedom, influenced by the American civil religion version of Christianity. This history and theology set the tone for the Korean/American church's ethos as the essential site of Protestant nationalism for Korea

---

[19] For example, Henry Gerhard Appenzeller, the first Methodist missionary to Korea, is a quintessential example who regarded the 19th-century American civil religion as the essence of Christianity. See Daniel M. Davies, *The Life and Thought of Henry Gerhard Appenzeller (1858–1902): Missionary to Korea* (Lewiston, NY: The Edwin Mellen Press, 1988).

[20] Ella Appenzeller, "Ella Appenzeller to Mrs. J. S. Wadsworth, May 14, 1886," quoted in Davies, *The Thought and Life of Henry Gerhard Appenzeller (1858–1902)*, 185.

[21] Yoo, *Contentious Spirits*, 17–33.

[22] David K. Yoo and Ruth H. Chung, *Religion and Spirituality in Korean America* (Chicago: University of Illinois Press, 2008), 3.

[23] Yoo and Chung, *Religion and Spirituality in Korean America*, 3.

[24] *Encyclopedia.com*, s.v. "Korean-American Religions," accessed June 19, 2022, https://www.encyclopedia.com/religion/legal-and-political-magazines/korean-american-religions.

and as centers for local and transnational politics.[25] Regarding this, Yoo analyzes that, "Korean/Americans viewed their role as preserving Korea as a distinct people and nation through a community of memory."[26]

As a diaspora community whose aim was the independence of their motherland, their focus was also on Japan as the colonizer. Thus, Korean/American Christians easily overlooked US colonialism. They regarded America as a Christian land of benevolence with freedom in an egalitarian society, as they learned from missionaries. These foundational ideologies then have fostered a denial of the US engagement in imperial projects at home and abroad, including the Korean peninsula.[27] Erika Lee, an Asian/American historian and Ethnic Studies scholar, points out that Asian migration in the late nineteenth and early twentieth centuries is closely connected to capitalism, imperialism, uneven economic development, and population displacement in Asia by the Western colonial power, including the United States. The powerful reach of the United States in many places in Asia, like the Philippines and Korea, continues even today, and it has been shaping global migration patterns beyond Asia.[28]

In addition to an idealized America and an overlooked US imperialism, Yoo observes that the hardship, racism, and exploitation in Hawai'i and the mainland directed most Korean/Americans to express their loyalties to Korea, which further shaped their meta-narratives of indifference and self-excuse.[29] Many were angry at white Christians who discriminated against them. Early Korean Christian immigrants were confused and perplexed about how their shared religious tradition with most Americans did not protect them from being racialized. They could not understand how fellow white Christians in the land built on Christian egalitarian values were discriminating against them through housing restrictions, discriminatory wage scales, and the racially motivated immigration quota system that kept them from being united with their families. Regarding this, Yoo argues that "the confluence of religion and race engaged the complexities and contradictions" of the early Korean/American immigrant experiences.[30]

Although more than a century has passed since the first Korean/Americans arrived in the United States, such legacy, historical ethos, and ideological narratives still implicitly but firmly provide the foundations for Korean/American Christian identity and peoplehood. Internalizing white supremacy, Christian nationalist rhetoric, and the racist myth of the model minority while constantly experiencing discrimination through the perpetual foreigner syndrome, Korean/American immigrant Christians have developed and deepened the attitude of

---

[25] Yoo and Chung, *Religion and Spirituality in Korean America* 3; Yoo, *Contentious Spirits*, 58–82.

[26] Yoo, *Contentious Spirits*, 9.

[27] Yoo, *Contentious Spirits*, 10.

[28] Erika Lee, "A Part and Apart: Asian American and Immigration History," *Journal of American Ethnic History* 34, no. 4 (Summer 2015): 34.

[29] Yoo, *Contentious Spirits*, 9.

[30] Yoo, *Contentious Spirits*, 12.

indifference or self-excuse from accountability for racism in general and for anti-black racism in the church and the larger society.

Indifference is one of the critical ways for non-White people to participate in perpetuating white supremacy, albeit unintentionally. According to Aggie J. Yellow Horse et al., who examined individual-level predictors of indifference to the Black Lives Matter (BLM) movement based on native status, a large proportion of Asian/Americans are indifferent to anti-black racism and the BLM movement.[31] They concluded that the main reason for the indifference is the lack of a sense of belonging. Particularly, foreign-born Asian/Americans were significantly more indifferent to the BLM movement than their US-born Asian/American counterparts. However, the impact of nativity was meaningless once the sense of belonging and acknowledgment of anti-Black racism was counted. Even among US-born Asian/Americans, the lower their sense of belonging, the higher their indifference level was. In fact, Yellow Horse et al. conclude that the level of sense of belonging was the only predictor of indifference among US-born Asian/Americans. They argue that Asian/Americans' indifference is rooted in internalized racism as an adaptive strategy to survive white supremacy. Indifference has led them to have less knowledge of the complexities of racial relations in the United States and willfully embrace colorblind ideologies.[32] The result is that Asian/Americans intentionally and unintentionally help to sustain white supremacy. This greatly resonates with Korean/Americans' double-edged experiences of America, a land of God's benevolence filled with racism. Such experiences have led them to pay significantly more attention to Korea than the United States. In sum, it is critical to interrogate the omnipresent white supremacy in US society in an examination of Korean/Americans' indifference to racial justice as a fundamental way to overcome it.

White supremacy is "a multipronged phenomenon that sustains White privilege through socioeconomic, legal, cultural, and materialist means," and other "normal" social systems, such as naturalization, citizenship, immigration, loans, housing, education, promotions, and other cultural systems designed to serve White people's interests in the name of convention.[33] As Yellow Horse et al. argue, Korean/Americans participate in the perpetuation of white supremacy through their indifference and self-excuse. Although there are compelling historical reasons why they have become a meta-narrative for Korean/American Christian identity formation, they need to remember that indifference is not value-free but a potent form of support that protects existing privilege.[34] In the United States, anti-black racism has been the backbone of white supremacy and

---

[31] Aggie J. Yellow Horse, et al., "Asian Americans' Indifference to Black Lives Matter: The Role of Nativity, Belonging, and Acknowledgement of Anti-Black Racism," *Social Sciences* 10, no. 5 (2021): 1–19.

[32] Yellow Horse, et al., "Asian Americans' Indifference to Black Lives Matter," 8.

[33] Yellow Horse, et al., "Asian Americans' Indifference to Black Lives Matter," 2.

[34] Fran Tonkiss, "The Ethics of Indifference: Community and Solitude in the City," *International Journal of Cultural Studies* 6, no. 3 (2003): 297–311, https://doi.org/10.1177/13678779030063004.

Christian nationalism. The indifference or complicity of Korean/Americans has helped to support anti-black racism regardless of their intentions. Simply put, it is not enough for Korean/Americans not to be racist. They must be "anti-racist" in the system of racial capitalism and white supremacy.[35] As Hammack says, "the problem of identity is not simply a matter of life-course timing. It is, rather, the substance of identity and its place in the larger process of cultural reproduction that is central to an integrative formulation."[36] The question for Korean/American Christians, then, is how they narrate their history with decolonial and anti-racist consciousness, particularly undoing anti-black racism prevailing in our communities and society.

2. *It's the time for us, Asian/Korean/Americans, to claim our equal rights and demand Asian/American-centered anti-racism education and movement."*

This declaration by the Korean/American male pastor is another typical response to anti-racist work in Korean/American churches. Putting it upfront, it is another form of supporting white supremacy, which tactically pits minoritized people against each other. Although minoritized communities throughout the United States and global history have been working together and in solidarity to disrupt racial hierarchies, white supremacy, exploitation, and other colonial projects, those stories and histories are often erased in both white and non-white people's discourse.[37] Opting into such false rhetoric further perpetuates anti-black racism as it makes each minoritized community compete with one another at the cost of African Americans at the bottom of the racial hierarchy. Deepa Iyer calls this a white supremacy tactic that maintains capitalism.[38]

Expanding Andrea Smith's three pillars of white supremacy, Iyer names the four central logics of white supremacy which are the foundation and driving force for all the oppressions we know: 1) slavery that underpins capitalism/anti-black racism; 2) settler colonialism, which enables and strengthens ongoing colonialism and imperialism; 3) Orientalism, which rationalizes the militarism and the necessity of war to continue and maintain the interests of imperialism; 4) Islamophobia/National Security that preserves the illusion of safety against non-Christians and immigrants of color. [39]

One axis of white supremacy is the logic of slavery. The logic is that, in essence, blacks are nothing more than possessions, and they were created to be enslaved, so it is natural for them to be discriminated against. Even though official slavery was abolished 150 years ago, anti-black racism is relived in contemporary societies in different forms. Iver argues that anti-black racism is the basic premise of sustaining capitalism, as it leads poor whites and non-blacks to falsely

---

[35] Yellow Horse, et al., "Asian Americans' Indifference to Black Lives Matter," 3.

[36] Hammack, "Narrative and the Cultural Psychology of Identity," 225.

[37] Yellow Horse, et al., "Asian Americans' Indifference to Black Lives Matter," 6.

[38] Deepa Iyer, *We Too Sing America: South Asian, Arab, Muslim, and Sikh Immigrants Shape Our Multicultural Future* (New York: The New Press, 2015), 103–109.

[39] Iyer, *We Too Sing America*, 104.

believe that they can get out of the bottom of capitalism as long as they are not black. This false belief "encourages" them to work for white capitalism by keeping blacks at the bottom of society.

The second axis of white supremacy is the logic of racial extinction. This logic is related to land ownership, which is associated with the extermination policy of the Indigenous people who claim original land ownership. To prevent indigenous people from claiming their rights to land, this logic creates a false myth that they have disappeared. Thus, it is legitimate for non-indigenous people to claim their ownership of indigenous people's land, resources, spirituality, and culture.

Iyer names the logic of Orientalism as the third pillar of white supremacy. This logic identifies certain people or nations as inferior beings who continue to threaten the well-being and interests of the empire. This logic sees non-white immigrants as a threat who might have allegiance to outsiders, especially during wartime, such as Japanese Americans confined to concentration camps until the end of World War II. At the same time, their property was confiscated. Nowadays, Muslim immigrants have been the subject of the most scrutiny and discrimination since the war on terrorism after 9/11.

The fourth pillar of white supremacy, closely related to Orientalism, is Islamophobia. It is a belief system that disparages Muslims and Muslim-appearing people for the illusion of collective safety. Iyer argues that in the name of security, white supremacy-based governing systems of the United States have created new laws to justify profiling, targeting, imprisoning, and deporting immigrants of color, particularly Muslim immigrants. This logic shows the connection between white supremacy and Christian nationalism.

In sum, irrespective of race, immigration history, economic class, and other statuses, every American is entangled in the white supremacy system. If they do not work in solidarity, minoritized people continue perpetuating each other's sufferings.[40] Korean/Americans are victims of orientalism that discriminates against immigrants of color. Yet they are part of an anti-black racist structure while also being an inherent part of settler colonialism as inhabitants of the land taken from Native Americans. Korean/Americans' lives are inherently connected and intertwined with others, especially other minoritized people. Their privileges and oppressions, resistance and healing, self-reflection and solidarity are concurrently formed and evolving in tangled, interwoven, and overlapping locations.

The response of the Korean male pastor and other similar ones have been more commonly found among Korean immigrant pastors since the pandemic. The rise of anti-Asian and xenophobic rhetoric and hate incidents toward Asian/Americans have become personal for Korean immigrants. These experiences have awakened many Asian/Korean immigrants who have been formed through indifference and self-excuse narratives of the community. However, as most

---

[40] Iyer, *We Too Sing America*, 105–106.

Korean immigrant Christians' identity formation in the United States has been framed in the nationalist history and orientation toward Korea, many immigrant Christians have neither paid close attention to nor have had many opportunities to learn about Asian/American involvement in anti-racism and civil rights movements and solidarity work with other BIPOC communities, especially, African American communities. The unfortunate consequence is perpetuating white supremacy, which further discriminates against themselves, and being accused of "not supporting mass movements for racial equality" and "trafficking in anti-Black racism," further dividing minoritized people.[41]

It is true that Korean/Americans are doubly marginalized and live within liminality, as reflected in their experiences with the model minority and the perpetual foreigner syndromes. However, in US society, where racial hierarchy frames socioeconomic-political policies and practices, Korean/Americans cannot solely focus on their marginalization and equality. For example, Laura Hyun Yi Kang argues that even among Asian/American women, there have been hierarchically structured differences along the line of race/ethnicity, class, and nationality ever since the era of Japanese imperial expansion at the end of the nineteenth century.[42] That hierarchy continues in various forms in Asia and the United States. As Korea's economic status has improved, so has the status of Korean/American women in the social hierarchy. According to the 2018 Report on the Gender Wage Gap by the Institute for Women's Policy, women of all major racial and ethnic groups earn less than men of the same group and less than White men.[43] Among women of all races, Asian/American women's earning power is the highest, being the third among all groups and just after White men and Asian men. That is, while Asian and Korean/American women experience discrimination, they are better off than other women and non-Asian racial minority men on the economic ladder of US society.[44]

---

[41] Yellow Horse, et al., "Asian Americans' Indifference to Black Lives Matter," 2.

[42] Laura Hyun Yi Kang, *Compositional Subjects: Enfiguring Asian/American Women* (Durham, NC: Duke University Press, 2002) 183.

[43] Ariane Hegewisch and Heidi Hartmann, *The Gender Wage Gap: 2018 Earnings Differences by Race and Ethnicity* (Washington, DC: Institute for Women's Policy Research, 2018). Available at https://iwpr.org/iwpr-issues/esme/the-gender-wage-gap-2018-earnings-differences-by-gender-race-and-ethnicity/.

[44] One important fact to remember is that among Asian Americans there are significant economic gaps depending on one's immigration status, educational level, English proficiency, countries of origin, etc. Often those statistics are based on survey with English speaking Asian Americans who are employed. According to the 2021 Pew Research Center's data, "there are large differences in poverty rates among Asian subgroups. Most of the Asian origin groups analyzed (12 of 19) had poverty rates that were as high as or higher than the U.S. average in 2019." Abby Budiman and Neil G. Ruiz, "Key Facts About Asian Americans, A Diverse and Growing Population" (Washington, D.C.: The Pew Research Center, 2021). Available at https://www.pewresearch.org/fact-tank/2021/04/29/key-facts-about-asian-americans/.

It is a known fact that one of the critical governing methods of all empires in human history was *divide et impera* (divide and rule).[45] This policy was used to prevent different subjugated groups from uniting. Using *divide et impera*, the ancient and modern-day empires have pitted people, especially the marginalized, against each other. This policy, coupled with the co-opting of the elites of the minoritized groups, has further complicated the existing internal hierarchical system, creating even more sociopolitical-economic classes at the bottom of society.[46] The above data on Asian/Korean/American women should challenge Korean/Americans to be more conscious of how *divide et impera* is at work in contemporary society. It urges them not to subscribe to the model minority myth, a tool to marginalize others further. Without such critical consciousness, they quickly fall prey to white supremacy logic, indifference, and self-excuse from anti-black racism-centered racial justice work.

The common claim among Korean/American Christians highlighting their victim status with an emphasis on bettering their people or their uniqueness and struggles is also a form of internalized racism and colonialism that supports anti-black racism and white supremacy. Internalized oppression is the acceptance by the oppressed people of the negative societal beliefs and stereotypes about themselves as a result of discrimination and oppression over a period of time.[47] Although unjust social structures and discriminatory cultural biases hinder them from achieving equal social standing, many marginalized communities can turn the experience of oppression inward and take for granted their lower status and unworthiness engineered by the oppressors of the white supremacist system. Internalized oppression at the group level can result in further harmful consequences for the oppressed. Rather than working in solidarity with others to challenge unjust situations and systems, marginalized groups tend to perceive each other as enemies with whom they must compete to achieve justice. Loretta Pyles, a scholar of social welfare, argues that when one marginalized group turns against another marginalized group, projecting internalized oppression onto other people of similar social status, it results in horizontal hostility and fighting between oppressed groups.[48] Horizontal hostility and internalized oppression

---

[45] Richard Morrock, "Heritage of Strife: The Effects of Colonialist 'Divide and Rule' Strategy upon the Colonized Peoples," *Science & Society* 37, no. 2 (1973): 129–151. Also, Angelo N. Ancheta, *Race, Rights, and the Asian American Experience* (New Brunswick, NJ: Rutgers University Press, 2006).

[46] Morrock, "Heritage of Strife,"129.

[47] The Center for Community Health and Development, "Healing from the Effects of Internalized Oppression," in *Community Toolbox: Tools to Change Our World* (Lawrence: University of Kansas, 2019). Available at https://ctb.ku.edu/en/table-of-contents/culture/cultural-competence/healing-from-interalized-oppression/main.

[48] Loretta Pyles, *Progressive Community Organizing: Reflective Practice in a Globalizing World*, 2nd ed. (New York: Routledge, 2013), 167.

together have the effect of *divide et impera*, which pits people against themselves and one another.

Discriminations Korean/American Christians have experienced and heightened hate crimes targeting them during the pandemic challenge them even more to consider the urgency of solidarity with other marginalized people. They need to be critically aware of their location in the hierarchical US society and the danger of subscribing to the myth of the model minority, a tool for horizontal hostility. As Benjamin Chang points out, while the pandemic has deepened the burdens of Korean/American Christians and other Asian/Americans, it has also afforded opportunities to see shared struggles across communities. Thus, Korean/Americans should ask why things are the way they are, and connect and mobilize with others, confronting and deconstructing false binaries and other essentialization of race and society.[49] It is time to critically review Korean/American Christian identity narratives and omitted histories.

Toward Solidarity-Based Identity Formation Narratives

Korean/American Christians are called to revisit their long-lived meta-narratives of indifference and self-excuse and develop solidarity-creating identity formation narratives that deconstruct white supremacy and Christian nationalism. However, they need to pay attention to Elizabeth Rubio's caution: do not fall into well-meaning racial liberalism but develop an abolitionist solidarity narrative. She defines racial liberalism as how-to anti-racism that

> sustains the tenuous promise that racism is something that one can challenge in interpersonal relationships and by following specific steps toward individualized behavior correction…"settling" anti-racism into a repertoire of predetermined steps, how-to-ism constrains the contradiction, anger, and uncertainty that is fundamental to forging the radical accountability central to abolitionist work.[50]

The root of racial liberalism is the innate American exceptionalism of white liberal allies and well-meaning people. It is more visibly expressed during heightened racial conflict times like the current pandemic and the Black Lives Matter movement. Convinced about racial equality as the telos of America as a country, white liberal allies try to restore a sense that racial injustice is something they should address and must resolve by following the proper steps and doing the right thing. They typically read literature "oriented toward restoring the 'rational' structuring of racial hegemony as a process of white liberal catharsis."[51] Robin DiAngelo's popular book, *White Fragility*, is a case in point that showcases the white racial liberalism industry's how-to behavioral products in recent years. Typically, they view

---

[49] Chang, "From 'Illmatic' to 'Kung Flu'," 752.
[50] Rubio, "Black-Asian Solidarities and the Impasses of 'How-To' Anti-racisms," 16.
[51] Rubio, "Black-Asian Solidarities and the Impasses of 'How-To' Anti-racisms," 17.

people of color as almost entirely powerless and are particularly condescending toward Black people.[52] They portray Black and other people of color as victims of white racist and colonial systems. Thus, they must "save" or at least "help" the powerless victims by doing the right thing. Rubio points out that such an approach—having done something about racial inequality and violence, starting with reading the relevant literature, is the very sign of the "underlying contradiction exposed in the moment of racial confusion for the restitution of American exceptionalism."[53] Reading racial liberalist literature usually is followed by a series of how-to behavioral programs for public education and legislative bills within the existing US systems. The consequence is the perpetuation of the same system, except that liberal white people feel good that they have done something about it. Then when another heightened racial conflict arises, the same cycle is repeated. The same system with the illusion of being improved continues without undoing racial hierarchy, white supremacy, and settler colonialism.

Rubio is critical of how frequently such how-to racial liberalism is found in Asian/American communities, including Korean immigrant societies. Particularly, it is prevalent in their relationship with African Americans and the solidarity movement with them. After analyzing scores of panels and conferences organized and hosted by Asian/Americans, she names three dominant logics that circulate in contemporary Asian/American efforts to express solidarity with African Americans—indebted, transactional, and self-reflexive:

> Solidarity rooted in indebtedness names the ways that Asian Americans are deeply indebted to Black liberation struggles historic and present. It often looks like quoting Black theorists, highlighting the origins of certain organizing tactics in Black resistance movements, or paying homage to the ways Asian Americans have benefitted from Black struggles. This vital sense of indebtedness leads to a second transactional logic that implies that Asian Americans should show up for Black-led protests, bump relevant social media content, or fight against anti-Black policies because we might need Black folks to show up for us one day. A third self-reflexive logic centers Asian American reckoning with anti-Blackness within ourselves and our communities. Self-reflexivity focuses on unlearning anti-Black behaviors and ways of thinking, while also acknowledging the ways Asian Americans benefit from Black oppression.[54]

Rubio emphasizes that acknowledging African Americans' fights and the paths they have paved for human rights for all are critical in Asian/American racial justice work. Critical self-reflections on racism and anti-black racism within Asian/American communities are also necessary for multiracial struggles over transactional attitudes. However, Rubio points out that these three logics are like the how-to white racial liberalism in that they have become a repertoire or predictable routine that Asian/Americans should follow for any racial justice work, centering solidarity

---

[52] John McWhorter, "The Dehumanizing Condescension of *White Fragility*," *The Atlantic*, July 15, 2020, https://www.theatlantic.com/ideas/archive/2020/07/dehumanizing-condescension-white-fragility/614146/.
[53] Rubio, "Black-Asian Solidarities and the Impasses of 'How-To' Anti-racisms," 17.
[54] Rubio, "Black-Asian Solidarities and the Impasses of 'How-To' Anti-racisms," 21.

with African Americans.⁵⁵ For example, one often hears Asian/American activists urge fellow Americans of Asian heritage to show up for other groups' justice work to unlearn their anti-Blackness. Rubio warns that such predictable "repertoire, while covering the important ground, puts brackets around the beginning and the end of the conversation, such that you come to know how it ends before it even begins."⁵⁶ This almost manual following approach easily creates false consciousness among Asian/Americans, as if the issue is Blackness, not white supremacy. In other words, the discourse on the necessity (or difficulty) of building solidarity movements with African Americans becomes central rather than deconstructing white supremacy, nationalism, and colonialism.

Such false consciousness also creates an ahistorical myth, as if there are equivalences between Asian and African American struggles. It also flattens diversity among Asian/Americans, with ethnic hierarchies, classism, sexism, homophobia, transphobia, classism, heteropatriarchy, and other oppressive systems and cultures. Solidarity building with African Americans and other BIOPC communities based on predictable manuals and how-to racial liberalism does not create solidarity. Because true solidarity, whose purpose is to deconstruct white supremacy and colonialism, requires collapsing all the oppressive systems and hierarchies among, between, and in our world and societies. It mandates us to give up our privileges gained at the white-led global hierarchical systems. It requires a new social order based on equity and equality for the liberation of all people, prioritizing the most minoritized people. In this sense, racial justice work through solidarity building should move toward abolitionist new world construction.

As Korean immigrant Christian churches revisit their histories and meta-narratives to build a just world for all, they need to remember lessons from abolitionist anti-racists that not being a racist is not enough, although it is the first step. They are called to be anti-racists and anti-black racists. For that, multiracial solidarity is a must. However, solidarity does not mean everyone is getting along. Instead, it mandates to be in struggles with one another and be accountable to one another.⁵⁷ If individual community members' identity only makes sense when their ideological narratives are aligned with the cultural meta-narratives, Korean immigrant Christians must re-narrate their stories to create abolitionist meta-narratives for the kin-dom of God as they pray "thy will be done on earth as it is in heaven." For that, Korean/Americans will have to ask different questions to unlearn their old meta-narratives with critical eyes for undoing white supremacy: What new educational mechanisms do they need to have to learn the complexities of racial dynamics of the United States from decolonial perspectives, which hardly are included in the US educational systems? How do Korean/Americans tell their histories, struggles, and perseverance as a part of Asian/American stories? What concrete action beyond racial liberalist approaches is needed to challenge anti-Asian discrimination in a

---

⁵⁵ Rubio, "Black-Asian Solidarities and the Impasses of 'How-To' Anti-racisms," 17–22.
⁵⁶ Rubio, "Black-Asian Solidarities and the Impasses of 'How-To' Anti-racisms," 22.
⁵⁷ Rubio, "Black-Asian Solidarities and the Impasses of 'How-To' Anti-racisms," 28.

way that does not subscribe to the divide and conquer strategies of white supremacy? To answer these questions, the first step would be to examine Korean and Korean/American experiences and histories in a global context to understand how white supremacy and its colonial projects have shaped their stories and experiences at the cost of many invisible others. Narrating Korean/American histories with a global consciousness means that they need to connect the dots between the British slavery abolition act and forced migrations of Asians, such as the presence of so-called "guest workers"—cheap laborers from British colonies like India and parts of China in North America, their solidarity and conflict with enslaved African people, migration of Korean labors to Hawai'i after the enactment of discriminatory laws against Chinese.[58] It also means demystifying the model minority myth, a project of white supremacy to which many Korean/Americans have unknowingly subscribed and thus participated in further discriminating against black and brown people. In sum, Korean/Americans must learn how to narrate their stories as a part of the larger narrative of the minoritized people in both America and the world. Without that first step, they will continue to be collaborators of white colonial projects, even when they want to resist it.

Discussion Questions

1. Reflect on your own and your family's immigration history. How is it connected to the larger history of other Asian/Americans and BIPOC Communities in the United States? What are the fundamental ideologies of your narratives?
2. How or how not are your identity narratives linked to white supremacy and anti-black racism? What are some of the evidence?
3. What stories do you and your communities need to tell as your identity and history to create solidarity with others as Christians?

Bibliography

Ancheta, Angelo N. 2006. *Race, Rights, and the Asian American Experience*. New Brunswick, NJ: Rutgers University Press.
Budiman, Abby, and Neil G. Ruiz. 2021. *Key Facts About Asian Americans, A Diverse and Growing Population*. Washington, D.C.: The Pew Research Center. https://www.pewresearch.org/fact-tank/2021/04/29/key-facts-about-asian-americans/.
The Center for Community Health and Development. 2019. Healing from the Effects of Internalized Oppression. In *Community Toolbox: Tools to Change Our World*. Lawrence: University of Kansas. https://ctb.ku.edu/en/table-of-contents/culture/cultural-competence/healing-from-interalized-oppression/main.

---

[58] ChangeLab, "A Different Asian American Time Line," https://aatimeline.com/intro?fbclid=IwAR1WqtZoYMoU6ZkMHI41VAXtoE3ijiafbIcgffxqDAiJylmXa1BHRBzPwBQ.

Chang, Benjamin. 2020. From 'Illmatic' to 'Kung Flu': Black and Asian Solidarity, Activism, and Pedagogies in the Covid-19 Era. *Postdigital Science and Education* 2: 741–756. https://doi.org/10.1007/s42438-020-00183-8.

ChangeLab. A Different Asian American Time Line. https://aatimeline.com/intro?fbclid=IwAR1WqtZoYMoU6ZkMHI41VAXtoE3ijiafbIcgffxqDAiJylmXa1BHRBzPwBQ.

Davies, Daniel M. 1988. *The Life and Thought of Henry Gerhard Appenzeller (1858–1902): Missionary to Korea*. Lewiston, NY: The Edwin Mellen Press.

Hegewisch, Ariane, and Heidi Hartmann. 2018. *The Gender Wage Gap: 2018 Earnings Differences by Race and Ethnicity*. Washington, DC: Institute for Women's Policy Research. https://iwpr.org/iwpr-issues/esme/the-gender-wage-gap-2018-earningsdifferences-by-gender-race-and-ethnicity/.

Hammack, Phillip L. 2008. Narrative and the Cultural Psychology of Identity. *Personality and Social Psychology Review* 12 (3): 222–247. https://doi.org/10.1177/1088868308316892.

Iyer, Deepa. 2015. *We Too Sing America: South Asian, Arab, Muslim, and Sikh Immigrants Shape Our Multicultural Future*. New York: The New Press.

Kang, Laura Hyun Yi. 2002. *Compositional Subjects: Enfiguring Asian/American Women*. Durham, NC: Duke University Press.

Lee, Erika. 2015. A Part and Apart: Asian American and Immigration History. *Journal of American Ethnic History* 34 (4): 34.

Lee, Sammy Seung-min, Boyung Lee, Chad Shomura, and Boram Jeong. 2022. inVISIBLE | hyperVISIBE: Art Exhibit, Public Lecture & Workshop on Asian America. September 10–October 10, 2021. The Red Line Contemporary Art Center in Denver, CO. https://www.redlineart.org/invisible-hypervisible; May 20-July 16. The Dairy Arts Center. Boulder, CO. https://thedairy.org/invisible-hypervisible/.

Liu, Marian Chia-Ming. 2022. States are Mandating Asian American History Lessons to Stop Bigotry. *The Washington Post*, May 20. https://www.washingtonpost.com/education/2022/05/20/asian-american-history-schools-aapi/.

McAdams, Dan P., and Kate C. McLean. 2013. Narrative Identity. *Current Directions in Psychological Science* 22 (3): 233–238.

McWhorter John. 2020. The Dehumanizing Condescension of *White Fragility*. *The Atlantic*, July 15. https://www.theatlantic.com/ideas/archive/2020/07/dehumanizing-condescension-white-fragility/614146/.

Morrock, Richard. 1973. Heritage of Strife: The Effects of Colonialist 'Divide and Rule' Strategy upon the Colonized Peoples. *Science & Society* 37 (2): 129–151.

The Pew Research Center. 2012. *The Rise of Asian Americans*. Washington, D.C.: The Pew Research Center. https://www.pewresearch.org/social-trends/2012/06/19/chapter-7-religious-affiliation-beliefs-and-practices/.

Pyles, Loretta. 2013. *Progressive Community Organizing: Reflective Practice in a Globalizing World*. 2nd ed. New York: Routledge.

Rubio, Elizabeth Hanna. 2021. Black-Asian Solidarities and the Impasses of 'How-To' Antiracisms. *Journal for the Anthropology of North America* 24 (1): 16–31.

Tonkiss, Fran. 2003. The Ethics of Indifference: Community and Solitude in the City. *International Journal of Cultural Studies* 6 (3): 297–311. https://doi.org/10.1177/13678779030063004.

Le Tran, Mai-Anh. 2010. Narrating Lives, Narrating Faith: "Organic Hybridity" for Contemporary Christian Religious Education. *Religious Education* 105 (2): 188–203. https://doi.org/10.1080/00344081003645186.

Horse, Yellow, J. Aggie, Karen Kuo, Eleanor K. Seaton, and Edward D. Vargas. 2021. Asian Americans' Indifference to Black Lives Matter: The Role of Nativity, Belonging, and Acknowledgement of Anti-Black Racism. *Social Sciences* 10 (5): 1–19.

Yoo, David K., and Ruth H. Chung. 2008. *Religion and Spirituality in Korean America*. Chicago: University of Illinois Press.

Yoo, David K. 2010. *Contentious Spirits: Religion in Korean American History, 1903–1945*. Stanford, CA: Stanford University Press.

11
Under the Master's Table: An Anti-darkness and Caste Interpretation of the Canaanite Woman

Sharon Jacob

In his book, *Annihilation of Caste: An Undelivered Speech*, B.R. Ambedkar writes, "Every Congressman who repeats the dogma of Mill that one country is not fit to rule another country, must admit that one class is not fit to rule another class."[1] Conversations on race in both Indian and Indian American communities remain incomplete and partial if they do not take the impact and influence of the caste system into consideration. Terms like Aryan and Dravidian are not only used to connect geographical locations to people but are used as signifiers that link caste with race.[2] Historians have noted the myth of the Aryan and Dravidian conquest narrative and its use to promote supremacy in which Dravidians, their languages, religions,

---

[1] B. R. (Bhimrao Ramji) Ambedkar, *Annihilation of Caste: An Undelivered Speech* (New Delhi: Arnold Publishers, 1990), 174–175. Also cf. Arundhati Roy, *The Doctor and the Saint: Caste, Race, and Annihilation of Caste: The Debate Between B. R. Ambedkar and M. K. Gandhi* (Chicago: Haymarket Books, 2017).

[2] Sonja Thomas, *Privileged Minorities: Syrian Christianity, Gender, and Minority Rights in Postcolonial India* (Seattle: University of Washington Press, 2018), 69. She writes, "'Aryan' signals both a Brahmin caste identity and lighter skin. In other words, 'Aryan' and 'Dravidians' are not just linguistic divisions but markers that intersect in profound ways with color and caste as well."

S. Jacob (✉)
Visiting Professor of New Testament and Postcolonial Studies, Claremont School of Theology, Claremont, CA, USA
e-mail: SJacob@cst.com

© The Author(s), under exclusive license to Springer Nature Switzerland AG 2023
K. C. Pae, B. Lee (eds.), *Embodying Antiracist Christianity*,
https://doi.org/10.1007/978-3-031-37264-3_11

customs, and their skin color are deemed inferior and undesirable.[3] Noted Indian historian Romila Thapar illustrates this point writing, "Racial separateness required a demarcating feature and conquest became the mechanism by which caste hierarchy and inequalities could be explained as a form of racial segregation."[4] The creation of "mythhistories" reifies the caste and color divide in the Indian context.

Furthermore, the complexity of India is further exacerbated when the lines connecting color and caste are not clear. Thus, to say that all fair-skinned people belong to the upper caste and all dark-skinned people are low caste is an oversimplification. Nikki Khanna writes, "There are varied degrees of skin tone in most castes, and skin color is more location specific than caste related…"[5] While it is true that color in India is location specific, we must not ignore the way in which caste intensifies and institutionalizes a dark skin bias that is deeply entrenched into the Indian consciousness. The bias towards dark skin, or what I will call "anti-darkness bias," is intensified to such an extent that it becomes difficult to distinguish caste from black skin and vice versa. Colorism as a concept is limited in capturing the nuances of caste in the Indian context, while "anti-blackness" is a term that is contextual to the United States and does not quite translate to situations in India.

Therefore, I suggest the term "anti-darkness" to help elicit these connections and nuances. This term "anti-darkness" or "dark skin bias," I argue, would help incorporate the bias against dark skin by drawing on colorism while integrating it with the caste system where having dark skin is not just a matter of ideal beauty standards but unconsciously connects color with the caste of a person.

Color, Caste, and Christianity

My reason for introducing the term "anti-darkness" is twofold. First, the term "anti-darkness" encapsulates the complex relationship between colorism, caste, and religion. Although terms like colorism are effective and helpful in the Indian context, they also effectively separate conversations of race from caste. As I will argue, such separations are unhelpful and problematic. Secondly, the introduction of "anti-darkness" sentiment can help map the trajectory in which bias towards dark skin rooted in the Indian context travels, transforms, and morphs into anti-blackness in

---

[3] Thomas notes that, "The very idea of Aryans in India begins with the Aryans migration theory. In colonial histories, the Aryans were depicted as a superior, fair-skinned, racially homogenous group that came from Iran and migrated to both Europe and India." Thomas, *Privileged Minorities,* 71. Thomas further notes in the book that the Aryan migration was quickly changed to the myth of Aryan conquest that helped support the supremacy myth of fair skinned Aryans over the dark-skinned Dravidians.

[4] Romila Thapar, *The Aryan: Recasting Constructs* (Gurgaon, India: Three Essays Collective, 2008), 33.

[5] Nikki Khanna, *Whiter: Asian and Asian American Women on Skin Color and Colorism*, ed. Nikki Khanna (New York: New York University Press) 17.

South Asian communities in the United States. Alice Walker describes colorism as "prejudicial or preferential treatment of same-race people based solely on their color."[6] Disdain for dark skin is native to the Indian context; words like *kaali, kaalu, kari, karupu* (often translated as black) are used to describe people with dark complexions.[7] Bias against dark skin in the Indian context is institutionalized through industries like Bollywood, where visual mediums tailor our gaze towards desiring *whiteness*.

Contempt for dark skin starts at an early age and is formalized through explicit and implicit messages on a daily basis that to have a dark complexion is to be lesser and inferior. Casual racism[8] is normalized and passed off as humor and entertainment in many mainstream Bollywood movies.[9] When dark-skinned actors are cast in films, they are often relegated to playing villains or sidekicks that provide comic relief. Meanwhile, dark-skinned women are relegated to playing sexually loose women with dubious moral standards.[10] More recently, this unease with blackness in the South Asian immigrant community was also seen with the election of Vice President Kamala Harris, who is half Indian and half black. The need to quickly accept Harris' Indian roots while sidelining her black roots indicates anti-black sentiments in diasporic South Asian communities, thereby suggesting that the roots of anti-blackness begin at home (India).[11] At the same time, one must ask why South Asian communities cringe at the expression person of color when they enter the United States. I would argue that the anti-black sentiment in South Asian

---

[6] Alice Walker, "If the Present Looks Like the Past, What Does the Future Look Like?" in *In Search of Our Mothers Gardens: Womanist Prose*. (San Diego: Harcourt Brace Jovanovich, 1983), 290.

[7] *Kaali, karupu, kaalu*, and *kari* are words often used in local Indian languages to describe dark skin individuals. These names are often used as first labels to describe an individual even before their names or other identity markers, thereby illustrating disdain and derision for dark skin individuals.

[8] I use the term "casual racism" to depict the almost matter of fact ways in which derogatory comments on dark skin are made in Indian contexts. For example, during my own growing years, I was often discouraged from playing outside in the sun, asked to wear dark color clothing, constantly advised to keep my coarse hair braided and oiled, and advised to consume milk or yogurt and apply lightning creams. As a dark skin girl, I too have succumbed to the addiction of bleaching creams in the hopes of becoming light. Also cf. Barkha Dutt, MOJO STOR, episode "Masaba Masaba Racism|Viv Richards, Neena Gupta|Feminism, Fashion, Films," November 21, 2020, YouTube, https://www.youtube.com/watch?v=JJCqivYcGXw.

[9] Staff Writer, "Racism is Embedded in Bollywood: It's Time to Change That," *Madras Courier*, June 24, 2022, https://madrascourier.com/opinion/racism-is-embedded-in-bollywood-its-time-to-change-that/. Also cf. Khanna, *Whiter*, 6. She writes, "lighter-skinned characters are depicted as intelligent, while those with darker skin are portrayed as 'clownish' and 'less intelligent'."

[10] Isha Aran, "Bollywood's shameful history of blackface," *Splinter*, April 14, 2016, https://splinternews.com/bollywood-s-shameful-history-of-blackface-1793856198. She observes, "Darker-skinned people, if they're even included in films, almost exclusively portray villains or sidekicks that provide comedic relief, or are generally subservient minor characters."

[11] Sakshi Venketaraman, "'Kamala auntie' prompts examination of anti-Blackness for South Asians," *NBC News*, August 19, 2020, https://www.nbcnews.com/news/asian-america/kamala-auntie-prompts-examination-anti-blackness-south-asians-n1237339.

communities is so deeply ingrained into the Indian consciousness that there is an unconscious attempt to connect the term not only to color but also to one's caste.

Connecting Color to Caste

The desire for whiteness in the Indian context is often connected to colonial history, in particular, the presence of the British empire. However, as Neha Mishra has aptly pointed out, "Public disdain for the Indian race created superiority based on 'white' skin color and deeply embedded race-based ideologies in nation's darker-skinned common man who was ruled by the whiter skin masters: first by Mughals then by other European rulers like the Portuguese and the British for over three hundred and fifty years."[12] A question remains then: If disdain for dark skin was a consequence of colonialism, how does one explain its occurrence even after colonialism ended? I argue that the introduction of the caste system, which predates colonialism, must be taken into consideration when speaking about race in the Indian context. Lighter skin in the Indian context is not only viewed as an upper caste marker but is also connected to the financial and social status of a person. Sudras, or lower caste people, were connected to manual labor and were expected to be poor as a result of their lower caste.[13] At the same time, it is important to understand that caste and color serve as a double whammy in the Indian context, where a person with a higher caste and darker skin is still considered socially more acceptable than a low caste person with dark skin.[14] Drawing parallels between race and caste, Sonja Thomas points out that "Racism and casteism have similar effects, including segregation, job discrimination, depictions of overly sexualized women (depictions that, all too often, are used as an excuse for sexual violence against Black and Dalit women)…"[15] Hira Singh and M.A. Kalam also point to the past and present ways that bias against dark skin in India has impacted people with dark complexions.[16] More recently, the

---

[12] Neha Mishra, "India and Colorism: The Finer Nuances," *Washington University Global Studies Law Review* 14, no. 4 (2015): 732.

[13] Mishra, "India and Colorism," 737. She writes, "Skin colour, therefore, was also viewed as related to financial and social status of a person. This automatically incorporated 'caste factor' into it because Sudras were expected to do manual labor, which made their skin darker than upper caste."

[14] Mishra, "India and Colorism, 737. She writes, "Therefore, it can be concluded that while the desirability of a person gets affected by their skin color, caste as a variable is intertwined with it and has to be seen together to understand the status and desirability, viz., higher caste with a darker skin tone may be acceptable more when compared to a lower caste and having a darker skin tone."

[15] Thomas, *Privileged Minorities,* 70.

[16] Hira Singh and M. A. Kalam, "India's Race Problem: Ignorance and Denial," *Social Scientist* 45, no. 9/10 (September/October 2017): 75. Singh and Kalam write, "India has a race problem made up of a combination of ignorance and denial. A case in point would be that the Bharatiya Janata Party leader and former Rajya Sabha member, Tarun Vijay's statement to a television channel that Indians could not be racist as they lived with 'black' South Indians is symptomatic of ignorance of race, and he is not alone. See "Tarun Vijay Lands in Trouble with 'Black People' Remarks, Later Apologises on Twitter," *The Hindu,* April 7 2017, https://www.thehindu.com/news/national/if-we-were-racist-why-would-we-live-with-south-indians-tarun-vijay/article17866698.ece.

horrific acts of violence against African students living in India are illustrative of the presence of anti-black sentiments.[17] Caste and colorism create a perfect mixture in the Indian context to shun blackness. Caste becomes the fundamental structure that upholds and institutionalizes dark skin bias. Thus, it is caste, along with color, that is used to cement a person's status and justify discrimination against them in society.

How anti-darkness is structuralized in the Indian context is similar to the ways in which anti-blackness is structuralized in the United States. Udit Raj, leader of the Indian Justice Party, which represents Dalits, the oppressed tribes and castes in the political system, says that "The hold of the caste system in India is deep, dark skin is the skin of the lowest castes, traditionally the subjugated people and, therefore, disagreeable."[18] Caste, more than color, is significant in the acceptance of a person in Indian society. Color can be transcended if a person is born in the "right" caste and economic strata. However, a dark-skinned person, who is both low caste and poor, is predestined to a life filled with humiliation and degradation. Apart from skin color, names also serve as another marker of caste.[19] Thus, if anti-blackness refers to the structural ways in which race and treatment of black people in the American context is institutionalized and normalized, "anti-darkness" creates a context in which bias against dark skin moves from personal prejudices into political, economic, and systematic intolerances in India. Caste is used to justify discrimination against people in housing, jobs, and access to water, as well as police brutality, sexual assault and rape of women and young girls, lynching, murder, and many other horrific human rights violations against people who are seen as belonging to the low caste and/or tribal group.[20] Dark skin becomes the first visual sign of a low caste person unless and until proven otherwise with further evidence such as last names, places of origin, etc.

---

[17] Abhishek Mishra, "India's Racial Prejudice is Jeopardizing Ties with African Nations," *Observer Research Foundation,* July 28, 2020, https://www.orfonline.org/research/indias-racial-prejudice-is-jeopardising-ties-with-african-nations/. Mishra writes, "In the light of recent attacks against foreigners in India, such as the one in Roorkee, the question of racial prejudice and biases has once again come to the forefront. Racial bias is the single most important challenge facing Africans living in India. With all our democratic values and internationalist outlook, the core Indian society is still overwhelmingly traditional, and stereotyping of African nationals creates difficulties. Also cf. Khanna, *Whiter,* 126. Khanna refers to this incident, which took place in 2017 where a group of African students were beaten by an Indian mob.

[18] Staff Writer, "Black is blemish in India," *Aljazeera*, October 7, 2003, https://www.aljazeera.com/news/2003/10/7/black-is-blemish-in-india.

[19] A very common question posed in discussions of Caste is how one determines a person's caste. As I have noted in my discussion, dark skin and caste are not always correlated. Thus, the next layer to determine a person's caste origins is levied in the form of last names. Meanwhile, Christians and Muslims are viewed with suspicion and distrust because they are often assumed to be of the low caste until and unless they can prove that they have high caste origins in their lineage. See Amrita Ghosh and Arun Kimar, "Casteism continues to thrive among Indians abroad –through surnames," *Scroll.in,* August 28, 2020, https://scroll.in/global/970262/casteism-continues-to-thrive-among-indians-abroad-through-surnames.

[20] Hilary Mayell, "India's "Untouchables" Face Violence and Discrimination," *National Geographic,* June 2, 2003, https://www.nationalgeographic.com/pages/article/indias-untouchables-face-violence-discrimination.

From Color to Caste to Religion: Christian Women's Cases

Another layer implicit in conversations concerning race and caste in India is religion. Often religion is subsumed under the caste system. For this reason, there is a failure to understand the complex ways in which religion and caste help cement anti-darkness bias in the Indian context. In a predominantly Hindu context, Christians and Muslims are often depicted as outsiders, foreign to the Indian soil and therefore suspect and unworthy of trust.[21] Popular conceptions of Christian women link us closer to the West, thereby creating an image of Christian women as sexual, erotic, and loose.[22] Crude remarks are often heard and then reinforced through films where Christian women are often depicted as willing to participate in premarital relations, thereby confirming the stereotype of Christian women as having loose and dubious morals.[23] Indian-Christian women often bear western sounding names, which serve as markers to discriminate, essentialize, stereotype, and ultimately "otherize." Once again, we see names being used as visual and oral markers that affirm the categorization of bodies in terms of religion, caste, gender, and even the geographical location of an individual. Indian-Christian women are depicted as the asexual elderly house help or sexually tantalizing sirens.[24] The Indian-Christian woman's body, placed in direct opposition against the Hindu upper class and caste woman, constructs a binary in which Hindu women are both idealized and idolized as a pure, chaste, and loyal, while Indian-Christian women are

---

[21] Thomas, *Privileged Minorities,* 75. Thomas writes, "The Hindu Right has tried to claim that the Aryans did not migrate to India but were indigenous to South Asia. If the authors of the Hindu Sanskrit texts were indigenous to India, then all others who migrated to South Asia at later dates—namely Christians and Muslims—could be painted as racially different and foreign."

[22] Sharon Jacob, "Neither Here nor There! A Hermeneutics of Shuttling: Reflections from a Postcolonial Biblical Critic," in *Asian and Asian American Women in Theology and Religion,* ed. Kwok Pui Lan (Cham, Switzerland: Palgrave Macmillian, 2020). I have written in length about the ways in which Christian women in the Indian context are overtly sexualized given their description as women with western sounding names and wearing western clothes.

[23] Deborah Grey, "The Stereotypes I live with as an Indian Christian woman," *Youth Ki Awaz*, December 12, 2016, https://www.youthkiawaaz.com/2016/12/stereotypes-about-indian-christian-women/. Grey writes, "Try renting a house and they respond with a volley of questions based on strange stereotypes, *"Oh. So you are Christian. That means you are allowed everything. Like boyfriends and short skirts?"* Now while I do have a boyfriend and wear short skirts, I wonder how that is an exclusive Christian privilege? Potential landlords would often gather these neighborhood aunties for my 'trial' before deciding to rent their homes to me. They have asked me the strangest questions like *"Why do your parents allow you to date? This is against Indian culture! How can they be so careless with you?"*

[24] Ryan D'Souza, *Representations of Indian Christians in Bollywood Movies* (Ph.D. diss., University of South Florida, 2019), 50, https://digitalcommons.usf.edu/etd/7772. D'Souza writes, "Bollywood movies, in particular, conflate Anglo-Indian and Christian with "Christian names" such as Julie, Mary, Monica, and Rosie. These characters drink alcohol, dance in bars for the pleasure of a predominantly male patronage, unsuccessfully seduce the Hindu protagonist who is committed to a Hindu woman, and, in general, are sleazy women" (50).

symbolized as sexual, unfaithful, and foreign.[25] Compound this religious difference with caste and color, and the situation becomes more complex and nuanced. Thomas observes that:

> The intersection between fairness and a girl's marriageability produces a version of female morality centered on gendered forms of control that police movements of upper-caste women and also make them always already suspect of sexual transgressions. On four different occasions, I was told a virtually identical story about dark skin and "fate" that involved assumptions about illicit unions between fair Syrian Christian women and dark lower-caste men.[26]

Thomas's words are illustrative of the ways in which both caste as well as anti-darkness bias seeps into other religions in the Indian context. In other words, caste and anti-darkness is not a Hindu problem, but rather an Indian problem. Pregnant women in India are often encouraged to partake in white foods and to post pictures of white babies with the intention that the gaze of whiteness through pictures and the intake of white foods like milk and yogurt will somehow lead to Indian women giving birth to fair-skinned babies. The advice to actively desire whiteness while implicitly discouraging the presence of darkness is also part of the Indian-Christian community. Thomas notes that "during pregnancy a Syrian Christian woman takes ayurvedic medicines, drinks milk mixed with gold flaked off the girl's mother's wedding ring, and is covered with a paste of green turmeric and bitter gourd juice, all to ensure that the child will have fair skin."[27] Desire for white skin coupled with derision for dark skin stirs a form of "caste supremacy," that can easily attach to the ideology of white supremacy in the American context. Thus, we must not ignore how caste, color, and religion intersect in the context of the United States. Nikki Khanna writes, "Perhaps the disdain for brown bodies, even their own, can be observed in former Louisiana governor Bobby Jindal, Indian American and brown-skinned, who made headlines in 2015, when a portrait of him hanging in the state capital portrayed him with white skin."[28] It is interesting to note that both Bobby Jindal and Nikki Haley, two important political figures from the South Asian community, deliberately take on a Christian identity in their political life.[29] While one

---

[25] Nivedita Mishra, "Sandra from Bandra to Oh Fanny re: the Changing Face of Christians in Films," *Hindustan Times*, September 12, 2014, https://www.hindustantimes.com/bollywood/sandra-from-bandra-to-oh-fanny-re-the-changing-face-of-christians-in-films/story-wH9aE6IymtN-FJkllEViSUJ.html. She writes: "Here was a film that was a superhit but it had all the possible stereotypes one could imagine. An Anglo-Indian Christian girl falls for a Hindu boy and in a moment of passionate encounter gets pregnant. While many will argue that it is work of fiction and such plots work, it's hard not to miss the stereotypes - girl with 'easy morals', unwed mother, Hindu boy with can have sex but take no responsibility for his act, the film was as clichéd as it gets.
[26] Thomas, *Privileged Minorities,* 86.
[27] Thomas, *Privileged Minorities,* 86.
[28] Khanna, *Whiter,* 131.
[29] Schuyler Kropf, "Nikki Haley, Bobby Jindal explain their faith during the Response prayer meeting Saturday," *The Post and Courier*, June 12, 2015, https://www.postandcourier.com/politics/nikki-haley-bobby-jindal-explain-their-faith-during-the-response-prayer-meeting-saturday/article_c48ab132-a0df-5044-a86f-97f32bd64e37.html.

may want to chalk up this conversion to pandering to the evangelical Christian community, we cannot ignore how Christianity in the United States is used as a tool of assimilation and a blatant gesture that speaks to the desire to be closer to whiteness.

Drawing on the anti-darkness or anti-dark skin bias as a lens, the next section will demonstrate how the story of the Canaanite woman can be read through a more nuanced light. My interpretation of this pericope will also draw on the ways in which anti-darkness sentiments in the Indian context similar to anti-Canaaniteness in the Matthean text. The text in Matthew's gospel uses conquest narratives passed down for generations to create systems that help institutionalize and justify acts of discrimination against those we perceive as others. My reading, utilizing the anti-darkness lens, will bring to light the ways in which conquest narratives are ultimately "mythhistories" that are constructed and used to produce a singular narrative that justifies the marginalization of certain people at the hands of those in dominant positions of power.

Anti-Canaaniteness: Reading Matthew 15:21-28 Through the Lens of Anti-darkness

The author of Matthew begins the gospel with a genealogy that attempts to connect Jesus to his Jewish roots. The all-male lineage is interrupted by five women, four of whom share a foreign lineage. Among the four women (Ruth, Tamar, Bathsheba, and Rahab) present in the genealogy, Tamar and Rahab are both Canaanites.[30] However, their Canaaniteness is never explicitly mentioned in the text; perhaps a sign signaling their assimilation into a predominantly Jewish genealogy. Meanwhile, the only woman to be explicitly named and identified as a Canaanite found in Matthew 15:21-28 remains both unnamed and acculturated at the end of the narrative.[31] The naming of the two Canaanite women in Mathew's genealogy could be considered the politics of the "acceptable ethnic other" whose body is acknowledged and even inserted into the mythhistories if their blackness, or in this case their Canaaniteness, is not too overt or overpowering to dominant histories.

Meanwhile, the Canaanite woman in Matthew 15:21-28 remains unnamed and isolated because her Canaanite heritage makes her an ethnic outsider and, therefore, an object of aversion. The interaction between Jesus and the Canaanite woman could easily be seen as one of the most cringeworthy exchanges in the New Testament.

---

[30] Glena S. Jackson, "Enemies of Israel: Ruth and the Canaanite Woman," *Hervormde Teologiese Studies* 59, no. 3 (September 2003): 786. Jackson writes, "While all four women are enemies of Israel (Canaanites Tamar and Rahab, Moabite Ruth, and Hittite Bathsheba) and get pregnant through unorthodox ways (Tamar poses as a prostitute for Judah's pleasure, Rahab is a harlot, Ruth seduces Boaz, and Bathsheba is seduced [or raped] by King David…"

[31] Grant LeMarquand writes, The woman of Matthew 15, then, is the only person in the New Testament who is explicitly called a 'Canaanite.'" Grant LeMarquand, *"The Canaanite Conquest of Jesus* (Matthew 15: 21-28)" *Arc: The Journal of the Faculty of Religious Studies* 33 (2005): 238.

Although this story first appeared in Mark, the author of Matthew makes a pointed decision to re-tell the narrative with significant alterations. Some of these differences include a change of the female character's ethnicity from Syrophoenician to Canaanite, the title given to Jesus by the woman, and, most importantly, the response by Matthew's Jesus, which is much harsher than that in the gospel of Mark.[32]

Along with other scholars, I argue that the conquest narratives of the Canaanites function as "mythhistories" in the text.[33] Mythhistories of conquest are used as justifications to marginalize certain groups because they promote this false notion that their inferiority is inherent to their skin color, language, religion, caste, etc. Moreover, the inherent inferiority of one group over the other is used to validate their conquest and, ultimately, their oppression and marginalization. The danger of these "mythhistories" or conquest narratives is that when they are taught or passed down from generation to generation without much critical thought or question. It is also important to take into consideration how these conquest narratives have the ability not only to turn people belonging to different races against one another but also to turn those belonging to the same race and ethnicity against each other. In the Indian context, conquest narratives of Aryans hailing from the North conquering Dravidians belonging to the South are passed down and taught widely, thereby institutionalizing the color and linguistic difference between these two groups. What is interesting and worth taking note of is that there is no archeological evidence to suggest that this conquest ever took place in history,[34] and yet the power of such mythhistories is that these narratives continue to promote anti-darkness and anti-dark skin bias.

Conquest narratives that supported the idea that Canaanites as an ethnic group were inferior and therefore deserved to be conquered and marginalized were not only formalized in written texts, but one could infer that such stories may have been

---

[32] Melanie S. Baffles, "What Do We Do with This Jesus? A Reading of Matthew 15:21–28 through the Lens of Psychoanalytic Theory," *Pastoral Psychology* 63 (2014): 249–263. Baffles observes, "The story appears also in Mark 7: 24–30, presumably the source of Matthew's version. But the author of Matthew has altered key elements of the story: (1) the woman, named in Mark as "Syrophoenician," is here called "Canaanite," most likely to heighten her marginalized status by associating her with the traditional enemy of Israel; (2) in both versions, the woman addresses Jesus as "Lord," yet only in Matthew does she refer to him as "Son of David," a title Matthew uses frequently to describe the "earthly" Jesus" (250).

[33] See, Exod 23:20-33; Lev 26:3-45; Num 14:39-45; 21:1-3; 31:1-20; Deut 7:1-5, 17-26; 9:1-5; 12:1-3; 13:12-18; 20:10-18, as well as the narratives (especially in the book of Joshua) in which the Canaanite genocide is, to a greater or lesser degree, carried out.

[34] Kanad Sinha, "The Question of Aryan Identity," *The Telegraph,* Jan 28, 2023, https://www.telegraphindia.com/culture/books/the-question-of-aryan-identity/cid/1696499. Sinha writes, "An 'Aryan invasion' was offered as a possible reason for the Harappan decline, facilitating a political interpretation which claimed that the Dravidians/South Indians/lower castes were sons of the soil and the upper-caste Hindus were invaders. However, no such massive invasion is attested to by archaeology. On the other hand, the Hindu nationalist claim portraying Aryans as the original inhabitants of India and originators of a 'uniform, continuous Hindu culture' tries to push back the dates of the Rig Veda to present the Vedic and Harappan civilizations as identical. But Jaya Menon shows that the archaeological cultures of North India in the period 2000-500 BCE depict multiplicity and movement, not uniformity and continuity."

passed down orally from generation to generation. The divinely sanctioned violence against the Canaanites embedded into the consciousness of the Israelites is the larger context that must be taken into account when interpreting Matthew 15:21-28. The mythhistories of the conquering of the ancient Canaanites must inform our interpretation of Jesus' harsh response to the Canaanite woman. The decision of the author of Matthew to change the woman's ethnicity from Syrophoenician to Canaanite must be seen as an attempt to evoke an anti-Canaanite sentiment.[35] While the word "Canaanite' was no longer in use at this time, Musa Dube notes that locations such as Jerusalem and Canaan were geographically loaded destinations that could evoke certain stereotypes and deliberate hostilities among readers. [36]

Although we will never know for sure what Jesus may or may not have heard while growing up, we could argue that the author of Matthew is evoking certain stereotypes and relying on certain conquest narratives as he re-tells and re-writes this narrative from the Markan text.

The author of Matthew imagines Israel as a nation that is limited and sovereign by creating a clear boundary between outsider and insider. Although the land of Canaan was seen as good, the Canaanites were seen as evil. In fact, the Canaanites were depicted as enemies of the Israelites who needed to be exterminated by the orders of God.[37] In the narrative, Jesus responds to the request of the Canaanite woman by telling her, "I was sent only to the lost sheep of Israel (Matthew 15:24)." In Matthew 15:27, the Canaanite woman responds to Jesus: "'Yes it is, Lord,' she

---

[35] Guy Nave, "Challenging Privilege through the Preaching and Teaching of Scripture," *Currents in Theology and Mission* 47, no. 3 (July 2020): 17. Nave writes, "The author's identification of the woman as "Canaanite" is significant because in the version of the story found in Mark (which is widely considered to be older than Matthew), the woman is identified as "Syrophoenician." He continues, "The author of Matthew invokes the memory of this violent historical past between Jews and Canaanites by identifying this woman as a Canaanite."

[36] Charlie Trimm, *The Destruction of the Canaanites: God, Genocide, and Biblical Interpretation* (Grand Rapids, MI: W. B. Eerdmans Publishing Company, 2022),32. Trimm makes a similar case writing, "During the early first millennium the term "Canaanite" dropped out of use and became a historical term rather than a way to refer to contemporary inhabitants of Canaan. The use of "Canaanite" in Matthew 15:22 is most likely designed to force the reader to think in Old Testament terms as this would be an unnatural way to refer to someone in New Testament times." Also cf. Musa Dube, *Postcolonial Feminist Interpretations* (St. Louis, MO: Chalice Press, 2000), 146.

[37] LeMarquand, "The Canaanite Conquest of Jesus (Matthew 15:21-28)," 242. He writes, "Clearly, although it views the land of Canaan as good, the Old Testament sees Canaanites themselves as evil. Matthew's use of the term 'Canaanite' to describe the woman known from Mark as a Syro-Phoenician highlights the nature of this woman and her daughter as the worst of outsiders. Canaanites are the quintessential enemies of Israel, the ones God had commanded them to exterminate because their sins were so extreme that contact with them, especially through intermarriage, would lead Israel into idolatry and immorality. The Canaanite woman is not merely a gentile, therefore, but a representation of those peoples who are God's, as well as Israel's, enemies." Also cf. Glenna Jackson, *'Have Mercy on Me': The Story of the Canaanite Woman in Matthew 15:21-28* (JSNTS up 228; Sheffield: Sheffield Academic Press, 2002), 80; In fact, as James Treat notes, if it were not for this story readers of the New Testament might assume that the genocide had been completely 'successful'; see "The Canaanite Problem," *Daughters of Sarah* (Spring 1994): 23; cf. Robert Allen Warrior, "A Native American Perspective: Canaanites, Cowboys, and Indians," in *Voices From the Margin: Interpreting the Bible in the Third World*, ed. R. S. Sugirtharajah (Maryknoll: Orbis, 1995), 277-85.

said. 'Even the dogs eat the crumbs that fall from their master's table.'" Her response is often read as the "Ah ha!" moment where her witty and quick response resisting Jesus' insults earns her daughter's healing. While such an interpretation is pertinent, I argue that an anti-darkness lens that takes the intersections of caste and color into consideration could present a more nuanced approach.

The Canaanite woman's words mark a remarkable shift in Jesus's attitude. Although the focus of this narrative begins with a request for the healing of the Canaanite woman's daughter, the story actually ends with Jesus being schooled and healed from the anti-Canaanite bias that he seems to carry when this narrative begins. Nave argues that " the challenge posed to Jesus by this 'Canaanite' woman forces him to at least reflect upon his own cultural privilege and consider how he uses that privilege."[38] Read through anti-black sentiments in the South Asian immigrant communities, I push Nave's observations even further to encapsulate the sordid and complex ways in which colonized peoples duplicate patterns of oppression acting out against people on the margins. To push even further, the Canaanite woman's response is a direct call, maybe even a dig at the privileged position occupied by Jesus in his context, courtesy of his religious and gender identity.

The Canaanite woman's response to Jesus is not just a reminder of his privilege but *a reminder of his own history*. This is similar to what Indian author and political activist, Arundhati Roy, writes: "South Indians who are mocked by North Indians for their dark skins in turn humiliating Africans for the very same reason. It's like falling into a borewell with no bottom."[39] Roy also notes that Indian racism towards Black folks is almost worse than white people's racism. Stephenson Humphries-Brooks writes, "The use of 'Canaanite' rather than 'Syrophoenician' as in Mark 7.26 emphasizes that the woman comes from an ethnicity Israel traditionally viewed as worthy of extermination (see Josh. 12.20)."[40] One could argue that the Canaanite woman's response to Jesus implies that his words of discrimination against her are almost worse than the treatment she is already subjected to at the hands of the empire. The ethnicity of the Canaanite is not just invoking Israel's history with these people, but also creating a hierarchy that people belonging to the land of Canaan are purposely placed lower in the collective imagination of the audience listening to and reading this narrative. The concept of mythhistory based on religion is useful here. As Thomas writes, mythhistories of religious origins "tend to highlight phenotypical differences to prove one's privileged status over others today. This racial positioning even happens with caste."[41] Applying the idea of mythhistories to the text, I argue that Matthew's Jesus is exposing the mythhistories present in his context. Furthermore, conquest narratives were passed down to create a hierarchy that supposedly assumes a posture of superiority and supremacy. In reading and interpreting

---

[38] Nave, "Challenging Privilege through the Preaching and Teaching of Scripture,"18.
[39] Staff Writer, "An Email Interview with Arundati Roy," *Dalit Camera,* June 8, 2020, https://www.dalitcamera.com/indian-racism-towards-black-people-is-almost-worse-than-white-peoples-racism/.
[40] Stephenson Humphries-Brooks, "The Canaanite Women in Matthew," in *Feminist Companion to Matthew*, ed. Amy-Jill Levine (New York: Bloomsbury Publishing, 2001), 142.
[41] Thomas, *Privileged Minorities*, 81.

this pericope, we also unconsciously duplicate and highlight a singular history of the Canaanites that is more complex, nuanced, and worthy of critical inquiry.

In Matthew 15:26, Jesus says, "It is not right to take the children's bread and toss it to the dogs." By calling the Canaanite woman a "dog," Matthew's Jesus relegates her to being lower while also constructing himself as higher than Canaanites. Perhaps, for a moment, he even feels satisfied in knowing that in his ideological hierarchy, he now has someone who is below him. The Canaanite woman responds to this remark stating, "Yes it is, Lord," she said. "Even the dogs eat the crumbs that fall from their master's table. (Mt 15:27)." It is interesting to note that Matthew's Jesus in his remarks to the Canaanite woman is about food, Israel, and dogs; they never mention a master. However, the Canaanite woman's response is ironic because her answer to Jesus is not about the children of Israel or food but the crumbs that fall from their master's table. In other words, it is the Canaanite woman who invokes the imagery of the "master" three times in the text (vs. 22, 25, & 27). The first two Κύριε (vs. 22 & 25) are in reference to Jesus, while the last Lord/Master appears to be more generic.

The Greek word often translated as "master," "κυρίων" in vs.27, can also be translated as "Lord." We cannot overlook the imperial underpinnings that are present in this title. As readers, we have a tendency to read the response of the Canaanite woman as a metaphor, where her use of the "master's/Lord's table" could be an allusion to the God of Israel. However, scholars using the lens of empire have often reminded us that titles such as Son of God, Lord, Redeemer, Savior of the World, etc., were titles given to Caesar, the Augustus.[42] Thus, I wonder why we have not read the Canaanite woman's response referring to "the master's table" as an allusion to Rome or the Roman empire? In other words, while Matthew's Jesus may want to see the Canaanite woman as the "Other," as suggested to him from his own "mythhistories of conquest narratives," the reference to the master's table is a firm reminder to Jesus of his own colonized status under Rome. Moreover, why would the Canaanite woman, in her response, as an outsider and not a convert, refer to the God of Israel as her master or Lord?[43] In fact, I argue that as a colonized person, the Canaanite woman's reference to the "master's table" is her censure on the inequality and hoarding of resources by the empire. Pushing this interpretation even further, I would argue that the Canaanite woman's response to Jesus is a reminder that "under the master/lord's table" (read as Rome), both she and Jesus are colonized people. And in their colonized status, Jesus and the Canaanite woman are subjected to the crumbs that fall from the table of the empire. In short, Rome would view both Jesus and the Canaanite women as the "proverbial dogs," the outsiders, the nobodies.

---

[42] John Dominic Crossan, "Roman Imperial Theology," in *In the Shadow of Empire: Reclaiming the Bible as a History of Faithful Resistance*, ed. Richard A. Horsley (London: Westminister John Knox Press, 2008), 73.

[43] For more discussion on this please see. Kwok, Pui Lan. *Postcolonial Imagination and Feminist Theology* (Louisville: WJK, 2005), 83. Also cf. Surekha Nelavela, "Dare Not! Or Fear Not! Reimagining the Story of the Canaanite-Noisy Woman (Matthew 15)" in *Mission and Context*, edited by Jione Havea, (Lexington Books/Fortress Academic, 2020) pp. 116. Nelavela drawing on the work of Pui Lan points out that, "the Canaanite is a woman of another faith, and her story is inscribed within the master discourse of the Christian canon and interpreted primarily to justify the mission to the Gentiles."

Conclusion

Commenting on the relationship between colonial India and color, Mishra writes, "Entry to restaurants and educational institutions was prohibited for 'Black Indians' with entry boards clearly stating 'Indians and dogs not allowed.'"[44] Denigrating Indian bodies and associating them with blacks and dogs was an important part of our colonial history and our struggle for independence from the British. This is a historical past that we South Asian immigrants seem to forget when we move to other parts of the globe. Shifting our eyes back to Matthew 15:21-27, the Canaanite woman's reference to the "master's table" is both a reminder and the reckoning moment in the text. It is a reminder that under the gaze of the κυρίου/Lord, Jesus' Jewishness is no different than this woman's Canaaniteness; they are both the foreigner, Other, and inferior. Matthew 15:21-28 ends with Jesus healing the daughter of the Canaanite woman. This healing happens without assimilation or accommodation, moving to contemporary contexts, the distrust between South Asian immigrant communities and Black communities stems from intergenerational mythhistories that continue to support and justify an anti-darkness bias that connects dark skin to low caste. As Tyrus Townsend points out, within Asian and Asian American communities, anti-blackness is entwined with an aversion to dark skin.[45] As South Asian immigrants, we can no longer depend on "dog moments" that put us in direct contact with our Black brothers and sisters to reflect back to us our own racist past and our anti-darkness bias. These moments of reckoning must begin in our own contexts, where we learn to confront and unlearn the racism that continues to promote anti-darkness/anti-dark skin bias. Thus, reading through the lens of anti-blackness/anti-Canaaniteness, the Canaanite woman's response becomes the visible moment when Jesus is reminded that, like the Canaanite woman, he too is a colonized subject under Rome: a dog, an outsider, and a perpetual foreigner. Thus, just as Rome would have conflated Jesus' Jewishness and this woman's Canaaniteness through a singular lens of colonization, under the American empire, the brownness of South Asian immigrants is conflated with the blackness of African Americans. We collectively are transformed and viewed through a singular white lens as people of color. Thus, the sooner we come to terms with our dark skins and disentangle the interconnectedness of caste and color, the faster we can begin to build bridges of solidarity that celebrate our commonalities rather than our differences.

Questions

1. Why is colorism a helpful but limited term to capture the nuances between caste, religion, and color in the Indian Context?

---

[44] Mishra, "India and Colorism: The Finer Nuances," 731.
[45] Khanna, "Anti-Blackness," 131.

2. How does anti-darkness or anti-dark skin bias translate to anti-blackness sentiments in the United States context? How do mythhistories create a color-conscious bias in the Indian context while also linking skin color to caste origins?
3. Did Jesus in Matthew 15:21-28 suffer from an anti-Canaanite bias? If so, how do mythhistories, particularly around conquest narratives, play in formalizing and institutionalizing these narratives both in ancient texts and current contexts?

Bibliography

Aran, Isha. Bollywood's shameful history of blackface 6. https://splinternews.com/bollywood-s-shameful-history-of-blackface-1793856198.
Ambedkar, B. R. (Bhimrao Ramji). 1990. *Annihilation of Caste: An Undelivered Speech*. New Delhi: Arnold Publishers.
Baffles, Melanie S. 2014. What Do We Do With This Jesus? A Reading of Matthew 15: 21–28 through the Lens of Psychoanalytic Theory. *Pastoral Psychology* 63: 249–263.
Crossan, John Dominic. 2008. Roman Imperial Theology. In *In the Shadow of Empire: Reclaiming the Bible as a History of Faithful Resistance*, ed. Richard A. Horsley, 59–73. London: Westminster John Knox Press.
D'Souza, Ryan A. 2019. *Representations of Indian Christians in Bollywood Movies*. Ph.D. diss., University of South Florida.
Dube, Musa. 2000. *Postcolonial Feminist Interpretations*. St. Louis, MO: Chalice Press.
Dutt, Barkha. Mojo Story. Masaba Masaba | Racism | Viv Richards, Neena Gupta | Feminism. 2020. Fashion, Films. YouTube video, 38:25. November 21. https://www.youtube.com/watch?v=JJCqivYcGXw
Ghosh, Amrita and Arun Kimar. 2020. Casteism Continues to Thrive Among Indians Abroad – Through Surnames. *Scroll.in*, August 28. https://scroll.in/global/970262/casteism-cotinues-to-thrive-among-indians-abroad-throu.
Grey, Deborah. 2016. The Stereotypes I Live with As an Indian Christian Woman. *Youth Ki Awaz*, December 12. https://www.youthkiawaaz.com/2016/12/stereotypes-about-indian-christian-women.
Humphries-Brooks, Stephenson. 2001. The Canaanite Women in Matthew. In *Feminist Companion to Matthew*, ed. Amy-Jill Levine, 138–156. New York: Bloomsbury Publishing.
Jackson, Glenna S. 2003. Enemies of Israel: Ruth and the Canaanite Woman. *Hervormde Teologiese Studies* 59 (3): 779–792.
Jacob, Sharon. 2020. Neither Here nor There! A Hermeneutics of Shuttling: Reflections from a Postcolonial Biblical Critic. In *Asian and Asian American Women in Theology and Religion*, ed. Kwok Pui Lan, 123–136. Cham, Switzerland: Palgrave Macmillan.
———. 2021. The Cost of Infinite Gratitude on Immigrant Workers in the Workplace and Beyond. *Medium*, June 4. https://medium.com/@sharonjacobpts/the-cost-of-infinite-gratitude-on-immigrant-workers-in-the-workplace-and-beyond-f370076c3ce1
Khanna, Nikki, ed. 2020. *Whiter: Asian and Asian American Women on Skin Color and Colorism*. New York: New York University Press.
Kropf, Schuyler. 2015. Nikki Haley, Bobby Jindal Explain Their Faith During the Response Prayer Meeting Saturday. *The Post and Courier*, June 12. https://www.postandcourier.com/politics/nikki-haley-bobby-jindal-explain-their-faith-during-the-response-prayer-meeting-saturday/article_c48ab132-a0df-5044-a86f-97f32bd64e37.html.
LeMarquand, Grant. 2005. The Canaanite Conquest of Jesus (Matthew 15:21-28). *Arc: The Journal of the Faculty of Religious Studies* 33: 237–247.

Mayell, Hilary. 2003. India's "Untouchables" Face Violence and Discrimination. *National Geographic*, June 2. https://www.nationalgeographic.com/pages/article/indias-untouchables-face-violence-discrimination.

Mishra, Abhishek. 2020. India's Racial Prejudice is Jeopardizing Ties with African Nations. *Observer Research Foundation*, July 28. https://www.orfonline.org/research/indias-racial-prejudice-is-jeopardising-ties-with-african-nations/

Mishra, Neha. 2015. India and Colorism: The Finer Nuances. *Washington University Global Studies Law Review* 14 (4): 725–750.

Mishra, Nivedita. 2014. 'Sandra from Bandra' to 'Oh Fanny re': the Changing Face of Christians in Films. *Hindustan Times*, September 12. https://www.hindustantimes.com/bollywood/sandra-from-bandra-to-oh-fanny-re-the-changing-face-of-christians-in-films/story-wH9aE6IymtNFJkllEViSUJ.html.

Nave, Guy. 2020. Challenging Privilege through the Preaching and Teaching of Scripture. *Currents in Theology and Mission* 47 (3): 15–18.

Roy, Arundhati. 2017. *The Doctor and the Saint: Caste, Race, and Annihilation of Caste: the Debate Between B. R. Ambedkar and M. K. Gandhi*. Chicago: Haymarket Books.

Singh, Hira, and M.A. Kalam. 2017. India's Race Problem: Ignorance and Denial. *Social Scientist* 45: 75–78.

Sinha, Kanad. 2023. The Question of Aryan Identity. *The Telegraph*, January 28. https://www.telegraphindia.com/culture/books/the-question-of-aryan-identity/cid/1696499.

Staff Writer. 2020. An Email Interview with Arundhati Roy. *Dalit Camera*, June 8. https://www.dalitcamera.com/indian-racism-towards-black-people-is-almost-worse-than-white-peoples-racism/.

———. 2003. Black Is Blemish in India. *Al Jazeera*, October 7. https://www.aljazeera.com/news/2003/10/7/black-is-blemish-in-india.

———. 2022. Racism Is Embedded in Bollywood: It's Time to Change That. *Madras Courier*, June 24. https://madrascourier.com/opinion/racism-is-embedded-in-bollywood-its-time-to-change-that/.

———, 2017. Tarun Vijay Lands in Trouble with 'Black People' Remarks, Later Apologises on Twitter. *The Hindu*, April 7. https://www.thehindu.com/news/national/if-we-were-racist-why-would-we-live-with-south-indians-tarun-vijay/article17866698.ece.

Thapar, Romila. 2008. *The Aryan: Recasting Constructs*. Gurgaon, India: Three Essays Collective.

Thomas, Sonja. 2018. *Privileged Minorities: Syrian Christianity, Gender, and Minority Rights in Postcolonial India*. Seattle: The University of Washington Press.

Taiwo, Wendy Thompson. 2020. What It Means to be Brown. In *Whiter: Asian and Asian American Women on Skin Color and Colorism*, ed. Nikki Khanna, 137–142. New York: New York University Press.

Trimm, Charlie. 2022. *The Destruction of the Canaanites: God, Genocide, and Biblical Interpretation*. Grand Rapids, MI: W. B. Eerdmans Publishing Company.

Venketaraman, Sakshi. 2020. 'Kamala Auntie' Prompts Examination of Anti-Blackness for South Asians. *NBC News*, August 19. https://www.nbcnews.com/news/asian-america/kamala-auntie-prompts-examination-anti-blackness-south-asians-n1237339.

Walker, Alice. 1983. If the Present Looks Like the Past, What Does the Future Look Like? In *In Search of Our Mothers Gardens: Womanist Prose*. San Diego, CA: Harcourt Brace Jovanovich.

12
Who Is Family? Where Asian North American Christians Are in Empathizing with Black People

Courtney T. Goto

Recently a Japanese American mother and daughter were arguing about whether to defund the New York City police department, an issue that has been a clarion call for the Black Lives Matter movement.[1] Daughter Yumi (age 26), who was born and raised on the Upper West Side, feels strongly about joining the protests. Laid off from her job because of Covid, Yumi was in the midst of applying for jobs when she decided to act. She said, "[I]t kind of felt a little meaningless to not put my body on the streets and, you know, join other people in the city to make our voices heard and to show everyone that we were upset. And me and a friend who lived close by, we would just go to every single protest that we could. Because it just felt like the most direct form of action that I've ever been able to be a part of."[2] After experiencing how police were treating the protesters, she became convinced that the police "truly don't care" and they "don't provide more safety."[3] While Yumi believes that the city's police force should be defunded and eventually "abolished," her mother

---

[1] The conversation between Yumiko Mannarelli and Misako Shimada was featured in Michael Barbaro, "Policing and the New York Mayoral Race," June 22, 2021, in *The Daily*, produced by Jessica Cheung, Rachel Quester and Rob Szypko, podcast, 38:42, https://www.nytimes.com/2021/06/22/podcasts/the-daily/new-york-city-mayoral-race-crime-policing.html. This chapter uses the adjective "Black" to refer to people of African descent, particularly in North America, to echo Black Lives Matter language as well as the term used by Yuri Kochiyama, who is discussed later. I find it difficult to be thoughtful about using one or another name (Black versus African American, for example) because each has its own histories, associations, and political implications.

[2] Barbaro, "Policing."

[3] Barbaro, "Policing."

C. T. Goto (✉)
Associate Professor of Religious Education, Boston University School of Theology, Boston, MA, USA
e-mail: cgoto@bu.edu

Misako vehemently disagrees.[4] Misako (age 57) was born in Japan and has lived in New York since she was 17, and she remembers how "seedy" her neighborhood was and how unsafe she felt walking alone at night, having been "smacked in the face" by a "homeless guy."[5] She believes that police presence is essential for deterring random acts of violence, for example, in the subway. She's concerned about the rise of anti-Asian violence, and she feels safer with police around. When Misako starts condemning the protesters for looting, Yumi says with exasperation, "Oh my god, no... Do you understand that the rich people loot from all of us by not paying their taxes?"[6]

On its surface, this situation involves two people hotly disagreeing about defunding the police, but it entails much more. This is a conflict between Asians, who happen to be in the same family, over whether to support Black (and Brown) people who are victimized by police. Yumi explains, "I think that the experience of others, like Black and Brown people, are significantly worse [when it comes to having run-ins with the police]. And that's what...gets me upset. Like I wasn't out there for me. Like I was out there for the other people."[7] When her mother disagrees, Yumi expresses frustration and judgment. The conflict is also generational. Yumi came of age in the United States, her mother in Japan. *Most importantly, they fundamentally disagree about who is in their clan.* With an expansive sense of "we," Yumi is willing to risk her bodily safety to engage in civil protest for Black (and Brown) people whom the police treat worse than her. In contrast, Misako has a narrower sense of who is in her clan. She is focused on people of Asian descent, feeling targeted and terrorized since the pandemic.

The conflict between Yumi and Misako illustrates a larger social problem felt within many Asian North American (ANA) families, including many church families. Some are solidly in support of Black lives, while others are more and less anti-Black without being willing to admit it. Since the killing of Michael Brown in Ferguson, many young progressive ANAs like Yumi have participated in the movement for Black lives, for example through organizations in the San Francisco Bay Area, New York City, San Diego, and the Twin Cities that were participating in or influenced by #Asians4BlackLives activism.[8] However, not only are the histories of relations between people of Asian and African descent complicated, ANAs are not of one mind when it comes to allying with Black and Brown people. Some members of Asian communities are preoccupied with proving their worth (exceptionalism), pursuing their own success, or advocating for their own victimhood.[9] I suspect that

---

[4] Barbaro, "Policing."

[5] Barbaro, "Policing."

[6] Barbaro, "Policing."

[7] Barbaro, "Policing."

[8] May Fu et al., "#Asians4BlackLives: Notes from the Ground," *Amerasia Journal* 45, no. 2 (May 4, 2019), 253–270.

[9] Wen Liu, "Complicity and Resistance: Asian American Body Politics in Black Lives Matter," *Journal of Asian American Studies* 21, no. 3 (2018), 421–451; Rachel Kuo, "Visible Solidarities: #Asians4BlackLives and Affective Racial Counterpublics," *Studies of Transition States and Societies* 10, no. 2 (2018), 40–54.

many ANA families cope with these differences among their members by avoiding the subject of solidarity with Black people.[10] They may feel ill-equipped to engage in productive discussions and/or anxious about the prospect of conflict.

If we're trying to increase empathy for Black people among ANA Christians, our impulse might be to argue, shame, or cajole (church) family members to change. We want people we love to join our side, that is, the good side. This is Yumi's strategy with Misako. She wants her mom to do right by Black (and Brown) people who suffer at the hands of police, but perhaps without saying so she also wants to experience her mom being *with* her. In the heat of the moment, people tend to approach conflict in binary terms, enacting often without words a certainty—that I know and you don't. While that may be all that we know how to do, trying to convince people of the error of their ways doesn't go very far. Just ask Yumi and Misako. A more fruitful approach, which I explore in this chapter, is to cultivate some curiosity and openness to what each of us does not know about ourselves, as well as what we do not know about one another.

Rather than focusing exclusively on the conflict between us, there's deeper, psychic work to take on within ourselves. Consider for a moment that Yumi and Misako represent not only factions in the same family (or congregation) that disagree. They also *represent conflicting voices within the same person.* In this sense, Yumi and Misako are metaphors for an experience we all have at times—being of multiple minds on an issue. For example, a person might tell herself that she supports Black struggle in principle (Yumi), but in action she is more concerned about her own safety and does not act (Misako). Acknowledging and exploring our own

---

[10] My assessment runs counter to Lee and Huang's claim that solidarity between Asians and Black people in the US is growing. They interpret a 2020 voter survey to show that Korean Americans have made progress in developing empathy for Black people. They write, "[M]ore than nine in ten Korean Americans believe that there is at least some discrimination against Black people in our society today. Seventy percent also agree that the government should do more to protect the civil rights of Black Americans, and 67 percent agree that local governments should shift spending from law enforcement to programs." They attribute these changing attitudes to community education in the decades since the LA riots. They also cite from the same study a finding that "half of Asian Americans across ten different national-origin groups feel they have 'something' or 'a lot' in common with Black Americans when it comes to government, political power, and representation." (Jennifer Lee and Tiffany Huang, "Why the Trope of Black-Asian Conflict in the Face of anti-Asian Violence Dismisses Solidarity," *How We Rise* (blog). *Brookings Institution*, March 11, 2021, https://www.brookings.edu/blog/how-we-rise/2021/03/11/why-the-trope-of-black-asian-conflict-in-the-face-of-anti-asian-violence-dismisses-solidarity/.) I tend to view the results of the 2020 Asian American Voter Survey in terms of the "glass half empty" rather than "half full." When asked "how much discrimination there is against Black people in our society today," fifty-one percent of Asian Americans indicate they believe that Black people experience "some" (28%), "only a little" (11%), or "no" discrimination (13%). Disaggregated data show even worse partial or lack of recognition for Black suffering among Chinese (56%) and Vietnamese (59%). (Gregg Orton, Karthick Ramakrishna and Janelle Wong, "2020 Asian American Voter Survey," AAPI Vote, AAPI Data, Asian Americans Advancing Justice, September 15, 2020, 39.) As a teacher, I would not call myself successful if half or more than half my students learned only some, a bit, or none of what I intended. In terms of education, the data suggest we have work to do.

hesitations, contradictions, and unresolved feelings can help disrupt binary thinking that leads to meltdown.

In this chapter, I guide readers toward engaging in rare, honest conversations among ANA Christians about what motivates and/or keeps us from deeper relationships with Black neighbors.[11] I use the metaphor of "family" to refer to people who deserve our care, concern, and empathy because they are part of the human family. Because these insights are difficult to foster, I am taking an indirect approach by introducing readers to a third person—the late Yuri Kochiyama (1921–2014).[12] Like Yumi and Misako, Kochiyama was a Japanese American New Yorker, though she was of a previous generation. Observing how she relates to members of her predominantly Black community and reflecting on our reactions and responses to Kochiyama (what I will later theorize as "introspection" [Kohut]) provide important clues about where each of us is in empathizing with Black people.

Kochiyama was an activist for radical justice through cross-racial solidarity, beginning with but not limited to collaborative action with Black leaders during the 1960s. As a Japanese American *nisei* (second generation) who was among the nearly 120,000 incarcerated without due process during World War II, Kochiyama could have easily returned upon release to San Pedro, the well-heeled, predominantly white community in which she was raised in southern California. Alternatively, she could have made a comfortable life among other Japanese Americans, as many former internment camp survivors did. However, Kochiyama and her husband Bill started their family in a low-income housing project in mid-town Manhattan, where 95% of the tenants were Black or Puerto Rican.[13] In 1960, they moved to a project in Harlem, where they raised their six children. As she became active in the community, Kochiyama slowly became politically aware of institutional racism, colonialism, and the need for self-determination for Black people. She eventually embraced Black nationalism. When she died in 2014 at age 93, scholars and activists paid homage to her legacy of civil and human rights activism, which started

---

[11] Afro-Asian solidarity has been approached through philosophical, historical and/or structural ways in Afro-Asian studies, ethnic studies including Asian American studies, as well as ANA theology. See Hope's helpful discussion of five traditions in literature on Afro-Asian solidarity. This body of work has been important to establish a context for and to identify challenges in Afro-Asian solidarity. Jeanelle K. Hope, "This Tree Needs Water!: A Case Study on the Radical Potential of Afro-Asian Solidarity in the Era of Black Lives Matter," *Amerasia Journal* 45, no. 2 (May 4, 2019): 223–224, https://doi.org/10.1080/00447471.2019.168480.

[12] Although Kochiyama's story may be less familiar among ANA Christians, I am not alone in finding it to be an important source from which to learn. Grace Y. Kao, "Setting the Captives Free: Yuri Kochiyama and Her Lifelong Fight Against Unjust Imprisonment," in *Can I Get a Witness?: Thirteen Peacemakers, Community-Builders, and Agitators for Faith and Justice*, eds. Charles Marsh, Shea Tuttle and Daniel P. Rhodes (Grand Rapids, MI: Eerdmans, 2019), Kindle; Ki Joo Choi, "Asian American Christian Ethics: The State of the Discipline," *Journal of the Society of Christian Ethics* 38, no. 2 (January 1, 2018): 42; Tat-siong Benny Liew and Vincent L. Wimbush, "Contact Zones and Zoning Contexts: From the Los Angeles 'Riot' to a New York Symposium," *Union Seminary Quarterly Review* 56, no. 1–2 (2002): 32.

[13] Diane C. Fujino, *Heartbeat of Struggle: The Revolutionary Life of Yuri Kochiyama* (Minneapolis: University of Minnesota Press, 2005), 83.

with being formed in the Black Liberation movement of the 1960s.[14] In 2005, she was nominated for a Noble Peace Prize for her remarkable contributions.[15]

In this essay, I proceed through three moves. First, I characterize Kochiyama as "saintly," drawing on the work of William James. Although you can read about Kochiyama's life without thinking of it as saintly, I find this frame helpful. In a Jamesian sense, saintly people are guides and catalysts for social change, taking risks most people are not willing to take. They are often ahead of their time. As Christians, we have in our diverse tradition a history of relating to saints, which is why James' discussion is apropos. Kochiyama's saintliness serves as an ethical yardstick by which to compare ourselves as a point of departure. The second move in this chapter introduces the practice of introspection within an intersubjective encounter. This is a tool that my co-researcher Chris Schlauch and I have been using in our teaching and research on relating across what we are calling "paradigms of racism." Within an intersubjective encounter, introspection is not simply solo self-reflection or critical reflection about something. In this chapter, it involves reflection in reaction and response to Kochiyama, your conversation partner(s), and with yourself. The third move is to facilitate three encounters with Kochiyama, posing questions to encourage theological reflection as well as introspection between and among members of ANA communities.[16]

My thesis is modest: *Relating to Kochiyama as a saintly figure can reveal where each of us is—and could become—in empathizing with Black people as family.* In a society that sees race in terms of black and white, where people of Asian descent are in relation to either is a fluid, ambiguous question fraught with political consequences. Identifying too much with white people earns the scorn of some fellow Asians. Identifying too much with Black people spells trouble with others. I assume that many ANAs have seldom asked themselves or one another: How honest can we be about where we are in empathizing with Black folk (or not)? How do we take seriously where other ANAs are, especially if they are not where we think they should be? My hope is that this reflection with ANAs about ourselves in response to Kochiyama will help to clarify who we are and who we could be in relation to Black people. A more advanced step would be to practice relating to African Americans, which is the direction to which this essay points but does not address. Ultimately, they are the judge of our empathy, as Schlauch says.[17]

My personal stake in this essay is to ponder how I respond to Kochiyama as she relates to Black members of her community and introduce readers to some concepts

---

[14] For tributes, see Mary Uyematsu Kao, "Salute to Yuri Kochiyama (May 19, 2021 - June 1, 2014)," *Amerasia Journal* 40, no. 2 (2014): 112–114.; Mary Uyematsu Kao et al., "Tributes to Yuri Kochiyama," *Amerasia Journal* 40, no. 3 (January 01, 2014): 1–33.

[15] Kochiyama was nominated through the 1000 Women for the Nobel Peace Prize Project, but she did not receive the Nobel. Kao, "Setting the Captives Free," Kindle.

[16] Some readers might recognize my practical theological approach, drawing on psychology and theology to open up lived experience.

[17] Chris R. Schlauch, "The Psychology of the Self and Cross Cultural Clinical Care," *Journal of Pastoral Theology* 17, no. 2 (2007): 83–117, https://doi.org/10.1179/jpt.2007.17.2.006.

from a larger project on relating across paradigms of racism.[18] I met Kochiyama several times between 1995–2000 at Japanese American community events in Manhattan. She was spry, sharp as a tack, witty, and quick to deflect being introduced to me as someone "famous." Although I was merely a friend of a friend, she was interested in learning who I was. I had no idea that I was meeting someone truly extraordinary and someone about whom I would write more than twenty years later.

Kochiyama as "Saintly"

Kochiyama is probably turning in her grave as I describe her as "saintly." For someone who habitually deflected attention from herself,[19] being associated with saintliness would likely make Kochiyama uncomfortable and would not be accurate to how she knew herself. Some critics might scoff at my associating Kochiyama with saintliness because she admired revolutionary leaders such as Mao Tse-tung.[20] To some detractors, the fact that Kochiyama moved away from the institutional Christianity in which she was raised or that she practiced Islam for a time might disqualify her from being characterized as saintly. Some Christians might associate saintliness with admirable virtues, values, and behavior that come from their faith tradition. However, James uses the notion of saintliness in an expansive sense, to describe an archetype that can be found in many "varieties."

By characterizing Kochiyama as saintly, I do not wish to imply that she was perfect. In fact, it's her humanness and flaws that make her a relatable and compelling figure. In paying tribute to Kochiyama, journalist Thandisizwe Chimurenga observes how she neither saved lives on the battlefield, nor possessed impressive job titles, nor busied herself with writing publications. Chimurenga writes, "She was, however, present. She reported for duty. She provided aid and comfort. Yuri did not practice solidarity with oppressed people and their movements for liberation: she lived and breathed it. It is for this reason that she will forever be respected and loved."[21] It's Kochiyama's *everyday* saintliness that is not only impressive but instructive.

---

[18] Schlauch and I are co-authoring a book whose working title is *Paradigms of Racism: Beyond Reacting Toward Relating*. The approach taken in this chapter is elaborated in the book but applied more broadly to everyday encounters involving race/racism.

[19] Fujino, *Heartbeat of Struggle*, 75, 100.

[20] Kao writes, "Yuri's admiration for revolutionaries remains one of the most controversial aspects of her legacy. She was drawn to Maoist philosophy after having received *The Little Red Book: Quotations from Chairman Mao Tse-tung* as a gift; supported the Peruvian militant communist group Shining Path; and favorably compared Osama bin Laden to Malcolm X, Che Guevara, Fidel Castro, and several others for fighting against US imperialism. Kao, "Setting the Captives Free," footnote 11, Kindle.

[21] Kao et al., "Tributes to Yuri Kochiyama," 18.

William James argues that humanity is indebted to saints for having lived among us because they are "authors, *auctores*, increasers, of goodness."[22] He writes,

> The saints, with their extravagance of human tenderness, are the great torchbearers of this belief [in the essential sacredness of every person], the tip of the wedge, the clearers of the darkness. Like the single drops which sparkle in the sun as they are flung far ahead of the advancing edge of a wavecrest or of a flood, they show the way and are forerunners. The world is not yet with them, so they often seem in the midst of the world's affairs to be preposterous. Yet they are impregnators of the world, vivifiers and animaters of potentialities of goodness which but for them would lie forever dormant. It is not possible to be quite as mean as we naturally are, when they have passed before us. One fire kindles another; and without that overtrust in human worth which they show, the rest of us would lie in spiritual stagnancy.[23]

In a Jamesian sense, saints are essential catalysts for social transformation—multipliers of goodness who lead others to do better. They show us a way forward by living what most of us cannot yet imagine or embody. They show us what is possible.

James portrays saints as an elite, albeit eccentric, group of people who are driven by a passion that keeps them focused on their God-given mission.[24] While ordinary folk are held back by hesitation and ambivalence about doing most anything, even the most commonplace of acts, people who are saintly live by what James describes as "excitement" that overrides any "inhibitions."[25] Readers might recognize what this phenomenon is like by imagining what's possible when a person's adrenaline is pumping. A teenager witnesses a car that has flipped over into a ditch and without hesitation runs to pull the driver out of the car. For someone with a saintly character, the impulse to act courageously is fueled by an intense excitement that is experienced not only under dangerous or extraordinary circumstances but rather every day. While most people are normally plagued with inhibitions, James writes, "[T]he genius with the inborn passion seems not to feel them at all; [s]he is free of all that inner friction and nervous waste."[26]

When Kochiyama was eighteen years old, she wrote a "creed" that expresses a passion that characterizes the kind of emotional energy that James describes. She writes:

---

[22] William James, "Lectures XIV and XV: The Value of Saintliness," in *The Varieties of Religious Experience a Study in Human Nature* (New York: Longmans, Green, and Co, 1902b), 349. I am indebted to Chris Schlauch for introducing me to this work.

[23] James, "The Value of Saintliness," 350.

[24] James writes, "The saintly character is the character for which spiritual emotions are the habitual centre [sic] of the personal energy." Across all religions, saintliness can be characterized by charity a knowing in one's bones "the existence of an Ideal Power", "a sense of the friendly continuity of the ideal power with our own," joy and freedom that comes with diminishment of ego, and a "shifting of the emotional centre [sic] towards loving and harmonious affections." William James, "Lectures XI, XII, XIII: Saintliness," in *The Varieties of Religious Experience a Study in Human Nature* (New York: Longmans, Green, and Co, 1902a), 266–267.

[25] James, "Saintliness," 256.

[26] James, "Saintliness," 260. Another interesting avenue to explore in the future is the degree to which Kochiyama pursues her cause with such zealousness that it is tantamount to the kind of asceticism that James identifies as a "practical consequences" of saintliness (Ibid., 268).

> To live a life without losing faith in God, my fellowmen, and my country…[T]o never break one link of friendship, regardless of the time or distance that separates me from that friend, even if that friendship is only a memory stored away in my heart and mind. / To never humiliate or look down on any person, group, creed, religion, race, employment, or station in life, but rather to respect. / To always keep in mind, that any opportunities, achievement, or happiness I have had, I owe to someone else. / To love everyone; to never know the meaning of hate, or have one enemy. (An enemy, to me, is only created in one's mind.)…[T]o never expect another to be indebted to help me, but should I be able to help anyone, to be grateful that I could be of use. / To give the advantage, but never to ask for it; to be strict with myself, but not with others…Dear Heavenly Father—Help me *live* [my philosophy of life.][27]

While Kao describes this creed as "Pollyannish,"[28] such an assessment underestimates how Kochiyama names a truth so central to her mission that she still finds the creed to be true of her late in life, when she writes her autobiography.[29] *Kochiyama's creed reveals a humble but fierce love and respect for fellow human beings.* Her creed illustrates the intense "affection" or "excitement" that James says is characteristic of saintliness.

Kochiyama practices love and respect for others with extraordinary zeal. According to Fujino, it was in Kochiyama's nature to "jump whole-heartedly into a project she believed in," including political activism. When she began to work for Black liberation, Kochiyama said, "I think a lot of other people like myself who had never been arrested were excited to be part of the actions [circulating petitions, protesting, and getting arrested], to be doing something concrete to help fight discrimination."[30] Where most ANAs (and most people in general) would hesitate to do anything that would lead to incarceration, Kochiyama found "exhilaration" in these risky actions, as Fujino describes it.[31] Kochiyama's excitement about being arrested is testament to the kind of saintly affect that overrides and redefines risk as simply "the right thing to do."[32]

Kochiyama never set out to become saintly, yet her actions and her words show how much of a saint she is. She faithfully abides by a vision that guides how and to whom she dedicates herself, in this case, Black neighbors who are agitating for fair treatment. She demonstrates a cross-racial solidarity that some of us may be carrying on, which others may not be able to imagine.

---

[27] Emphasis in the original. Kochiyama writes, "My family found something I wrote long ago as a teenager. While my religious and political beliefs have changed quite a bit since 1939 [when the creed was written], my basic personal values and philosophy of life have remained the same." Yuri Kochiyama, *Passing It On: A Memoir* (Los Angeles, CA: UCLA Asian American Studies Center Press, 2004), xxiv.

[28] Kao, "Setting the Captives Free," Kindle.

[29] Kochiyama, *Pass It On*, xxiv.

[30] Fujino, *Heartbeat of Struggle*, 120. On this occasion, she is referring to protesting employment discrimination practices at the Downstate Medical Center in Brooklyn during the summer of 1963 (Ibid., 119). Kochiyama frames other protest action as "exciting" (Ibid., 229).

[31] Fujino, *Heartbeat of Struggle*, 120.

[32] Fujino, *Heartbeat of Struggle*, 230.

Practicing Introspection Within Intersubjective Encounters

As you've encountered Kochiyama, you may have been engaged in running sidebar conversations. You might have said to yourself, "I could never do what she did." Or, "That sounds like something I would do." If readers are like me, there's always a chorus voicing impressions, opinions, and questions within the confines of my mind. In a sense, you were responding to Kochiyama. If you read her biography or memoir, she would be speaking even more directly to you, and presumably, you'd have more to say/ask in response. In this sense, you've been experiencing an intersubjective encounter, where she is relating to you and you are reacting and responding.

In my co-research with Schlauch, I have learned that introspection is a practice that strengthens the "observing ego," which is not the chattering chorus but the "I" that can stand back and observe, moment to moment the flow of thoughts, feelings, and sensations.[33] Thanks to an observing ego, I can track my own experience of relating, which then allows me to reflect on how and why I'm reacting and responding as I do. Introspection, Schlauch tells me, is a necessary step toward empathy, which is the ultimate goal of cross-racial solidarity. Without the practice or discipline of seeking to be present to one's own experience, it's impossible to imagine accurately someone else's or being present to them in their experiencing.

In the next section, I facilitate three encounters with Kochiyama that create occasions to practice introspection with ANA conversation partners. As you read, summon your observing ego to catch yourself in the midst of experiencing Kochiyama. Notice how you are responding to her as she relates to Black people. Be alert to thoughts, bodily sensations, and emotions. Take time to pause and reflect on the questions I pose, rather than speeding through them as you might be in the habit of doing. It might be helpful to write your responses and share them. These questions are designed for you to slow down and open up what you are experiencing (introspection) and compare with others.

I am inviting readers to pay attention and share your responses to Kochiyama's relating to Black people in order to reveal something about yourselves to yourselves. This invitation to readers to collaborate and track your relating to Kochiyama is inspired by Schlauch's expertise in the work of psychoanalyst Heinz Kohut, who takes a thoroughly relational view of human being and becoming.[34] By attending to our relating to Kochiyama, there is the possibility of unearthing, strengthening and/

---

[33] Heinz Kohut, "Introspection, Empathy, and Psychoanalysis: An Examination of the Relationship between Mode of Observation and Theory," *Journal of the American Psychoanalytic Association* 7, no. 3 (1959): 459–483.

[34] Chris R. Schlauch, "The Therapeutic Relationship in Pastoral Psychotherapy," in *Transforming Wisdom: Pastoral Psychotherapy in Theological Perspective*, eds. Felicity Brock Kelcourse and K. B. Lyon (Eugene, OR: Cascade Books, 2015), 183–198; Chris R. Schlauch, "Do I Hear what You Hear? Thinking about Psychotherapy and Spirituality from a Self Psychological Approach: The Spiritual Horizon of Psychotherapy," *Journal of Spirituality in Mental Health* 11, no. 1–2 (2009): 26–50; Chris R. Schlauch, *Faithful Companioning: How Pastoral Counseling Heals* (Minneapolis, MN: Fortress Press, 1995); Chris R. Schlauch, "Empathy as the Essence of Pastoral Psychotherapy," *Journal of Pastoral Care* 44, no. 1 (January 1, 1990): 3–17.

or challenging assumptions that shape how often, well, or poorly we relate to Black people—assumptions by which we live but may not consider critically. This work is meant to be practiced with other ANA conversation partners who provide support and potentially challenge one another in the process.

Encounter 1: "Becoming a Presence"

When Kochiyama begins to attend meetings for the civil rights movement in her community, she is the only person of Asian descent among a majority of Black people with some Latinx. Naturally, they are wary or "skeptical."[35] We can imagine at first some Black activists wondering why Kochiyama is there, whether she is trustworthy, or how she will take to Black leadership in the Movement. They might question how politically savvy she is when it comes to Black people agitating for change. If they are "all in," meaning they are fully invested in the Movement, some leaders might question how far *she* is willing to go since she isn't Black.

Fujino provides insight about how Kochiyama relates to Black activists in the Movement when she is a newcomer. She writes: "Although Yuri may have felt hesitant to involve herself in this new arena, she was not one to act with shyness when she saw a need. She would not have tried to pass herself off as a politically experienced activist, nor would she have tried to act Black to fit in…Instead, she demonstrated her seriousness through her hard work, dependability, and enthusiasm."[36] Evidently, Kochiyama is humble yet secure enough in herself to relate to Black activists as she knows herself—a member of the community who should be concerned about the wellbeing of others. Any inhibitions about being inexperienced or in the minority are overridden by the directive to do something if people are not being loved and respected, as her creed dictates. In working with the mostly Black Harlem Parents Committee, Kochiyama recalls, "The people were so wonderful. Even though we weren't Black, we never felt we were different. It was just that we were part of the community."[37] People accept Kochiyama because she develops a history with the community, "bec[oming] a presence."[38]

I invite readers to inventory the range of thoughts, images, sensations, and questions you had in this encounter with Kochiyama. For some readers, being a minority among Black people is a regular, familiar situation. For others, it is a rare occurrence, if ever.

- At what point(s) did you "identify" with Kochiyama? When did you feel like you could or could never do what she did?

---

[35] Fujino, *Heartbeat of Struggle*, 122.
[36] Fujino, *Heartbeat of Struggle*, 122.
[37] Fujino, *Heartbeat of Struggle*, 122.
[38] Fujino, *Heartbeat of Struggle*, 123.

- If you are in the habit of working with Black allies for a common cause, recall a time when you were new to cross-racial solidarity, like Kochiyama was at this point in her life. What factors facilitated or inhibited your forming that trust?
- If being in the minority among Black people is rare, what is it like to imagine working within a Black community?

Kochiyama does not seem preoccupied with racial difference, at least not in relation to the Black and Brown people in her community. She is becoming politically aware of structural racism, most likely preoccupied with the oppressive power of white institutions. Rather than seeing Black experiences of race as so distinct from her own as Japanese American, she prefers to recognize her own experience of racism in theirs to create the possibility of solidarity.[39] She places greater weight on the common life she has with Black people—the fact they are all part of the same community—as the reason to participate.

As readers:

- How do you relate to Kochiyama as one who is more or less inclined to see the differences between Black people and Asian people as a problem?
- How did you come to perceive the truth of what you know?

One way to reflect theologically about this encounter with Kochiyama is through the story of Ruth. When Naomi presses her daughter to return to her people, Ruth refuses and says, "Where you go, I will go; where you lodge, I will lodge; your people shall be my people, and your God my God."[40] This is a story of women who are not from the same country. Naomi is from Judah, while Ruth is from Moab. For Ruth not to return to her homeland and be with her kind is a significant sacrifice. She is faithful, not allowing Naomi to dissuade her from staying with her. In her saintliness, Kochiyama displays a similar dedication to the predominantly Black community in which she lived. Both Ruth and Kochiyama are minorities either in the land of Judah or in Harlem, making these seemingly foreign places their adopted home. Ruth insists on staying with Naomi because of their deep relationship, which is not unlike Kochiyama's dedicated relationship with her Harlem community. Members of the community gather at her home for parties every Saturday night, where there is food, music, conversation, and even a place to stay when needed. Later Kochiyama hosts educational, cultural, or political meetings at her house. Kochiyama has close relationships with Black folk. They are part of her life and she and her family a part of theirs.[41]

---

[39] Kochiyama writes, "I see the parallel between the way African Americans were treated in the segregated South and the way Japanese Americans were evacuated and relocated en mass to remote internment camps across the U.S. In each instance there were senseless degradation, brutality, and hatred wrought by fear and ignorance caused by racism. So I remain passionately committed to doing whatever I can and saying whatever I must to eliminate racist assumptions and ideas." Kochiyama, *Pass It On*, 7.

[40] Ruth 1:17 (NRSV).

[41] Kochiyama's everyday life in her predominantly Black community is well documented in Fujino, *Heartbeat of Struggle*.

This encounter with Kochiyama in light of the biblical text inspires another set of reflections.

- What does God ask of us (ANAs) in relating to Black people in our respective communities?
- When do you feel most and least summoned to do as Ruth and Kochiyama have done?
- If you're a woman, how do they speak to you as an ANA Christian woman?

In responding to these questions, track and share what you are learning about you with an ANA conversation partner (or partners). Compare what in your experience or character allows as well as inhibits you from imagining carrying out the kind of cross-racial solidarity that Kochiyama performs.

Encounter 2: Holding the Wounded

As Kochiyama becomes politically aware and active in Black liberation work, she becomes an informal student and a friend of Malcolm X.[42] Through numerous conversations, he challenges her to see the need for self-defense and autonomy for Black people, the need for socialism, and the connection between their struggle and that of colonized, oppressed peoples throughout the world. Kochiyama does not embrace all that Malcolm believes in, but she is deeply influenced by his thinking. Each of them invests energy in the relationship. Malcolm makes an unannounced appearance at a meeting of *hibakusha* (Japanese survivors of the atomic bomb) at Kochiyama's apartment, despite the risk to his personal safety, having received death threats. They correspond with one another, despite Malcolm's busy international travel schedule.

On the day that Malcolm is assassinated, he is making a speech, and Kochiyama is in the audience. When shots are fired, there is chaos, with most people scattering and taking cover. In contrast, Kochiyama leaps on stage toward Malcolm, who is bleeding from gunshot wounds. She cradles his head as he is dying. There is a saintliness in Kochiyama's uninhibited action, as she disregards her safety in order to do what is good and right, especially for her friend. In Jamesian terms, Kochiyama's compassion illustrates saintly "extravagances of human tenderness," which make people like her "prophetic."[43]

Encountering Kochiyama in this scene with Malcolm may or may not be familiar to readers. Once again:

- What is your experience of imagining Kochiyama bolting on stage and holding Malcolm?

---

[42] See Chapter 5, Fujino, *Heartbeat of Struggle*.
[43] James, "The Value of Saints," 349.

- To what extent can you identify with what she did? To what degree were her actions foreign to you, as something you would or could not do?

The image of Kochiyama cradling Malcolm's wounded body is reminiscent of Michaelangelo's *Pietà*, in which Mary holds Jesus' crucified body. The *Pietà* is not based on any biblical text. Nonetheless, Michelangelo's masterpiece is beloved among generations of Christians for expressing great loss and deep sorrow over the brutal murder and suffering of Jesus. To associate the *Pietà* with Kochiyama's holding Malcolm is not to make simple correspondences of Malcolm as Jesus or Kochiyama as Mary. In contrast, the art captures a universal human truth—a mother's agony in holding her dying or dead child slain by violence. The *Pietà* helps the faithful to imagine Mary's experience, and by association Kochiyama's.

There is something profoundly intimate about a mother holding her dying child, or anyone cradling someone who is dying, especially a person one loves. In Kochiyama's case, she is holding not her son but her teacher and friend. In my imagination, the din of the chaos is muted as Kochiyama's eyes are locked onto Malcolm's eyes in which the light is fading. She pleads with him, "Please, Malcolm! Please, Malcolm! Stay alive!"[44] It is an intimate moment between them because it is not only desperate but also tender, to use James' expression. Kochiyama must be fully present to the dying one, to not become lost in her own reactions, so that Malcolm does not feel alone. In being present, Kochiyama is open to experiencing Malcolm's suffering so that he might experience her staying with him.

Returning to the exercise of relating to Kochiyama invites another layer of introspection. Perhaps you're imagining what it would be like to hold a Black friend who is suffering—maybe even dying. Many, if not most of us, have Black friends.

- What thoughts, feelings, and images emerge for you as you contemplate the prospect of holding this person?
- What other Black bodies around you need and would welcome being "held" in ways that matter to them? How open are you to their suffering?
- What would motivate you or keep you from doing this work?

Reflect and compare with your conversation partner(s) what these questions bring up for each of you.

Encounter 3: Making Hard Choices

In this next encounter, Kochiyama is not the sole focus, but rather she is working with her husband and children in a labor of love—a newsletter sent to the hundreds of friends they had made over the years. Because responding individually to letters they receive is prohibitive, a newsletter makes sense, especially given Kochiyama

---

[44] Kao et al, "Tributes to Kochiyama," 19.

and her husband Bill's background in journalism.[45] Keeping in touch with friends is important to Kochiyama, but the more she becomes involved in the Black community in New York, the more she becomes disconnected from the lived reality of many people whom she knew in her previous life. At a certain point, Kochiyama makes a hard choice about to whom to be closest—her newer friends or some of her long-time friends.

In 1950, Kochiyama, her husband Bill, and her children publish a family newsletter called *Christmas Cheer*, and they go on to produce 19 issues in all. Kochiyama explains it as a "newsy family paper relaying our season's cheers, while focusing on family and friends, weddings and births, sports and performing arts, events, ministories, and whatever else popped into our minds. As the children became older, they would have their own columns. One of the features was excerpts from editorials, essays, poems, and so forth that would best exemplify Christmas, its meaning, or its spirit."[46] The Kochiyamas choose playful themes and clever names for themselves to make readers smile. They express hope and holiday wishes, even while acknowledging hardship and injustice in the world.

It took me a while to realize I had mistakenly assumed *Christmas Cheer* is like the kind of newsletters I receive during the holidays. In my experience, they're a kind of "brag report," where people share the adventures and milestones of the family that writes and sends it. In contrast, *Christmas Cheer* is "more about the activities and accomplishments of others than it is about the Kochiyama family."[47] Fujino observes that the newsletter's outward focus "reflects the borderlessness of Yuri's definition of family."[48]

If readers are Millennials or younger, it may be difficult to fathom how much time, energy, and money Kochiyama and her family pour into producing *Christmas Cheer*. This is long before word processing, desktop publishing, image editing, and email. Imagine typing without a delete-key. In the 1950s, it takes the Kochiyamas' working non-stop from September to late November to write, copyedit, lay out, print, fold, stuff, stamp, and mail the newsletters. They perform how much they value their friends as well as how important it is to stay connected. Some of their readers respond with offers to help, including donations to defray the cost of production since the cost is a burden to the family.[49]

In 1963, editorials in *Christmas Cheer* turn more political in substance and in tone, which reflects the increasing political activism of all the Kochiyamas. They write passionately about the plight of Black people and critique American policies and institutions for engaging in "war, racism, and imperialism."[50] While it may have been well received by some, friends begin to express dismay, bafflement, and out-

---

[45] Fujino, *Heartbeat of Struggle*, 100.
[46] Kochiyama, *Pass It On*, 107.
[47] Fujino, *Heartbeat of Struggle*, 100.
[48] Fujino, *Heartbeat of Struggle*, 100.
[49] Fujino, *Heartbeat of Struggle*, 102.
[50] Kochiyama, *Pass It On*, 114.

rage at the perspectives in the newsletter. Kochiyama receives comments such as, "I showed your newspaper to my brother-in-law, and he told me that Christmas Cheer was Communist influenced."[51] Or "I am shocked to say the least. I do not appreciate your kind of Christmas editorials."[52] Or "I came out of my mother's womb a white baby. I grew up in a white man's society, but I fight for the Negroes too. I fight for everybody. I am not a yes-man to anybody. And you and anybody else won't tell me, how, when, and where to turn to."[53] The Kochiyamas were simply being themselves, sharing what they passionately believed in, assuming friends would appreciate what they wrote. Kochiyama writes, "It never occurred to me at the time that I might lose friendships or that our friends would not understand the real issues at hand."[54] Eventually, the Kochiyama's decide to cease publication of *Christmas Cheer*.

Sit with your responses to this encounter:

- What comes up for you, as you imagine friends revealing their racism and ignorance to Kochiyama?
- To what extent have you experienced the cost of relating to, supporting, or befriending Black people?

Kochiyama's situation reminds me of Jesus' teaching about what it takes to follow him. It is written, "Many people were traveling with Jesus. He said to them, 'If you come to me but will not leave your family, you cannot be my follower. You must love me more than your father, mother, wife, children, brothers, and sisters—even more than your own life! Whoever will not carry the cross that is given to them when they follow me cannot be my follower.'"[55] In this passage, Jesus is alluding to faith that requires making hard choices between commitments. It is only natural to love members of one's family or to love one's own life. However, Jesus requires the faithful to love God in following their God-given mission above all else, even if it means leaving loved ones behind.

The decision to follow Jesus is not without sacrifice, just as Kochiyama's decision to continue speaking out against racial oppression and empire rather than catering to what old friends expected. I imagine this was a painful decision. Remember in her creed she swears "never to break one link of friendship," and yet she feels that she must protect herself from friends who misunderstand and philosophically undermine the principles to which she dedicates her life. Yuri says, "Our old friends told us, 'We liked when [*Christmas Cheer*] was just about Xmas.' This is when I decided to put a distance between myself and my hometown. I didn't want them to influence me into their way of thinking. They wanted me to stay the way they knew me. But I had changed."[56]

---

[51] Kochiyama, *Pass It On*, 114.
[52] Kochiyama, *Pass It On*, 114.
[53] Kochiyama, *Pass It On*, 115.
[54] Kochiyama, *Pass It On*, 114.
[55] Luke 14: 25–27 (NRSV).
[56] Fujino, *Heartbeat of Struggle*, 133–134.

Interestingly, the Kochiyamas decision to stop communicating with certain friends is aligned with saintly behavior. According to James, "It costs...nothing to drop friendships, to renounce long-rooted privileges and possessions, to break with social ties."[57] James' notion that a saint feels no pain in ending friendships seems a bit exaggerated in Kochiyama's case.

Reflect for a moment:

- Kochiyama changes to a point that some of her old friends don't recognize her. To what degree are you willing (or have been willing) to allow cross-racial solidarity to change you? What would fuel (or fuels) you to stay the course even if sacrifices must be made?
- When it comes to racism, to whom does God call you to be empathic? Does empathy to Black people mean being less empathic to others, including one's own clan? How do you think about this?

If answering some of these questions for yourself and/or with someone else is challenging, that would be normal. Much depends on how comfortable partners feel and the space they've created for difficult conversations. Your responses to the same questions may change over time if you return to them.

Where Are We in Empathizing with Black People as Family?

Reflect with your conversation partner(s) on moments of matching and/or mismatching between you and Kochiyama, who was highly attuned to the suffering and struggles of Black people in her community. While you may have been able to relate to her at times, I assume that some of her experiences, attitudes, or behaviors were less or not resonant with your own. For example, Kochiyama became who she was because of the people with whom she lived, while many of us have never and probably will never live in a predominantly Black community. Most of us may never have the intense contact with Black neighbors that she had. Furthermore, Kochiyama was able to dedicate her life to raising her family and engaging in volunteer work, but most of us can't afford not to work for a salary. These moments of mismatch might lead you to discount or minimize the implications of Kochiyama's example for your life.

Those moments when you and/or your ANA partner(s) could not relate to Kochiyama may be decentering enough that you become aware of your own habits of relating. As Kochiyama's actions reveal who she considers family, you might have asked yourself "Whom do *I* treat as family?" She performs an expansive understanding of family, which is not limited to the people who look like her or the people back home, but the community of Black and Brown people in whom she becomes invested. Kochiyama acts as family in holding a bleeding Malcolm. She stands with her expanded family, even if it means no longer maintaining close ties with *Christmas*

---

[57] James, "Saintliness," 259.

Cheer readers who do not support her political views. Each of these encounters invites us to think of Black people who are family to us. Perhaps there are many, a handful, or none. These encounters with Kochiyama invite us to ask ourselves and one another, "To what lengths would I go to help and protect the Black people I call family? How far would you go?" If I bring to mind Norbert, Wylin, and their daughter Amani, I know I would "move mountains" to help and protect these loved ones. If you were my conversation partner, you might gently suggest that my first response may be too facile. Our discussion might challenge me to consider how much wider my heart might stretch to embrace more people. We might wonder how far we could go to struggle with and for Black people who are strangers.

Unfortunately, there are common habits that keep us from becoming more like Kochiyama. Among the ugliest ones (for some ANAs more than others) are anti-Blackness and investment in the model minority myth.[58] In both cases, we may or may not be aware of the degree to which we practice either or both habits.[59] ANA Christians are not immune to fearing Black people, believing Asians are superior, looking after our own, and committing microaggressions and worse. We have inherited anti-Black bias along with white Christianity and North American culture, as well as the Asian cultures from which we hail. Many ANA Christians are also deeply invested in pursuing the American Dream, which encourages people to look out for themselves and at most one's clan.[60]

As I said in Yumi and Misako's case, it's easy to fall into trying to "help" [READ: reform] ANA (church) family members by directly challenging their bad behavior, in this case anti-Blackness and/or complicity with the model minority myth. However, (church) family members with whom we do not agree would not experience us taking seriously the truth of what they know. They could experience us as disrespecting them, which does not help people change. If we were more honest with ourselves, we might acknowledge that it's easier to recognize unsavory habits in others than in ourselves, even if we practice them or others to a lesser degree. If we were more alert to our own ambiguity, we might be more open to the possibility that others are more complex than we know—that they are not reducible to the behavior we reject. I'm not trying to excuse anti-blackness and/or complicity with

---

[58] Liu discusses how Chinese Americans in New York City are split "between those *for* and *against* the centering of Black Lives." The author identifies how one coalition uses four strategies to attack Black Lives Matter and justify their own interests: "racial victimology, ethnic empowerment and deservingness, the American Dream, and anti-Blackness" (Liu, "Complicity and Resistance," 421, emphasis in the original; 427). These sound like additional, plausible habits that can be found in many other ANA communities that would hinder solidarity with Black people.

[59] ANA theorists, including authors in this book, help us to understand how and why anti-Blackness and maintaining the model minority myth are detrimental for other people of color, including Black people, but also for ANAs.

[60] For a recent literature of Asian American's captivity to the American Dream see Seungyoun Jeong, "A Psalmic-Theological Homiletic for the Korean Immigrant Congregation" (PhD diss., Boston University School of Theology, 2019), https://buprimo.hosted.exlibrisgroup.com/permalink/f/g23ind/TN_cdi_proquest_journals_2130838387.

the model minority myth. I'm suggesting that perhaps we could be more patient and work more skillfully with those with whom we disagree.

It may be more constructive to explore the *plausibility* and *reasonableness* of anti-Blackness and/or complicity with the model minority myth. To progressive ANA Christians, doing so might sound like giving up ground in the fight for anti-racism. However, understanding why such habits are compelling is a necessary step. Habits of anti-Blackness and/or complicity with the model minority myth persist because they serve important (albeit self-serving) purposes having to do with ANA survival, safety, and strategy within Black-white binary thinking that dominates US and possibly North American culture. For example, anti-Blackness and taking advantage of being perceived as a model minority are tactics used by some ANAs to avoid racism that victimizes Black people.[61] From an egocentric (self-centered) point of view, survival is a reasonable demand. So is needing to feel safe or wanting prosperity for our family and our descendants.

The plausibility and reasonableness of anti-Blackness and/or complicity with the model minority myth need to be acknowledged in order for such habits to be challenged over time. Kochiyama is saintly because she managed to overcome the need for constant safety or self-interest, throwing out inherited anti-Black stereotypes or performing as a model minority (before it had a name). She is proof that it's possible *not* to remain captive to habits that do harm to Black people directly and ANAs indirectly by leaving racism unchallenged.

ANA churches could provide helpful spaces to become aware of anti-Blackness and/or complicity with the model minority myth by encountering Kochiyama on an extended basis. For example, a congregation might read and discuss her biography and/or autobiography over multiple sessions. Participants might engage her and one another as you have done (and as I have engaged you) in this chapter. A congregation might create pairs or small groups that mixes generations.

ANA churches might use the approach I've outlined, posing questions that open up a range of responses to Kochiyama as she relates to Black people. This would create opportunities for participants to probe moments of matching and mismatching with Kochiyama and possibly one another. Participants could wonder and compare about what motivates and/or holds them back from the saintly work of starting or deepening cross-racial solidarity work. They could explore how they have been formed collectively, generationally, and/or individually in ecclesial, North American, and Asian cultures in anti-Black bias and/or the model minority myth, where

---

[61] For an intriguing discussion of "The Parable of the Shrewd Manager" (Luke 16) in terms of the model minority myth and its implications for ANA Christians, see Jonathan Tran, "Moral Innovation and Ambiguity in Asian American Christianity," *Theology Today* 75, no. 3 (2018): 347–357, https://doi.org/10.1177/0040573618791749.

applicable.[62] Participants would need help to acknowledge the safety/survival needs and self-interest that fuel harmful habits of relating to Black people, while also challenging one another whether these habits are as warranted and/or as effective in bringing about safety and security as they assume. Participants may discover, for example, that anti-Black sentiment does not make ANAs safer or more prosperous.

ANA Christians could identify what small step Kochiyama is inspiring them to take collectively and individually to act as if all Black people were family. They could reflect on Kochiyama as a counterexample to habits that keep Black and Asian communities apart. Such work is no substitute for relating to Black people in real time, but ideally, this side work enables us to be better partners as we seek greater solidarity with them.

If Kochiyama were alive, I imagine she would encourage us to build on the long legacy of Asian and Black solidarity that preceded her. In her words, we need to "break down barriers, obstacles and phobias" between Asians and Black people so that "we become one, for the future of humanity."[63] African-Asian relations were a favorite topic on which she spoke publicly. Typically, she made the case by citing a well-documented history of cooperation between Asians and Black people. Passing on the wisdom of Malcolm X, she advocated for Asians and Black people to study history to learn about themselves and one another, finding more in common than they might expect.[64]

Questions for Discussion

1. After reading this chapter, where would you situate yourself currently in empathizing with Black people (or not) and where would you like to "be" in relation to Black people?
2. This chapter suggests that Asian North American churches could provide helpful spaces to become aware of anti-Blackness and/or complicity with the model minority myth by encountering Kochiyama on an extended basis. In what ways you do think your church can provide such space? What are some challenges?

---

[62] For an inspiring example of saintliness among some Asian American high school graduates, explore why they give up their admission to Harvard to make room for Black and underrepresented Brown students. Jonathan Tran, "'The Spirit of God was Hovering Over the Waters': Pressing Past Racialization in the Decolonial Missionary Context; Or, Why Asian American Christians should Give Up their Spots at Harvard." *Can "White" People be Saved?: Triangulating Race, Theology, and Mission*, eds. Love L. Sechrest, Johnny Ramírez-Johnson, and Amos Yong (Downers Grove, IL: IVP Academic, 2018), 229–249.

[63] Fujino, *Heartbeat of Struggle*, 301.

[64] Fujino, *Heartbeat of Struggle*, 301.

3. What is your understanding of everyday saintliness? What actions and practices may constitute everyday saintliness to dismantle structural racism and to build up solidarity among diverse people of color?
4. Kochiyama suggests paying attention to our experiences of racism rather than seeing Black experiences of race as distinct from our own to create the possibility of solidarity. Reflect on your experiences of racism that can serve as an entry point to an empathy-based solidarity-building movement.

Bibliography

Barbaro, Michael. 2021. Policing and the New York Mayoral Race. Produced by Jessica Cheung, Rachel Quester, and Rob Szypko. *The Daily*, June 22, podcast 38:42, https://www.nytimes.com/2021/06/22/podcasts/the-daily/new-york-city-mayoral-race-crime-policing.html.

Choi, Ki Joo. 2018. Asian American Christian Ethics: The State of the Discipline. *Journal of the Society of Christian Ethics* 38 (2): 33–44.

Fu, May, Simmy Makhijani, Anh-Thu Pham, Meejin Richart, Joanne Tien, and Diane Wong. 2019. #Asians4BlackLives: Notes from the Ground. *Amerasia Journal* 45 (2): 253–270. https://doi.org/10.1080/00447471.2019.1671158.

Fujino, Diane C. 2005. *Heartbeat of Struggle: The Revolutionary Life of Yuri Kochiyama*. Minneapolis: The University of Minnesota Press.

Hope, Jeanelle K. 2019. This Tree Needs Water!: A Case Study on the Radical Potential of Afro-Asian Solidarity in the Era of Black Lives Matter. *Amerasia Journal* 45 (2): 222–237. https://doi.org/10.1080/00447471.2019.1684807.

James, William. 1902a. Lectures XI, XII, XIII: Saintliness. In *The Varieties of Religious Experience a Study in Human Nature*, 254–319. New York: Longmans, Green, and Co.

———. 1902b. Lectures XIV and XV: The Value of Saintliness. In *The Varieties of Religious Experience a Study in Human Nature*, 320–369. New York: Longmans, Green, and Co.

Jeong, Seungyoun. 2019. A Psalmic-Theological Homiletic for the Korean Immigrant Congregation. Ph.D. diss. Boston University School of Theology. https://buprimo.hosted.exlibrisgroup.com/permalink/f/g23ind/TN_cdi_proquest_journals_2130838387.

Kao, Grace Y. 2019. Setting the Captives Free: Yuri Kochiyama and Her Lifelong Fight Against Unjust Imprisonment. In *Can I Get a Witness?: Thirteen Peacemakers, Community-Builders, and Agitators for Faith and Justice*, ed. Charles Marsh, Shea Tuttle, and Daniel P. Rhodes. Grand Rapids, MI: Eerdmans.

Kao, Mary Uyematsu. 2014. Salute to Yuri Kochiyama (May 19, 2021 - June 1, 2014). *Amerasia Journal* 40 (2): 112–114.

Kao, Mary Uyematsu, Audee Kochiyama-Holman, Eddie Kochiyama, Ryan Kochiyama, Kai Williams, Karen Tei Yamashita, Thandisizwe Chimurenga, Renee Tajima-Peña, and Diane C. Fujino. 2014. Tributes to Yuri Kochiyama. *Amerasia Journal* 40 (3): 1–33. https://doi.org/10.17953/amer.40.3.j15t28t25n22m130.

Kochiyama, Yuri. 2004. *Passing it on: A Memoir*. Los Angeles, CA: UCLA Asian American Studies Center Press.

Kohut, Heinz. 1959. Introspection, Empathy, and Psychoanalysis: An Examination of the Relationship between Mode of Observation and Theory. *Journal of the American Psychoanalytic Association* 7 (3): 459–483.

Kuo, Rachel. 2018. Visible Solidarities: #Asians4BlackLives and Affective Racial Counterpublics. *Studies of Transition States and Societies* 10 (2): 40–54.

Lee, Jennifer and Tiffany Huang. 2021. Why the Trope of Black-Asian Conflict in the Face of Anti-Asian Violence Dismisses Solidarity. *How We Rise* (blog). *Brookings*

Institution, March 11. https://www.brookings.edu/blog/how-we-rise/2021/03/11/why-the-trope-of-black-asian-conflict-in-the-face-of-anti-asian-violence-dismisses-solidarity/.

Liew, Tat-siong Benny, and Vincent L. Wimbush. 2002. Contact Zones and Zoning Contexts: From the Los Angeles 'Riot' to a New York Symposium. *Union Seminary Quarterly Review* 56 (1-2): 21–40.

Liu, Wen. 2018. Complicity and Resistance: Asian American Body Politics in Black Lives Matter. *Journal of Asian American Studies* 21 (3): 421–451. https://doi.org/10.1353/jaas.2018.0026.

Orton, Gregg, Karthick Ramakrishna, and Janelle Wong. 2020. 2020 Asian American Voter Survey, AAPI Vote, AAPI Data, Asian Americans Advancing Justice, September 15. https://www.apiavote.org/sites/default/files/2020-09/2020%20Asian%20American%20Voter%20Survey%20-%20Sept%2015.pdf.

Schlauch, Chris R. 2009. Do I Hear What You Hear? Thinking About Psychotherapy and Spirituality from a Self Psychological Approach: The Spiritual Horizon of Psychotherapy. *Journal of Spirituality in Mental Health* 11 (1-2): 26–50.

———. 2007. The Psychology of the Self and Cross Cultural Clinical Care. *Journal of Pastoral Theology* 17 (2): 83–117. https://doi.org/10.1179/jpt.2007.17.2.006.

———. 1990. The Psychology of the Self. Empathy as the Essence of Pastoral Psychotherapy. *Journal of Pastoral Care* 44 (1): 3–17.

———. 1995. *Faithful Companioning: How Pastoral Counseling Heals*. Minneapolis: Fortress Press.

———. 2015. The Therapeutic Relationship in Pastoral Psychotherapy. In *Transforming Wisdom: Pastoral Psychotherapy in Theological Perspective*, ed. Felicity Brock Kelcourse and K.B. Lyon, 183–198. Eugene, OR: Cascade Books.

Tran, Jonathan. 2018a. Moral Innovation and Ambiguity in Asian American Christianity. *Theology Today* 75 (3): 347–357. https://doi.org/10.1177/0040573618791749.

———. 2018b. 'The Spirit of God was Hovering Over the Waters': Pressing Past Racialization in the Decolonial Missionary Context; Or, Why Asian American Christians should Give Up their Spots at Harvard. In *Can "White" People be Saved?: Triangulating Race, Theology, and Mission*, ed. Love L. Sechrest, Johnny Ramírez-Johnson, and Amos Yong, 229–249. Downers Grove, IL: IVP Academic.

Name Index

A
Addams, Jane, 125
Ahmed, Sarah, 41
Althaus-Reid, Marcella, 4, 145
Ambedkar, B.R., 195
Appenzeller, Ella, 183
Appenzeller, Henry, 183
Arundati, Roy, 205
Avison, Oliver R., 43
Ayuyang, Rina, 69

B
Bayard, Thomas (Senator), 24, 26, 27
Bayoumi, Moustafa, 1
Bray, Karen, 64
Brock, Rita Nakashima, 88, 89, 170
Brown, Jeffrey A., 65
Butler, Judith, 135

C
Chen, Kuan-Hsing, 96
Cho, Grace M., 105–107, 132, 143, 144
Cockburn, Cynthia, 84, 85
Cone, James, 118, 119
Crossan, John Dominic, 206

D
Davenport, John, 19, 20
Day, Iyko, 49, 141
Dooner, Pierton, 28, 29, 32
Dube, Musa, 204
DuBois, W. E. B., 1, 151

E
Eng, David L., 102, 152
Enloe, Cynthia, 4

F
Fawaz, Ramzi, 59, 60, 69
Fraser, Nancy, 114
Fujikane, Candace, 50, 140

G
Garrett, Greg, 59
Gordon, Avery F., 106
Green, Michael Cullen, 80

H
Haley, Nikki, 201
Hammack, Phillip, 179, 180, 186
Haritaworn, Jin, 152, 168
Harris, Cheryl, 44
Harris, Kamala, 197

I
Iwamura, Jane, 61, 62
Iyer, Deepa, 139, 186, 187

J
James, William, 215–218, 223, 226
Jennings, Willie James, 56–57, 116
Johnson, Lyndon B., 44, 80

K
Khanna, Nikki, 196, 199, 201
Kim, Jodi, 65, 76
Klein, Christina, 59, 80
Knackfuss, Herman, 30, 31
Kochiyama, Yuri, 10, 211, 214–229
Kohut, Heinz, 10, 214, 219
Kwok, Pui-Lan, viii, 56, 89, 200
Kwon, Heonik, 75

L
Le, Quynh Nhu, 42, 45, 46, 140
Lee, Erika, 50, 73, 103, 184
Lee, Jin-Kyung, 143
Lee, Sunisa, 75, 76
Lie, John, 46, 47
Locke, John, 45, 98

M
Malcolm X, 216, 222, 229
Man, Simeon, 84
Melamed, Jodi, 138, 141
Meyers, Ruth, 64, 65
Mills, Anthony R., 57–60, 62
Milton, John, 29, 45
Moon, Seungsook, 75
Morrison, Toni, 8, 95–108
Moy, Zac, 54

N
Nave, Guy, 204, 205
Neha, Mishra, 198
Nguyen, Mimi Thi, 102, 138

P
Padoongpatt, Mark, 157, 160, 162, 163, 165, 172
Park Hong, Cathy, 7, 63–66
Pate, SooJin, 83
Patton, Laurie L., 89
Peckruhn, Heike, 9, 56
Pieris, Aloysius, 89

R
Richardson, Beulah (Beah), 85, 87
Robeson, Paul, 82, 84
Rubio, Elizabeth Hanna, 178, 190–192

S
Santa Ana, Jeffrey, 48, 49
Saunders, Ben, 58
Skidmore, Joey, 58
Skidmore, Max J., 58
Stanford, Leland, 24
Stewart, William (Senator), 27
Sumner, Charles (Senator), 27

T
Thapar, Romila, 196
Thobani, Sunera, 140
Thomas, Sonja, 196, 198, 200, 201, 205
Tran, Jonathan, 114, 229
Tran, Mai-Anh Le, 74, 180
Tsing, Anna, 124, 126
Tuck, Eve, 140

V
Vesely-Flad, Rima, 85

W
Walker, Alice, 197
Wilcox, Melissa, 10
Williams, Andy, 41
Williams, George (Senator), 23, 27
Wolfe, Patrick, 43
Wolter, Robert, 29, 32
Wong, Jessica Wai-Fong, 8, 10, 85, 86

Y
Yang, Jeff, 53, 55, 67
Yang, K. Wayne, 140
Yellow Horse, Aggie J., 185
Yoo, David, 178, 182–184

Subject Index[1]

A

Affect, 5, 9, 63, 64, 66, 84, 136, 139, 152–156, 162, 163, 171, 218
African Americans, 8, 42, 63, 76, 78–84, 87, 96, 97, 99, 100, 102, 103, 107, 134, 152, 181, 186, 188, 191, 192, 207, 211, 215, 221
Afro-Asian relations, 74, 76, 80
Alien land laws, 44
American civil religion, 183
American Dream, 15, 49, 102, 139, 145, 227
American exceptionalism, 43, 45, 48, 101, 190, 191
American Forces Korean Network (AFKN), 40, 41, 48
American popular music, 7, 41
Angel Island, 3, 33, 34
Anti-Asian hate/violence, v–vii, 2, 8, 69–70, 80, 86, 131–146, 178, 179, 212
Anti-Asian immigration, v, 24
Anti-Black racism/anti-Blackness, vi, vii, 2, 6, 9, 73, 74, 76–77, 82, 85, 97, 119, 139, 178–192, 196, 197, 199, 207, 227, 228
Anti-Canaaniteness, 202–207
Anti-darkness, 9, 195–207
Anti-dark skin bias, 202, 203, 207
Antiracism, vii, viii, 8–11, 131–146
Anti-racist identity formation, 177–193
Antiwar feminism (antiwar feminist theology), 7, 73–90
Apocalypse, 15, 18, 29

Aryan, 79, 195, 196, 200, 203
Asian, v–vii, 2, 7, 8, 23, 34, 40–51, 53–55, 60–70, 75, 76, 78–81, 83, 86, 87, 89, 97, 102, 131–133, 135, 136, 138–144, 151–153, 155, 156, 158, 159, 161–166, 168, 169, 171, 180–182, 187, 188, 192, 193, 212, 213, 215, 220, 221, 227–229
Asian American identity, 75, 76, 165
Asian American women or Asian/American women, vi, viii, 5, 88, 89, 132, 133, 136, 142, 155, 188
Asian and Asian Americans or Asian/Americans, v–vii, 11, 55, 61, 65, 88, 131–134, 138–140, 142, 177, 178, 180–182, 184, 185, 187, 188, 190–192, 207
Asian migration, 184
Asian settler colonialism, 42
Asia-Pacific, 73–75, 79, 80, 82, 84, 97, 102, 106
Assimilation, 43–47, 50, 53, 60, 62–64, 66–70, 125, 152, 162, 202, 207
Atlanta spa shootings, 132, 133, 135, 139, 142
Authenticity, 159, 160, 163, 166

B

Belonging/kinship, 7, 8, 42–44, 47–51, 53–70, 99, 101, 103, 105–107, 113–115, 117–119, 121–123, 127, 139, 152–154, 157, 160–163, 165, 167, 169–172, 185, 199, 203, 205

---

[1] Note: Page numbers followed by 'n' refer to notes.

Black body, 83–85, 101, 223
Black, Indigenous, and People of Color (BIPOC), 4, 5, 54, 178, 180–182, 188
Black Lives Matter (BLM), 117, 185, 190, 211, 212, 214, 227
Blackness, 42n8, 76, 86, 113, 113n5, 116, 117, 151, 192, 197, 199, 202, 207
Body of Christ, 18, 123, 127
Bollywood, 197
British Empire, 198
Brown baby crisis, 81
Bubonic plague, 3, 4

C
Canaanite woman, 9, 195–207
Caste, 9, 195–207
Caste supremacy, 201
Chinese Exclusion Act, v, 24–26, 32, 33
Chinese immigrants, 3, 15, 16, 22–25, 29, 32–34, 44, 49, 134
Christian internationalism, 7, 74, 86–89
Christian missionaries, 46–48
Christian nationalism, 9, 181, 186, 187, 190
Citizenship, v, 22, 23, 27, 44, 59, 68, 79, 124, 139–141, 145, 167, 172, 185
Co-constitution, 57
Cold War, 7, 58, 60, 74–76, 80, 81, 84, 87, 90, 96, 139, 161
Colonial, colonialism, vi, vii, 2, 4, 6, 7, 9, 42–51, 54–58, 62–64, 66, 68–70, 73, 75, 83, 96, 97, 106, 113, 116, 137–142, 146, 154, 158, 159, 168, 170, 178, 182–184, 186, 187, 189, 191–193, 196, 198, 207, 214
Colorism, 196–199
Columbus, Christopher, 16, 18–20, 33
Comics Bronze Age, 59
Comics Code Authority (CCA), 58
Comics Golden Age, 58–61, 58n15, 64
Comics Silver Age, 58–61, 58n15, 60n24
Community organizing, 127
Conquest narratives, 195, 202–206
Contamination, 118, 123–126
Cosmopolitics, 7, 53–70
COVID-19, v, 2–5, 55, 90, 134, 137, 177
Cross-racial solidarity, vi, 5, 6, 8, 105–107, 214, 218, 219, 221, 222, 226, 228
Culinary colonialism, 158, 160–161, 163, 166

D
Dalit, 198, 199
Dawes Act, 44, 45

Diaspora, 47, 95, 97, 105, 106, 132, 135–137, 142, 184
Disorder, 86, 116, 117, 126
Divide et impera (divide and rule), 189, 190
Dravidian, 195, 196, 203

E
Ebony, 81, 82
Economy of abundance, 128
Economy of scarcity, 120, 128
Emotions, 7, 9, 41, 42, 49, 63, 152–155, 170, 217, 219
Empathy, 10, 120, 213–215, 219, 226
Empire, v, vi, 15, 47, 73–90, 97, 102, 106, 140, 158, 187, 189, 198, 205–207, 225
Ethnic other, 160, 163, 202
Executive Order 9066, 80
Exile, 20, 49, 50, 76

F
Floyd, George, 111
Fluxability, 60
Formation process, 154, 178
Foundational narratives, 182

G
Gatekeeping, 15, 119, 127
Geary Act, 25, 32
Gender, viii, 4–7, 84, 87, 90, 99, 132, 133, 136–138, 145, 146, 163, 166, 168, 170, 172, 200, 205
GI bride, 105, 106
God of interstices, 74, 89, 90
Gospel of John, 8, 95–108
Gospel of Matthew, 26
Grievability, 135, 145

H
Happiness, 48, 49, 218
Haunting, 97, 105–107
Hawai'i, 50, 183, 184
Healing, 8, 97, 99, 101, 103, 105–107, 187, 205, 207
Heteronormativity, 163
Hmong, 75
Home (homecoming), 7, 18, 19, 29, 32, 33, 41–43, 49, 50, 53, 74, 81, 83, 90, 95–108, 156, 158, 160–162, 164, 167, 170–172, 183, 184, 197, 200, 221, 226

Subject Index

Homophobia, 73, 136, 192
Horizontal hostility, 189, 190
Human identity, 180

I

Identity, 7–9, 15, 23, 34, 42, 43, 45, 54, 55, 57, 60, 65–69, 75, 76, 88, 89, 98, 112–115, 117, 119, 120, 124–126, 132, 133, 137, 139, 141, 142, 146, 151–173, 177–193, 195, 197, 201, 205
Imagination, 3, 7, 15, 18, 19, 29, 33, 46, 53–70, 152, 154, 157, 165, 168, 169, 171, 205, 223
Immigrants, v, vii, 3, 7, 9, 15, 16, 19, 22–25, 29, 32–34, 40–46, 48–50, 76, 86, 114, 124, 125, 134, 138, 139, 141, 143–145, 158, 162, 165, 167, 168, 177–193, 197, 205, 207
Immigrants of color, vii, 186, 187
Immigration, v, 6, 7, 15, 24, 26, 29, 33, 34, 44, 68, 78, 80, 81, 86, 140, 141, 143, 153, 162, 163, 168, 184, 185, 187, 188
Imperialism, 27, 42, 54–59, 62, 64, 84, 85, 107, 139, 161, 168, 183, 184, 186, 216, 224
Indian Americans, 195, 201
Indian Christian Women, 200
Indians, 9, 19, 73, 125, 137, 195–203, 205, 207
Indifference, vi, 9, 181, 182, 184–187, 189, 190
Indigenous, 4, 5, 7, 19, 42–47, 51, 60, 63, 125, 138–141, 178, 181, 187, 200
Innocence, 3, 4, 42, 43, 45–46, 48, 58, 66
Internalized oppression, 189
Intertextual, 97, 106, 107
Introspection, 10, 62, 112, 214, 215, 219–220, 223
Islamophobia, 138, 186, 187

J

Japanese American, 67–68, 74, 81, 180, 187, 211, 214, 216, 221
Japanese colonization, 48, 96
Japanese imperialism, 183
Japan/Imperial Japan/Japanese Empire, 31, 46, 47, 61, 67, 74, 75, 77–80, 88, 182–184, 212
Jews, 86, 123, 126, 204
Johnson-Reed Act, 44

K

Kingdom of God, 127
Knowledge production (racial identity), 152, 156, 170
Korean/American (Christian) identity, 178–190, 192, 193
Korean/American meta-narratives, 9, 184, 190, 192
Korean/American racial formation, 179
Korean churches, 134, 135, 181
Korean Immigrant Churches, 40, 43, 177–193
Korean War, 8, 47, 74, 77, 78, 81–83, 87, 88, 90, 95–97, 105–107
  as forgotten war, 105, 106
  police action, 106, 107
K-pop, 42, 48

L

Liminality, 188

M

Malcolm X, 216, 222, 229
Masculinity, 98, 168
McCarran-Walter Act, 79, 80
McCarthyism, 7, 74, 82, 87
Meta-narrative, 9, 178–180, 185, 190, 192
Militarism, vii, 7, 74, 81, 84, 85, 87, 90, 106, 133, 142, 161, 186
Minor feelings, 7, 55, 63–68
Minoritized people/communities, vi, 8, 9, 63, 65, 97, 107, 133, 178, 186–188, 192, 193
Minority/minorities, 2, 4, 6, 9, 53–70, 75, 76, 80, 81, 83, 87, 136–139, 142, 145, 146, 164, 165, 167, 184, 188–190, 193, 220, 221, 227, 228
Minority nationalism, 8, 132, 133, 137–142, 145
Mixed race ambiguity, 152
Model minority, 6, 53–70, 75, 80, 138, 142, 145, 146, 184, 188–190, 193, 227, 228
Multiculturalism, 138, 141, 142, 152, 162, 163, 169, 172
Mythhistories, 196, 202–207

N

Narrative identity formation, 9, 178
National belonging, 8, 55, 69, 132, 137–142
New Immigration Act of 1965, 80
New Jerusalem, 6, 15–34
Nostalgia, 40, 42, 48–51, 166

O

Okinawa, 78
Order, 6, 9, 11, 20, 33, 34, 41, 42, 44, 50, 53, 54, 57, 64–67, 80, 84, 99, 102, 113, 116–127, 132, 139, 144, 159, 161–163, 165, 192, 204, 219, 222, 228
Order of God, 8, 120–122, 124, 126–128
Orientalism, 27, 61, 142, 186, 187
Oriental Monk, 61, 62
Other, 25, 50, 57, 97, 102, 106, 107, 159, 169, 170, 206, 207

P

Page Law, 24
Pentecost, 126
Perpetual foreigner syndrome, 184, 188
Plantation logic, 124–126
Police, 5, 74, 85, 96, 98, 107, 144, 201, 211–213
Police brutality, 106, 199
Pop culture, 7, 53, 55, 61
Postcolonial, 56
Post-traumatic stress disorder (PTSD), 100, 102
Power, 3, 4, 7, 8, 10, 17, 28, 55, 56, 58, 60–62, 65, 66, 69, 70, 73, 75, 78, 80, 82–84, 107, 113, 116, 119–122, 126, 137, 142, 143, 152–154, 156, 158–160, 163–165, 167, 169, 172, 182, 184, 188, 202, 203, 213, 217, 221
Productive contamination, 123–125
Protestant Christianity, 178, 182, 183
Puritans, 19, 22, 57
Purity, 3, 7, 20, 34, 58, 59, 63, 79, 86, 113, 118, 122–128, 133, 144

R

Race, 1, 6, 8–10, 24, 26, 27, 34, 57, 78–80, 82, 84, 86, 87, 90, 97, 99, 104, 111–118, 120, 123, 125, 127, 132, 137, 151–167, 169, 170, 172, 178, 184, 187, 188, 190, 195, 196, 198–200, 203, 215, 218, 221
  concept of, 8, 112–114
Racial, 2–11, 42, 45, 54, 62, 63, 75, 76, 78, 80–83, 85, 87, 88, 90, 96, 98, 99, 104, 105, 107, 111–128, 132, 137, 139, 141, 142, 151–158, 160, 162–172, 177, 179, 180, 182, 185, 186, 188, 190–192, 196, 199, 205, 221, 225

extinction, 187
hierarchy, 82, 85, 86, 155, 186, 188, 191
identity formation, 165
Racialized affect, 63, 84, 152, 152n8, 155–157, 172
Racial justice, vi, vii, 6, 8, 88, 111–128, 142, 177, 178, 185, 189, 191, 192
  antiracist, vi, 5–11, 73–90, 113, 114, 117–119, 125, 127, 133, 186
  for Asian Americans, 6, 8, 111, 177, 178, 191
  for Black Americans, 8, 112
  identitarian approach, 115, 117, 121, 125
  indifference, 185
Racial liberalism, 138, 178, 190–192
Racial logic, 113, 116, 117, 119
Racial logic, modern, 116
Racial politics, 74, 80–82
Racism, v–viii, 2–7, 9–11, 42, 50, 54, 56, 60, 66, 68, 73, 74, 76–77, 82–85, 90, 96–99, 102, 103, 106, 107, 115, 118, 119, 126, 132–139, 142–144, 152, 153, 157, 160, 164, 165, 167, 170, 177–191, 197, 198, 205, 207, 214, 216, 221, 224–226, 228
Radical Black Peace Activism, 84, 85
R&R business, 78, 82
Remembering, 8, 40–51, 69, 97, 101, 105
Revelation, 7, 15, 16, 18, 26–34
Roman Empire, 97, 206

S

Saintliness, 215–218, 221, 222, 229
Secret Identities, 67
Secret war, 75
Self-excuse, 9, 182, 184, 185, 187, 189, 190
Self-reflexivity, 191
Sensory formation, 161
Settler colonialism, vi, vii, 2, 6, 7, 42–48, 54, 56–58, 64, 68, 70, 75, 139–142
Settler racial tense, 45
Sexual, 2, 6, 28, 79, 105, 106, 132, 136, 139, 143–145, 164, 168, 198–201
Sex work, 143–145, 164, 169
Shame, 7, 55, 63, 65–69, 100, 144, 145, 152, 153, 213
Siloing racial/racially isolationist/coalition solidary, 113, 119, 120
Slavery, v, 100, 102, 142, 183, 186, 193
Social construction of race, 152, 154–155, 158, 161, 171
Social imagination, 57, 58, 157
Social reform movement, 124

Subject Index

Solidarity, vi–viii, 5–8, 42, 51, 59, 63, 67–69, 81, 85, 88–90, 105–107, 111–128, 131–134, 136, 139, 140, 142, 145, 146, 158, 162, 165, 172, 177–193, 207, 213, 214, 216, 218, 219, 221, 222, 226–229
Solidarity-creating narratives, 177–193
South Asians, 9, 86, 197, 201, 205, 207
Spirit of God, 125
Stop AAPI Hate, 4–5
Subjectivity, 42, 95, 96, 107, 169

T
Thai, 151, 157–172
Thai food, 9, 151, 156–166, 169–171
Theological imagination, 7, 53–70
Theology, v, vii, viii, 4–7, 9, 56, 57, 59, 73–90, 112, 132, 144–146, 183
 of decency, 8, 132, 144–146
Transcontinental railroad, 21, 23
Transnationalism, 105
Trauma, 8, 96–103, 105, 106, 120, 157, 169

U
Ungrievable lives, 135, 143
US as God's benevolent land, 182
US Colonialism, 184
US Empire
 exceptionalism, 43, 45, 48, 101, 190, 191, 212
 imperialism, 42, 54–59, 62, 64, 168, 184, 216

US military
 integrated army, 99
 occupation, 158
 US involved war, 102

V
Violence, v, vi, 1, 4–6, 8, 11, 15, 21, 23, 25, 42, 48, 55, 57, 62–64, 66, 69–70, 74, 76, 79, 80, 82, 85, 89, 90, 96–99, 103, 105, 106, 121, 131–146, 151, 152, 162, 164, 165, 171, 181, 191, 198, 199, 204, 212, 223

W
White allyship, 119
Whiteness, 44, 67, 86, 113, 115–117, 120, 124, 139, 141, 158, 160, 163, 165, 171, 197, 198, 201, 202
White settler colonialism, vi, 6, 56–58, 64, 70, 73
White supremacy, vi, viii, 5, 9, 54, 55, 66, 68, 73, 74, 76, 85, 97, 178, 181, 182, 184–193, 201
Women's International Democratic Federation (WIDF), 7, 74, 86–89

Y
Yanggongju, 106
 military prostitution, 77, 79
 Western Princess, 105
Yellow Peril, 16, 25–33, 61, 62

SPRINGER NATURE

GPSR Compliance

The European Union's (EU) General Product Safety Regulation (GPSR) is a set of rules that requires consumer products to be safe and our obligations to ensure this.

If you have any concerns about our products, you can contact us on ProductSafety@springernature.com

In case Publisher is established outside the EU, the EU authorized representative is:

Springer Nature Customer Service Center GmbH
Europaplatz 3
69115 Heidelberg, Germany

The manufacturer's authorised representative in the EU is Springer Nature Customer Service Centre GmbH, Europaplatz 3, 69115 Heidelberg, Germany. If you have any concerns regarding our products, please contact ProductSafety@springernature.com

Printed and bound by CPI Group (UK) Ltd, Croydon, CR0 4YY
25/03/2026
02078185-0010